ANSWERING JEWISH OBJECTIONS *to* JESUS

Volume 2

Theological Objections

MICHAEL L. BROWN

Baker Books
A Division of Baker Book House Co
Grand Rapids, Michigan 49516

Published by Baker Books
a division of Baker Book House Company
P.O. Box 6287, Grand Rapids, MI 49516-6287

Second printing, June 2002

Printed in the United States of America

Library of Congress Cataloging-in-Publication Data

Brown, Michael L., 1955–
    Answering Jewish objections to Jesus : theological objections / Michael L. Brown.
       p. cm.
    Includes bibliographical references (p.) and indexes.
    ISBN 0-8010-6334-5 (paper)
    1. Apologetics. 2. Jews—Conversion to Christianity. 3. Jesus Christ—Messiahship. I. Title.
    BV4922.B76 2000
    239—dc21   99-046293

For current information about all releases from Baker Book House, visit our web site:
http://www.bakerbooks.com

ANSWERING
JEWISH
OBJECTIONS
to
JESUS

Also by Michael L. Brown

   Revolution! The Call to Holy War

   Answering Jewish Objections to Jesus: General and Historical
      Objections

   Go and Sin No More: A Call to Holiness

   Let No One Deceive You: Confronting the Critics of Revival

   From Holy Laughter to Holy Fire: America on the Edge of Revival

   Israel's Divine Healer

   It's Time to Rock the Boat: A Call to God's People to Rise Up and
      Preach a Confrontational Gospel

   Our Hands Are Stained with Blood: The Tragic Story of the
      "Church" and the Jewish People

   Whatever Happened to the Power of God: Is the Charismatic
      Church Slain in the Spirit or Down for the Count?

   How Saved Are We?

   The End of the American Gospel Enterprise

   Compassionate Father or Consuming Fire: Who Is the God of the
      Old Testament?

Michael L. Brown is a Jewish believer in Jesus and has a Ph.D. in
Near Eastern Languages and Literatures from New York University.
He is the president of the Brownsville Revival School of Ministry in
Pensacola, Florida, and has served as a visiting professor at Trinity
Evangelical Divinity School and Fuller Theological Seminary. He has
written over twelve books and is a contributor to the *Oxford Diction-
ary of Jewish Religion*.

Dedicated to
my fellow Jewish believers in Jesus
around the world

Joshua 1:9
2 Corinthians 13:8
Hebrews 13:11–14

Contents

Preface

In November of 1971, as a rebellious, proud, heroin-shooting, rock-drumming, Jewish sixteen-year-old, I discovered something that I was not looking for and the course of my life was completely altered. I found out that Jesus was the Jewish Messiah! I learned that he was the one spoken of in the Hebrew Scriptures, that he was God's way of salvation for Jew and Gentile alike, and that through faith in him my life could be transformed—even though I didn't want it to be transformed. I loved my sinful ways! But God's goodness overcame my badness, and in a matter of weeks, I was a brand-new man.

My parents were thrilled—and relieved—to see the tremendous change in my life. I had fallen so far, so quickly, since my bar mitzvah at age thirteen, and my parents had been deeply concerned. But the positive transformation was more radical and dramatic than was the fall. The only problem for my parents—especially for my father—was that in their opinion I had joined a foreign religion. So my father, thrilled with the change in my life but very much wanting me to come back to our traditions, brought me to the local Conservative rabbi in early 1972 (I was still not yet seventeen). But rather than attacking my beliefs, this twenty-six-year-old rabbi befriended me. He told me that in his opinion he was not as spiritual a person as I was, although his beliefs were right and mine were wrong. In his view, Judaism, meaning traditional, Orthodox, observant Judaism, was the only true faith for our people, and he felt that the key for me would be to meet some very religious—and zealous—traditional Jews. And so the journey began!

In the summer of 1973, the rabbi brought me to Brooklyn to spend an afternoon with some ultra-Orthodox rabbis. It was a real eye-opener for me! I was impressed with the devotion and kindly demeanor of these men, and I was challenged by their scholarship. How could I, just eighteen years old and barely able to read the Hebrew alphabet, tell them what our sacred Hebrew texts meant? They had been studying the Scriptures all their lives; I had been a believer less than two years, although by then I had read the Bible cover to cover roughly five times and memorized more than four thousand verses. But they had memorized the original; I was dependent on English translations. What business did I have telling them that Jesus was actually the fulfillment of the prophecies of our Hebrew Bible?

This was my predicament: I was sure that my faith was sound and that Jesus really was our Messiah, but I could find almost no literature (and almost no people) to help me. When I did find solid academic works by Christians dealing with Messianic prophecy and related subjects, they tended to be insensitive to the traditional Jewish objections I was hearing. On the other hand, the few books (really, booklets) I found specifically addressing Jewish objections tended to be popular, short, and nonscholarly in their approach. I was in a quandary!

How could I effectively answer the questions of the rabbis and refute their objections? And what about my own conscience? Could I really be at peace with myself without being able to provide intellectually solid responses to my own people, especially when the rabbis told me that if I could read the original texts, I would never believe in Jesus? So it was that I began to study Hebrew in college, ultimately making it my major and continuing with graduate studies until I earned a doctorate in Semitic languages. And all through my college and graduate years, I was constantly dialoging with rabbis and religious Jews, sometimes in public debates, other times one on one. I wanted to understand exactly why my own people rejected Jesus— Yeshua—as Messiah, and I wanted to answer them with truth as well as with love.

In the providence of God, I became somewhat of a specialist in Jewish debate and dialogue, and in the late 1980s and early 1990s, my Messianic Jewish friends and colleagues began to ask me, "When are you going to put all this in writing?" In fact, one friend in particular, Sid Roth, lovingly badgered me for years, asking me almost every time we talked, "So, Mike, when are you going to write *the* book"— implying that everything else I was writing was of secondary importance! Finally, in 1996 I felt the release to begin the work in earnest, and as word started to get out, I was amazed at the level of interest expressed by many of my Christian friends: "I want to read your book and then give it to one of my Jewish friends who doesn't believe in Jesus! When is it coming out?" At last I can answer, "Now," with only one caveat. It's no longer a book; it's a series of three books. There was simply too much material to cover, and after all this time—especially given the fact that no comparable work exists—I felt that it was better to be too thorough than not thorough enough.

Volume 1 dealt with general and historical objections (covering thirty-five objections in all, numbered respectively as 1.1–1.19 and 2.1–2.16) and was released in December 1999. The current volume deals with theological objections (twenty-eight in all, and numbered here 3.1–3.28). Volume 3, scheduled for release in 2001, will deal with objections based on Messianic prophecy (thirty-nine total), objections to the New Testament (thirty-four total), and objections arising from Jewish tradition (eighteen total). If there is sufficient reader interest, these three volumes will then be combined into a one-volume reference edition, with some special studies and further notes added. The table of contents in each volume lists the specific objections covered in that specific volume, enabling the reader to get an overview of the material at a glance and also making it easy to locate each individual objection.

To briefly summarize the material treated in this series, *general objections* boil down to the perception that "Jesus is not for Jews! Our religion is Judaism, not Christianity. No true Jew would ever believe in Jesus." *Historical objections* tend to be more substantial and deal with the very purpose of the Messiah (in other words, the claim that the Messiah was to bring peace to the world) or the alleged failure of the church ("Christian" anti-Semitism; the state of the "church" worldwide, including divisions and scandals). The heart of these objections is, "Jesus cannot be the Messiah because we are obviously not in the Messianic age." *Theological objections,* treated at length in the current volume, cut to the heart of the differences between traditional Judaism and the Messianic Jewish/Christian faith. They revolve around the nature of God (the Trinity, the deity of Jesus, the person of the Holy Spirit), the nature of man and the need for salvation, and sin and the means of atonement. In sum, these objections claim, "The religion of the New Testament is a completely foreign religion that is not only un-Jewish but is also unfaithful to the Hebrew Bible."

The *objections based on Messianic prophecies* arise from traditional Judaism's rejection of our standard Messianic prophetic "proof texts," either denying that they have anything to do with Jesus, claiming that they have been mistranslated, misquoted, or taken out of context by the New Testament authors or traditional Christian apologists, or arguing that none of the *real* Messianic prophecies—the so-called "provable" prophecies—were ever fulfilled by Jesus. In short, these objections say, "We don't believe Jesus is the Messiah because he didn't come close to living up to the biblical description of the Messiah." Jewish *objections to the New Testament* can be broken down into several categories: The New Testament misquotes and misinterprets the Old Testament, at times manufacturing verses to suit its purposes; the genealogies of Jesus given by Matthew and Luke are hopelessly contradictory (at best) and entirely irrelevant anyway; the New Testament is filled with historical and factual errors (especially Stephen's speech); the teachings of Jesus are impossible, dangerous, and un-Jewish (and Jesus as a person was not so great either); and the New Testament is self-contradictory. To sum up rather bluntly: "Only a fool would believe in the divine inspiration of the New Testament." Finally, *objections based on traditional Judaism* are founded on two key points: (1) "Judaism is a wonderful, fulfilling, and self-sufficient religion. There is no need to look elsewhere"; and (2) "God gave us a written and an unwritten tradition. We interpret *everything* by means of that oral tradition, without which the Bible makes no sense." (For further background to the history of these objections, see the introduction to volume 1.)

Each of the volumes follows a similar format. I begin with a concise statement of the objection, followed by a concise answer to the objection, which is then followed by an in-depth answer, including citations of important sources as needed and consideration of possible objections to the answers. For those interested in more detailed discussion, substantial notes have been provided. Other readers may choose to skip the notes and concentrate on the main text.

In dedicating this volume to my fellow Jewish believers scattered around the world, it is my hope that the material provided here will strengthen your faith and provide you with a needed resource that will, at last, silence many formidable objections that have been raised against our beliefs throughout the centuries. I am also confident that interested Christian readers—including theologians and biblical scholars—will find much here of value as well, including important Jewish concepts that provide background and illumination for doctrines that you cherish.

And to every Jewish reader who does not yet believe in Yeshua (Jesus), I ask you to study this volume carefully with Bible in hand (especially a Hebrew Bible if you have one). And as you read, pray a simple prayer that the psalmist prayed more than twenty-five hundred years ago: "Open my eyes that I may see wonderful things in your Torah" (Ps. 119:18). God will answer that prayer! Every word that follows speaks directly to you, my Jewish friend, and if I can be of help to you in your search for truth, don't hesitate to contact me. Let the journey begin!

Note on citations and sources: Rabbinic literature is cited using standard conventions (e.g., the letter "m." before a rabbinic source means "Mishnah" while "b." stands for "Babylonian Talmud"). When there is a difference in the numbering of biblical verses between some Christian and Jewish versions, the Jewish numbering is in brackets (e.g., Isa. 9:6[5]). Bear in mind, however, that the actual verses are identical; only the numbering is different. Also, in keeping with the stylistic conventions of the publisher, all references to deity are lowercase. However, in keeping with traditional Jewish conventions, other words (such as Rabbinic, Temple, and Messianic) have been capitalized. Unless otherwise noted, all emphasis in Scripture quotations is my own.

PART 3

THEOLOGICAL
OBJECTIONS

3.1. Jews don't believe in the Trinity. We believe in one God, not three.

> Just as Messianic Jews probably misunderstand some of the things you believe, I think you misunderstand some of the things we believe. We do not in any way believe in three gods. Our God is one, and his name is the LORD (or Yahweh, known to Orthodox Jews as HaShem). He revealed himself to us through his Son, the Messiah, who is the very image and reflection of God, and he touches us and speaks to us by his Spirit. These are deep, spiritual truths. Later theologians labeled this relationship the Trinity—God as a triune One. But the word *Trinity* is not found anywhere in the New Testament, and it may confuse the issues for you.

Christians and Messianic Jews emphatically believe in one God and only one God. This is expressed clearly in the doctrinal confession signed by Church of England clergy: "There is but one living and true God, everlasting, without body, parts, or passions; of infinite power, wisdom, and goodness; the Maker and Preserver of all things both visible and invisible."[1] As noted by some contemporary Christian theologians, "One thing Christians are not willing to give up is their full acceptance of the Bible's teaching that God is one. This is simply not negotiable. It is a fact firmly entrenched in Scripture."[2] And again, "The unity of God is, in fact, one great pillar on which the whole Christian faith is built. We do not and cannot deny that God is one."[3] Would any religious Jew have a problem with such statements about the unity of God?

But the God we worship and adore is far greater than anything we can fathom with our natural minds. In Jewish mystical literature he is called the *Eyn Sof*, the Infinite One (literally, "without end"), and traditional Jewish thought recognizes that there are different aspects to his being. You could say that he is one and he is more than one. Our Lord has many different dimensions! We can't put him in a little box and subject him to mathematical analysis.[4] There are mysteries about the eternal nature of God, as all monotheistic believers would gladly admit, and we in our finitude can hardly describe God in his infinitude. As one Jewish intellectual once said to me, "With our own minds, we know as much about God as a fly does about nuclear science."[5]

As always, though, the question is, What does the Hebrew Bible say? The opinions of Christians and Jews carry weight only if they agree with the Word of God. So we need to start at the beginning and build our understanding from the foundation up. And remember, the concept of the Trinity came about when followers of Jesus looked at all the pieces of the puzzle and tried to put together the evidence of the Scriptures. We need to look first at that evidence before drawing any kind of conclusion, negative or positive.

The fundamental Jewish confession of faith, called the Shema, is taken from Deuteronomy 6:4. As traditionally understood, it reads, "Hear, O Israel: The LORD our God, the LORD is one" (we will discuss other possible translations below). Messianic Jews often claim that the Hebrew word for "one" that is used here, 'echad, actually means a compound unity, while traditional Jews often argue their case as if the word meant an absolute unity.

Actually, 'echad simply means "one," exactly like our English word "one." While it *can* refer to compound unity (just as our English word can, as in one team, one couple, etc.), it does not specifically refer to compound unity. On the other hand, 'echad certainly does not refer to the concept of absolute unity, an idea expressed most clearly in the twelfth century by Moses Maimonides, who asserted that the Jewish people must believe that God is *yachid*, an "only" one.[6] There is no doubt that this reaction was due to exaggerated, unbiblical, "Christian" beliefs that gave Jews the impression Christians worshiped three gods. Unfortunately, the view of Maimonides is reactionary and also goes beyond what is stated in the Scriptures. In fact, *there is not a single verse anywhere in the Bible that clearly or directly states that God is an absolute unity*.

What then does the Shema mean? According to the common, traditional understanding—and that is what most Jews are familiar with—the text is declaring emphatically that God is 'echad. Therefore, we should take a more in-depth look at the biblical usage of this word. According to Genesis 2:24, when a man is united to a woman, the two become "one *('echad)* flesh," clearly a compound unity. So also, in Exodus 36:13, God instructs Moses to join the many pieces of the tabernacle together so that it will be "one" (*'echad;* see also Exod. 26:6, 11; 36:18). There are many components but one, unified tabernacle.

The Bible also speaks of Israel being "one nation" (*goy 'echad;* see 2 Sam. 7:23; Ezek. 37:22), just as in the Pledge of Allegiance we in America speak of being "one nation under God." In fact, we state that as "one nation" we are "indivisible." Yet we number 270 million people! America is one nation made up of millions of people; ancient Israel was one nation made up of hundreds of thousands of people. Each can be described as *'echad,* just as the people who joined together to build the Tower of Babel could be called "one people" (*'am 'echad;* Gen. 11:6) and the uniting of the Shechemites and Israelites would have made them "one people" (*'am 'echad;* Gen. 34:16, 22). There can be many aspects to oneness!

More examples from the Hebrew Bible could easily be given,[7] but the basic point should be clear: To say that Yahweh, the God of Israel, is *'echad* does not tell us anything about his essential nature—whether he is one in one or ten in one. In fact, this really wasn't an issue at all, since every god was "one." The problem was that there were *so many* gods competing for our people's worship and adoration. This was Israel's battle, as God warned in the Ten Commandments, and as Moses and Joshua often repeated:

> I am the LORD your God, who brought you out of Egypt, out of the land of slavery. You shall have no other gods before me.
>
> Exodus 20:2–3

> Do not bow down before their gods or worship them or follow their practices. You must demolish them and break their sacred stones to pieces.
>
> Exodus 23:24

> Do not associate with these nations that remain among you; do not invoke the names of their gods or swear by them. You must not serve them or bow down to them.
>
> Joshua 23:7

The Shema was not addressing philosophical issues such as the absolute or compound unity of God. (Would anyone even be thinking of such a question?[8]) Rather, it was saying to our people Israel that the LORD *alone* was to be our God—he and no other.

This is exactly what *'echad* means elsewhere in Scripture. Look, for example, at 1 Chronicles 29:1: "Then King David said to the whole assembly: 'My son Solomon, the one whom God has chosen, is young and inexperienced.'" Or as translated more idiomatically in the New Jewish Publication Society Version: "God has chosen my son Solomon alone." So *'echad* can mean "one" in the sense of "that one alone."[9]

For this reason, the NJPSV translates Deuteronomy 6:4 as, "Hear, O Israel! The LORD is our God, the LORD alone." In fact, the footnote in the NJPSV reminds us that this is also the understanding of the revered, medieval commentators Abraham Ibn Ezra and Rashbam (Rabbi Shmuel Ben Meir). Therefore, it is not just a later "Christian" argument that Deuteronomy 6:4 does not specifically teach that God is an absolute unity.[10] In fact, Moshe Weinfeld, a leading Jewish biblical scholar who for technical grammatical reasons translates, "Hear, O Israel! YHWH our God is one YHWH,"[11] entitles his discussion of Deuteronomy 6:4–25, "Exclusive Allegiance to YHWH." *The entire thrust of Deuteronomy 6:4 was that the Lord alone was to be Israel's God.*

This is also in harmony with the famous midrash to this passage (see b. Pesahim 56a; Sifre Deuteronomy 31; Genesis Rabbah 98:4), which uses "Israel" to refer to Jacob. The midrash relates that as Jacob neared death, he wanted to reveal to his sons the things to come but found the presence of God had departed from him. He expressed his fear that possibly one of his sons would not remain faithful to the Lord. His sons all replied to him, "Hear, O Israel [i.e., Israel/Jacob, our father], the LORD is our God, the LORD alone. Just as in your heart there is only One *('echad)* so also in our hearts there is only One *('echad).*" To this Jacob replied, "Blessed be his Name, whose glorious kingdom is forever and ever."[12] Once again, this has nothing whatsoever to do with the issue of God's essential nature. Rather, it is a profession of faith that the Lord alone—the God of Jacob/Israel— would be the only God of Jacob's descendants.

This was also the message and call of the prophets:

> Do not tremble, do not be afraid.
> Did I not proclaim this and foretell it long ago?
> You are my witnesses. Is there any God besides me?
> No, there is no other Rock; I know not one.
>
> Isaiah 44:8

> I am the LORD, and there is no other;
>   apart from me there is no God.

Isaiah 45:5

> For this is what the LORD says—
> he who created the heavens,
>   he is God;
> he who fashioned and made the earth,
>   he founded it;
> he did not create it to be empty,
>   but formed it to be inhabited—
> he says:
> "I am the LORD,
>   and there is no other."

Isaiah 45:18

> Turn to me and be saved,
>   all you ends of the earth;
>   for I am God, and there is no other.

Isaiah 45:22

Every follower of Jesus fully affirms these words. The Lord alone is our God. (See 3.4 for more on this.) Our only concern is to know what the Lord is like. What do the Scriptures say? He is known by different names in the Bible and is described in different ways. What do these names and descriptions mean? Are there any indications in the Hebrew Scriptures that God is in any sense a "compound unity." In other words, just as a husband and wife are *'echad* and the Tabernacle with its many parts is *'echad* and a nation with its millions of people is *'echad*, is God complex in his oneness?[13]

Remember, the issue is not how many gods we worship, three or one. No. There is only one true God! The God of the New Testament is the same as the God of the Hebrew Scriptures. But what is he like? How does he make himself known to us? In what sense is he one? Is it a simple matter of "spiritual mathematics," or is there mystery involved? The universe is "one," the ocean is "one," and God is "one," but what exactly does this mean?

Maybe the problem is not really about the nature of God as much as it is about a gut-level, negative reaction to anything "Christian." Maybe the problem lies with an overemphasis on the often misunderstood—and frequently poorly explained—term *Trinity*. Perhaps it would help if, for just one moment, we stopped thinking about what

Christians believe—since not everything labeled "Christian" is truly Christian or biblical—and pictured instead an old Jewish rabbi unfolding the mysteries of God. Listen to him as he strokes his long, gray beard and says, "I don't talk to everyone about this. These things are really quite deep. But you seem sincere, so I'll open up some mystical concepts to you."

And so he begins to tell you about the ten Sefirot, the so-called divine emanations that act as "intermediaries or graded links between the completely spiritual and unknowable Creator and the material sub-lunar world." When you say, "But doesn't that contradict our belief in the unity of God?" he replies, "God is an organic whole but with different manifestations of power—just as the life of the soul is one, though manifested variously in the eyes, hands, and other limbs. God and his Sefirot are just like a man and his body: His limbs are many but He is one. Or, to put it another way, think of a tree which has a central trunk and yet many branches. There is unity and there is multiplicity in the tree, in the human body, and in God too. Do you understand?"[14]

Now think of this same rabbi saying to you, "Consider that in our Scriptures, God was pictured as enthroned in heaven, yet at the same time he manifested himself in the cloud and the fire over the Tabernacle while also putting his Spirit on his prophets. And all the while the Bible tells us that his glory was filling the universe! Do you see that God's unity is complex?"

And what if this rabbi began to touch on other mystical concepts of God such as "the mystery of the three" (Aramaic, *raza' di-telatha*), explaining that in the Zohar there are five different expressions relating to various aspects of the threefold nature of the Lord? What would you make of the references to "three heads, three spirits, three forms of revelation, three names, and three shades of interpretation" that relate to the divine nature? The Zohar even asks, "How can these three be one? Are they one only because we call them one? How they are one we can know only by the urging of the Holy Spirit and then even with closed eyes."[15] These issues of "the Godhead" are deep!

Through the ages, followers of Jesus have pointed to plural references to God found in the Hebrew Bible as proof of the Trinity. For example, in the very first verse of Genesis, God is called *'elohim*, which is a plural form. Then, in Genesis 1:26, God says, "Let *us* make man in *our* image, in *our* likeness." In a similar way, the Lord says in Genesis 3:22, "The man has now become like one of *us*," while in Genesis 11:7 (with reference to the building of the Tower of Babel), he says,

"Come, let *us* go down and confuse their language." So also Isaiah 6:8 records the Lord saying, "Whom shall I send? And who will go for *us*?"

Does all this indicate that God is a compound unity? The response of the rabbis, as far back as the Talmud (b. Sanhedrin 38b), has been to point out that whenever the plural form is used, it is immediately followed by the singular. So the Scriptures often use a plural noun for God (like *'elohim*) with a singular verb (like *bara'*, "God created" in Gen. 1:1), or, after saying, "Let us make man" (plural) the Bible then says, "So God created" (singular) (Gen. 1:26–27).[16]

Whose argument is correct?

Actually, the fact that God is called *'elohim* (translated as "God" when referring to the Lord and as either "god" or "gods" when referring to idols) is not unusual. In the Ancient Near East, it was common to refer to the deity in the compound plural,[17] and when speaking of an owner or master, it was often the rule to speak of him in such terms. To give you just a few examples, Abraham's servant speaks of his master in the plural in Genesis 24 (*'adonim*, literally, "lords"), Joseph speaks of his master Potiphar in the plural in Genesis 39, and David the king is spoken of as "lords" in 1 Kings 1:11. In Exodus 21, to translate literally and incorrectly, the law speaks of a slave and his masters (*'adonim*, referring to just one master), in Isaiah 19:4, the prophet tells Israel that God will hand them over to a cruel lord (Hebrew, *'adonim qasheh*, a plural noun with a singular adjective), and Isaiah 1:3 tells us that a donkey knows the feeding crib of its masters (*ba'alim*, referring to just one person; cf. the first half of the verse in which reference is made to an ox's owner—in the singular).

These examples, which are really very common, show clearly that compound plurals were often used to speak of leaders, owners, masters, or kings. How much more then could similar expressions be used to speak of *the* Lord, *the* Master, *the* King, and *the* God. To bring this out with my own hyper-literal translation, in Malachi 1:6 God asks, "If I am a Lords where is my honor?" while the psalmist exclaims in Psalm 8:1, 9, "O YHWH, our Lords," and Deuteronomy 10:17 hails YHWH as "the Gods of gods and the Lords of lords."

But before you conclude from all this that plural nouns for God have no bearing on the question of his unity, consider this simple truth: Hebrew, along with other Semitic languages, sometimes expressed greatness, supremacy, exaltation, majesty, and fullness by means of compound plural nouns. Plurality could express prominence, ownership, or divinity, all with reference to a single person or single deity. This means that the very concept of "compound unity" or "plurality in unity" was part of the language of the Tanakh. Such concepts would not be foreign to the biblical mind.[18] So while these references to God or Lord in the plural do not in any way *prove* Trinitarian beliefs, they are certainly in perfect harmony with everything we are trying to say here, namely, that in some way the Lord's unity is complex.

What about God saying, "Let *us* make man in *our* image . . . The man has become like one of *us* . . . Let *us* go down . . . Who will go for *us*?" Do these verses prove the Trinity? Many answers have been given to this question by both Christians and Jews. For example, the Father was speaking to the Son and the Spirit (or to the Son *or* the Spirit), the Lord was speaking to the angels, he was deliberating with himself, the Hebrew is once again using the so-called majestic plural, and so on. The list of answers is almost endless, and the list of objections to these answers is just as long.[19] So what is a person to believe?

My suggestion again is simple: Recognize that these verses from the Hebrew Scriptures *could* refer to God's plurality or diversity within his unity, but other explanations are possible. These verses are certainly in harmony with Trinitarian beliefs and could easily support such beliefs, but they don't prove them. On the other hand, these verses most definitely do not exclude such beliefs.

At this point, you may think I'm opening the door too wide and being too open-minded to views about God's compound unity. You may feel that somewhere, somehow there must be a verse in the Hebrew Bible that decisively refutes all this and definitely points to God's absolute unity. After all, belief in the unity of God is considered to be *the* foundation of Judaism.[20] It is in this context that Zechariah 14:9 is often quoted, taken to mean, at the end of this age, "the LORD shall be king over all the earth: in that day shall there be one LORD" (that is, recognized as an absolute unity) "and his name one" (reemphasizing the fact that he is in no way "more than one"). So when it all gets sorted out in the end, everyone will know that God is an absolute unity, not a compound unity or complex unity or triunity. Period.[21]

But is that what Zechariah was saying? The word used for "one" in this verse is—you guessed it!—*'echad*, hardly the right word to choose if the prophet wanted to say anything about God's essential nature and absolute unity. Just look back to Zechariah 11:8, where he uses *'echad* to speak of "one month." What does that tell us about the essential nature of a month? Does it mean that a month does not have thirty days because it is one?

It is therefore with good reason that the footnote in the New Jewish Publication Society Version to Zechariah 14:9 explains the verse to mean, "the LORD alone shall be worshiped and shall be invoked by His true name." Exactly. It is a prophecy of all peoples turning to Yahweh, forsaking their idols and false religions and worshiping him alone.[22] It tells us nothing about the nature of his oneness. All it says is that he, the one true God, will be worshiped by all. This is exactly what the New Testament teaches.

Consider these well-known passages. When Jesus was asked by a Jewish teacher of the law, "Of all the commandments, which is the most important?" He replied, "The most important one . . . is this: 'Hear, O Israel, the Lord our God, the Lord is one. Love the Lord your God with all your heart and with all your soul and with all your mind and with all your strength'" (Mark 12:28–30). When he was praying shortly before his crucifixion, he uttered these words: "Now this is eternal life: that they may know you, the only true God, and Jesus [the Messiah], whom you have sent" (John 17:3). Yes, Jesus himself taught that his Father was the one and only God!

Peter preached the same message emphatically, and Paul taught it clearly: The one true God, our Father and Creator, appointed his Son, Jesus, to be Messiah and Lord.

First, the words of Peter: "Men of Israel, listen to this: Jesus of Nazareth was a man accredited by God to you by miracles, wonders and signs, which God did among you through him, as you yourselves know. . . . God has raised this Jesus to life, and we are all witnesses of the fact. . . . Therefore let all Israel be assured of this: God has made this Jesus, whom you crucified, both Lord and [Messiah]" (Acts 2:22, 32, 36). Next, the words of Paul: "We know that an idol is nothing at all in the world and that there is no God but one. For even if there are so-called gods, whether in heaven or on earth (as indeed there are many 'gods' and many 'lords'), yet for us there is but one God, the Father, from whom all things came and for whom we live; and there is but one Lord, Jesus [the Messiah], through whom all things came and through whom we live" (1 Cor. 8:4–6).[23] "For there is one God and one mediator between God and men, the man [Messiah] Jesus, who gave himself as a ransom for all men—the testimony given in its proper time" (1 Tim. 2:5–6). And so Paul wrote to the Thessalonians, reporting how everyone had heard ". . . how you turned to God from idols to serve the living and true God, and to wait for his Son from heaven, whom he raised from the dead—Jesus, who rescues us from the coming wrath" (1 Thess. 1:9–10).

This is one of the central reasons why God sent his Son into the world, that through Jesus the Messiah people in every nation and land would forsake their idols and dead religious traditions and turn to the living and true God. The New Testament is most definitely monotheistic, and it further clarifies the monotheism of the Hebrew Bible. The only true God is one, and yet his oneness is complex, unique, and beyond human understanding.

Here are some important points for you to consider. We'll expand on them in answering the next few objections:

- The Hebrew Bible states that no one can see God, and yet at times it says that people saw him. Who was it that they saw?
- The Hebrew Bible speaks of God occasionally manifesting himself on the earth, apparently in human form. Yet, as God, he sits enthroned in the highest heavens. How can both of these things be true?
- The Hebrew Bible sometimes describes the Holy Spirit as a personal being and not just as an impersonal force. Is the Holy Spirit merely a synonym for God, or does the term describe part of his very nature, his own Spirit?
- The Hebrew Bible makes reference to God's Word as a concrete entity, worthy of praise, sent on divine missions, and active in the world. What is meant by this "Word"? (If you take a good look at the next objection, you'll learn what the rabbis had to say about "the Word" of the Lord, in Aramaic, his *memra'*).

The rabbis spoke much about the Shekhina, the Divine Presence, corresponding also to the feminine, motherly aspects of God.[24] They taught that the Shekhina went into exile with the Jewish people, suffering with "her" children in foreign lands (for more on this, see the next objection). According to this concept, God cannot be "whole" again until his people return from their physical and spiritual wanderings and the Temple is rebuilt. The rabbis based this idea on verses that spoke of God being with his people (corporately or individually) in their trouble, distress, and exile (see Mekhilta deRabbi Yishmael, Massekhta dePiskha, 14).

In fact, Rabbi Akiva went as far as saying that, *according to the Scriptures*, when God redeemed his people, he had, as it were, redeemed himself (ibid.). Some Hasidic Jews, joining the concept of the Shekhina with the mystical concept of the Sefirot, took this one step further. They believed (and still believe) that

> the purpose of the performance of the *mitzvot* [commandments] is to help the *Shekhinah* to unite with *Tiferet* [the Sefira of glory or beauty], the male principle. The sins of Israel hinder this union and prevent the "reunification of worlds," which is a necessary prerequisite for the coming of God's kingdom.
>
> The hasidim, in accordance with this belief, adopted the formula (much deplored by their opponents), "For the sake of the unification of the Holy One, blessed be He, and his *Shekhinah*," which they recited before the performance of *mitzvot*.[25]

For now, according to this Hasidic Jewish view, God is in some kind of "disunity." And you thought that God's oneness was such an elementary subject! Why should we try to minimize the mystery?

As we said up front, these are lofty, spiritual concepts. God's unity or tri-unity isn't easily understood. In fact, if you ask ten Christians whether they expect to see three different divine persons in heaven— God the Father, Jesus, and the Holy Spirit—you'll get many different answers. Why? Because God's tri-unity is not some neatly spelled out doctrine or a trite little teaching to be explained in thirty seconds or less. It's like asking a Hasidic rabbi, "Is the Shekhina God?" or, "Is the Memra' (i.e., the Word) God?", or, "Are the Sefirot God?"[26] (I've gotten different responses to these kinds of questions too.) These are deep theological and philosophical issues.

Consider these verses from the last book of the New Testament, the Book of Revelation. In Revelation 3:21, Jesus declares that he sat down with the Father on his throne, but what does that mean? According to Revelation 4:2, John, who wrote the Book of Revelation, is caught up in the Spirit and sees "a throne in heaven with someone sitting on it." It was "the Lord God Almighty, who was, and is, and is to come" (4:8). Next, John sees "a Lamb [representing Jesus], looking as if it had been slain, standing in the center of the throne" (Rev. 5:6). And as the heavenly drama unfolds, John records: "Then I heard every creature in heaven and on earth and under the earth and on the sea, and all that is in them, singing: 'To him who sits on the throne and to the Lamb be praise and honor and glory and power, for ever and ever!'" (Rev. 5:13).

Did you notice those words? "To him who sits on the throne and to the Lamb." Now pay careful attention. In Revelation 7:9, John sees a multitude "standing before the throne and in front of the Lamb," and they cry out, "Salvation belongs to our God, who sits on the throne, and to the Lamb" (7:10). The general picture is clear, but the specifics are not as easy to decipher: God sits on his throne, and with him is the Lamb, yet this Lamb is "at the center of the throne" (5:6; 7:17). What exactly does this mean? There is some mystery involved, without doubt.

Then we come to the end of the book, and in a real sense, the end of the story. Revelation 22:1 speaks of "the river of the water of life, as clear as crystal, flowing from the throne of God and of the Lamb." Mark those words carefully: *the throne* of God and of the Lamb. And now look at these astounding verses: "The throne of God and of the Lamb will be in the city [i.e., the New Jerusalem], and his servants will serve him. They will see his face, and his name will be on their foreheads" (22:3–4).

What an incredible description! There is one throne for God and the Lamb (not two thrones), and his servants (not their servants) will serve him (not them) and see his face (not their faces). One throne, one God, and one face. This is profound, glorious, monotheistic truth at its best. Our God is complex and unique! And so the angel exhorts John in Revelation 22:9, "Worship God!" *not* "Worship gods." Perish the thought. The one God of Abraham and Moses is the one God of Peter and Paul.[27]

In answering the next few objections, I'll provide many important insights from the Tanakh, the New Testament Scriptures, and even the Rabbinic writings. We'll look more closely at the individual pieces of the puzzle. For now, it is sufficient to understand this: The Hebrew Bible nowhere teaches that our Lord, who is the only true God, is an absolute unity, while it does give indications that his unity is complex or compound.

Next we'll respond to specific questions concerning the deity of Jesus, the meaning of "Son of God," and the nature of the Holy Spirit. Then you can put all the evidence together for yourself. You're in for a wonderful surprise.

3.2. If you claim that Jesus is God then you are guilty of making God into a man. You are an idol worshiper!

> We believe that the eternally preexistent Son of God, through whom the universe was made, came forth from God his Father and was clothed with human flesh, making

himself known to us as Yeshua the Messiah. He lived on this earth, died, rose from the dead, and returned to his Father. He now sits enthroned in heaven next to God. We understand that Jesus, the Son of God, is the very image of God, the one in whom God caused his fullness to dwell, the one through whom he revealed himself completely to mankind. Since the Son came forth from the Father and shares his divine nature, in one sense it is quite correct to say that Jesus is God (or divine or deity), always bearing in mind that the overwhelming testimony of the New Testament writings is that Jesus is the Son of God. I can show you from the Hebrew Scriptures that there is absolutely nothing idolatrous about what we believe. God has always revealed himself to his people. He did it most permanently and most fully through Jesus his Son.

The question of the deity of Jesus—is he or is he not God—is one of the most important issues a traditional Jew and a Jewish follower of Jesus can possibly discuss. Emotions run high over this, and misunderstanding is the rule not the exception. The objections raised here are sometimes crude, such as, "Your god wore diapers. Our God sits enthroned in heaven." At other times, they are more sophisticated, such as, "You say, 'Jesus is God,' the Bible says, 'God is not a man' (Num. 23:19), therefore, your faith is contrary to the Bible." There is even a Rabbinic precedent for this argument that claims that Numbers 23:19 was uttered "because Balaam foresaw that a certain man would lead mortals astray by claiming to be God."[28] How can we respond to these objections in a rational and honest way?

It's only fair to say that I fully understand how our faith may look to someone viewing it from the outside. It may seem that the Jesus of Christianity is no different than some guru, holy man, or deluded religious fanatic claiming to be god. In fact, in March of 1996 I was scheduled to be in the city of Anantapur in Andhra Pradesh, India, a city famous for its worship of Satya Sai Baba, a so-called god-man. Therefore, I read this report, filed in December 1995 by Paul Murphy for the Religion News Service, with special interest:

Followers of Sai Baba regard the Hindu leader, who was born in 1926, as the reincarnation of Sai Baba of Shirdi and as personification of the Hindu divinities Shiva and Shakti. According to Michael Goldstein, who led the American mission [that visited Sai Baba's headquarters in

Puttaparthi, India, in November 1995], "The beautiful, pure, profound grace one gets in his presence is testimony to his all-knowing love."

Now, when I read something like that I say, "That's absurd. Some man living in India is not God." And when I see that it was presumably a Jew (Michael Goldstein) who led the delegation to worship Sai Baba, I feel even more grieved. "How could a Jew believe such a thing?"

"Exactly!" you say. "That's how I feel when I hear that you people worship Jesus. Such things are off limits for us as Jews." Well, let's talk it over and see what the Bible says. If our beliefs in Yeshua are just like people's beliefs in Sai Baba, then we're completely off base. But if our beliefs are thoroughly biblical, even answering many questions and filling in gaps found in the Rabbinic literature, then you're going to have to do some fresh, serious thinking. So let me explain precisely what we believe. I'll start by repeating a famous Jewish quote: "No one has ever seen God."

Do you know who wrote those words? It was none other than John (or Yochanan, as he would have been known to his family and friends), the Jewish fisherman who became one of Jesus' most loyal followers and, to be quite candid, one of the most spiritual Jewish teachers the world has ever known. He made several significant statements in his important book that we know today as the Gospel (or Good News) according to John.

Before explaining that "no man has ever seen God," he wrote, "In the beginning was the Word, and the Word was with God, and the Word was God. He was with God in the beginning" (John 1:1–2). Whoever this "Word" was, he was uniquely related to God. John says twice that he was *with God* in the beginning, and yet he also says that he *was God*. Then John explains, "Through him all things were made; without him nothing was made that has been made" (John 1:3). This preexistent "Word" did not make all things himself; rather, all things were made *through* him. That is reminiscent of Paul's teaching quoted in the previous answer: "For us there is but one God, the Father, from whom all things came and for whom we live; and there is but one Lord, Jesus [the Messiah], through whom all things came and through whom we live" (1 Cor. 8:6; see also Heb. 1:2). So all things came *from* God, the Father, and *through* Jesus the Messiah, called "the Word" by John.

Now, think back to the creation account in Genesis 1. What does it say there? How did God create the universe? He created all things by his spoken word. Over and over we read, "And God *said* . . ." For example, "And God *said*, 'Let there be light,' and there was light" (Gen. 1:3); "and God *said*, 'Let the water under the sky be gathered to one place, and let dry ground appear.' And it was so" (Gen. 1:9). In fact, Psalm 33:6 states, "By the *word of the LORD* were the heavens made, their starry host by the breath of his mouth." So God made all things through his word. In Genesis 1, the emphasis is on God's spoken word; in John 1, the emphasis is on the Word "himself"—a divine entity, with God and yet God. What does this actually mean?

Let's ask an obvious question: Why did God *speak* when he created the universe? Why didn't he "just do it" without utterance or sound? To whom or for whom was he speaking? Was there even a language that he used? It seems clear that there was a creative, dynamic force to his words, a power and energy in his command, a tangible release of his divine life. He spoke, and it was so. His word was an extension of his nature, an expression of his will—alive, powerful, and effective—not just letters, syllables, and sounds. There is a vibrant quality to his word!

Now, look at these verses from the Tanakh, not twisted or taken out of context in any way. Each of them speaks of the divine word being sent on a mission.

> Then they cried to the LORD in their trouble,
>   and he saved them from their distress.
> He sent forth his word and healed them;
>   he rescued them from the grave.
>
> Psalm 107:19–20

> As the rain and the snow
>   come down from heaven,
> and do not return to it
>   without watering the earth
> and making it bud and flourish,
>   so that it yields seed for the sower and bread for the eater,
> so is my word that goes out from my mouth:
>   It will not return to me empty,
> but will accomplish what I desire
>   and achieve the purpose for which I sent it.
>
> Isaiah 55:10–11

> He sends his command to the earth;
>   his word runs swiftly.
> He spreads the snow like wool

> and scatters the frost like ashes.
> He hurls down his hail like pebbles.
> Who can withstand his icy blast?
> He sends his word and melts them;
>   he stirs up his breezes, and the waters flow.

Psalm 147:15–18

What is the significance of these statements? They are just another way of explaining how God, the invisible Spirit, carries out his will on earth. It is by his word. This is how he communicates with us, and this is how he reveals himself. On the one hand, he has done this through the Bible, his written Word. We learn his will through his Word, and his Word reveals his nature and character to us. (Read Psalm 119 for many statements about this.) We know God through his Word. His Word is even worthy of praise: "In God, whose word I praise, in God I trust; I will not be afraid. What can mortal man do to me?" (Ps. 56:4).

But there's more. The most common Hebrew expression for "word" is *davar*, which can mean "word, thing, matter, affair." There is *content* and *reality* to one's "words." The simple analogy of Old Testament scholar G. A. F. Knight is worth citing:

> In a children's comic, the words that people utter are usually written with a line ringing them round and are connected by another line with the mouth of the speaker. Their words have a very objective and solid look about them, framed as they are on the comic strip. You feel that the contents of the frame are now out of the speakers in actuality, that words that came out as thin sounds have condensed like steam into very tangible clouds, and that it is now too late to do anything about them. You cannot push the words back into the mouths of the speakers—they have solidified and become objectified. You can only deal with them for good or for evil. So also in the OT. Once a word, coming from the heart of man or God, is uttered, it condenses, so to speak, and becomes objective, it becomes a thing [see, e.g., Genesis 27].[29]

The rabbis took this one step further. Since God was often perceived as somehow "untouchable," it was necessary to provide some kind of link between the Lord and his earthly creation. One of the important links in Rabbinic thought was "the Word," called memra' in Aramaic (from the Hebrew and Aramaic root, "to say" *['mr]*, the root used throughout the creation account in Genesis 1, when God *said* and the material world came into existence). We find this memra' concept hundreds of times in the Aramaic Targums, the translations and paraphrases of the Hebrew Scriptures that were read in the synagogues before, during, and after the time of Jesus. These Targums arose because, in some locations, many of the Jewish people no longer understood Hebrew. Instead, they grew up speaking and reading Aramaic, so they could follow the public reading of the Scripture only with Aramaic translation.

To use Genesis 3:8 as an example, most of the people who were listening to the public reading of the Scriptures would not have understood the Hebrew, which said, "And they heard the sound of the LORD God as he was walking in the garden." Rather, they would have understood the Targum, which said, "And they heard the sound of *the Word of the LORD God* walking in the midst of the garden." What a difference an extra "word" makes! To speak of the Lord walking in the garden seemed too familiar, too down to earth. So the Targum made an adjustment: It was not the Lord who was walking in the garden, it was the Memra' (Word) of the Lord! This Word was not just an "it"; this Word was a him.[30]

Now, I want you to look carefully at the following verses. The translation of the Hebrew text is followed immediately by the translation of the Aramaic Targum. Keep in mind when reading that these Targums were the official translations used in the *synagogues*. Therefore, the Targums took on great significance in the religious life of the people, just as English versions of the Bible take on great significance for English speakers today. Here are several examples:

Genesis 1:27	God created man.	The Word of the Lord created man. (Targum Pseudo-Jonathan)
Genesis 6:6–7	And it repented the Lord that he made man on the earth.	And it repented the Lord through his Word that he made man on the earth.
Genesis 9:12	And God said, "This is the sign that I set for the covenant between me and you."	And the Lord said, "This is the sign that I set for the covenant between my Word and you."
Genesis 15:6	And Abraham believed in the Lord.	And Abraham believed in the Word of the Lord.
Genesis 20:3	And God came to Abimelech.	And the Word from before the Lord came to Abimelech.

Genesis 31:49	May the Lord keep watch between you and me.	May the Word of the Lord keep watch between you and me.
Exodus 14:31	And they believed in the Lord.	And they believed in the Word of the Lord.
Exodus 20:1	And the Lord spoke all these words.	And the Word of the Lord spoke all these words.
Exodus 25:22	And I will meet with you there.	And I will appoint my Word for you there. [31]
Leviticus 26:9	And I will turn to you.	And I will turn through my Word to do good to you.
Numbers 10:35	Rise up, O Lord!	Rise up, O Word of the Lord!
Numbers 10:36	Return, O Lord!	Return, O Word of the Lord!
Numbers 11:23	Is the hand of the Lord shortened?	Is the Word of the Lord detained?
Numbers 14:35	I the Lord have spoken.	I the Lord decreed through my Word.
Deuteronomy 1:26	And you rebelled against the mouth of the Lord your God.	And you rebelled against the Word of the Lord your God.
Deuteronomy 1:30	The Lord your God who goes before you, he himself will fight for you.	The Lord your God who leads before you, his Word will fight for you.
Deuteronomy 18:19	I myself will require it of him.	My Word will require it of him.
Deuteronomy 31:3	The Lord your God will pass before you.	The Lord your God, his Word will pass before you.
Joshua 1:5	As I was with Moses I will be with you.	As my Word was in support of Moses, so my Word will be in your support.
Judges 11:10	The Lord will be witness between us.	The Word of the Lord will be witness between us.
Isaiah 45:17	Israel will be saved by the Lord.	Israel will be saved by the Word of the Lord.

As if these examples aren't enough (and there are many more), just consider Genesis 28:20–21, Jacob's vow. In Hebrew, it reads, "If *God* will be with me and will watch over me on this journey I am taking and will give me food to eat and clothes to wear so that I return safely to my father's house, then *the LORD will be my God*." The Targum says, "If the *Word of the LORD* will be with me . . . then *the Word of the LORD will be my God*." The Word of the Lord will be Jacob's God! And this was read in the synagogues for decades, if not centuries. Week in and week out, the people heard about this walking, talking, creating, saving, delivering Word, this Word who was Jacob's God.

Risto Santala, a Finnish Christian scholar fluent in Hebrew and Rabbinic sources, summarizes the combined evidence from the Targums: "'The LORD's Memra will be my God'; 'I will save them through their God, the LORD's Memra'; Abraham was justified through the Memra; the Memra gave Israel the Law; Moses prayed to the Memra; Israel was justified through the Memra's instrumentality and the Memra even created the world."[32] In fact, according to Targum Neofiti, representing important, early traditions, man was created in the image of the Memra' of the Lord! Consider also Targum Pseudo-Jonathan—a Targum printed in all Rabbinic Bibles (called *Mikra'ot Gedolot*). Deuteronomy 4:7 in the Hebrew reads, "What other nation is so great as to have their gods near them the way the LORD our God is near us whenever we pray to him?" The Targum instead says, "The Memra of Yahweh sits upon his throne high and lifted up and hears our prayer whenever we pray before him and make our petitions." That is just some of the Targumic concept of "the Word."

Now, let's go back to the profound truths that open the Gospel according to John: "In the beginning was the Word, and the Word was with God, and the Word was God. He was with God in the beginning. Through him all things were made; without him nothing was made that has been made. In him was life, and that life was the light of men" (John 1:1–4). This is sounding quite Jewish! (Try rereading this with "the Memra'" in place of "the Word" and "him." It becomes even clearer.)

Of course, even though John as a Galillean Jew would have been completely familiar with the Aramaic concept of the Memra', he wrote his Gospel in Greek, and the Greek expression he used for "word" was *logos*. Interestingly, Philo of Alexandria, the greatest Jewish philosopher of the day and a man who was, roughly speaking, a contemporary of Jesus, had much to say about the *logos*. As explained in *The Oxford Dictionary of Jewish Religion:*

Although in a sense an aspect of the Divine, the Logos often appears as a separate entity, namely, a half-personal emanation of God. The concept was appropriated by Philo in order to bridge the gap between the transcendent God of Judaism and the divine principle experienced by human beings. This view of the Logos as a mediating principle between God and material creation could link up with biblical references to the creative "Word of God," by which the heavens were made (Ps. 33:6) and with the concept of *meimra* (Aram.; "word") in Targum literature (especially as it appears in Targum Onkelos).[33]

Although Philo spoke of the *logos* more than fourteen hundred times in his writings, there are a few examples that are especially important. To quote New Testament scholar Larry Hurtado:

Philo calls the Logos "the second god" *(ton deuteron theon)* and states that the "God" in whose image Adam was created in Gen 1:27 is actually the Logos, which the rational part of the soul resembles. It is impossible (according to Philo) to think of anything earthly being a direct image of God himself . . . [and] Philo also calls the Logos "mediator" *(mesites)*.[34]

Philo also refers to the *logos* as "firstborn" *(protogonon)*, "archangel," "Name of God," and "governor and administrator of all things," stating that the "Divine Word" *(theios logos)* is the "chief" of God's powers.[35] The unique revelation that John is bringing is that this Word (Hebrew, *davar;* Aramaic, *memra';* Greek, *logos*) actually became flesh and made his dwelling among us.[36] "The Word became flesh and made his dwelling among us. We have seen his glory, the glory of the One and Only, who came from the Father, full of grace and truth" (John 1:14). Jesus came to bring God near! The *logos* became flesh and blood.

While Philo's description of the *logos* may have been philosophical, speaking of divine attributes in highly personified terms,[37] John's usage was very real. Through Jesus, the living Word, God made himself known. The Memra'/Logos, an extension of the Lord himself—in one sense God and in another sense with God—came down among us.

If John simply wrote, "God became a human being," that would have given a false impression, leading one to think that the Lord was no longer filling the universe or reigning in heaven, having abandoned his throne to take up residence here. Instead, John tells us that it was *the divine Word* that became a human being, and through the Word we know God personally.

You may say, "All of this is a little difficult to understand." Maybe so, but the Rabbinic concepts of the Memra', Shekhina, and Sefirot are a little difficult to understand too. The fact is, as we keep emphasizing, God cannot be put into a little box. But this much is sure. Objections such as "Your god wore diapers" are as worthless as they sound and completely miss the point. So let's get back to John 1. Things will keep getting clearer as we go along.

We pointed to the important expression in John 1:14: "The Word became flesh and *made his dwelling* among us." The Greek verb for "made his dwelling" literally means "lived in a tent," and to carry out the imagery here, we could say that God pitched his tent among us and temporarily settled in our midst through Jesus the Messiah.

Let's examine this in more depth. When Solomon dedicated the Temple of the Lord he said, "The LORD has said that he would dwell in a dark cloud; I have built a magnificent temple for you, a place for you to dwell forever" (2 Chron. 6:1–2). Solomon had constructed a gorgeous, physical building for God to dwell in, an earthly "house" for the Lord. (In Hebrew, the Temple is often referred to as a "house.") Of course, Solomon understood the limitations of such a building: "But will God really dwell on earth with men? The heavens, even the highest heavens, cannot contain you. How much less this temple [Hebrew, house] I have built!" (2 Chron. 6:18).

Still, he knew the promise God had given to Israel through Moses: "Then have them make a sanctuary for me, and I will dwell among them" (Exod. 25:8). The God whom the heavens could not contain would dwell in the midst of his people in the Tabernacle and Temple. How? He would "pitch his tent" among them. (Remember that the Tabernacle was *literally* an elaborate tent.) That's exactly how the Septuagint put it in 2 Chronicles 6:1–2. It translated the words *dwell* in both verses with the Greek verb "to pitch a tent"—the very word that John used in 1:14!

So just as God "pitched his tent" in the midst of his people Israel through the Tabernacle and Temple—while remaining God in heaven and filling the universe with his presence—so he pitched his tent among us through his Son—while remaining God in heaven and filling the universe with his presence. As one Catholic scholar put it, Jesus is the replacement of the ancient Tabernacle.[38]

This is the ultimate answer to the question of the Talmudic rabbis, Jewish philosophers, and medieval mystics as to how Almighty God could dwell in our midst: He came to us through his Word, Yeshua the Son of God. In a very real sense, God was *in* his Temple, and in a very real sense, God was *in* his Son. The glory of God filled them both, and the glory of God was manifested in both.

When the Tabernacle of Moses was completed, the Torah says, "Then the cloud covered the Tent of Meeting, and the glory of the LORD filled the tabernacle. Moses could not enter the Tent of Meeting because the cloud had settled upon it, and the glory of the LORD filled the tabernacle" (Exod. 40:34–35). When the Temple of Solomon was completed, the Scripture says, "When Solomon finished praying, fire came down from heaven and consumed the burnt offering and the sacrifices, and the glory of the LORD filled the temple. The priests could not enter the temple of the LORD because the glory of the LORD filled it" (2 Chron. 7:1–2). And when Jesus the Messiah walked the earth, John records, "We have seen his glory, the glory of the One and Only, who came from the Father, full of grace and truth" (1:14).

As he went around healing the sick, raising the dead, having compassion on the weak and helpless, setting the captives free, comforting the afflicted, lifting the burdens of the oppressed, demonstrating the Father's love and making his truth known, he manifested the glory of God. Paul also spoke of this: "For God, who said, 'Let light shine out of darkness,' made his light shine in our hearts to give us the light of the knowledge of the glory of God in the face of [the Messiah]" (2 Cor. 4:6). When we see Messiah's "face," we see the glory of God.

At this point, before we go any further and provide other examples from the Tanakh and Rabbinic literature, let's listen to more of what the New Testament says about Jesus-Yeshua our glorious Messiah:

> In the past God spoke to our forefathers through the prophets at many times and in various ways, but in these last days he has spoken to us by his Son, whom he appointed heir of all things, and through whom he made the universe. The Son is the radiance of God's glory and the exact representation of his being, sustaining all things by his powerful word. After he had provided purification for sins, he sat down at the right hand of the Majesty in heaven.
>
> Hebrews 1:1–3

> He is the image of the invisible God, the firstborn over all creation. For by him all things were created: things in heaven and on earth, visible and invisible, whether thrones or powers or rulers or authorities; all things were created by him and for him. He is before all things, and in him all things hold together. And he is the head of the body, the church; he is the beginning and the firstborn from among the dead, so that in everything he might have the supremacy. For God was pleased to have

all his fullness dwell in him. . . . For in [Messiah] all the fullness of the
Deity lives in bodily form.

Colossians 1:15–19, 2:9

Not a single word here could be called "idolatrous." In fact, even
the concept of God's "fullness" dwelling in the Messiah in bodily form
presents no problem when properly understood.[39] For just as the glory
of God filled the Tabernacle and Temple without in any way emptying, depleting, or lessening God, so also his glory filled his Son, without in any way emptying, depleting, or lessening him. Isaiah 6:3 also
teaches that the whole earth is *filled* with his glory, while in the New
Testament, it is written that the church—the worldwide congregation of true believers in Yeshua—is *"the fullness* of him who fills everything in every way" (Eph. 1:23). Does this diminish God?

The fullness of the Father filled Jesus the Son, who "is the radiance
of God's glory and the exact representation of his being" (Heb. 1:3), and
when we see Jesus, we see God. The Son is the Father's mirror image.

Now John's words are becoming crystal clear: "No one has ever
seen God; the only Son, who is in the bosom of the Father, he has
made him known" (John 1:18 RSV). Or as translated by New Testament scholar G. R. Beasley-Murray, "God no one has ever seen. The
only Son, by nature God, who is ever close to the Father's heart, has
brought knowledge of him."[40]

Shortly before his death, Jesus had this dialogue with his disciples:

If you really knew me, you would know my Father as well. From now
on, you do know him and have seen him. Philip said, "Lord, show us
the Father and that will be enough for us." Jesus answered: "Don't you
know me, Philip, even after I have been among you such a long time?
Anyone who has seen me has seen the Father. How can you say, 'Show
us the Father'? Don't you believe that I am in the Father, and that the
Father is in me? The words I say to you are not just my own. Rather,
it is the Father, living in me, who is doing his work. Believe me when
I say that I am in the Father and the Father is in me; or at least believe
on the evidence of the miracles themselves."

John 14:7–11

Whoever has seen the Son has seen the Father. Do you understand?

Let's look back to Jewish tradition for a moment. What were some
of the Rabbinic answers to the question of how a human being could
see the Lord and live? According to Exodus 33:20, God said to Moses,
"You cannot see my face, for no one may see me and live." Yet in Exo-

dus 24:9–11, less than ten chapters earlier, we read, "Moses and Aaron, Nadab and Abihu, and the seventy elders of Israel went up [Mount Sinai] and saw the God of Israel. Under his feet was something like a pavement made of sapphire, clear as the sky itself. But God did not raise his hand against these leaders of the Israelites; they saw God, and they ate and drank."

How can this be explained? Abraham Ibn Ezra interpreted the text to mean that they saw God in a prophetic vision. Then why did God tell them in 24:1 to actually go up the mountain *to the Lord,* remaining at a distance from him while Moses alone drew near? And why does the text point out that God did not lift his hand against them, as would have been expected? Obviously, this was far more than a prophetic vision.

The Targum also had a problem with these verses and could not translate them directly,[41] rendering instead, "They saw the glory of the God of Israel . . . they saw the glory of the LORD."[42] Yet the text says, "They saw the God of Israel . . . they saw God." What is the answer? Let's keep looking at the texts. There's more evidence to consider.

According to a story in the Talmud (b. Sanhedrin 38b), a man identified as a schismatic—here a clear reference to a Jewish follower of Jesus—was talking to a rabbi about Exodus 24:1, the beginning of the passage we are looking at, in which God said to Moses, "Come up to the LORD [Hebrew, YHWH]." It seems that they were having a discussion similar to our own! The Jewish believer was trying to argue that it seemed odd that God said to Moses, "Come up to YHWH," rather than, "Come up to me." Didn't this seem to indicate more than one divine Person? (It was as if I said to you in a conversation, "You should call Mike Brown," instead of, "You should call me.")

Now, the rabbi could have simply replied, "Such usage is not that unusual in the Hebrew Bible." Instead, because he too sensed that there were some theological issues to be addressed, the rabbi answered that God was not speaking here of himself but rather of Metatron, the most powerful angel in Rabbinic literature, "whose name is as his Master." In other words, when God said, "Come up to YHWH," he did not mean, "Come up to me" but "Come up to Metatron whose name is YHWH." So according to this Talmudic interpretation, Metatron was called YHWH! Talk about going to all kinds of lengths to avoid the obvious.[43]

The simple fact is that when God said, "Come up to the LORD," that's exactly what he meant. He was inviting Moses to come into his very own presence—not merely that of an angel.

"Well," you might say, "what about Exodus 3. Doesn't that chapter equate seeing the angel of the Lord with seeing God?" You're getting very close! The relevant verses read:

> Now Moses was tending the flock of Jethro his father-in-law, the priest of Midian, and he led the flock to the far side of the desert and came to Horeb, the mountain of God. There the angel of the LORD appeared to him in flames of fire from within a bush. Moses saw that though the bush was on fire it did not burn up. So Moses thought, "I will go over and see this strange sight—why the bush does not burn up." When the LORD saw that he had gone over to look, God called to him from within the bush, "Moses! Moses!" And Moses said, "Here I am." "Do not come any closer," God said. "Take off your sandals, for the place where you are standing is holy ground." Then he said, "I am the God of your father, the God of Abraham, the God of Isaac and the God of Jacob." At this, Moses hid his face, because he was afraid to look at God.
>
> Exodus 3:1–6

How does Targum Onkelos translate the end of verse 6? Moses "was afraid to look beside the glory of the LORD." Once again, the Targum found it impossible to say what the Scripture said. It was too direct, too clear. Another Targum, called Pseudo-Jonathan, took this even further, translating that Moses was afraid to look at "the glory of the *Shekhina* of the LORD."

This is reminiscent of the Targum's rendering of Exodus 25:8. The Hebrew says, "Then have them make a sanctuary for me, and I will dwell among them." The Targum renders, ". . . and my *Shekhinah* will dwell in their midst."[44] It seems that there is a clear pattern emerging. And notice how the text in Exodus 3 completely intertwines the angel of the Lord with the Lord himself: *The angel of the LORD* appeared to Moses in the flaming bush, but *the LORD* saw that Moses went over to look, so *God* called to him from within the bush, and Moses hid his face because he was afraid to look at *God*. It seems that God was somehow "in" this angel (remember that the Hebrew word for angel simply means "messenger") and that seeing the angel was equated with seeing God.

According to the Jewish biblical scholar Nahum Sarna, "From several texts it is clear that the demarcation between God and his angel is often blurred [citing examples from Gen. 16:7–9, 11; 22:11–12, 15–18; Exod. 3:2, 4; Judg. 6:11–23]. At the Exodus from Egypt it is now God (Exod. 13:21), now his angel (14:9) who goes ahead of the Israelite camp."[45]

And how does Sarna account for the doctrine of angels (called angelology) in ancient Israel? He offers three scholarly views. One view is to see Israelite angelology as borrowing from Near Eastern mythology, hardly a compelling view for Bible believers. "Another view regards the angel as the personified extension of God's will, or the personification of his self-manifestation. A third theory sees the angel as a conceptual device to avoid anthropomorphism [i.e., speaking of God in human terms]. He serves as a mediator between the transcendent God and His mundane world."[46]

Now, if we look beyond Sarna's rational, slightly technical explanation—since he is trying to explain in human terms how and why the ancient biblical authors "came up" with the concept of angels—we can see at once that he is saying much of what we are saying. Angels can appear as "the personification of his self-manifestation"—i.e., as the concrete, visible embodiment of the glorious God—and angels can serve as mediators "between the transcendent God and His mundane world." This is particularly true in certain key passages, in which it is clear that we are not dealing with any ordinary angel but with one who is especially identified with the Lord. Once again, this teaching explains how the infinite and invisible God can interact with finite, earthly people.

Let's look at Genesis 32:24–30. We read that in the midst of a deep crisis, Jacob was left alone in his tent at night, and there he wrestled with a man until daybreak. (According to Hosea 12:4 this "man" was actually an angel.) After a fierce battle, this mysterious visitor blessed Jacob, changing his name to Israel. "So Jacob called the place Peniel, saying, 'It is because I saw God face to face, and yet my life was spared'" (Gen. 32:30; Peniel means face of God). Not surprisingly, the Targum translated with, "I have seen the angel of the LORD face to face." Yet Jacob said, "I have seen God face to face"!

This is reminiscent of Judges 6, in which Gideon saw the angel of the Lord—sometimes referred to as "the LORD" in the account—and was afraid that he would die:

> Gideon went in, prepared a young goat, and from an ephah of flour he made bread without yeast. Putting the meat in a basket and its broth in a pot, he brought them out and offered them to him [i.e., the angel] under the oak. The angel of God said to him, "Take the meat and the unleavened bread, place them on this rock, and pour out the broth." And Gideon did so. With the tip of the staff that was in his hand, the angel of the LORD touched the meat and the unleavened bread. Fire

flared from the rock, consuming the meat and the bread. And the angel of the Lord disappeared. When Gideon realized that it was the angel of the Lord, he exclaimed, "Ah, Sovereign Lord! I have seen the angel of the Lord face to face!" But the Lord said to him, "Peace! Do not be afraid. You are not going to die."

Judges 6:19–23

Even clearer is Judges 13, in which Manoah, the father of Samson, equated seeing the angel of the Lord with seeing God himself:

Then Manoah took a young goat, together with the grain offering, and sacrificed it on a rock to the Lord. And the Lord did an amazing thing while Manoah and his wife watched: As the flame blazed up from the altar toward heaven, the angel of the Lord ascended in the flame. Seeing this, Manoah and his wife fell with their faces to the ground. When the angel of the Lord did not show himself again to Manoah and his wife, Manoah realized that it was the angel of the Lord. "We are doomed to die!" he said to his wife. "We have seen God!" [This is rendered again by the Targum as, "We have seen the angel of the Lord."] But his wife answered, "If the Lord had meant to kill us, he would not have accepted a burnt offering and grain offering from our hands, nor shown us all these things or now told us this."

Judges 13:19–23

Now, let's stop for a moment and review. According to Exodus 33:20, no one can see God or his face and live. Yet the Hebrew Bible preserves numerous instances of people "seeing God." Look again at the Rabbinic explanations:

- In Exodus 25:8, God says that he will dwell in Israel's midst. The Targum translates this to mean his *Shekhina* will dwell among them.
- Exodus 24:9–11 states that Moses and a select group of Israelites saw God, who did not strike them down. The Targum says that they saw *the glory of God.*
- According to Exodus 24:1, God said to Moses, "Come up to the Lord." The Talmud states that "the Lord" here refers to the angel *Metatron,* whose name is as his Master.
- Jacob, who wrestled with the angel of the Lord, said that he had seen God face to face (Gen. 32:30). The Targum changed this to, "I have seen *the angel of the Lord* face to face." The exact same change is made in Judges 13:22.

- In Exodus 3:1–6, the angel of the Lord, equated with the Lord himself in the text, appeared to Moses in flaming fire in a bush, and Moses looked away because he was afraid to look at God. The Targum says that he was afraid to look near *the glory of the Lord*.

Obviously, these texts presented some problems for the rabbis. (We won't even mention passages such as Isaiah 6 and Ezekiel 1, in which the prophets said that they saw the Lord, since someone could argue that these were just prophetic visions.) How could God actually dwell in the midst of his people? How could anyone see him and not die? And why was seeing his angel the same as seeing him? Speaking for the ancient rabbis you might reply, "He dwells in our midst by his Shekhina, his glorious presence, and he reveals himself to us through his angel, who bears his name. Seeing him is like seeing God, just not directly."

Good response. You're really close now. The only problem is that seeing the angel of the Lord is *not* seeing God—unless that angel is more than just an angel. And no angel is called "the Lord"—not Metatron, not Michael, not Gabriel, not anyone—unless he is, in some sense, the Lord. And God said that he himself—not merely his Shekhina—would dwell among his people.[47] So what's the answer? It was always the Son whom they saw. As Paul wrote, Yeshua "is the image of the invisible God." We quote once more John 1:18, this time as translated in the Jewish New Testament: "No one has ever seen God; but the only and unique Son, who is identical with God and is at the Father's side—he has made him known."

Yes, it is the Son, who "is the radiance of God's glory and the exact representation of his being" (Heb. 1:3) who has made the Father known. As he said, "Anyone who has seen me has seen the Father" (John 14:9).

No one would argue that various individuals in the Bible saw "the glory of God" as opposed to God himself. In fact, that is exactly what the New Testament tells us happened as Stephen was being stoned to death: "But Stephen, full of the Holy Spirit, looked up to heaven and saw *the glory of God*, and Jesus standing at the right hand of God" (Acts 7:55).

There are similar expressions found in the Tanakh. Look, for example at these verses in the Book of Exodus:

So Moses and Aaron said to all the Israelites, "In the evening you will know that it was the Lord who brought you out of Egypt, and in the morning you will see the glory of the Lord, because he has heard your grumbling against him. Who are we, that you should grumble against us?" . . . While Aaron was speaking to the whole Israelite community, they looked toward the desert, and there was the glory of the Lord appearing in the cloud.

Exodus 16:6–7, 10

Or consider Exodus 24:15–17, verses that are especially important when we remember that it was in this very chapter, just a few verses earlier, that we read that Moses and the elders *saw God.* Here the language is very different:

When Moses went up on the mountain, the cloud covered it, and the glory of the Lord settled on Mount Sinai. For six days the cloud covered the mountain, and on the seventh day the Lord called to Moses from within the cloud. To the Israelites the glory of the Lord looked like a consuming fire on top of the mountain.

Exodus 24:15–17

It is one thing for Scripture to say that people "saw God" and another thing to say that they "saw the glory of God." The Bible makes a clear distinction. The problem arises when the Bible explicitly says that people saw God and the traditional translators and commentators tell us something different. Once again, I emphasize that it is Jesus the Messiah—the divine Son, the image of the invisible God, the Word made flesh, the exact representation of the Father's being—who solves the riddle and explains how someone could really see God, even though God cannot be seen. The Messiah is the visible representation of the invisible, the living manifestation of the glory of God.

I want to give you one more example, possibly the clearest example in the entire Hebrew Bible. At the end of Genesis 17, we read how Abraham and his entire household were circumcised in obedience to the command of the Lord. Genesis 18:1–2 says, "The Lord [Hebrew, YHWH] appeared to him by the terebinths of Mamre; he was sitting at the entrance of the tent as the day grew hot. Looking up, he saw three men standing near him" (NJPSV).

According to the Talmud (b. Bava Mesia 86b), God himself was paying Abraham a personal sick call, checking on him after the ordeal of circumcision. Here is the expanded translation of Rabbi Adin Steinsaltz (the actual words of the Talmud are in bold). We read that Abraham went out

and saw the Holy One, blessed be He, standing at the door of his tent, as the verse says, "And the Lord appeared to him by the terebinths of Mamre." **This is what the verse** is referring to when it **says** (Gen 18:3): "And he said, 'O Lord, if now I have found favor in Your sight, **do not,** I pray you, **pass by Your servant.'"** In this verse Abraham was speaking to God Himself (and so addressed Him as Lord and referred to himself as His servant). **When God saw that** Abraham **was** busy **tying and untying** the bandages of his circumcision, **He said** to Himself, **"It is not fitting** that **I stay here** while Abraham is taking care of His wound." He was about to remove His presence when Abraham pleaded with Him to stay a little longer. And **this is** also **what the verse** refers to when it **says** (Genesis 18:2): **"And he raised his eyes and looked, and,** behold, **three men stood by him; and when he saw them, he ran to meet them."**[48]

Now, here we have a biblical text that indisputably says that the Lord—Hebrew, YHWH—appeared to Abraham, and the Talmud even relates in story form how Abraham actually saw "the Holy One, blessed be He," addressing him as Lord. Yet, just a few words later, this very same biblical text says that Abraham looked up and saw *three men,* the Talmud giving the impression that God himself appeared to Abraham, only to be replaced by these men.

Who were the three men? Some Christian teachers, quite naturally, have suggested that the three men represented the Father, the Son, and the Holy Spirit, but this cannot work for a number of reasons. First, it would mean that Abraham actually saw God the Father, something that would be contrary to Scripture; second, the Bible—Old Testament or New Testament—never pictures God as three separate people; third, as we will see, the context is against this trinitarian reading, since it is only one of the three "men" who is addressed as Lord.

According to the Talmud, the three men were the angels Michael, Gabriel, and Raphael, each with his own special task. Michael came to give Sarah the good news that she would soon have a son, Raphael came to heal Abraham, and Gabriel went to overthrow the cities of Sodom and Gomorrah (although the Talmud says that Michael went along with Gabriel so as to rescue Lot). But there are problems with this view too. First, the text nowhere says that these angels replaced or represented the Lord. Instead, the Bible says that the Lord appeared to Abraham, that he saw three men, and that he addressed one of them both as Lord *('adonai)* and as YHWH. Second, the context indicates clearly that two of the men went on to Sodom—where they are identified as angels—and that Abraham stayed before YHWH, with whom he had an extended dialogue. To be faithful to the Scriptures, we must say that the Lord, with two angels, appeared to Abraham, and all three appeared as human beings who spoke, ate, and drank with Abraham and Sarah.

Let's watch the text unfold. In verse 3, we read that Abraham said, "'adonai, if it please you, do not go on past your servant." According to the traditional Jewish punctuation, and as understood by the Talmud and many Rabbinic commentators, 'adonai here means Lord, indicating that Abraham already understood who one of his guests was. Other traditional commentators suggest that this is unlikely, changing the vowels to read 'adoni, "my lord," as if Abraham simply addressed the apparent leader of the group without knowing who he was. Which view is correct? It really doesn't matter if we keep reading. One of these "men" is YHWH himself!

The text states that Abraham hurried to Sarah, told her to start cooking, and then ran to the herd to get a calf to slaughter. (Abraham's running around makes the Talmudic story a little unlikely too, since a man who was just circumcised would hardly be running around.) After preparing the meal, Abraham watched as the men ate:

> They said to him, "Where is your wife Sarah?" And he replied, "There, in the tent." Then one said, "I will return to you next year, and your wife Sarah shall have a son!" Sarah was listening at the entrance of the tent, which was behind him. Now Abraham and Sarah were old, advanced in years; Sarah had stopped having the periods of women. And Sarah laughed to herself, saying, "Now that I am withered, am I to have enjoyment—with my husband so old?" Then the LORD [YHWH] said to Abraham, "Why did Sarah laugh, saying, 'Shall I in truth bear a child, old as I am?' Is anything too wondrous for the LORD [YHWH]? I will return to you at this time next year, and Sarah shall have a son." Sarah lied, saying, "I did not laugh," for she was frightened. But He replied, "You did laugh."
>
> Genesis 18:9–15 NJPSV

There is only one honest way to read these verses. *One of these three men was the Lord.* Notice carefully: *One of them* promises to return next year so that Sarah will have a son; she laughs out loud when she hears this seemingly impossible promise; *the Lord* then addresses Abraham, asking him why his wife laughed and doubted his promise that he would graciously visit her the coming year; Sarah *heard* what he said, denying that she laughed; then he replied to her. There is absolutely no way around it. Abraham, Sarah, and the Lord were all there together.

And, as if we needed any more proof, here is the clincher. Verse 16 states that "the men set out from there and looked down toward Sodom, Abraham walking with them to see them off" (NJPSV), explaining in the next verses that the Lord then filled Abraham in on what he was about to do. This brings us to verse 22, "The men went on from there to Sodom, while Abraham remained standing before the LORD" (NJPSV), to whom he intercedes on behalf of Sodom through verse 32. So, *the men* went on to Sodom while *the Lord* remained with Abraham.

Now brace yourself for the last verse of chapter 18 and the first verse of chapter 19: "When the LORD had finished speaking to Abraham, He departed; and Abraham returned to his place. The two angels arrived in Sodom in the evening, as Lot was sitting in the gate of Sodom" (NJPSV). The Scripture tells us that *the Lord* appeared to Abraham, then it says that Abraham saw *three men* by his tent, then it identifies *one* of those three as *the Lord*, who holds a conversation with Abraham and Sarah. The Bible then says that Abraham walked with the men as they went on their way to Sodom, that *the Lord* then informed Abraham of his intentions to destroy Sodom and Gomorrah, that *the men* (i.e., the other two men)[49] continued on to Sodom while Abraham stayed and talked with *the Lord*, and that when they were done, *the Lord* left and Abraham went home, and that *two angels* then arrived in Sodom. I'll say it again: One of those three men was YHWH, the Lord.

The awesome and exciting thing about this text is that it explicitly tells us that Abraham and Sarah talked with the Lord, that he appeared in human form to them, dusty feet and all (see Gen. 18:4), and that he even sat down and ate their food.[50] Yet all the while he remained God in heaven!

I wonder what our critics would do with this passage if it was not in the Hebrew Bible but rather in the New Testament Scriptures alone. They certainly would try to attack it as crass, asking us if God gained any weight when he ate and if he had to relieve himself when he was finished. After all, those are the kind of objections we hear when we talk about Jesus the Messiah being the Son of God in the flesh.

The fact is, Genesis 18 clearly and indisputably teaches that God can come to earth in human form for a period of time if he so desires. And if he could do this for a few hours, in temporary human form, he could do this for a few years, in permanent human form. This is what theologians call the incarnation, God coming down to earth as a man in the person of his Son.[51] And it is only when we recognize the Son—the exact representation of God, and yet God himself—that we can explain how God remained the Lord in heaven while also appearing as the Lord on earth in Genesis 18. Even if you study all the Rabbinic commentaries you want, you won't find another explanation that works.

I well remember talking about Jesus the Messiah with a rabbi at Phil's Kosher Delicatessen in Smithtown, Long Island. Suddenly a light went on within him and he said, "So Jesus was like a walking Shekhina!" Exactly! The Lord, who remained hidden in heaven just as he always had, walked among us in his Son, the Messiah, the true messenger of the Lord and the bearer of his glory.

Could it be that when Moses and the elders saw the unseen God they actually saw his Son? Could it be that when Gideon and Manoah saw the angel of the Lord—somehow identified with the Lord himself—it was the Son whom they saw? And could it be that it is not Metatron—an angel mentioned nowhere in the Bible—who bears the name of the Lord, but the Son of God who does? Yes, yes, and yes!

Listen to more of the words of Jesus the Messiah, the Son of God: "Do not believe me unless I do what my Father does. But if I do it, even though you do not believe me, believe the miracles, that you may know and understand that the Father is in me, and I in the Father. . . . I and the Father are one" (John 10:37–38, 30). Once more, there is nothing idolatrous here. In fact, these words of our Messiah put a lot of the pieces together!

After his resurrection, Jesus said to the women who had come to his tomb, "I am returning to my Father and your Father, to my God and your God" (John 20:17). Notice that he called him "my Father" and "my God." Yet when Thomas saw him a short while later he exclaimed, "My Lord and my God!" (John 20:28). It makes perfect sense. Seeing Jesus was seeing God, yet Jesus did not call himself God. He called himself God's Son—the one in whom the fullness of God dwells in bodily form. This contradicts nothing that we saw in numerous texts from the Hebrew Scriptures. Rather, it opens up the meaning of these texts in a way that answers the questions that neither the Targums, nor the Talmud, nor the Rabbinic commentators could answer.

You may, however, still be wondering about something. You might say, "Okay, I see that in one real sense Jesus makes God known, and in another real sense, he himself is divine. But doesn't this mean that

God is somehow divided? And you never explained where this 'Son of God' came from?" I'm glad you asked. In fact, we devote the next answer to the specific subject of the "Son of God" question. But there are a few important points to make right now.

John the Immerser said of the Messiah, "A man who comes after me has surpassed me because he was before me" (John 1:30), and Jesus himself spoke about the relationship he had with the Father before the world began: "Now this is eternal life: that they may know you, the only true God, and Jesus [the Messiah], whom you have sent. I have brought you glory on earth by completing the work you gave me to do. And now, Father, glorify me in your presence with the glory I had with you before the world began" (John 17:3–5).

The Scriptures state that "Jesus knew that the Father had put all things under his power, and that he had come from God and was returning to God" (John 13:3), and he himself said to his disciples, ". . . the Father himself loves you because you have loved me and have believed that I came from God. I came from the Father and entered the world; now I am leaving the world and going back to the Father" (John 16:27–28).

That's why Jesus could say, "You are from below; I am from above. You are of this world; I am not of this world" (John 8:23), and "before Abraham was, I am" (John 8:58). The idea of a preexistent Messiah who will come down from heaven is even found in traditional Jewish sources (see below, 3.22, for references); the New Testament just gives us the rest of the story.

The most detailed statement of this comes from the pen of Paul, the brilliant Jewish scholar and teacher. He explains the incarnation:

> Your attitude should be the same as that of [Messiah] Jesus: Who, being in very nature God, did not consider equality with God something to be grasped [i.e., held on to], but made himself nothing, taking the very nature of a servant, being made in human likeness. And being found in appearance as a man, he humbled himself and became obedient to death—even death on a cross! Therefore God exalted him to the highest place and gave him the name that is above every name, that at the name of Jesus every knee should bow, in heaven and on earth and under the earth, and every tongue confess that Jesus [the Messiah] is Lord, to the glory of God the Father.
>
> Philippians 2:5–11

So where did the Messiah come from? He came from God. Is he divine? Yes, because he is the Son of God. (We'll explain this concept more fully in the next objection.) Is he also human? Yes, since he took on human nature and as a man became the mediator between God and mankind, expressing the amazing breadth and depth of God's love for a sinning world. To save us and deliver us, he joined himself with us.

Now, you will remember our discussion about the Shekhina (above, 3.1), what the Israeli scholar Ephraim Urbach calls "The Presence of God in the World." The Shekhina was one of the most important Rabbinic ways of explaining how the infinite and transcendent God could really be *with* his people in this world.[52] We explained previously how the rabbis believed that "at the time of the destruction of the Temple *(mishkan)*, the Shekhinah went into exile, as it were, and was thought to accompany the Jewish people in their wanderings—sharing their sufferings and longing with them to be reunited once more with the Holy Land."[53]

God, so to speak, is experiencing internal "disunity" until his people are fully restored. In that sense, their physical regathering and spiritual renewing will mean the complete restoration of his unity. This is actually very close to a New Testament concept, namely, that the Son of God, who came forth from his Father, joined himself to us in our human nature, died, rose again, and returned to his Father in heaven, will in the end submit himself back to his Father "so that God will be all in all": "For he [God] 'has put everything under his [Jesus'] feet' [Ps. 8:6(7)]. Now when it says that 'everything' has been put under him, it is clear that this does not include God himself, who put everything under [Messiah]. When he has done this, then the Son himself will be made subject to him who put everything under him, so that God may be all in all" (1 Cor. 15:27–28). It begins with one God, and it will end with one God. Jesus the Messiah, the Son of God, makes him known to man.

So the next time someone says to you, "God is not a man, so Jesus cannot be God," you have a sound answer to give: "Of course, God is not a man. But can he reveal himself in and through a man? Can he temporarily pitch his tent among us? Can his fullness dwell in a virgin-born human? The scriptural answer is yes."

And if someone hits you with, "Your god wore diapers; our God sits enthroned in heaven," tell them, "My God, who is the God of Abraham, Isaac, and Jacob, always has and always will sit enthroned in heaven. But his divine Word became flesh and blood. It's really quite a lofty spiritual concept!"

You are now ready to teach them. In fact, you can begin by quoting John 1:18.

3.3. God doesn't have a son.

> It all depends on what you mean by the word *son*. In the Hebrew Bible, Israel was called God's son, the king was called God's son, and the angels were called God's sons. Is it any wonder that the Messiah, the ideal representative of Israel, the king of all earthly kings, and the one more highly exalted than the angels, should be called God's Son? More than anyone else who has walked this earth, Jesus the Messiah is uniquely entitled to be called the Son of God.

Obviously, none of us believe that God had a son in the same way that a human father would have a son. We are fully aware that the creator of the universe wasn't married. What then do we mean when we say that Jesus is the "Son of God"?

Christian theologians often explain that Jesus was "eternally begotten of the Father," yet that is not the easiest concept to grasp. Technical terms such as *circumincession, coinherence, subordinationism,* and *prolation* don't help us much either. (To tell you the truth, I'm not too sure *I* can even tell you precisely what each of these words means.)[54] So rather than getting too theological, let's think through some issues with regard to the concept of "son of God" in the Bible, and as we study these issues, remember this one important fact: We believe that the Son of God is truly divine, eternal, and not created. When he came down to earth, he took on human form, and from that point on, we have known him as Jesus the Messiah. The eternal Son of God made himself known to us as Yeshua, the Jewish carpenter, rabbi, Messiah, and Savior of the world.

Turning to the biblical concept of "son," any student of the Semitic languages knows that the word *son* (Hebrew, *ben;* Aramaic, *bar;* Arabic, *ibn*) has many different meanings. It can refer to literal offspring (such as one's physical son or distant descendant) as well as to metaphorical offspring (such as "the sons of the prophets," meaning the disciples of the prophets). When applied to the Israelite king, it means "son" by divine adoption (e.g., 2 Sam. 7:14: "I will be his father, and he will be my son"), and it can even apply to the people of Israel as a whole, since they were specially chosen by God (see Exod. 4:22–23: "Then say to Pharaoh, 'This is what the LORD says: Israel is my first-born son, and I told you, "Let my son go, so he may worship me"'"). In this sense, it could also apply to the obedient people of Israel as individuals (Hosea 1:10: "They will be called 'sons of the living God.'").

Another meaning of "son" has to do with those who belong to the same class of being. Thus the angels are called *benei 'elohim,* "sons of God," meaning those who share in the qualities of *'elohim:* partaking of heavenly, spirit nature as opposed to the earthly, flesh nature of humans.

Therefore, the angels, the kings, and the nation could be called "sons of God." In the Hebrew Scriptures, it seems that God had many sons! And Israel was even called his "firstborn." But neither the angels nor the king nor the people of Israel were *literally* sons of God, as if the Lord consorted with a goddess who then gave birth, the way the gods and goddesses did in pagan mythology. Unfortunately, some traditional Jewish teachers have understood the concept of Jesus the Messiah as "Son of God" in a crassly literal way, and some segments of the church may have contributed to this. It is important, then, that we understand in exactly what ways the Messiah is the Son of God.

Israel, the Lord's "firstborn son," was specially singled out by God and appointed to a specific mission. In a unique sense, God himself was Israel's Father. So, too, Jesus the Messiah was specially singled out and appointed to a specific mission, and in a unique sense, God was his Father. But, quite obviously, the sonship of Jesus goes well beyond the sonship of Israel. What about the sonship of Israel's king? There are a number of important Scripture passages to consider.

I previously quoted 2 Samuel 7:14, in which the Lord tells David that he will establish a dynasty for him, treating the future ruling sons of David as his own sons. Speaking of Solomon he said, "I will be his father, and he will be my son." In Psalm 2:7, the king (David? Solomon? a later descendant of David?) says, "I will tell of the decree. The LORD said to me, 'You are My son; this day have I begotten you.'"[55] When did the Lord utter those words? They were probably spoken by a prophet at the time of the king's coronation, when the descendant of David became recognized as a "son" of God, and they may have become a regular feature of that momentous ceremony, whenever a new king would begin his reign.[56]

But there's something more. Note carefully those final words: "today I have begotten you" (*'ani hayyom yelidtika; yalad* is the standard Hebrew verb used for a woman giving birth to a baby or a man fathering a child). Either this is a direct prophecy of Jesus (and there are many Christians who would say it is!), or else it indicates that when David (or one of his sons) became king, his adoption by God was recognized as some kind of divine begetting.[57] The choice of words is quite bold! "Today I have begotten you."

But the plot thickens. Many times in the psalms, the Lord *and* his anointed king are described in equally exalted terms, and similar reverence is required for both. Consider these following clear parallels (which I have translated for greater clarity): In Psalm 83:18, God is "the Most High over all the earth," while in Psalm 89:28, it is the Davidic king, designated significantly as "firstborn," who has been appointed "the most high of the kings of the earth." In Psalm 86:9, "all nations will bow down" to the Lord, yet in 72:11, the foreign kings will bow down to the Davidic king. First Chronicles 29:20 is even more to the point: "They [i.e., the people] bowed down and did obeisance to the LORD and to [David] the king." So also in Psalm 2:11 and 100:2, the rulers and peoples are exhorted to worship/serve the Lord, while in 18:44 and 72:11, it is the Davidic king whom they must worship/serve.

Both God and his anointed king are worthy of praise (see Ps. 67:4, where the peoples are called on to extol God, and 45:17[18], where it is the king whom they will extol forever), and both are clothed with "glory and honor" (cf., e.g., Ps. 96:6 with 21:6). Of the royal king it can be said, "All kings will bow down to him and all nations will serve him" (Ps. 72:11); for "I will also appoint him my firstborn, the most exalted *['elyon]* of the kings of the earth" (Ps. 89:27[28]). "I will set his hand over the sea, his right hand over the rivers" (Ps. 89:25[26]), and "I will establish . . . his throne as long as the heavens endure" (Ps. 89:29[30]). "Therefore the nations will praise [him] for ever and ever" (Ps. 45:17[18]).

God's "son," the Davidic king, was quite an exalted figure! Is it any wonder that Scripture declares that in the Messianic era the people "will serve the LORD their God and David their king" (Jer. 30:9)?

Let me state these facts again clearly: According to the Hebrew Bible, the Davidic king was called God's son and firstborn, and he was described as begotten by God. He was to be praised, extolled, served, and adored.[58] How much more could this be said of the supreme Davidic king, the Messiah, the ultimate "Son of God"?

We know, of course, that as Jews we are to have no other gods aside from the Lord. That is the first of the Ten Commandments, and, as we saw in answering the last objection, a true, New Testament faith in Jesus the Messiah agrees with this both in letter and in spirit. But here is something interesting to consider: Even if you didn't understand that the Messiah was both divine and human (and therefore, in praising and adoring him we really *are* praising and adoring God), you would still need to recognize that every major Hebrew word for worship, praise, service, adoration, and obeisance that is used in the

Bible with reference to God is also used with reference to the Messiah, the Davidic king. These are indisputable facts.[59]

This is in harmony with what Jesus taught in John 5:22–23: "Moreover, the Father judges no one, but has entrusted all judgment to the Son, that all may honor the Son just as they honor the Father. He who does not honor the Son does not honor the Father, who sent him."

These words are in complete harmony with the verses we just read from the Tanakh: God and his Son, the Davidic Messiah, are to be honored and revered. This is also the picture painted in John's heavenly visions in Revelation 5:13: "Then I heard every creature in heaven and on earth and under the earth and on the sea, and all that is in them, singing: 'To him who sits on the throne and to the Lamb be praise and honor and glory and power, for ever and ever!'" These words are the fulfillment of that which was promised in the psalms: All peoples will praise and glorify God and his anointed one, the Messiah.

The reason I quote these New Testament verses here is so that you can see firsthand exactly what these Scriptures declare, helping to do away with prejudice and misunderstanding. If you really adhere to the words of the Hebrew Bible, you will have no problem adhering to the words of Jesus and his followers as recorded in the New Covenant Scriptures.

For now, however, we will return to Psalm 2 in the Tanakh in light of a homiletical Rabbinic commentary called *Midrash Tehillim*. The midrash is addressing the words, "I will declare the decree. The Lord said to me, 'You are my son; today I have begotten you.'" Which decree, the rabbis ask, is being referred to here? First, it is answered, the text refers to "the decree of the Torah," Exodus 4:22, where God calls Israel his firstborn son. In other words, just as Israel was God's son, so also the king was God's son. Next, it refers to "the decree of the Prophets," citing Isaiah 52:13 ("Behold, my servant will act wisely") and Isaiah 42:1 ("Here is my servant, whom I uphold, my chosen one in whom I delight"). Now, what is interesting here is that neither of these verses makes reference to the term *son*, yet they are among the most famous Messianic prophecies in the entire Bible, often pointed to by Christians with ultimate reference to Jesus. And the midrash ties them in with the king being called God's son in Psalm 2:7!

Next, the rabbis point to "the decree of the Writings" (i.e., the remainder of the Tanakh), citing Psalm 110:1, "The Lord said to my lord, 'Sit at my right hand,'" a verse quoted by Jesus himself to demonstrate that as Messiah, he was more than just David's son, since David in Psalm 110 called him "my lord" (see Matt. 22:42–45). And all this is given in explanation of "the decree" proclaiming the Davidic king as God's son. But it gets even better.

The final verse cited is Daniel 7:13: "In my vision at night I looked, and there before me was one like a son of man, coming with the clouds of heaven." Thus, in light of this Rabbinic compilation of Scripture, the exalted figure coming in the clouds of heaven is none other than the Davidic king, the Son of God! (Remember this is *Rabbinic* midrash not New Testament commentary.) From a Messianic standpoint, this verse in Daniel is of critical importance. It goes on to say:

> He [i.e., this one like a son of man] approached the Ancient of Days and was led into his presence. He was given authority, glory and sovereign power; all peoples, nations and men of every language worshiped him. His dominion is an everlasting dominion that will not pass away, and his kingdom is one that will never be destroyed.
>
> Daniel 7:13–14

What an exalted figure!

Now, let's put this all together: According to this Midrash, the justification for calling the king the son of God is based on: (1) God calling Israel his firstborn son; (2) prophecies from Isaiah referring to the faithful servant of the Lord, clearly Messianic references; and (3) a royal psalm in which God says to the king, "Sit at my right hand," and the glorious "son of man" prophecy from Daniel. If I didn't read this myself in the Hebrew *Midrash Tehillim*, I would have thought that a Messianic Jew put these verses together. They are some of the most common texts that we quote, all with reference to Jesus the Messiah. And here the rabbis tie them in with the Davidic king as son of God. In fact, Rabbi Yudan states explicitly that the words "you are my son" refer to the Messiah.

There were a number of Davidic kings in our history, some of whom were great, like David, Solomon, Hezekiah, and Josiah, and each of whom would have been called "God's son." But none of them sat down at God's right hand (Psalm 110), none of them were (or are) worshiped and adored by people of every nation and tongue (Daniel 7), and only Yeshua, who called himself both "Son of man" and "Son of God," will return in the clouds of heaven (again, Daniel 7). He fulfills that which was prophetically spoken of the Davidic king, the anointed *(mashiach)* of the Lord, in the Prophets and Psalms.

In fact, according to Psalm 45 and Isaiah 9, this anointed king was even called "God." Let's look first at Psalm 45. To help you understand this psalm, spoken to the Davidic king, I will leave the Hebrew word *'elohim* ("God") untranslated in the following verses:

> You are the most excellent of men
>> and your lips have been anointed with grace,
>> since *'elohim* has blessed you forever. . . .
> In your majesty ride forth victoriously
>> in behalf of truth, humility and righteousness;
>> let your right hand display awesome deeds. . . .
> Your throne, O *'elohim,* will last for ever and ever;
>> a scepter of justice will be the scepter of your kingdom.
> You love righteousness and hate wickedness;
>> therefore *'elohim,* your *'elohim,* has set you above your
>> companions
>> by anointing you with the oil of joy.

> Psalm 45:2, 4, 6, 7[3, 5, 7, 8]

So this royal descendant of David is called *'elohim:* "Your throne, O God *['elohim],* will last for ever and ever"! To attempt to translate the key verse with "your divine throne" or "your throne is God" is forced, to say the least. The most natural and obvious meaning is, "Your throne, O God," spoken to the Davidic king!

When I first started studying Hebrew in college, I asked my professor, a very friendly Israeli rabbi, to translate for me the words *kis'aka 'elohim 'olam wa'ed.* He replied immediately, "Your throne, O God, is for ever and ever," explaining, "These are praises to the Almighty." I then asked him to read the rest of the psalm, clearly addressed to the king, and his face dropped. How could this earthly king be called *'elohim*? To repeat: This is the most natural and obvious meaning of the Hebrew, and no one would have questioned such a rendering had the entire psalm been addressed to God.[60] How then can the earthly king be called "*'elohim*"?

Obviously, when we apply this verse to Jesus the Messiah, there is no question or difficulty. In fact, he is the *answer* to the question and the *solution* to the difficulty. But this psalm was originally addressed to an entirely human "son of God" and later applied in its fullest sense to Jesus, the last and greatest Davidic king. How can this be?

Jewish scholars have sometimes forced the translation of the key words in order to avoid the powerful implications of the text. This is seen clearly in the 1917 Jewish Publication Society Version, which rendered Psalm 45:6[7] as, "Your throne, *given of God,*" even though the translators created the words "given of God" out of thin air.[61] On the other hand, Christian scholars, in applying the words to Jesus alone, have sometimes failed to explain the original context of the psalm, which was addressed to an earthly king. How can we be faithful to both the original text and the original context?

The answer is very important and helps to provide a key to understanding Messianic prophecy. The word *'elohim* can mean God, god, gods, or angels, all of which refer in some sense to "divine beings." It is also important to note that in the Ancient Near East, the kings of Mesopotamia and Egypt were considered gods themselves.[62] This, however, was not the case in Israel. Rather, the Davidic king was a highly exalted human, recognized as God's unique son. Here in Psalm 45, the Hebrew language was stretched to its limit, speaking of the Davidic king as *'elohim,* a "divine one."[63] But this daring concept serves as the perfect introduction to the *real* divine sonship of the Messiah. He truly is *'elohim*! So this verse applied in a limited sense to the earthly, Davidic king, and it applies in its full sense to Jesus, the Davidic Messiah.[64]

This may seem a little complex, but it really is very simple. Every time a new Davidic king was installed, there was an elaborate ceremony, and it appears that psalms such as Psalm 2 were read, proclaiming the king to be God's son, the anointed *(mashiach)* of the Lord (cf. Ps. 2:2), and promising him rulership over the entire world (see Ps. 2:8–9). Eventually, these psalms became part of our Hebrew Bible, and as each new king failed to live up to the high prophetic expectations, disappointment set in. But these were God's words and God's promises. How could they fail to reach their fulfillment? It was this kind of tension that caused the people of Israel to begin to look for a greater son of David, the anointed one *(mashiach)* par excellence.

When Jesus *the* Messiah finally came into the world, these royal psalms reached their goal. Here was one who truly was God's Son, who in a unique way was *'elohim* among us, and who was David's lord, to be worshiped and served by all mankind. Thus, the royal psalms had their *partial application* to the earthly sons of David, but they were only *fulfilled* through Yeshua, the greater son of David. This understanding alone does justice to the truth of the Hebrew Bible and the truth of history.

The same principle applies to Isaiah 9:6–7[5–6], a prophetic announcement of the birth of a new Davidic king whose kingdom would be established forever, words that became famous around the world through Handel's *Messiah*. The NIV, a traditional Christian translation, reads:

For to us a child is born,
   to us a son is given,
   and the government will be on his shoulders.
And he will be called
   Wonderful Counselor, Mighty God,
   Everlasting Father, Prince of Peace.
Of the increase of his government and peace
   there will be no end.
He will reign on David's throne
   and over his kingdom,
establishing and upholding it
   with justice and righteousness
   from that time on and forever.
The zeal of the LORD Almighty
   will accomplish this.

Who is this child and what is the meaning of his name? The verses preceding this glorious prophecy refer to the fall of Assyria, the great enemy of the Jewish people seven hundred years before Jesus. So the birth announcement *could* refer to a Davidic king born in that general time frame. But no king born at that time fulfilled what was promised. Just read the verses again, ignoring for a moment the names of the child. The only godly king of that era, Hezekiah, hardly lived up to any of the promises given, and before he was dead, the prophet Isaiah informed him that his descendants would be taken into exile in Babylon (see Isaiah 39). Other interpreters, both Jewish and Christian, have argued that this is a Messianic prophecy, plain and simple, since the prophets always saw the Messiah coming on the immediate horizon of history. In this vein, the Targum explicitly calls the child born "Messiah."

Actually, I believe there is truth to both interpretations: These prophetic words, spoken over a Davidic king born in Isaiah's day, were never fulfilled. They only reached their goal when the Messiah came into the world. It really is simple. It's not that the prophets spoke falsely or the psalmists wrote falsely. Instead, they were sometimes inspired by the Spirit to speak of *each* Davidic king as if he were *the* Davidic king, painting a picture for us of who the Messiah would be and what he would do. This helps to clear up many misunderstandings that both Jewish and Christian scholars have had with these texts. These verses had their immediate, incomplete application in the days when they were spoken, and they have their final, complete application in the Messianic era, an era that began when Jesus came into the world.

But let's look back at the names of the child according to Isaiah 9:6[5]. How can he be called "Wonderful, Counselor, Mighty God, Father Forever, Prince of Peace"? There is no problem with "Wonderful" and "Counselor," nor does "Prince of Peace" present any problem for a human being. As for "Father Forever" (which is a better translation of the Hebrew 'abi 'ad), when it is understood that the king as shepherd, protector, and leader of the people was their "father," then this too can be applied to a human being. But "Mighty God"?

The Targum, in a valiant but futile attempt to get around this, paraphrases, "And his name will be called before the Wonderful Counselor, the Mighty God who exists forever, 'Messiah,' for peace will abound upon us in his days." So instead of heaping up names on this royal child—a common ancient Near Eastern practice at the time of enthronement—the Targum heaps the names on the Lord! This is not only farfetched, it is a grammatical monstrosity, as is widely recognized by translators and commentators of every background.

Modern Jewish versions attempt to find different solutions to the problem,[65] but the most obvious reading of the Hebrew text—just as in Psalm 45—is that the titles are descriptive of the king himself, including "Mighty God" ('el gibbor), and this view is commonly found in the Talmud (b. Sanhedrin 94a) and later Rabbinic writings,[66] and it is expressly supported by the brilliant medieval commentator Abraham Ibn Ezra. In fact, in section nine of the *Huppat Eliyahu* in *Otsar Midrashim*, all of these names are given as titles of the Messiah.[67] Ibn Ezra, reflecting views expressed elsewhere in Rabbinic literature, explains the words as follows:

> The correct view in my opinion is that all these are names of the child.[68] *pele'*—because the Lord did wonders in his days; *yo'ets*—such was Hezekiah [as it is written], "And the king took counsel" [see 2 Chron. 30:2]; *'el gibbor*—because he was strong, and the kingdom of the house of David was prolonged because of him; *['abi] 'ad*—the word *'ad* has the same meaning as "dwelling in eternity" [in Isa. 57:15]; *sar shalom*—because there was peace in his days.

There is only one problem with Ibn Ezra's interpretation: He explains how the word *gibbor* (strong one, hero, warrior) could apply to Hezekiah, but he fails to explain how the word *'el*, "God" could refer to him![69] Once again, we are faced with a problem that only Jesus the Messiah can solve, namely, how the Davidic king could be human and yet more than human, David's son and yet David's lord, both son of

God and Son of God. In this text, the prophet Isaiah, almost bursting the bounds of the Hebrew language, called the Davidic king, "mighty God," a title reserved elsewhere for Yahweh alone (see Isa. 10:21). That's the gospel truth. The text says what it says, and there is no way to get around this profound fact: No Davidic king could bring to reality the full meaning of these words except Jesus the Messiah. It is the Hebrew Bible itself that indicates that the Davidic Messiah would be the "Son of God" in a unique way, even bearing divine qualities and in a real sense being divine.

Once again, we see that it is only through Jesus the Messiah that all the varied pieces of the puzzle fit together. Far from being idolatrous, the New Testament doctrine of the Son of God is the culmination of the dream of Israel's prophets and psalmists, the fulfillment of the Hebrew Scriptures, the hope of mankind. And the doctrine of the virgin birth is not some borrowed, pagan myth.[70] Rather, it explains how the eternal Son of God could enter our world as a "divine human." His origins were both earthly and heavenly, as the angel Gabriel announced to Miriam, the Messiah's mother: "The Holy Spirit will come upon you, and the power of the Most High will overshadow you. So the holy one to be born will be called the Son of God" (Luke 1:35).[71]

As you read through the New Testament on your own, you will learn that Jesus is called the Son of God because he came forth from God the Father, because he was born to a young Jewish virgin, because he had an intimate and unique relationship with his Father, and because he was the Davidic king. This is what Paul meant when he spoke of Yeshua, "who as to his human nature was a descendant of David, and who through the Spirit of holiness was declared with power to be the Son of God by his resurrection from the dead: Jesus [the Messiah] our Lord" (Rom. 1:2–4).

Later church theologians, trying to explain the mystery of how the Son of God could also be God the Son, stated that he was eternally begotten, not made. But such a statement does not *lessen* the mystery of God and his Son. Rather, it heightens the mystery, the wonder, and the awe. One with God, and yet God; called the Son, and yet eternal; and now, in the person of Jesus the Messiah, forever uniting God with man. It really is profound, wouldn't you agree?

I leave you with this riddle, written more than twenty-five hundred years ago, and found in our Hebrew Bible in Proverbs 30:4. It says, "Who has gone up to heaven and come down? Who has gathered up the wind in the hollow of his hands? Who has wrapped up the waters in his cloak? Who has established all the ends of the earth? What is his name, and the name of his son? Tell me if you know!"

Do you know the name of his son? I do![72]

3.4. According to the Law (Deuteronomy 13), Jesus was a false prophet because he taught us to follow other gods (namely, the Trinity, including the god Jesus), gods our fathers have never known or worshiped. This makes all his miracles utterly meaningless.

> Have you ever read what Jesus and his followers taught? They emphasized, "Love the Lord your God with all your heart and with all your soul and with all your mind and with all your strength" (Mark 12:30). Follow him. Obey him. Jesus pointed everyone to God his heavenly Father— by his miracles, by his message, and by his life. He lived, died, and rose again for the glory of his Father. Thus, Jesus was a faithful and true prophet.

We have already discussed in depth the issues of the tri-unity of God and the divinity of the Messiah, demonstrating clearly that such beliefs, when properly understood, are in complete harmony with the Hebrew Scriptures and are thoroughly monotheistic. Of course, there have been all kinds of misunderstandings between Christians and Jews through the years. Early Rabbinic literature seemed to think that the followers of Jesus worshiped three gods,[73] while the statues of Jesus, Mary, and the saints that were made by the Catholic Church certainly departed from the purity of the New Testament faith. But these are misunderstandings and aberrations, and no honest reader of the New Testament could come to any other conclusion but that Jesus and his followers pointed all people to worship the one true God.

Since we have spent so much time on these issues already, I will list here a representative sampling of New Testament verses. This way, you can see for yourself that Jesus was in no way, shape, or form a false prophet who led people to worship foreign and strange gods. Rather, he pointed all people to the Lord.

His ministry of healing and miracles brought glory to God:

Great crowds came to him, bringing the lame, the blind, the crippled, the mute and many others, and laid them at his feet; and he healed them. The people were amazed when they saw the mute speaking, the crippled made well, the lame walking and the blind seeing. And they praised the God of Israel.

Matthew 15:30–31

Everyone was amazed and gave praise to God. They were filled with awe and said, "We have seen remarkable things today."

Luke 5:26

When he came near the place where the road goes down the Mount of Olives, the whole crowd of disciples began joyfully to praise God in loud voices for all the miracles they had seen.

Luke 19:37

His teaching brought glory to God (these are a few examples out of scores):

Let your light shine before men, that they may see your good deeds and praise your Father in heaven. . . . Love your enemies and pray for those who persecute you, that you may be sons of your Father in heaven. He causes his sun to rise on the evil and the good, and sends rain on the righteous and the unrighteous. . . . Be perfect, therefore, as your heavenly Father is perfect.

Matthew 5:16, 44–45, 48

Be careful not to do your "acts of righteousness" before men, to be seen by them. If you do, you will have no reward from your Father in heaven.

Matthew 6:1

This, then, is how you should pray: "Our Father in heaven, hallowed be your name, your kingdom come, your will be done on earth as it is in heaven."

Matthew 6:9–10

His Father's kingdom and his Father's will were the entire focus of his life and ministry. He himself was the way to the Father—not to some new, strange god, but to our Creator and Lord: "I am the way and the truth and the life. No one comes to the Father except through me" (John 14:6). He pointed all people to his Father:

You Samaritans worship what you do not know; we worship what we do know, for salvation is from the Jews. Yet a time is coming and has now come when the true worshipers will worship the Father in spirit and truth, for they are the kind of worshipers the Father seeks.

John 4:22–23

I have come in my Father's name, and you do not accept me; but if someone else comes in his own name, you will accept him. . . . If God were your Father, you would love me, for I came from God and now am here. I have not come on my own; but he sent me.

John 5:43; 8:42

It is only natural, then, when John the Immerser, the forerunner of the Messiah, was born, his old father, Zechariah, spoke these Spirit-inspired words:

> Praise be to the Lord, the God of Israel,
>   because he has come and has redeemed his people.
> He has raised up a horn of salvation for us
>   in the house of his servant David
> (as he said through his holy prophets of long ago),
> salvation from our enemies
>   and from the hand of all who hate us—
> to show mercy to our fathers
>   and to remember his holy covenant,
>   the oath he swore to our father Abraham:
> to rescue us from the hand of our enemies,
>   and to enable us to serve him without fear
>   in holiness and righteousness before him all our days.

Luke 1:68–75

At last, God was sending his redeemer so that his Jewish people— and the Gentiles too—could "serve him without fear in holiness and righteousness before him all our days." This is hardly some kind of idolatrous, new religion! This is the fulfillment of the Mosaic faith.

When we look at the words of the Jewish followers of Jesus as recorded in the rest of the New Testament, we see the exact same themes and the exact same emphasis: Through Jesus the Messiah, we can come into an intimate relationship with the one true God, and it is the responsibility of those who follow the Messiah to make God known to the entire world.

- On the feast of Shavuot (Pentecost), when the disciples were filled with the Holy Spirit, the assembled people from several different countries heard them "declaring the wonders of God in our own tongues" (Acts 2:11). Moments later, when Peter addressed the crowd, he stated that "Jesus of Nazareth was a man accredited by God to you by miracles, wonders and signs, which God did among you through him, as you yourselves know" (Acts 2:22).

- As the number of these Jewish followers of Jesus began to grow rapidly, it is reported that "every day they continued to meet together in the temple courts. They broke bread in their homes and ate together with glad and sincere hearts, praising God and enjoying the favor of all the people" (Acts 2:46–47).
- When the lame man at the Temple was healed, "he jumped to his feet and began to walk. Then he went with [Peter and John] into the temple courts, walking and jumping, and praising God" (Acts 3:8). This is the explanation given by Peter: "The God of Abraham, Isaac and Jacob, the God of our fathers, has glorified his servant Jesus" (Acts 3:13). Such is the early record of the assembly of believers.
- To the recently transformed Thessalonians believers—formerly idolators but now worshipers of the one true God—Paul wrote, "Finally, brothers, we instructed you how to live in order to please God," explaining, "It is God's will that you should be sanc-tified: that you should avoid sexual immorality; that each of you should learn to control his own body in a way that is holy and honorable, not in passionate lust like the heathen, who do not know God. . . . For God did not call us to be impure, but to live a holy life. Therefore, he who rejects this instruction does not reject man but God, who gives you his Holy Spirit" (1 Thess. 4:1, 3–5, 7–8). Obedience to God was the issue.
- In like manner, Peter exhorted his readers to "live such good lives among the pagans that, though they accuse you of doing wrong, they may see your good deeds and glorify God on the day he visits us," further encouraging them to "live as servants of God" and "fear God" (1 Peter 2:12, 16–17).

Similar examples could be given almost without end. In fact, there are more than twelve hundred references to God—meaning the God of Abraham, Isaac, and Jacob—in the New Testament. Thus, the point is clear: Jesus the Messiah, the true and faithful prophet, directed all mankind to worship the one true God. In that regard—and this is something to ponder—he has been the most successful and effective

Jewish prophet who has ever walked the earth. Hundreds of millions of Gentiles now love, adore, worship, and serve the God of Israel because of him.

3.5. The Holy Spirit is not the so-called Third Person of the Trinity.

Rather than discuss the Trinity again (see 3.1, above), let's focus on one question: Is the Holy Spirit only a "what," or are there dimensions in which the Spirit is a "who"? From Scripture, it can be demonstrated that God's Spirit is more than just an abstract power. The Holy Spirit is part of God's very essence and clearly has personality. The New Testament simply expands on these established, biblical truths, which, interestingly enough, are treated in a similar way in some later Rabbinic traditions.

What does the Hebrew Bible say about the Spirit of God? It is well known that the Hebrew word *ruah,* just like the Greek word *pneuma,* can mean "breath" or "wind" as well as "spirit."[74] It is also true that the Tanakh speaks of people being "filled with the Spirit" (which means empowered or equipped by the Spirit), and that it makes reference to the Holy Spirit being "poured out" (Joel 2:28[3:1]). The New Testament uses the exact same phrases and images when referring to the Holy Spirit (see below). But there are other important biblical references that speak clearly of God's *personal interaction* with mankind by his Spirit. The Holy Spirit teaches and instructs, is rebelled against, and is grieved. This speaks clearly of personality not just power.

It is also helpful to remember that the Bible refers to (1) "spirits" among God's heavenly host (e.g., 1 Kings 22:20ff.), referring to angels, good or bad; (2) "evil spirits" (e.g., 1 Sam. 16:14), which are personal demonic beings not just abstract powers; (3) the human "spirit," speaking of inner attitudes, emotions, and the will (e.g., 1 Chron. 5:26; Pss. 32:2; 51:10; 73:21; Prov. 15:13; 18:14), or the inner being in general (e.g., 2 Kings 5:26). As there is a human spirit, there is also a divine Spirit.[75]

According to Psalm 106:32–33, when the children of Israel sinned in the wilderness, it was against God's Spirit that they rebelled: "By the waters of Meribah they angered the Lord, and trouble came to Moses because of them; for they rebelled against the Spirit of God, and rash words came from Moses' lips."[76] The identical theme is found in Isaiah 63:10: "Yet they rebelled and grieved his Holy Spirit. So he turned and became their enemy and he himself fought against them."

Here we learn that Israel's rebellion against God *grieved* the Holy Spirit. It is no surprise then that Micah 2:7 raises the question of whether the Spirit of the Lord can become impatient, helping us to understand that the Spirit refers not only to God's outward power but also to his "inmost being." (Remember: What makes us human is our spirit, our personal, inner being.)

Nehemiah also makes mention of the activity of the Spirit during the wilderness wanderings: "You gave your good Spirit to instruct them. You did not withhold your manna from their mouths, and you gave them water for their thirst" (Neh. 9:20). From this passage we learn that God *gave* his Spirit to the Israelites in the wilderness (cf. Ps. 104:30) *to instruct* them (cf. also Ps. 143:10, and see Zech. 7:12). So his Spirit teaches too! And if the Spirit can be given, then it is possible for the Spirit to be taken away: "Hide your face from my sins and blot out all my iniquity. Create in me a pure heart, O God, and renew a steadfast spirit within me. Do not cast me from your presence or take your Holy Spirit from me" (Ps. 51:9–11).

Now, at this point, it is fair to ask, Is the "Spirit of God" the same as "God"? Yes and no. The Spirit clearly has personality, since the Holy Spirit instructs the people of Israel and can be grieved or angered. Yet the Holy Spirit is the Spirit *of God*—i.e., God's very Spirit, not a separate being. So, in some way, when God gives his Spirit, he is both giving himself as well as giving of himself. The key is always this: God touches us, teaches us, interacts with us, and empowers us *by his Spirit*.

Look carefully at Isaiah 63:11–14:

> Then his people recalled the days of old,
>   the days of Moses and his people—
> where is he who brought them through the sea,
>   with the shepherd of his flock?
> Where is he who set
>   his Holy Spirit among them,
> who sent his glorious arm of power
>   to be at Moses' right hand,
> who divided the waters before them,
>   to gain for himself everlasting renown,

who led them through the depths?
　Like a horse in open country,
　　they did not stumble;
like cattle that go down to the plain,
　they were given rest by the Spirit of the Lord.
This is how you guided your people
　to make for yourself a glorious name.

We see once more reference to the presence of the Holy Spirit in the wilderness wanderings, with the new insight that it was the Spirit of the Lord who gave the Israelites rest.

Putting all this together with Nehemiah 9:19–20, we understand that the Spirit of God was the one who was manifest in the cloud by day and the fire by night: "Because of your great compassion you did not abandon them in the desert. By day the pillar of cloud did not cease to guide them on their path, nor the pillar of fire by night to shine on the way they were to take. You gave your good Spirit to instruct them."

God dwells among us by means of his Spirit. (In a sense, as expressed in Psalm 139:7, God's Spirit is his presence, which is everywhere on the earth.) On the one hand, he sits enthroned in heaven, separate from this earth. On the other hand, he is intimately involved with our daily affairs, right here in our midst. How? By his Spirit. That is why his Spirit can be grieved, and that is why his Spirit is the one who deals with us.

This also explains why there are a number of specific references to the Spirit in the context of the exodus from Egypt and wilderness wanderings: At that time in particular, more than any other period in ancient Israelite history, God was supernaturally manifest in the midst of his people. And so there are more references to the Spirit's presence during this time period. The Spirit of the Lord was right there!

We learn about other aspects of the work of the Holy Spirit in verses such as 2 Samuel 23:2: "The Spirit of the Lord spoke through me; his word was on my tongue." This is unmistakably personal. The Spirit speaks, which indicates a "someone" and not a "something." To make the Spirit in this verse merely synonymous with God's power would be incorrect.

Similar to this is 1 Chronicles 28:11–12:

Then David gave his son Solomon the plans for the portico of the temple, its buildings, its storerooms, its upper parts, its inner rooms and the place of atonement. He gave him the plans of all that the Spirit had put in his mind for the courts of the temple of the Lord and all the surrounding rooms, for the treasuries of the temple of God and for the treasuries for the dedicated things.

Notice here that the Spirit gave David specific plans for the building of the Temple.

According to the prophet Ezekiel, the Spirit of the Lord came upon him and God told him what to say: "Then the Spirit of the LORD came upon me, and he told me to say: 'This is what the LORD says'" (Ezek. 11:5). Do you see how God is identified with his Spirit? The Spirit of the Lord comes on the prophet, and the Lord tells him to speak. This is similar to Nehemiah 9:30: "For many years you were patient with them. By your Spirit you admonished them through your prophets." When the prophets instructed and rebuked, it was the Spirit speaking through them. (See also Micah 3:8 and Isaiah 30:1.)

Interestingly, there are several references in the Rabbinic literature to the Holy Spirit speaking, announcing, crying out, rebuking, and even serving as the counsel for the defense.[77] For example:

- The Talmud (m. Sotah 9:6; b. Sotah 46a) states that when the elders performed the rite of the red heifer (Deut. 21:1–9), "They did not have to say, 'And the blood shall be forgiven them' [Deut. 21:8], instead the Holy Spirit announces to them, 'Whenever you do this, the blood shall be forgiven to you.'"

- Commenting on Exodus 1:12, "But the more they [i.e., the Israelites] were oppressed [by the Egyptians], the more they multiplied and spread," the Talmud states (b. Pesahim 117a) that the Holy Spirit announced to them, "So will he [Israel] increase and spread out!" This is explained by Rashi and other major Jewish commentators to mean that the Holy Spirit said to the Egyptians, "Just as you seek to oppress them more, the more so will they increase and spread out!"[78]

- In Pirkei D'Rabbi Eliezer 31, as Ishmael (Abraham's son) and Eliezer (his steward) argue about who will be Abraham's heir— seeing that they are going together with Abraham to sacrifice Isaac to the Lord (Genesis 22)—the Holy Spirit answers them and says, "Neither this one nor this one will inherit."

- In a late midrash cited in Yalkut Reubeni (9d) to Genesis 1:26, after Ben Sira shared secret, mystical teachings with his son Uzziah and his grandson Joseph, the Holy Spirit called out, "Who is it that revealed My secrets to mankind?" Ben Sira replied, "I, Buzi, the son of Buzi." The Holy Spirit said to him, "Enough!"[79]

- Lamentations Rabbah 3:60, §9 relates that after the Roman emperor Hadrian indiscriminately executed two Jews, the Holy Spirit kept crying out, "You have seen, O LORD, the wrong done to me. Uphold my cause! You have seen the depth of their vengeance, all their plots against me" (Lam. 3:59–60). This provides an example of the Spirit making intercession.[80]

- According to Leviticus Rabbah 6:1, the Holy Spirit is a defense counsel who speaks to Israel on behalf of the Lord and then speaks to the Lord on behalf of Israel. To Israel the Spirit says, "Do not testify against your neighbor without cause" (Prov. 24:28), and to the Lord the Spirit says, "Do not say, 'I'll do to him as he has done to me'" (Prov. 24:29).[81]

In all these citations, which can be easily multiplied (see, e.g., Genesis Rabbah 84:11; Song of Songs Rabbah 8:16; Lamentations Rabbah 1:48), there can be no question that we are dealing with a "who" and not just with a "what," with a personal dimension of God and not just with an impersonal power, with God himself and yet with a "separate" entity who can mediate between God and man.[82] And these citations closely parallel some of the New Testament descriptions of the Holy Spirit, although virtually all the Rabbinic texts cited were written many years later.[83] Now, it's time to compare.

To summarize the teaching of some key New Testament texts, we read that the Holy Spirit empowers (e.g., Luke 24:49; Acts 1:8), comes upon people (e.g., Luke 2:25; Acts 8:16; 10:44; 19:6), anoints (Luke 4:18, quoting Isa. 61:1; Acts 10:38), fills (e.g., Luke 1:15; 1:41; Acts 2:4; 4:8; 4:31), reveals (e.g., Luke 2:26; 1 Cor. 2:10), and leads (e.g., Matt. 4:1; Acts 20:22; Rom. 8:14), just as in the Hebrew Bible. The Holy Spirit speaks through the disciples (Matt. 10:20; Acts 6:10), just as the Spirit spoke through the prophets of old (see Matt. 22:43; Acts 1:16; 11:28; 2 Peter 1:21). And just as the Rabbinic literature at times describes the Holy Spirit as speaking, saying, and communicating directly, the New Testament describes the exact same activity (Acts 10:19; 11:12; 13:2).

Verses such as Acts 4:25 ("You spoke by the Holy Spirit through the mouth of your servant, our father David") or Acts 28:25 ("The Holy Spirit spoke the truth to your forefathers when he said through Isaiah the prophet") reflect the typical understanding of the New Testament authors, an understanding that is in perfect harmony with the teaching of Moses and the prophets. We read in Nehemiah 9:30 that God "admonished" his people by the Holy Spirit, while Acts 9:31 says that the early believers were "encouraged" by the Holy Spirit. In Acts 20:23, Paul speaks of being "warned" by the Holy Spirit, apparently referring to prophetic utterances.

The Holy Spirit is given to the believers (e.g., Luke 11:13; John 7:39; Acts 2:38; cf. Neh. 9:20), just as the Spirit was given to Moses and the elders (see Num. 11:16–17, 24–30). The Holy Spirit is poured out, just as Joel promised (Acts 2:17–18; see also Acts 2:33; 10:45), and through the death and resurrection of Jesus, the Spirit now lives within God's holy people (e.g., John 14:17; Rom. 8:9, 11; 1 Cor. 3:16; 6:19; 2 Cor. 5:5), as the prophets declared (see below).

The Holy Spirit teaches (e.g., Luke 12:12; John 14:26; see also Acts 15:28) and is a Counselor (John 14:16–17; remember Leviticus Rabbah 6:1). The Spirit testifies to the truth about the Messiah (John 15:26; cf. Isa. 11:2) and leads his followers into all the truth (John 16:13). Just as David received instructions about the building of the Temple through the Holy Spirit, so also Jesus the Messiah, after his resurrection, gave his disciples instructions through the Holy Spirit (Acts 1:2).

In light of the evidence from the Hebrew Scriptures and the Rabbinic literature, are the words of Jesus in John troubling at all? He explained to his disciples that

> the Counselor, the Holy Spirit, whom the Father will send in my name, will teach you all things and will remind you of everything I have said to you. . . . When the Counselor comes, whom I will send to you from the Father, the Spirit of truth who goes out from the Father, he will testify about me. . . . But when he, the Spirit of truth, comes, he will guide you into all truth. He will not speak on his own; he will speak only what he hears, and he will tell you what is yet to come.

> John 14:26; 15:26; 16:13

Remember also that the Hebrew Bible helps us to understand that whatever is done to the Lord is done to his Spirit. The New Testament expands on these themes. Echoing the words of Isaiah 63:10, Paul urges us not to "grieve the Holy Spirit" (Eph. 4:30), and just as both Psalms and Isaiah speak of "rebelling" against the Spirit, Jesus warns us not to "blaspheme" the Holy Spirit (Mark 3:28–29)—meaning to willfully attribute the mighty works of the Holy Spirit to demonic powers. Lying to the Holy Spirit means lying to God (Acts 5:3–4), while sinful people "test" (Acts 5:9) and "resist" the Spirit (Acts 7:51).

Why is there much more talk about the Holy Spirit in the New Testament than in the Old Testament? It is because the Messiah has come and inaugurated the first stages of the Messianic age, a time of the Holy Spirit's special activity among mankind. It is a time when the plea of Moses begins to see its realization (Num. 11:29: "I wish that all the LORD's people were prophets and that the LORD would put his Spirit on them!"), a time of the outpouring of the Spirit predicted by Joel,[84] a time when verses such as Leviticus 26:12 and Ezekiel 37:27 begin to reach their fulfillment (see 2 Cor. 6:16–18).[85] This also explains why Jesus, during his time on earth, gave his disciples further teaching about the person and work of the Spirit, preparing them for the new empowering that they were about to receive.

We must remember that, according to the prophets, the Messiah himself was characterized by a special anointing of the Spirit, a picture confirmed in depth by the testimony of the Gospels (see Isa. 11:1–3; also Isa. 42:1; 61:1–3; Matt. 12:28; Luke 4:14; Acts 10:38; of course, we all know that "Messiah" simply means "anointed one"). The New Testament promises that the Messiah's followers would be characterized by a similar anointing—meaning special qualities and supernatural abilities given by the Holy Spirit (see 1 Cor. 12:7–11; Gal. 5:22–23).[86]

In Ezekiel 36 and 37, chapters filled with Messianic imagery, God promised to put his Spirit in us so that we would walk in his ways and keep his commandments. This has happened through the coming of the Messiah. The Holy Spirit, not simply an abstract influence, but rather the essence of God's own being, now lives in us. That's why it becomes completely "natural" to keep the commandments of God, because he—by his Spirit—lives in our hearts. It is in this light that the New Testament makes reference to the "fellowship of the Holy Spirit" (2 Cor. 13:14), and the Hebrew Scriptures, the Rabbinic writings, and the New Testament all associate the Holy Spirit with the joy of the Lord (e.g., Ps. 51:11–12; Pesikta Rabbati 12a; Rom. 14:17).

Paul describes this new life in the Spirit in great detail in Romans 8:1–27. These verses form an inspired commentary to Ezekiel 36:25–27, a future promise still to be realized by the people of Israel as a whole but experienced in great measure by all those—Jew and Gentile alike—who have received new life through the Messiah. God said through Ezekiel:

I will sprinkle clean water on you, and you will be clean; I will cleanse you from all your impurities and from all your idols. I will give you a new heart and put a new spirit in you; I will remove from you your heart of stone and give you a heart of flesh. And I will put my Spirit in you and move you to follow my decrees and be careful to keep my laws.

This glorious experience of the indwelling Holy Spirit has become real to millions around the world through Jesus the Messiah. Once, their very nature was bent on sin, destruction, and selfish satisfaction. Now, they live to give glory to God. Where there was hate, there is love; where there was anger, there is peace; where there was lust, there is self-control; where there was darkness, there is light. That is the effect of the Holy Spirit in the lives of God's people!

To summarize, then, the real question here is *not* whether the Holy Spirit is "the Third Person of the Trinity"—words found nowhere in the New Testament—but whether the New Testament teaching on the subject of the Holy Spirit is in harmony with the evidence of the Hebrew Scriptures, and whether it even has some common ground with later Jewish traditions. The answer is emphatically yes. The Holy Spirit is a "who" and not just a "what," the Holy Spirit is identified directly with God, the Holy Spirit is spoken of as distinct from God. Based on this, theologians have concluded that the Holy Spirit is "the Third Person of the Trinity."[87]

In any case, this much is perfectly clear: There is nothing unbiblical about the New Testament doctrine of the person and work of the Holy Spirit, and even a religious Jew can find parallels to these concepts in the Rabbinic writings.

3.6. According to Isaiah 43:11, God alone is our Savior. We don't need or recognize any other saviors.

Isaiah 43:11 is written with reference to other "gods," and it teaches emphatically that the Jewish people will not be saved by any other so-called god or deliverer. This is clear. It is also clear that God saves through whom he wills to save—whether it be earthly deliverers (such as kings or warriors), angelic messengers, or the Messiah.

The answer to this objection is self-evident if we consult a Hebrew concordance, since the word *moshi'a* (savior) occurs more than thirty times in the Bible, almost every time with reference to someone *other than* Yahweh. So, for example, it is written in Judges 3:9 that when the Israelites cried out to the Lord, he raised up a savior (or deliverer) for them (cf. also Judg. 3:15; 12:3), and in Isaiah 19:20, God promises that he will one day send Egypt a savior and defender who will rescue them—again with reference to someone other than the Lord. In a similar way, Isaiah 33:22 says that God is our lawgiver, judge, and king, but we know, of course, that he used Moses to give us the law, that he raised up numerous judges for Israel, and that the Messiah is known as King Messiah. There is no contradiction here at all.

The simple point is this: God, the only Savior, uses whom he will to deliver his people, and both traditional Judaism and the New Testament recognized that the Messiah would be the Lord's appointed Savior par excellence. Thus, the prayer for the Davidic Messiah in the Amidah (also called the Shemoneh Esreh, i.e., the eighteen foundational petitions in Judaism) talks about waiting for God's salvation to come through his Messiah, the one literally called "the horn of salvation." In fact, the footnote to this benediction in the *ArtScroll Siddur* (reflecting traditional Jewish scholarship) reads, "Here we are taught that the ultimate salvation of the Jewish people is possible only through the Davidic Messiah."[88] Well said!

3.7. We are righteous by what we do, not by what we believe. Christianity is the religion of the creed, Judaism the religion of the deed.

> The New Testament clearly teaches that faith without works is dead. But it also teaches that without faith there can be no meaningful works, and the first thing God wants from us is our total trust and dependence. That is called faith, and it is foundational to the Hebrew Scriptures as well. Our forefathers died in the wilderness because of their unbelief, and being pronounced righteous by God begins with absolute faith in him. So right living is the result of right believing. As a Jew, you should also remember that "the creed" is important in traditional Judaism too.

Believing in the Lord and keeping the commandments of the Lord are interrelated. True faith is marked by godly acts, and godly acts are the result of true faith. Does anyone seek to carefully follow the commandments of God without first *believing* that he exists and that he has, in fact, given us these instructions for life? And can anyone truly put his trust in the Lord without taking on his lordship in his life? The two go hand in hand.[89] As Jacob (James) wrote in the New Testament almost two thousand years ago:

> What good is it, my brothers, if a man claims to have faith but has no deeds? Can such faith save him? Suppose a brother or sister is without clothes and daily food. If one of you says to him, "Go, I wish you well; keep warm and well fed," but does nothing about his physical needs, what good is it? In the same way, faith by itself, if it is not accompanied by action, is dead. But someone will say, "You have faith; I have deeds." Show me your faith without deeds, and I will show you my faith by what I do.
>
> James 2:14–18

The importance of good works was also emphasized numerous times by Paul, even in contexts when he was careful to point out that we are not saved by our works. Rather, God has had mercy on us and redeemed us from our sins *so that* we might give ourselves to good works:

> For it is by grace you have been saved, through faith—and this not from yourselves, it is the gift of God—not by works, so that no one can boast. For we are God's workmanship, created in [Messiah] Jesus to do good works, which God prepared in advance for us to do.
>
> Ephesians 2:8–10

> But when the kindness and love of God our Savior appeared, he saved us, not because of righteous things we had done, but because of his mercy. He saved us through the washing of rebirth and renewal by the Holy Spirit, whom he poured out on us generously through Jesus [the Messiah] our Savior, so that, having been justified by his grace, we might become heirs having the hope of eternal life. This is a trustworthy saying. And I want you to stress these things, so that those who have trusted in God may be careful to devote themselves to doing what is good. These things are excellent and profitable for everyone.
>
> Titus 3:4–8[90]

The problem is that we cannot become righteous in God's sight simply by doing good—we are not good enough!—and this is what makes faith so fundamentally important. We all fall short of the mark continually (see 3.20 for more on this). So the first thing God is looking for is our trust and dependence. He wants us to look to him, to believe what he says about himself. After all, he is our Savior and Deliverer, and without his help, we are doomed. We look to his goodness before we try to be good ourselves. That's where the relationship starts. And having truly put our faith in him—to help us, to guide us, to change us, to forgive us, to save us, to keep us—we live obedient lives as his children.

In that sense, as Paul so often emphasized, we are pronounced righteous before God (i.e., "not guilty," acquitted of all charges, in right standing) *by faith* and not by any amount of good works we could possibly do. It's all because of his mercy! Then, as God's forgiven and accepted people, we give ourselves to him heart and soul, mind and strength, demonstrating our faith by our works.

Scripture makes this plain with regard to our father Abraham. In a well-known passage, it is recorded that when the Lord promised Abraham (then known as Abram) that he would have a son in his old age, "Abram believed the LORD, and he credited it to him as righteousness *[tsedaqah]*" (Gen. 15:6). When Abram took God at his word, believing that he would be faithful to accomplish the impossible thing he promised, God credited it to Abram's account as righteousness.[91] It's as if the Lord said, "That man is righteous! He trusts my word explicitly." Our relationship with God begins by faith, and every righteous person in the Bible has been a believer first and a doer second.

This is how the Lord dealt with our people as a whole. He delivered our ancestors from Egypt with a mighty hand and an outstretched arm, making himself known as the only true God, and then he gave us his statutes and laws. In fact, the Ten Commandments do not begin with a prohibition against idolatry but rather with a statement of who our God is: "I am the LORD your God, who brought you out of Egypt, out of the land of slavery" (Exod. 20:2). In light of this, he then said, "You shall have no other gods before me" (Exod. 20:3). First, know me; then, serve me. First, believe me; then, obey me.

"But what about Deuteronomy 6:25?" you ask. "Doesn't that verse state clearly that we are righteous by what we do, without any reference to the concept of faith?" Let's look at this verse in context:

> In the future, when your son asks you, "What is the meaning of the stipulations, decrees and laws the LORD our God has commanded you?" tell him: "We were slaves of Pharaoh in Egypt, but the LORD brought us out of Egypt with a mighty hand. Before our eyes the LORD sent miraculous signs and wonders—great and terrible—upon Egypt and Pharaoh and

his whole household. But he brought us out from there to bring us in and give us the land that he promised on oath to our forefathers. The LORD commanded us to obey all these decrees and to fear the LORD our God, so that we might always prosper and be kept alive, as is the case today. And if we are careful to obey all this law before the LORD our God, as he has commanded us, that will be our righteousness."

Deuteronomy 6:20–25

Once again, the pattern is the same: The response we are told to give to our children begins with a statement of the great and mighty things our God did in rescuing us from Egypt, and based on this fact, explains why we do what we do. In other words, the God of the law precedes the law of God.[92]

We must also remember that the law of God included the entire atonement system for Israel, part of the very heart of the Five Books of Moses.[93] It would be unthinkable for an Israelite to say to himself, "The Lord will accept me as righteous if I keep some of the commandments, even though I refuse to enter into the sacrificial rites or participate in the Day of Atonement." Nonsense! That would be like saying, "I'm sure God will accept me as righteous if I offer sacrifices and pray, even though I'm a thief and I don't honor my parents." Rather, *both* atonement for sins (i.e., a means for forgiveness, a way to become righteous before God) and directives for life (i.e., a path for obedience, a way to live righteously before God) are included in the Torah. The special emphasis in the New Covenant is this: Because our people failed miserably when it came to keeping the law, continually breaking the commandments and living unrighteous lives, the Messiah has come and paid for our sins, taking away our guilt and pronouncing us clean by faith—so that from here on, we can do the will of God.

This is what Paul explained when writing to the Romans:

For what the law was powerless to do in that it was weakened by the sinful nature, God did by sending his own Son in the likeness of sinful man to be a sin offering. And so he condemned sin in sinful man, in order that the righteous requirements of the law might be fully met in us, who do not live according to the sinful nature but according to the Spirit.

Romans 8:3–4

It is little wonder, then, that Christianity has been known as the religion of good works—feeding the poor, building hospitals, founding schools—all because of our faith (see also vol. 1, 2.5, and 3.25).

You see, throughout biblical history, it was our unbelief that opened the door for a deluge of other sins, leading to judgment and disaster. For example, it was because of our unbelief that we made the golden calf right at the foot of Mount Sinai, failing to trust the Lord and his servant Moses (see Exod. 32). And it was because of our unbelief in God's ability to bring us into the Promised Land that one entire generation died in the wilderness (see Numbers 13–14). But the people who truly believed were the ones who loyally obeyed (see, e.g., the example of Joshua and Caleb in Numbers 13–14). Again, belief and obedience, just like unbelief and disobedience, go hand in hand. In fact, it was unbelief that kept Moses and Aaron out of the land of Canaan: "And the LORD said to Moses and Aaron, 'Because you did not believe in me, to sanctify me in the eyes of the people of Israel, therefore you shall not bring this assembly into the land which I have given them'" (Num. 20:12 RSV; for Talmudic comments on this sin bringing about the death of Moses before his time, see b. Yoma 87a; b. Shabbat 55b). This is no light matter![94]

And this leads us to one last classic text in the Hebrew Bible dealing with faith, namely, Habakkuk 2:4, a verse quoted twice in the New Testament (see Rom. 1:17; Gal. 3:11) as well as in an important discussion in the Talmud (see Makkot 23b–24a). The Talmudic passage has to do with the number of commandments that God gave the Jewish people. First is the famous remark of Rabbi Simlai, setting the number at 613—365 negative commandments (365 "You shall not" commands, one for each day of the year) and 248 positive commandments (in other words, 248 "You shall" commands, one for each of the bones of the body).[95] I'll translate for you the discussion that continues:

> David came and established the number [of commandments] at eleven, as it is written, "A psalm of David. LORD, who may dwell in your sanctuary? Who may live on your holy hill? He whose walk is blameless and who does what is righteous, who speaks the truth from his heart and has no slander on his tongue, who does his neighbor no wrong and casts no slur on his fellowman, who despises a vile man but honors those who fear the LORD, who keeps his oath even when it hurts, who lends his money without usury and does not accept a bribe against the innocent. He who does these things will never be shaken" (Ps. 15:1–6).
>
> Isaiah then came and established the number [of commandments] at six, as it is written, "He who walks righteously and speaks what is right, who rejects gain from extortion and keeps his hand from accepting bribes, who stops his ears against plots of murder and shuts his

eyes against contemplating evil" (Isa. 33:14). Micah then came and established the number [of commandments] at three, as it is written, "He has showed you, O man, what is good. And what does the LORD require of you? To act justly and to love mercy and to walk humbly with your God" (Mic. 6:8). Amos then came and established the number [of commandments] at one, as it is written, "Seek the LORD and live" (Amos 5:6a).

But the Talmudic discussion is not quite over. Rav Nachman bar Yitzhaq took exception to this citation from Amos, claiming that the divine command to "seek me" runs throughout the entire Torah. Rather, it is Habakkuk who came and established the number [of commandments] at one, as it is written, "The righteous will live by his faith" (Hab. 2:4). Shades of the writing of Paul in the New Testament! This is what he explained to the believers in Jesus living in Rome: "I am not ashamed of the gospel, because it is the power of God for the salvation of everyone who believes: first for the Jew, then for the Gentile. For in the gospel a righteousness from God is revealed, a righteousness that is by faith from first to last, just as it is written: *'The righteous will live by faith'*" (Rom. 1:16–17).[96]

Yes, Paul points to this verse from the Hebrew Scriptures as an important text in his argument that both Jew and Gentile are pronounced righteous before God by faith, while the Talmud cites this very same verse as the summary of all the other commandments of the Torah. It seems that faith, righteousness, and obedience to the Torah go hand in hand!

And what is the context for this verse in Habakkuk? This prophetic book begins with the words, "How long, O LORD, must I call for help, but you do not listen?" (v. 2). The prophet wondered how long God would look at Judah's sin without doing anything about it. His faith—and the faith of the righteous Jews in general—was being challenged. But the divine answer was even harder to accept: God would send the Babylonians to bring judgment on Judah, but the atrocities they would commit would be far worse than the sins that had been committed by the Jewish people. Now what? It is in this context—patient, expectant waiting for a divine answer in the midst of apparent injustice—that the Lord speaks to his prophet:

> Then the LORD replied:
>   "Write down the revelation
>   and make it plain on tablets
>   so that a herald may run with it.

> For the revelation awaits an appointed time;
>> it speaks of the end
>> and will not prove false.
> Though it linger, wait for it;
>> it will certainly come and will not delay.
> See, he is puffed up;
>> his desires are not upright—
>> but the righteous will live by his faith."

Habakkuk 2:2–4

Now, there are some translations that understand the word *faith* here to mean "faithfulness," while others even understand "faithfulness" to refer to *God's* faithfulness (i.e., the righteous will live by the Lord's faithfulness).[97] But all these concepts completely overlap: We are faithful because of our faith (that's how we "keep on keeping on"), and our faith is in his faithfulness. That is how we live: by faith. In any case, the passage as a whole is clear. God is saying to all his righteous people, "I am trustworthy! What I said I will do. When everything seems unjust, trust my justice still. Put your faith in me and don't waver. That's how my righteous ones live."

The simple truth is that it is the creed that leads to the deed, and it is the combination of faith and works that produces a life that pleases God.[98] Of course, because Christianity emphasizes believing, it can produce empty professions of faith without accompanying deeds if it becomes a dead religion. But Judaism, with its emphasis on the commandments, can produce hypocritical works devoid of living faith if it becomes a dead religion. Both extremes are to be avoided, and the biblical pattern should be adhered to: True faith will be followed by good works. That's how you can live a righteous life in God's sight.

I should also remind you of the fact that Judaism *has* placed importance on credal confessions, although not to the point that the church did throughout history.[99] That's why traditional Jews have been martyred with the Shema, the fundamental creed of Judaism, on their lips as they died.[100] (In similar fashion, many Christians throughout the ages have been martyred with the confession of Jesus as Messiah on their lips.) And for hundreds of years now, the creed of Maimonides, articulating the Thirteen Principles of faith, has been recited in prayer by traditional Jews on a daily basis.[101] So it is clearly an overstatement to deny any importance to the creed in Judaism, just as it is a mistake to deny the great importance attached to good works in Christianity.

Interestingly, many observant Messianic Jews find themselves in a catch-22 situation with the traditional Jewish community with regard to these issues. First they are told, "If Jesus is really the Jewish Messiah then why have you departed from following the Torah?" In reply, these Messianic Jews say, "We *haven't* departed from the Torah. We find that following Yeshua has actually *strengthened* our desire to live Torah-observant lives in accordance with what is written in our Scriptures." And then the traditional community says to us, "You're just a bunch of hypocrites and deceivers. All this Torah-observance stuff is just an outward performance to lure unsuspecting and innocent Jews into Christianity."[102] Not at all! On the contrary, the New Testament explicitly teaches that faith does not nullify the law; it upholds it (see Rom. 3:31).[103]

It is also worth remembering that Judaism has always recognized the importance of grace and mercy, never relying completely on justification by works. As stated in the Midrash to Psalm 119:123–24:

> "My eyes long for your salvation and for your righteous word" (v. 123): [The verse refers] to this word which you spoke to Israel, "When you walk through the fire, you will not be burned . . ." (Isa. 43:2). Why? "Because I am the LORD your God, the Holy One of Israel, your Savior" (Isa. 43:3), and it is written, "And I will save my flock . . ." (Ezek. 34:22). Save us, as you have spoken, "for my eyes fail [in waiting for my God]" (Ps. 69:4[3]). Although you delight in our good works, if there is neither merit nor [good] works among us, then act towards us with grace *[hesed]*, as it is said, "Act towards your servant with grace" (v. 124). The former generations whom you redeemed, you did not redeem according to their works, but you acted towards them with grace and redeemed them. And thus [the scripture] says, "You led by your grace [the people whom you redeemed]" (Exod. 15:13). As you acted towards the former generations, so act towards us! Thus [the scripture] says, "Act towards your servant with grace."[104]

Without grace, where would we be? Actually, the Torah addresses that question, telling us that it is because of his grace and mercy— totally undeserved by us—that he called our people to himself. *In light of that grace,* he calls us to obedience:

> The LORD did not set his affection on you and choose you because you were more numerous than other peoples, for you were the fewest of all peoples. But it was because the LORD loved you and kept the oath he swore to your forefathers that he brought you out with a mighty hand

and redeemed you from the land of slavery, from the power of Pharaoh king of Egypt. Know therefore that the LORD your God is God; he is the faithful God, keeping his covenant of love to a thousand generations of those who love him and keep his commands. But those who hate him he will repay to their face by destruction; he will not be slow to repay to their face those who hate him. Therefore, take care to follow the commands, decrees and laws I give you today. If you pay attention to these laws and are careful to follow them, then the LORD your God will keep his covenant of love with you, as he swore to your forefathers.

Deuteronomy 7:7–12

It is therefore right to say that Christianity and Judaism are religions of *both* grace and good works, faith and law, the former emphasizing grace and faith without minimizing the importance of good works and law, the latter emphasizing good works and law without minimizing the importance of grace and faith. But given the state of the human race, the track record of our people Israel, and the corruption of each of our hearts, it makes a great deal of sense to put our hope in the grace of God more than in our works, no matter how righteously we may live.

All of us would do well to echo both the petitions and the sentiments of our forefathers as expressed in the psalms:

> O LORD, hear my prayer,
>   listen to my cry for mercy;
> in your faithfulness and righteousness
>   come to my relief.
> Do not bring your servant into judgment,
>   for no one living is righteous before you.

Psalm 143:1–2

> O Lord, hear my voice.
> Let your ears be attentive
>   to my cry for mercy.
> If you, O LORD, kept a record of sins,
>   O Lord, who could stand?
> But with you there is forgiveness;
>   therefore you are feared.

Psalm 130:2–4

Do you really want to seek justification before God based *primarily* on your works? I strongly recommend that you trust the Messiah first as your Savior and Deliverer, and then, by his help and grace, seek to live a life that pleases the Lord. Then and only then can you be fully acceptable in his sight.

3.8. Scripture clearly tells us that "to do what is right and just is more acceptable to the Lord than sacrifice" (Prov. 21:3).

> Amen! Who would argue with Scripture? Elsewhere the Bible teaches that obedience is better than sacrifice (1 Sam. 15:22). But these passages do not denigrate the importance of sacrifices, as some anti-missionaries would claim. Rather, throughout the Bible God opposes religious hypocrisy and formal, outward observance of religious rites. He would rather have our simple obedience than our lengthy prayers or costly sacrifices if our hearts are not right with him. And he prefers that we just do what he says rather than sin, repent, and bring a sacrifice for our sins. The sad fact is that we all sin grievously and we all need atonement for our sins, a subject that Scripture clearly affirms and teaches.

I am in full agreement with your point, and I have no objection to the translation of Proverbs 21:3 that you cited. My problem is with the misuse and misinterpretation of this verse, as if it were denigrating the importance of sacrifice and offerings. It is simply saying that morality is more important to the Lord than the observance of religious rituals.

How then can this verse be quoted as an *objection* to the New Testament faith? Actually, the objection is based on a fundamental misunderstanding of the Messianic Jewish view of the death of Jesus. Somehow, our beliefs are interpreted to mean that the only thing that matters is simply believing that the Messiah died for our sins—in other words, that he gave himself as the perfect sacrifice on our behalf—and that moral living is therefore no longer important. Or to put this in everyday terms, it is as if the believer in Jesus says to himself, "Why should I bother to live right and do right if my sins have all been paid for?" But that is not what followers of Jesus believe.

In the previous objection (3.7, immediately above), we saw that Christianity is not just a religion of the creed (i.e., believing in a specific set of dogmas) but also of the deed. Still, you might argue that our constant emphasis on Yeshua's sacrificial death completely undercuts and overshadows our emphasis on morality and holiness. Ask a traditional Jew what's most important regarding his faith, and he'll tell you that it's observing the Torah—in other words, doing what is just and right. Ask a Christian or Messianic Jew what's most important, and he'll tell you that it's believing in Jesus the Messiah—in particular, his death on the cross. So the argument goes.

The problem is that there is no substance to this argument. Proverbs 21:3, like many other Scripture passages, is counteracting the attitude of religious hypocrisy that takes refuge in the observance of forms and ceremonies while at the same time one lives in greed, or lust, or selfishness, or idolatry, or injustice, or lies. The verse could just as well say, "To do what is right and just is more acceptable to the LORD than saying your prayers, or attending synagogue, or giving to charity, or studying Talmud." As we will see below (3.9), the prophets strongly rebuked religious hypocrites, speaking out against their prayers, their observance of Sabbath, and their celebration of holy days and feasts, along with their offering of sacrifices, since with their mouths they drew near to the Lord but their hearts were far from him (Isa. 29:13). God despises this.

Similar sentiments are expressed elsewhere in Proverbs. See, for example, Proverbs 15:8: "The LORD detests the sacrifice of the wicked, but the prayer of the upright pleases him," where the contrast is between the religious activities of the righteous and the religious activities of the wicked, prayer and sacrifice being good things in themselves. Similarly, Proverbs 21:27 teaches that "the sacrifice of the wicked is detestable—how much more so when brought with evil intent." These verses are telling us that even a sacrifice—something of great importance in the Torah—is unacceptable to God if it is brought with an evil heart and an evil intent.

Related to this is the Rabbinic concept that for repentance to have value, it must be sincere: "He who says, 'I will sin and repent, I will sin and repent,' repentance is not vouchsafed to him."[105] Obviously, the concept of repentance is not the problem. It is one of the core teachings of Judaism. The problem has to do with religious hypocrisy and moral shallowness. Again, that's what Proverbs 21:3 is addressing, and we could just as well say, "He who says, 'I will sin and sacrifice, I will sin and sacrifice,' atonement is not vouchsafed to him.'" God prefers that you and I live right rather than lie, cheat, steal, hate, lust, and then fast, pray, repent, and offer sacrifices. He prefers obedience.

It's also important for you to remember that there were various functions for sacrifices in the Hebrew Bible, including purgation, purification, dedication, thanksgiving, and intercession, as well as expiation (see below, 3.12). So Proverbs 21:3 should not be interpreted as an attack on the Torah's system of blood atonement. Rather, God prefers obedience to sacrifices of any kind, which is exactly what Samuel told Saul in 1 Samuel 15:22–23: "Does the Lord delight in burnt offerings and sacrifices as much as in obeying the voice of the Lord? To obey is better than sacrifice, and to heed is better than the fat of rams. For rebellion is like the sin of divination, and arrogance like the evil of idolatry."

The New Testament teaches exactly the same thing:

> One of the teachers of the law came and heard them debating. Noticing that Jesus had given them a good answer, he asked him, "Of all the commandments, which is the most important?" "The most important one," answered Jesus, "is this: 'Hear, O Israel, the Lord our God, the Lord is one. Love the Lord your God with all your heart and with all your soul and with all your mind and with all your strength.' The second is this: 'Love your neighbor as yourself.' There is no commandment greater than these." "Well said, teacher," the man replied. "You are right in saying that God is one and there is no other but him. To love him with all your heart, with all your understanding and with all your strength, and to love your neighbor as yourself is more important than all burnt offerings and sacrifices." When Jesus saw that he had answered wisely, he said to him, "You are not far from the kingdom of God."
>
> Mark 12:28–34

> And do not forget to do good and to share with others, for with such sacrifices God is pleased.
>
> Hebrews 13:16

So on this point we totally agree!

3.9. The prophets indicated clearly that God did not care for blood sacrifices. In fact, they practically repudiated the entire sacrificial system, teaching that repentance and prayer were sufficient. The Talmudic rabbis simply affirmed this biblical truth.

Some later rabbis may have taught this, but the prophets certainly did not. Everything the prophets did, they did out of allegiance to the Torah and to reinforce what it said. There is no possible way that they would have repudiated the God-given, God-ordained, God-sanctioned system of atonement as laid out in the Torah—especially with the Temple standing. The prophets would not have contradicted Moses. What the prophets repudiated was hypocritical religion. In other words, they rejected the performance of sacred rites and the keeping of special days when those practicing them had polluted hearts. They were perfectly clear on this. It's also interesting to note that every traditional Jew around the world prays daily for the restoration of the Temple and the sacrificial system. If sacrifices were really unnecessary and unimportant, and if the prophets utterly repudiated them, why pray daily for their restoration?

The prophetic books contain many strong statements that say the Lord rejects the sacrifices and offerings brought by his people. There are also sentiments expressed in Psalms and Proverbs indicating that the Lord would rather have inward devotion than outward sacrifices. But there are also equally strong statements and sentiments in those books denouncing every form of hypocritical religious observance, including passages in which God is said to utterly reject his people's prayers and Sabbath observance. Does this mean the Lord is against prayer? Of course not. And would a traditional Jew think for a moment that God was anti-Sabbath? Never.

What the prophets and psalmists were saying was that God did not want empty and meaningless observance of his laws—whether those laws pertained to sacrifices, feasts, Sabbaths, holy days, or prayer. All the outward observance in the world is meaningless if the heart is far from God, and all the sacrifices in the world cannot take the place of godly conduct. Thus, the prophets taught that sacrifices without mercy and justice were vain and that bringing an offering without a repentant and contrite heart was unacceptable. On this point all of us—the prophets, traditional Jews, and Messianic Jews—agree. In fact, this was a theme emphasized by Yeshua as well, and one of his favorite texts was Hosea 6:6: "For I desire mercy, not sacrifice, and acknowledgment of God rather than burnt offerings" (see Matt. 9:13; 12:7).

The prophets and psalmists also taught that prayer and worship could be accepted by God in the same way as (not instead of) sacrifices and incense, a theme also repeated in the New Testament (see

Heb. 13:15–16). But it would be entirely wrong to suggest that the prophets or psalmists denigrated or rejected the sacrificial system itself. In fact, it was *because* sacrifices were so powerful and meaningful in Israelite religious practice that the prophets had to remind the people that the sacrifices had no atoning or blessing power unless they were coupled with repentant and devoted hearts. That is the meaning of Hosea 5:6: "When they go with their flocks and herds to seek the LORD, they will not find him; he has withdrawn himself from them."[106] In other words, even when the disobedient Israelites brought all their sacrifices to the Lord, he still would not listen to them. (From a parallel New Testament perspective, we could emphasize that even the ultimate sacrifice—the Messiah laying down his very life for us—has no life-changing value at all unless it is joined with repentance and faith; see vol. 1, 1.11.)

Let's consider just how central the sacrificial system was to the people of Israel before we discuss the words of the prophets and psalmists. According to the Tanakh, here are some undeniable facts:

- Over and over in the Torah, sacrifices and offerings are described as a *pleasing aroma* to God (see Gen. 8:21; Exod. 29:18, 25, 41; and twenty-eight more occurrences of this phrase in Leviticus and Numbers). Leviticus 1:9 gives a good example of the typical language used to describe these sacrifices: "It is a burnt offering, an offering made by fire, an aroma pleasing to the LORD."[107] The Lord obviously welcomed and enjoyed sacrificial offerings when his people brought them with holy hearts. He took pleasure in them, according to the clear testimony of Scripture.

- Sacrifices were so important to Israelite religion that when the Lord sent Moses and Aaron to Pharaoh, he sent them with this message: "The God of the Hebrews has met with us. Now let us take a three-day journey into the desert to offer sacrifices to the LORD our God, or he may strike us with plagues or with the sword" (Exod. 5:3). The very reason God gave for calling his people out of Egypt was to offer sacrifices to him.

- A careful study of the Five Books of Moses indicates that more chapters are devoted to the subject of sacrifices and offerings than to the subjects of Sabbath observance, high holy days, idolatry, adultery, murder, and theft combined.

- The sacrifices, more frequently than anything else in the Torah, are described as "lasting ordinances" or being established "for the generations to come." (Similar language is used to describe other priestly rituals, along with circumcision and the observance of the Sabbath and holy days.) If anything was *not* to be replaced, it was the sacrificial system. Consider the weight of verses such as these: "Once a year Aaron shall make atonement on [the altar's] horns. This annual atonement must be made with the blood of the atoning sin offering for the generations to come. It is most holy to the LORD" (Exod. 30:10; cf. similar language with regard to circumcision [Gen. 17:7–14] and Passover observance [Exod. 12:14–17, 42]). That's why Messianic Jews so strongly emphasize the fact that Jesus the Messiah fulfilled the requirements of the sacrificial system by laying down his life on our behalf (see below, 3.10, 3.14).[108] It is unthinkable to us—based on the Torah—that the sacrificial system was simply discarded and replaced with prayer.

- After Hosea, Amos, Isaiah, and Jeremiah had delivered their prophecies—prophecies that are quoted by anti-missionaries to prove that the prophets repudiated sacrifices—the prophets Haggai and Zechariah strongly encouraged the exiles who returned to Jerusalem to get on with the rebuilding of the Temple: "Now Haggai the prophet and Zechariah the prophet, a descendant of Iddo, prophesied to the Jews in Judah and Jerusalem in the name of the God of Israel, who was over them. Then Zerubbabel son of Shealtiel and Jeshua son of Jozadak set to work to rebuild the house of God in Jerusalem. And the prophets of God were with them, helping them" (Ezra 5:1–2; see also Haggai 1). They too were eager for the Temple to be rebuilt and for sacrificial worship to be restored.

- Malachi, who was the last of the prophets of the Tanakh and who lived in the days of the Second Temple, emphasized the importance of Temple sacrifices, soundly rebuking the priests for bringing defective offerings to the Lord (see Mal. 1:6–14). And Zechariah, prophesying in the very days in which the Second Temple was being built, declared that at the end of this age, "Every pot in Jerusalem and Judah will be holy to the LORD Almighty, and all who come to sacrifice will take some of the pots and cook in them" (Zech. 14:21; see below, 3.17). This, in fact, parallels the promise in Malachi, namely, that after the Lord purifies and refines the Levites, then he will "have men who will bring offerings in righteousness, and the offerings of

Judah and Jerusalem will be acceptable to the Lord, as in days gone by, as in former years" (Mal. 3:3–4). The prophets hardly repudiated the sacrificial system!

What then were the prophets saying? What exactly was their problem with the sacrifices? In order to give a sound, biblical answer to these questions, we'll look at every relevant verse in the Hebrew Scriptures, at the same time testing the accuracy of the anti-missionary claim that "the prophets loudly declared to the Jewish people that the contrite prayer of the penitent sinner replaces the sacrificial system."[109]

Let's begin our survey with the prophet Micah.

> With what shall I come before the Lord
>   and bow down before the exalted God?
> Shall I come before him with burnt offerings,
>   with calves a year old?
> Will the Lord be pleased with thousands of rams,
>   with ten thousand rivers of oil?
> Shall I offer my firstborn for my transgression,
>   the fruit of my body for the sin of my soul?
> He has showed you, O man, what is good.
>   And what does the Lord require of you?
> To act justly and to love mercy
>   and to walk humbly with your God.

Micah 6:6–8

Now, Micah was a Judean prophet living in the eighth century B.C.E., which means that he lived in proximity to the Temple in Jerusalem. In his day, the Temple was fully operative and the Jewish people were not in exile. Thus, no one can argue that Micah was addressing the question of how his people could come into right relationship with God when the Temple was destroyed or inaccessible. That was not the issue here. Rather, Micah was writing to people who had full access to the Temple, and this means that at the very time he was preaching and prophesying, daily sacrifices were being offered at the Temple in Jerusalem and special sacrifices were being offered on the holy days and feast days. And these sacrifices, as we have just noted, were being offered by divine directive, as laid out explicitly in the Torah.

Does anyone think that Micah was repudiating these divinely ordained sacrifices?[110] Does anyone think that Micah was saying to his fellow Jews, "The entire sacrificial system as outlined in the Torah is utterly meaningless to the Lord! The Five Books of Moses don't count. Their words have no meaning. Forget about them, ignore them, don't even think about following them." Can you imagine Micah saying such things?

Ironically, anti-missionaries often argue that Jesus was not a true prophet because, they claim, he ignored or violated the Torah and led others to ignore or violate the Torah (see vol. 3, 5.28). Yet if this passage from Micah means what some anti-missionaries claim it means, then Micah was a false prophet too. In fact, he would have to be considered a false prophet of the worst kind, since, it is alleged, he aggressively spoke against sacrifices and offerings. Obviously, this cannot be the case.

What then was Micah saying? He was reproving his sinful people and telling them (with some obvious hyperbole) not to think that they could please God merely by bringing thousands of sacrifices and offerings or to imagine that the Lord would want them to sacrifice their own sons to pay for their sins. Rather, what God was looking for was justice, mercy, and humility, something that some of them apparently overlooked in their zeal to bring sacrifices and special offerings. They put their emphasis on the wrong thing, emphasizing the outward ceremonies and ignoring the inward corruption. Such is human nature.

Yeshua rebuked hypocritical religious leaders for similar practices in his day, saying to them, "You give a tenth of your spices—mint, dill and cummin. But you have neglected the more important matters of the law—justice, mercy and faithfulness. You should have practiced the latter, without neglecting the former" (Matt. 23:23). Our Messiah was saying, "You are scrupulously careful to tithe on every last crop, but you completely overlook matters that are of far more importance to the Lord: justice, mercy, and faithfulness. You've got your priorities all wrong."

Similarly, Paul had to straighten out some zealous Christians who were excited about spiritual gifts (such as prophecy) but neglected love. He explained to them, "If I speak in the tongues of men and of angels, but have not love, I am only a resounding gong or a clanging cymbal. If I have the gift of prophecy and can fathom all mysteries and all knowledge, and if I have a faith that can move mountains, but have not love, I am nothing" (1 Cor. 13:1–2). In other words, I may be a great miracle worker, but if I don't have love, it's all a big, empty display. He even went as far as saying, "If I give all I possess to the poor and surrender my body to the flames, but have not love, I gain nothing" (1 Cor. 13:3).

All these voices—Micah, Yeshua, and Paul—express the identical sentiment: What good are our tithes, our offerings, our exercising of spiritual gifts, or even our personal sacrifice if we don't practice justice, mercy, love, and humility? *Those* are the qualities that God really requires.

Of course, it's easy to see how Micah's strong prophetic language could be misunderstood by people living centuries after the biblical era, just as the language of Yeshua and Paul has been misunderstood by some. But for Jews living in Micah's day, there was no possible way they would think he was saying, "Forget about Moses! Throw out the Torah! No longer observe the Day of Atonement! Disregard the Passover lamb! Forget about the daily, prescribed offerings! Get rid of the priests and their sacrifices!" Instead, his meaning was clear: "Sinner, God wants you to live right, not bring him endless—and pointless—sacrifices and offerings." And to underscore his point, Micah used exaggerated, sarcastic language, speaking of offering up "thousands of rams . . . ten thousand rivers of oil" and even the sinner's "firstborn" son. His argument is clear.

It's also important to note that the prophets often used either-or language to drill home their point. That's why Hosea could say on behalf of the Lord, "For I desire mercy, not sacrifice, and acknowledgment of God rather than burnt offerings" (Hosea 6:6), when in reality the Lord wanted *both* mercy and sacrifice, acknowledgment of him *and* burnt offerings.[111] Remember, the Torah described the burnt offering as "an offering made by fire, an aroma pleasing to the LORD" (e.g., Lev. 1:9, quoted in full above), and it represented the complete dedication of the worshiper to the Lord. This was something of worth when done with a right heart. And remember also that it was after Noah offered up sacrifices that the Torah records, "The LORD smelled the pleasing aroma and said in his heart: 'Never again will I curse the ground because of man, even though every inclination of his heart is evil from childhood. And never again will I destroy all living creatures, as I have done'" (Gen. 8:21; many other similar examples could be given from the Tanakh). There is nothing negative here.

You see, the Lord *did* desire sacrifices and offerings from his people—as long as they were brought with obedient or repentant hearts. But if his people continued to live in sin, then it was the height of self-deception for them to think that their sacrifices would make a difference to God. Absolutely not. Instead, those offerings were utterly repulsive to him, looking more like a bribe than an act of worship and devotion.

In contemporary terms we might say, "What's the use of your going to the synagogue (or church) and fasting and praying and giving large gifts to the building program if you're watching pornography at home and you cheat on your job? God hates your attendance at synagogue (or church) and he despises your acts of sacrifice. They are unacceptable to him! What he wants from you is obedience." (See further, 3.8, above.)

We see a similar emphasis in the writings of Isaiah, a contemporary of Micah and a man who also lived in proximity to the Temple. Speaking by divine inspiration, he said:

> Hear the word of the LORD,
>> you rulers of Sodom;
> listen to the law of our God,
>> you people of Gomorrah!
> "The multitude of your sacrifices—
>> what are they to me?" says the LORD.
> "I have more than enough of burnt offerings,
>> of rams and the fat of fattened animals;
> I have no pleasure
>> in the blood of bulls and lambs and goats.
> When you come to appear before me,
>> who has asked this of you,
>> this trampling of my courts?
> Stop bringing meaningless offerings!
>> Your incense is detestable to me.
> New Moons, Sabbaths and convocations—
>> I cannot bear your evil assemblies.
> Your New Moon festivals and your appointed feasts
>> my soul hates.
> They have become a burden to me;
>> I am weary of bearing them.
> When you spread out your hands in prayer,
>> I will hide my eyes from you;
> even if you offer many prayers,
>> I will not listen.
> Your hands are full of blood;
>> wash and make yourselves clean.
> Take your evil deeds
>> out of my sight!
> Stop doing wrong,
>> learn to do right!
> Seek justice,
>> encourage the oppressed.
> Defend the cause of the fatherless,
>> plead the case of the widow."

Isaiah 1:10–17

The meaning of Isaiah's words is obvious: God is sick of his people's hypocrisy. He is saying, "Enough! I don't want any more of your sacrifices, your prayers, your Sabbaths, or your holy days. What I want from you is that you repent and live right."

Would anyone, Messianic Jew or traditional Jew, argue with this? And would anyone take this passage to be a blanket statement indicating that God completely rejected the sacrificial system, along with prayer, worship, and Sabbath and Holy Day observance? Certainly not.[112] Rather, when sacrifices are brought with a sinful heart, they are meaningless offerings, a stench in God's nostrils. When sinful hands are lifted in prayer, the Lord hides his eyes and shuts his ears. Even when his people come to the Temple to worship, if their hearts are not right, God sees their presence as an intrusion—literally, a trampling of his courts—and he regards all their religious observance as an unbearable burden.

But when his people's hearts are right, then their sacrifices are a sweet smelling aroma to him, as emphasized above. And when his people have clean hands, then their prayers are his delight (see Prov. 15:8; and contrast Prov. 28:9, "If anyone turns a deaf ear to the law, even his prayers are detestable."). Jeremiah 14:12 is also in harmony with this, where the Lord tells his prophet, "Although they fast, I will not listen to their cry; though they offer burnt offerings and grain offerings, I will not accept them. Instead, I will destroy them with the sword, famine and plague." Yes, God will even reject our fasting— along with our prayers and offerings—if our hearts are far from him.

In this regard, Psalm 51 is especially enlightening. This psalm of repentance is attributed to King David after he committed adultery with Bathsheba and had her husband, Uriah, killed. After fully acknowledging his guilt and pleading for mercy, David exclaimed, "You do not delight in sacrifice, or I would bring it; you do not take pleasure in burnt offerings. The sacrifices of God are a broken spirit; a broken and contrite heart, O God, you will not despise" (Ps. 51:16–17[18–19]).

But does the psalm end there? Not at all. Instead, the very next verses contain a prayer, possibly added later by another author, closing with these words: "In your good pleasure make Zion prosper; build up the walls of Jerusalem. Then there will be righteous sacrifices, whole burnt offerings to delight you; then bulls will be offered on your altar" (Ps. 51:18–19[20–21]).[113] This is quite a statement!

When sacrifices are brought in righteousness, they are a delight to the Lord; when they are brought in sin—or as a replacement for repentance—they are an abomination. It is also in this light that we should understand the words of Psalm 40, where the psalmist wrote, "Sacrifice and offering you did not desire, but my ears you have pierced [or opened];[114] burnt offerings and sin offerings you did not require. Then I said, 'Here I am, I have come—it is written about me in the scroll. I desire to do your will, O my God; your law is within my heart'" (vv. 6–7).

It seems that the psalmist received a revelation, apparently while meditating on the words of the Torah. When he considered what was written there concerning the sacrificial system, he realized that what God really wanted was his own life, his own devotion, the surrender of himself to the Lord—as opposed to the mere offering up of a sacrifice. That's what he meant when he said, "it is written *about me* in the scroll."[115] In other words, "When you command me to bring an offering to you, that offering symbolizes my own life being given over to you, my own soul being poured out to you. That's what you really want!"[116]

In the New Testament, Paul used similar language: "I urge you, brothers, in view of God's mercy, to offer your bodies as living sacrifices, holy and pleasing to God—this is your spiritual act of worship" (Rom. 12:1).[117] That's what the psalmist was saying for himself: "Here I am, Lord, offered up wholly to you!" What the psalmist was *not* saying was, "The Day of Atonement, with its special sacrifices and offerings as given to Moses by the Lord himself, is not wanted by God. The special offerings for the Feast of Tabernacles—given in great detail by the Lord—are irrelevant to him. He doesn't want the offerings for purification, thanksgiving, dedication, and atonement as outlined in the Torah. No. He wants devotion." Clearly, this was not his point.

Jeremiah 6:19–20 underscores this well: "Hear, O earth: I am bringing disaster on this people, the fruit of their schemes, because they have not listened to my words and have rejected my law. What do I care about incense from Sheba or sweet calamus from a distant land? Your burnt offerings are not acceptable; your sacrifices do not please me." As the Christian Old Testament scholar David Talley noted:

> In Mal 3:4; Jer 6:20; Hos 9:4 the acceptability or unacceptability of the sacrifices is not based on the sacrifices themselves, but rather on the obedient lifestyle of the ones who offer them. It does not matter how much the sacrifices might cost (i.e., imported incense and sweet cane

or the amount of the sacrifice that is for the Lord), when sin is not for-saken, the sacrifices are worthless.[118]

From all this we are reminded of an important spiritual truth, one that recurs often throughout the Word of God: Even things as pre-cious as prayer, sacrifices, worship, fasting, and observance of the Sabbaths and holy days are utterly distasteful to the Lord when per-formed with a sinful, hypocritical heart. In fact, the Torah addressed this as well, specifically with reference to sacrifices and offerings.

As we noted earlier, God repeatedly referred to the sacrifices and offerings as a pleasing aroma to him, describing voluntary offerings, offerings for holy days, and daily, fixed offerings in these very terms. To give just one example, we read in Numbers that the Lord gave his people these instructions: "Prepare one lamb in the morning and the other at twilight, together with a grain offering of a tenth of an ephah of fine flour mixed with a quarter of a hin of oil from pressed olives. *This is the regular burnt offering instituted at Mount Sinai as a pleas-ing aroma, an offering made to the LORD by fire"* (28:4–6).

This is a sacred rite. The sacrifices and offerings were to be a vital, holy, and glorious part of Israel's worship and devotion. That is what the Torah taught, and we read here that these words came from Mount Sinai itself. But the Lord also said in the Torah that if we sinned against him and fell into idolatry, "I will turn your cities into ruins and lay waste your sanctuaries, *and I will take no delight in the pleas-ing aroma of your offerings"* (Lev. 26:31). It's all laid out in advance! The very problem the prophets were addressing was already addressed in the Torah. Sacrifices and offerings were not the problem. Sin was the problem. It spoiled everything, including Israel's sacrifices and offerings, making them unacceptable to the Lord. So it is written in the law of God. The words of the prophets were actually a fulfillment of the words of the Torah.

This, quite obviously, is a far cry from saying that God (and/or his prophets) repudiated the sacrificial system. Rather, as we have been emphasizing, God no more repudiated sacrifices than he repudiated prayer, worship, or the Sabbath. But he accepted *nothing* from those whose hearts were far from him, a truth that Yeshua affirmed as well. "You hypocrites!" he said to sinful leaders in his day. "Isaiah was right when he prophesied about you: 'These people honor me with their lips, but their hearts are far from me. They worship me in vain; their teachings are but rules taught by men'" (Matt. 15:7–9, quoting Isa. 29:13). The Messiah hated hypocrisy too.[119]

So as we have clearly seen, even though the Torah commanded that the Israelites keep the feasts, observe the new moons and Sabbaths, and offer various kinds of sacrifices—corporately, and under certain circumstances, individually—God would have none of it from sinners and hypocrites.

We find an almost identical message from the northern Israelite prophet Amos. Through him the Lord said:

> I hate, I despise your religious feasts [Hebrew, *hag*];
>   I cannot stand your assemblies [Hebrew, *'assevet*].
> Even though you bring me burnt offerings and grain offerings,
>   I will not accept them.
> Though you bring choice fellowship offerings,
>   I will have no regard for them.
> Away with the noise of your songs!
>   I will not listen to the music of your harps.
> But let justice roll on like a river,
>   righteousness like a never-failing stream!
>
> Amos 5:21–24

Now, if you have had any doubt whatsoever about my line of reasoning so far, this should settle things completely for you, since here the Lord rejects his people's religious feasts and assemblies (the Hebrew words here included Sabbaths, new moons, Passover, Tabernacles, and the other holy days and festivals), sacrifices and offerings, and music and songs. And why did he reject all these forms of worship and devotion? It was because the Israelites were steeped in sin—including idolatry, immorality, and injustice—and therefore all their acts of worship were abhorrent to the Lord. He wanted justice and purity, not songs, services, Sabbaths, and sacrifices. Add to this the fact that even the worship of Yahweh in northern Israel was mixed with the worship of other gods,[120] and you can see why he wanted nothing to do with their zealous religious activity—even when the choicest of offerings were brought to him or the most beautiful songs were sung to him.

The Israeli biblical scholar Shalom M. Paul summarized the message of Amos, noting that

> this total disavowal of the cult is expressed anthropomorphically [i.e., speaking of God in human terms] by the Lord's shutting off, so to speak, several of his own senses: smell (v 21 . . .), sight (v 22 . . .), and hearing (v 23 . . .) . . . representing a complete and comprehensive repudiation. . . .

Ritual per se, with all its paraphernalia and panoply, simply cannot substitute for the basic moral and ethical actions of humans. When these are lacking, religious life, with all its ritual accoutrements, becomes a sham. What is required above all else is justice and righteousness.[121]

That is what Amos was saying, and it was in harmony with the message of the rest of the prophets. As Charles Lee Feinberg, a Jewish Christian biblical scholar, noted:

sacrifices were always meant to be of secondary importance to obedience and godliness. Neither Jeremiah nor any other prophet decried sacrifices as such. They meant that moral law is always paramount to the ritual law. It is significant that when Leviticus 6–8 is read in the synagogue, this passage in Jeremiah is read as the concluding portion, called the Haphtorah.[122]

"But wait one second," you say. "You didn't quote the entire passage from the Book of Amos. If you continue reading, you will see that he claimed that the Israelites never even brought the Lord sacrifices during their forty years of wandering in the wilderness. And yet God took care of them that entire time, proving that sacrifices were simply not a big deal. In fact, Jeremiah went one step further, telling us that God never really wanted our sacrifices in the first place, even in the beginning when he gave us the law."

Let's look at those passages right now:

"Did you bring me sacrifices and offerings forty years in the desert, O house of Israel? You have lifted up the shrine of your king, the pedestal of your idols, the star of your god—which you made for yourselves. Therefore I will send you into exile beyond Damascus," says the LORD, whose name is God Almighty.

Amos 5:25–27

"This is what the LORD Almighty, the God of Israel, says: Go ahead, add your burnt offerings to your other sacrifices and eat the meat yourselves! For when I brought your forefathers out of Egypt and spoke to them, I did not . . . give them commands about burnt offerings and sacrifices, but I gave them this command: Obey me, and I will be your God and you will be my people. Walk in all the ways I command you, that it may go well with you."

Jeremiah 7:21–23[123]

What are these verses saying? Writing in the *Encyclopedia Judaica,* Anson F. Rainey, a professor at Tel Aviv University and a foremost biblical and Semitic scholar, provided these important insights:

> The prophets of the First Temple period often spoke out against sacrificial ritual (Amos 5:21–27; Hos. 6:6; Micah 6:6–8; Isa. 1:11–17; Jer. 6:20; 7:21–22). Righteous and just behavior along with obedience to the Lord are contrasted with the conduct of rituals unaccompanied by proper ethical and moral attitudes (Amos 5:24; Micah 6:8; Isa. 1:16–17; Jer. 7:23). It has thus been assumed by many scholars that the prophets condemned all sacrificial rituals. [The Catholic biblical scholar Roland] De Vaux has shown the absurdity of such a conclusion since Isaiah 1:15 also condemns prayer. No one holds that the prophets rejected prayer; it was prayer offered without the proper moral commitment that was being denounced; the same holds true for the oracles against formal rituals. Similar allusions in the Psalms which might be taken as a complete rejection of sacrifice (e.g., 40:7–8; 50:8–15) actually express the same concern for inner attitude as the prophets. The wisdom literature sometimes reflects the same concern for moral and ethical values over empty sacerdotal acts (Prov. 15:8; 21:3, 27).
>
> Certain other statements by Amos (5:25) and Jeremiah (7:22) have been taken to mean that the prophets knew nothing of a ritual practice followed in the wilderness experience of Israel. De Vaux has noted that Jeremiah clearly knew Deuteronomy 12:6–14 and regarded it as the Law of Moses. The prophetic oracles against sacrifice in the desert are really saying that the original Israelite sacrificial system was not meant to be the empty, hypocritical formalism practiced by their contemporaries. The demand by Hosea for "mercy and not sacrifice . . . knowledge of God more than burnt offerings" (Hos. 6:6; cf. Matt. 9:13; 12:7) is surely to be taken as relative, a statement of priorities (cf. also I Sam. 15:22). The inner attitude was prerequisite to any valid ritual expression (Isa. 29:13). Foreign elements that had penetrated the Israelite sacrificial system were, of course, roundly condemned by the prophets. Such was especially the case with Israel (Amos 4:5; Hos. 2:13–15; 4:11–13; 13:2) but also in Judah (Jer. 7:17–18; Ezek. 8; et al.).[124]

Rainey correctly rejects two impossible views: First, that the prophets completely repudiated the sacrificial system; and second, that the prophets knew nothing about a sacrificial system in conjunction with Israel's wilderness wanderings.[125] We should also point out that the Book of Jeremiah does *not* take a negative view of sacrifices and offerings. Just look at Jeremiah 17:24–26.

But if you are careful to obey me, declares the LORD, and bring no load through the gates of this city on the Sabbath, but keep the Sabbath day holy by not doing any work on it, then kings who sit on David's throne will come through the gates of this city with their officials. They and their officials will come riding in chariots and on horses, accompanied by the men of Judah and those living in Jerusalem, and this city will be inhabited forever. People will come from the towns of Judah and the villages around Jerusalem, from the territory of Benjamin and the western foothills, from the hill country and the Negev, *bringing burnt offerings and sacrifices, grain offerings, incense and thank offerings to the house of the LORD.*

What a promise! And what a reminder that the prophets did not denigrate or reject sacrifices per se. In fact, here is another promise from Jeremiah that is even more dramatic:

This is what the LORD says: "You say about this place, 'It is a desolate waste, without men or animals.' Yet in the towns of Judah and the streets of Jerusalem that are deserted, inhabited by neither men nor animals, there will be heard once more the sounds of joy and gladness, the voices of bride and bridegroom, and the voices of those *who bring thank offerings to the house of the LORD,* saying, 'Give thanks to the LORD Almighty, for the LORD is good; his love endures forever.' For I will restore the fortunes of the land as they were before," says the LORD.

Jeremiah 33:10–11

For Jeremiah, a restored Jerusalem meant a restored sacrificial system too.

And here is yet another promise of restored sacrifices from Jeremiah, also presupposing that the sacrifices were divinely ordained and positive: "For this is what the LORD says: 'David will never fail to have a man to sit on the throne of the house of Israel, nor will the priests, who are Levites, ever fail to have a man to stand before me continually to offer burnt offerings, to burn grain offerings and to present sacrifices'" (Jer. 33:17–18).

In light of these verses, there can be no question that Jeremiah did not reject the importance of sacrifices and offerings earlier in his book.

"Then why don't the rabbis agree with your position?"

Many of them do! According to Dr. J. H. Hertz, the late Chief Rabbi of the British Empire and the author of *the* English commentary on the Torah and prophetic readings used in Conservative synagogues worldwide, "Jeremiah by no means opposed sacrifice brought in the right spirit. In his picture of the Restoration (Jer. xxxiii, 18), due place is given to the Temple worship and priestly sacrifices."[126] With regard to the "widespread misunderstanding [that] exists in regard to the attitude of the Prophets to the sacrificial cult," Hertz notes:

> The Prophets do not seek to alter or abolish the externals of religion as such. They are not so unreasonable as to demand that men should worship without aid of any outward symbolism. What they protested against was the fatal tendency to make these outward symbols the whole of religion; the superstitious *over-estimate* of sacrifice as compared with justice, pity and purity; and especially the monstrous wickedness with which the offering of sacrifices was accompanied.[127]

In the words of Abraham Joshua Heschel, one of the most respected Jewish thinkers of the twentieth century:

> Sacrifice, the strength and the measure of piety, acts wherein God and man meet—all this should be called obnoxious?
>
> Of course, the prophets did not condemn the practice of sacrifice in itself; otherwise, we should have to conclude that Isaiah intended to discourage the practice of prayer (Isa. 1:14–15). They did, however, claim that deeds of injustice vitiate both sacrifice and prayer. Men may not drown out the cries of the oppressed with the noise of hymns, nor buy off the Lord with increased offerings. The prophets disparaged the cult when it became a substitute for righteousness. It is precisely the implied recognition of the value of the cult that lends force to their insistence that there is something far more precious than sacrifice. . . .
>
> What they [i.e., the prophets] attacked was, I repeat, extremely venerable: a sphere unmistakably holy; a spirituality that had both form and substance, that was concrete and inspiring, an atmosphere overwhelming the believer—pageantry, scenery, mystery, spectacle, fragrance, song, and exaltation. In the experience of such captivating sanctity, who could question the presence of God in the shape of a temple?[128]

In support of this last statement, Heschel cites Psalm 132:

> "Let us go to his dwelling place;
>   let us worship at his footstool—

arise, O Lᴏʀᴅ, and come to your resting place,
    you and the ark of your might.
May your priests be clothed with righteousness;
    may your saints sing for joy." . . .
For the Lᴏʀᴅ has chosen Zion,
    he has desired it for his dwelling:
"This is my resting place for ever and ever;
    here I will sit enthroned, for I have desired it."

Psalm 132:7–9, 13–14

God himself welcomed his people to his holy Temple, and the psalmist reveled in the wonder and awe of this joyful, sacred celebration. The prophets did not repudiate this. Rather, as we have clearly seen, it was because sacrifices were so significant in the biblical world that the prophets' attacks on their misuse sounded utterly shocking. Listen again to Heschel:

In the sacrifice of homage, God was a participant; in the sacrifice of expiation, God was a recipient. The sacrificial act was a form of personal association with God, a way of entering into communion with him. In offering an animal, a person was offering himself vicariously. It had the power of atonement. . . .

It is hard for us to imagine what entering a sanctuary or offering a sacrifice meant to ancient man. The sanctuary was holiness in perpetuity, a miracle in continuity; the divine was mirrored in the air, sowing blessing, closing gaps between the here and beyond. In offering a sacrifice, man mingled with mystery, reached the summit of significance: sin was consumed, self was abandoned, satisfaction was bestowed upon divinity. Is it possible for us today to conceive of the solemn joy of those whose offering was placed on the altar?
Then will I go to the altar of God,
to God my exceeding joy.
I will praise Thee with the lyre,
O God, my God (Ps. 43:4; cf. Deut. 12:18–19; 31:11; Exod. 34:23–24; Isa. 1:12).[129]

What a delight it was to go to the Temple and sacrifice at God's altar! What a joy, what a privilege, what a sacred transaction. These are biblical truths we must keep before us as we analyze and interpret the words of the prophets regarding the misuse and abuse of the sacrificial system.

Turning to the specific interpretation of Jeremiah 7:21–23, verses that have raised questions for both Jewish and Christian scholars,

there are several possible views: (1) In the Ten Commandments themselves, there is no mention of sacrifices and offerings, since morality
came before sacrificial rites, and it is the Ten Commandments (or
Exod. 19:5, one chapter before the Ten Commandments) to which
Jeremiah is referring.[130] (2) When the Lord brought our people out of
Egypt, he did not speak *only* about sacrifices and offerings—which
is the impression given by the overemphasis put on these rites by Jeremiah's contemporaries—but he also spoke about morality and obedience.[131] (3) It is a typical, prophetic overstatement that should be
taken to mean "that the original Israelite sacrificial system was not
meant to be the empty, hypocritical formalism practiced by their contemporaries" (A. F. Rainey, as quoted above).[132] (4) It is a strong rebuke
to individual Israelites who were not *commanded* to bring burnt offerings in the Torah but rather were given the privilege of doing so. The
stinging rebuke is found in God's words, "eat the meat for yourselves,"
since the burnt offering was to be consumed totally by the flames on
the altar, whereas God is saying here that their offerings are not
acceptable to him because of their sin, so they might as well eat the
sacrificial meat themselves.[133]

Which view is correct? That can be debated, but in reality, not one
of these views helps the anti-missionary argument, since none of the
positions just presented claims that God or his prophets ultimately
rejected or denigrated sacrifices and offerings. We have room, therefore, to differ on the exact interpretation of these verses. In fact, in
his commentary on Jeremiah, Charles Feinberg, writing from a Christian perspective, affirmed the first view cited above, even though that
view has been championed by leading rabbis through the ages.[134]
However, I believe it is important to offer some qualification to that
same view, since the casual reader might actually think that God
gave no specific commandments about sacrifices and offerings when
he brought our people out of Egypt. That is simply not what the
Torah says.

It was in Exodus 12, while the Israelites were still in Egypt—and
that means *before* the Ten Commandments were given—that the Lord
commanded them to sacrifice a lamb for each house, inaugurating
the annual Passover ritual. And this sacrificial ritual was to be established as a lasting ordinance for all generations (see especially Exod.
12:14). In Exodus 20:24, immediately *after* the giving of the Ten Commandments, the Lord said to his people, "Make an altar of earth for
me and sacrifice on it your burnt offerings and fellowship offerings,
your sheep and goats and your cattle. Wherever I cause my name to

be honored, I will come to you and bless you." Right from the start the Lord was speaking about sacrifices and offerings. In fact, in Exodus 20–24, called by scholars the Book of the Covenant (see Exod. 24:7), there are three more commandments regarding sacrifices and offerings (see Exod. 22:20, 29; 23:18; see also Exod. 24:1–8 and immediately below, 3.10). So we see that sacrifices and offerings were, in fact, part of God's laws to Israel immediately before and after the exodus from Egypt.

In this light, the comments of Rabbi Dr. H. Freedman, summarizing the major traditional Jewish commentaries to Jeremiah, are applicable. I quote here the relevant portions of his commentary to Jeremiah 7:21–23:

> **21.** *add your burnt offerings,* etc. Burnt-offerings were wholly consumed on the altar, whilst of other sacrifices parts were eaten by the priests and offerers. The meaning is: There is no sanctity in offerings brought by guilty men; they are merely *flesh* so you might as well eat your burnt offerings too! (Rashi; Metusdath David).
>
> **22.** *for I spoke not,* etc. Sacrifices were only of secondary importance and subordinate to moral conduct. But neither Jeremiah nor the prophets opposed sacrifices as a religious institution. This is made clear from the whole passage. . . . Some non-Jewish commentators have likewise recognized that Judaism has always given precedence to the moral over the ritual law [citing 1 Sam. 15:22 here; see above, 3.8]. Indeed, this selection of the Prophets has been chosen to read [in the weekly synagogue reading of Scripture] along with Lev. vi–viii as the Haphtarah [i.e., the supplemental reading from the Prophets that relates to the weekly Torah portion], to indicate that it is better to obey God rather than to sin and bring a sacrifice [with reference here to the commentary of Levush; note also the similar observation of Feinberg, cited above].
>
> **23.** *in the day . . . Egypt.* . . . the context makes it evident that a contrast is drawn between offerings on the altar and the moral laws enjoined in the Decalogue (verse 9); and it is true that there is no mention of sacrifices in the Ten Commandments. Daath Mikra [a classic Rabbinic commentary] suggests a different rendering of the text: 'I spake not unto your fathers . . . for the sake of burnt offerings,' i.e. I did not bring you out of Egypt because I wanted your sacrifices, although these are certainly part of the system of Divine worship.[135]

These comments speak for themselves, reinforcing that there is nothing in these verses—even according to the standard traditional commentaries—to support the anti-missionary argument that the prophets denigrated and rejected the sacrificial system.

As for Amos 5:25, I have no problem with your interpretation, namely, that the children of Israel did not bring sacrifices to the Lord during their wilderness wanderings, yet he still guided and kept them by his grace and mercy. It is clear that the contemporaries of Amos put some kind of mystical emphasis on sacrifices, offerings, worship, and the observance of Sabbaths and festivals, imagining that these rites could counteract their persistent sins and transgressions and somehow secure the favor of God. Amos is telling them in no uncertain terms that such an emphasis is nonsense, plain and simple. This is in complete harmony with everything we have read so far in the prophetic books.[136]

As we have seen, the prophets sought to counteract the *misunderstanding* and *misuse* of the sacrificial system, not its rightful use. Similar to this is the language of Psalm 50, in which the Lord says:

> "Hear, O my people, and I will speak,
>   O Israel, and I will testify against you:
>   I am God, your God.
> I do not rebuke you for your sacrifices
>   or your burnt offerings, which are ever before me.
> I have no need of a bull from your stall
>   or of goats from your pens,
> for every animal of the forest is mine,
>   and the cattle on a thousand hills.
> I know every bird in the mountains,
>   and the creatures of the field are mine.
> If I were hungry I would not tell you,
>   for the world is mine, and all that is in it.
> Do I eat the flesh of bulls
>   or drink the blood of goats?
> Sacrifice thank offerings to God,
>   fulfill your vows to the Most High,
> and call upon me in the day of trouble;
>   I will deliver you, and you will honor me."
>
> Psalm 50:7–15

Here the Lord is acknowledging that his people are wonderfully zealous when it comes to bringing sacrifices and offerings (just as Jesus acknowledged a similar zeal from the Jewish leaders of his day with regard to tithes and ceremonial purity). That was not the problem. The problem was their sin (see vv. 16–21 in this psalm) and their notion that somehow the Lord actually *needed* their sacrifices (as if they would satisfy his "hunger"). But this psalm cannot possibly be construed as an attack on the sacrificial system in general. Just look at verses 14, 15, and 23. "*Sacrifice thank offerings to God,* fulfill your vows to the Most High, and call upon me in the day of trouble; I will deliver you, and you will honor me. . . . *He who sacrifices thank offerings honors me,* and he prepares the way so that I may show him the salvation of God."

Here, bringing thanksgiving offerings is commanded and commended, not condemned and cast aside. The meaning of these verses is clear, and it is also clear that so far we have found no support for the anti-missionary claim that "the prophets loudly declared to the Jewish people that the contrite prayer of the penitent sinner replaces the sacrificial system." On the contrary, as we have seen, the prophets indicated that the Lord rejected *both* prayer and sacrifice—along with Sabbath observance and all forms of worship—from unrepentant sinners. As Chief Rabbi Hertz summarized, "The Prophet's call is not, Give up your sacrifices, but, Give up your evil-doing."[137]

"But," you say, "there are other passages that state clearly that prayer *does* replace sacrifice."

Let's finish our discussion, then, by turning to those verses that have sometimes been interpreted to mean that penitent prayer replaces sacrifice. We'll consider evidence from the Book of Psalms, the Book of Hosea, and the prayer of Solomon in 2 Chronicles 7 and 1 Kings 8.

In Psalm 141:2, David prayed, "May my prayer be set before you like incense; may the lifting up of my hands be like the evening sacrifice." The meaning of this petition is clear: "Lord, receive my prayers just as you receive the incense burned before you by the priests; receive my uplifted hands just as you receive the evening sacrifice."

How then can this verse be interpreted to mean that "prayer replaces sacrifice"? According to the psalm's superscription, it was David who uttered these words, the very man who wanted to build a Temple for the Lord, the man who wrote out the plans for that Temple and left a huge fortune for it to be erected by his son Solomon (see 1 Chronicles 29). It was the same David who brought the ark of the Lord back to Jerusalem, who invested so much time and effort to enhance the Tabernacle rituals (see 1 Chronicles 15; 28), who offered sacrifices to God to stop a plague of judgment (see 2 Sam. 24:25; 1 Chron. 21:26–28).

In fact, it was the Lord himself who instructed David to offer those sacrifices before he would stop the plague of judgment:

> When the angel stretched out his hand to destroy Jerusalem, the LORD was grieved because of the calamity and said to the angel who was afflicting the people, "Enough! Withdraw your hand." The angel of the LORD was then at the threshing floor of Araunah the Jebusite. When David saw the angel who was striking down the people, he said to the LORD, "I am the one who has sinned and done wrong. These are but sheep. What have they done? Let your hand fall upon me and my family." On that day Gad went to David and said to him, "Go up and build an altar to the LORD on the threshing floor of Araunah the Jebusite." So David went up, as the LORD had commanded through Gad. . . . David built an altar to the LORD there and sacrificed burnt offerings and fellowship offerings. Then the LORD answered prayer in behalf of the land, and the plague on Israel was stopped.
>
> 2 Samuel 24:16–19, 25

How important sacrifices and offerings were! Surely no one among David's descendants—for hundreds of years following—would have thought he was suggesting that prayer replaced sacrifice. It was those very descendants who were so faithfully involved in Temple worship and Temple offerings. And it was the beauty and glory of sacrifices and incense that provided the backdrop for David's prayer.

This verse does not teach that prayer replaces sacrifice (or just the evening sacrifice, since that's all the verse mentions), nor can it be interpreted as a secret biblical reference whose real meaning was only discovered centuries later when the Temple was destroyed. If that were the case, then it would be only fair to ask why the Jews who returned to Jerusalem one generation after the Babylonians destroyed the First Temple were so eager to rebuild that very Temple and begin to offer sacrifices to the Lord. If prayer replaced sacrifice, or if prayer was superior to sacrifice, then why were our forefathers so eager to reinstitute the sacrificial system? In fact, we must ask why Ezra and Nehemiah and their fellow workers risked life and limb to rebuild the Temple and restore the altar of the Lord. Why do this if God had prepared a better (or at the least, alternate) way? (For more on this, see below, 3.17.)[138]

Perhaps the anti-missionaries have a stronger case in the Book of Hosea? Rabbi Tovia Singer, representing the anti-missionary position, would answer with an emphatic yes. He writes:

In fact, in Hosea 3:4–5, the prophet foretold with divine exactness that the nation of Israel would not have a sacrificial system during the last segment of Jewish history until the messianic age. [Rabbi Singer then quotes Hosea 3:4–5, following the King James Version almost verbatim: "For the children of Israel shall abide many days without king or prince, without sacrifice or sacred pillar, without ephod or teraphim. Afterward the children of Israel shall return and seek the LORD their God and David their king, and shall fear the LORD and His goodness in the latter days."]

In the words of the Bible, this period of time would last for many days. Yet, despite the repeated proclamations of the church that the crucifixion of Jesus serves as a sin sacrifice today, the words of Hosea were meticulously fulfilled, and we are without an animal sacrificial system today.

Given the spiritual magnitude of this remarkable prophecy, Hosea was compelled to reveal how the ecclesiastical temple functions were to be replaced. In essence, if the prophet is testifying that the nation of Israel will indeed be without a sacrificial system during their long exile until the messianic age, what are we to use instead? How are the Jewish people to atone for unintentional sin without a blood sacrifice during their bitter exile? What about all the animal sacrifices prescribed in the Book of Leviticus? Can the Jewish people get along without animal offerings? Missionaries claim they cannot. The Bible disagrees.

For this reason, the statement in Hosea 14:2–3 is crucial. In these two verses, Hosea reveals to his beloved nation how they are to replace the sacrificial system during their protracted exile. The prophet declares that the Almighty wants us to "render for bulls the offering of our lips." Prayer is to replace the sacrificial system. Hosea 14:2–3 states, "Take words with you, and return to the LORD. Say to him, 'Take away all iniquity; receive us graciously, For we will render for bulls the offering of our lips.'"[139]

Are Rabbi Singer's claims true? Certainly not. Let's review his interpretation, working backward from Hosea 14 to Hosea 3.

First, it is quite natural to take Hosea 14:1–2[2–3] figuratively, just as Psalm 141:2, in which David, as we saw, asks that his prayer be set before God *as* incense and that the lifting up of his hands be *as* the evening sacrifice. So even following the traditional Jewish translation, God's people could be saying, "We will fulfill the vows of our lips as if they were bulls being offered up in sacrifice." The New Testament letter to the Messianic Jews (known as Hebrews) draws on the imagery of this verse in a similar fashion: "Through Jesus, therefore, let us continually offer to God a sacrifice of praise—the fruit of lips that confess his name" (Heb. 13:15).

Second, and more importantly, there are difficulties in the translation of Hosea 14:2[3], since the Hebrew literally reads, "Forgive all iniquity, and take good, and we will pay [Hebrew, *shillem*] bulls our lips." For that reason, there are leading Jewish scholars (such as Robert Gordis)[140] who suggest that the oldest Jewish translation of this verse, namely, the Septuagint, should be followed here, reading the word "fruit" *(peri)* instead of "bulls" *(parim)*—thereby undercutting the entire anti-missionary argument.[141] Not only so, but a careful reading of the Hebrew text—even leaving the word *bulls* intact—indicates that the verse has *nothing* to do with offering sacrifices, since the Hebrew verb *shillem* is never used in the entire Bible with reference to making an animal sacrifice. Rather, it is most frequently used in the context of paying a vow, and its actual meaning—which is not disputed in any Hebrew dictionary I have found—is "to fulfill, complete, pay, repay, compensate," as in Ecclesiastes 5:4[3]: "When you make a vow to God, do not delay in *fulfilling* it *[shillem]*. He has no pleasure in fools; *fulfill [shillem]* your vow." Therefore the meaning of the phrase is, "We will pay the vows of our lips to God," as opposed to, "We will replace animal sacrifices with the offerings of our lips."[142]

All this should give us pause for thought, since it would be highly unlikely—to put it mildly—that the Lord would hang a major, life-critical, Torah-revising revelation on just one verse, especially when that verse in the original Hebrew is somewhat obscure grammatically and clearly does not mean what the anti-missionaries claim it means.[143]

Third, there is a fatal flaw in Rabbi Singer's use of Hosea 3, and it is seen in the key verse from Hosea that he failed to quote. You will remember that he argued that according to Hosea 3:4–5, "the nation of Israel would not have a sacrificial system during the last segment of Jewish history until the messianic age." According to this interpretation, Hosea 3:5 describes the end of this period when Israel will again have sacrifice and king: "Afterward the Israelites will return and seek the LORD their God and David their king. They will come trembling to the LORD and to his blessings in the last days" (Hosea 3:5). Rabbi Singer then explains that during this period "the prophet declares that the Almighty wants us to 'render for bulls the offering of our lips.' Prayer is to replace the sacrificial system," referring to Hosea 14:1–2[2–3]. But he never actually quotes verse 1[2], which reads, "Return, O Israel, to the LORD your God. Your sins have been your downfall!" And this is the verse that leads into the exhortation to "take words with you. . . ."

So Hosea 14 is speaking of the *end* of the period described in Hosea 3:4–5, the time when Israel *returns* to the Lord, the time when sacrifices and offerings are restored. Look again at Hosea 3:5: "Afterward the Israelites will *return* [Hebrew, *shuv*] and seek the Lord their God and David their king." Then compare this with Hosea 14:1–2[2–3]: "*Return [shuv]*, O Israel, to the Lord your God. . . . Take words with you and *return [shuv]* to the Lord." Then keep reading in Hosea 14. God says:

> "I will heal their waywardness
>   and love them freely,
>   for my anger has turned away from them.
> I will be like the dew to Israel;
>   he will blossom like a lily.
> Like a cedar of Lebanon
>   he will send down his roots;
>   his young shoots will grow.
> His splendor will be like an olive tree,
>   his fragrance like a cedar of Lebanon.
> Men will dwell again in his shade.
>   He will flourish like the grain.
> He will blossom like a vine,
>   and his fame will be like the wine from Lebanon."

> Hosea 14:4–7[5–8]

What a wonderful passage! It is hardly a picture of Israel in exile, separated from the Temple and unable to offer sacrifices and offerings. Rather, it is a picture of Israel restored, gloriously blessed by the Lord, a picture that many traditional Jews would equate with the Messianic age, meaning the age of the building of the Third Temple, with its sacrifices and offerings (see below, 3.17). So Hosea is actually saying the *opposite* of what Rabbi Singer claims he says. Contrary to the assertion, then, that "the prophets loudly declared to the Jewish people that the contrite prayer of the penitent sinner replaces the sacrificial system," we have seen that not only did the prophets not declare this "loudly," they didn't declare it at all.[144]

Yet there is a final passage marshaled by Rabbi Singer and other anti-missionaries, taken this time from the prayer of Solomon as recorded in 2 Chronicles 6 and 1 Kings 8. Interestingly, it was the Lord's reply to this very prayer that was pointed to by the Talmudic rabbis for scriptural justification of their position that prayer had replaced sacrifice. As noted in the *Encyclopedia Judaica*, "After the destruction of the Temple and the consequent cessation of sacrifices, the rabbis declared, 'Prayer, repentance, and charity avert the evil decree,'"[145] and they based their position on one scriptural text, namely, 2 Chronicles 7:14, in which the Lord said to Solomon, "If my people, who are called by my name, will humble themselves and pray and seek my face and turn from their wicked ways, then will I hear from heaven and will forgive their sin and will heal their land."

With reference to this Talmudic concept, Rabbi Singer writes:

> The prophets never instruct the Jews to worship any crucified messiah or demigod. Nor does scripture ever tell us that an innocent man can die as an atonement for the sins of the wicked. Such a message is utterly antithetical to the teachings of the Jewish scriptures. [Actually, this very message is found both in the Hebrew Bible and the Talmud. See below, 3.15.] Rather, it is the lips of the sinner that would become as bulls of the sin offerings.
>
> King Solomon echoes this sentiment as well. In I Kings 8:46–50 [which is an exact parallel to 2 Chron. 6:36–40], King Solomon delivers a startling prophetic message as he inaugurates the first temple that had just been completed. In his inauguration sermon, King Solomon forewarns that one day the Jewish people would be driven out of the land of Israel, and be banished to the land of their enemies, far or near. During their exile they will fervently desire to repent of their sins. King Solomon then declares that they will face Jerusalem from their exile, confess their sins, "and God will hear their prayers in Heaven, and forgive them for all their transgressions."
>
> There was no mention of a cross or a dead messiah in King Solomon's prophetic message.[146] Only the contrite and repentant prayer of the remorseful sinner can bring about a complete atonement. Although King Solomon's timeless message stands out as a theological impossibility in Christian terms, it remains the centerpiece of the Jew's system of atonement throughout his long and bitter exile.[147]

"Well," you say, "it seems that at last there is support for my argument, since these verses explicitly state that when the children of Israel are in exile—and that means without Temple or sacrifice—that their prayers directed to the Temple are sufficient. God will forgive them when they repent and ask for mercy, without sacrifices of any kind."

Are you sure? Have you read these verses in context? You see, rather than speaking of a time when there are no Temple sacrifices being offered, these verses are predicated on the fact that the Temple *would* be standing and that sacrifices *would* be offered. That's why prayer toward the Temple was so important. And the ancient rabbis, knowing full well that a destroyed Temple indicated that something was amiss, instituted prayers for the restoration of the Temple, and these prayers are prayed daily around the world by traditional Jews. In fact, one petition is so important that it forms the last of the Eighteen Benedictions, called the Amidah or Shemoneh Esreh: "Be favorable, O LORD our God, toward Your people Israel and toward their prayer, and restore the service to the Holy of Holies of Your Temple. The fire-offerings of Israel and their prayer accept with love and favor, and may the service of Your people Israel always be favorable to You."[148]

This petition is also recited every day:

> May it be Your will, O LORD our God, and the God of our forefathers, that You have mercy on us and pardon us for all our errors, atone for us all our iniquities, forgive all our willful sins; and that You rebuild the Holy Temple speedily, in our days, so that we may offer to You the continual offering that it may atone for us, as You have prescribed for us in Your Torah through Moses, Your servant, from Your glorious mouth, as it is said: [Num. 28:1–8 then follows].[149]

So rather than simply teaching that prayer replaces sacrifice, the rabbis longed for the day when they could offer sacrifices again. As the note in the *ArtScroll Siddur* explains: "We are about to begin 'offering' our communal sacrifices, as it were. Before doing so, we recite a brief prayer that God end the exile and make it possible for us to offer the *true offerings*, not just the recitations that take their place."[150] Even the Prayerbook recognizes how important the Temple sacrifices were.

Let's look carefully at 2 Chronicles 7, God's response to Solomon's prayer (the prayer strangely referred to by Rabbi Singer as Solomon's prophetic message and inauguration sermon). To bring out some key points, I have highlighted them in the text:

> When Solomon had finished the temple of the LORD and the royal palace, and had succeeded in carrying out all he had in mind to do in the temple of the LORD and in his own palace, the LORD appeared to him at night and said: "*I have heard your prayer and have chosen this place for myself as a temple for sacrifices*. When I shut up the heavens so that there is no rain, or command locusts to devour the land or send a plague among my people, if my people, who are called by my name, will humble themselves and pray and seek my face and turn from their wicked ways, then will I hear from heaven and will forgive their sin and will heal their land. Now my eyes will be open and my ears attentive to the prayers offered in this place. I have chosen and consecrated this

temple so that my Name may be there forever. My eyes and my heart will always be there. As for you, if you walk before me as David your father did, and do all I command, and observe my decrees and laws, I will establish your royal throne, as I covenanted with David your father when I said, 'You shall never fail to have a man to rule over Israel.' *But if you turn away and forsake the decrees and commands I have given you and go off to serve other gods and worship them, then I will uproot Israel from my land, which I have given them, and will reject this temple I have consecrated for my Name. I will make it a byword and an object of ridicule among all peoples. And though this temple is now so imposing, all who pass by will be appalled and say, 'Why has the* Lord *done such a thing to this land and to this temple?' People will answer, 'Because they have forsaken the* Lord*, the God of their fathers, who brought them out of Egypt, and have embraced other gods, worshiping and serving them—that is why he brought all this disaster on them.'"*

2 Chronicles 7:11–22

Let's take this one step at a time. We must first remember that the prayer of Solomon was the prayer of the dedication of the Temple. In response to this prayer, the Lord appeared to Solomon and said, "I have heard your prayer and have chosen this place for myself as a Temple for sacrifices." And it is this fact, namely, that the Lord chose this Temple as a house for sacrifices, that leads into the famous promise of verse 14: "If my people, who are called by my name, will humble themselves and pray and seek my face and turn from their wicked ways, then will I hear from heaven and will forgive their sin and will heal their land." Yet this is the very verse quoted in the Talmud to prove that when the Temple was *not* standing, prayer, repentance, and charity replaced sacrifice. Isn't this amazing? A verse based on God's acceptance of the centrality of the Temple sacrifices is used to prove that those very sacrifices were replaced.[151]

But there's more. The verses we just read state clearly that Solomon's prayer would be answered only as long as the Temple was standing. Otherwise, if the people of Israel went too far in their sin, then the Lord would uproot them from their land and destroy the very Temple he had consecrated for his name.[152] And so, rather than being an object of veneration and respect, the destroyed Temple would be an object of ridicule and reproach, a sign to the nations that God's people "have forsaken the Lord, the God of their fathers, who brought them out of Egypt, and have embraced other gods, worshiping and serving them—that is why he brought all this disaster on them." A destroyed Temple would be a sign of severe divine judgment. It would mean that Israel, as a nation, was temporarily rejected by God.[153] At such times the words of the psalmist must have been on the lips of many: "Awake, O Lord! Why do you sleep? Rouse yourself! Do not reject us forever. Why do you hide your face and forget our misery and oppression?" (Ps. 44:23–24). Yes, the pain and grief and shame were almost unbearable.

Just consider the biblical response, found in the Book of Lamentations, to the destruction of the First Temple:

> Jerusalem has sinned greatly and so has become unclean. All who honored her despise her, for they have seen her nakedness; she herself groans and turns away. . . . Zion stretches out her hands, but there is no one to comfort her. The LORD has decreed for Jacob that his neighbors become his foes; Jerusalem has become an unclean thing among them. . . .
>
> The Lord is like an enemy; he has swallowed up Israel. He has swallowed up all her palaces and destroyed her strongholds. He has multiplied mourning and lamentation for the Daughter of Judah. He has laid waste his dwelling like a garden; he has destroyed his place of meeting. The LORD has made Zion forget her appointed feasts and her Sabbaths; in his fierce anger he has spurned both king and priest. *The Lord has rejected his altar and abandoned his sanctuary.* He has handed over to the enemy the walls of her palaces; they have raised a shout in the house of the LORD as on the day of an appointed feast. . . . *The LORD has done what he planned; he has fulfilled his word, which he decreed long ago.* He has overthrown you without pity, he has let the enemy gloat over you, he has exalted the horn of your foes.
>
> Lamentations 1:8, 17; 2:5–7, 17[154]

In light of descriptions such as this, the Talmudic use of 2 Chronicles 7:14 must be seen as misguided at best and presumptuous at worst, since the Rabbinic sages claimed that prayer had replaced sacrifice *immediately after the Temple was destroyed.* It is reminiscent of the words of the people of Israel who failed to feel the weight of God's judgments centuries before. They said, "The bricks have fallen down, but we will rebuild with dressed stone; the fig trees have been felled, but we will replace them with cedars" (Isa. 9:10). Or in the present context, "The Temple has been destroyed, but we will replace it with something else!"[155] On the contrary, with the Temple in ruins, there is no national system of atonement, and either the Messiah has come and fulfilled the purpose of the sacrifices and offerings, or else as a people we have no atonement.[156]

In this connection, there is an interesting tradition found in Rashi's commentary to Genesis 15:6 ("Abram believed the LORD, and he credited it to him as righteousness"). Rashi explains:

> **6 And he believed in the Lord** He did not request of Him a sign regarding this, but regarding the inheritance of the land, he did request of Him a sign, and he said to Him, "How will I know? [from b. *Nedarim* 32a] **and He accounted it to him as righteousness** The Holy One, blessed be He, accounted it to Abram as a merit and as righteousness for the faith that he believed in Him (Targum Jonathan). Another explanation for: "How will I know?" He did not ask Him for a sign but he said before Him, "Let me know with what merit will they [my descendants] remain therein [in the Land]?" The Holy One, blessed be He, replied, "With the merit of the sacrifices."[157]

What a concept! Abraham's descendants would be able to stay in the Promised Land through the merit of the sacrifices. How important, then, were the sacrifices, even in traditional Jewish thinking?

Not surprisingly, some of the Talmudic rabbis, fully aware of the magnitude of the destruction of the Temple and of the disastrous consequences that followed, stated that since the day the Temple was destroyed, the gates of prayer were closed and there was an iron wall between God and his people (see b. Berakhoth 32b, with reference to Ezek. 4:3). In fact, it was even taught that since the day Jerusalem and the Temple were destroyed, there was not a day that went by that had no curse in it (see Midrash Psalms 9:7; Tanhuma [Buber] Tezaveh 10) and there was no joy in God's presence until such time that Jerusalem would be restored with Israel in her midst (see Midrash Zuta, Eicha, 1:7). Despite all this, however, the Rabbinic view that became normative was that with the Temple's destruction, prayer replaced sacrifice.

The sad, painful fact is that there have been times in our history when God refused to forgive us as a nation. Just consider these verses from Jeremiah, shortly before the Temple was destroyed: "So do not pray for this people nor offer any plea or petition for them; do not plead with me, for I will not listen to you" (Jer. 7:16). "Do not pray for this people nor offer any plea or petition for them, because I will not listen when they call to me in the time of their distress" (Jer. 11:14). "Then the LORD said to me, 'Do not pray for the well-being of this people. Although they fast, I will not listen to their cry; though they offer burnt offerings and grain offerings, I will not accept them. Instead, I will destroy them with the sword, famine and plague'" (Jer. 14:11–12).

Just consider how hopeless the anti-missionary argument is that with the Temple destroyed, God ordained that prayer would replace sacrifice. The Temple was destroyed because of our sins as a people, sins that were so grievous to God that he said, "Enough! No amount of prayer, sacrifice, or fasting will stop me. I will reject my city and my sanctuary, and I will judge my people, banishing them from my presence." How ludicrous to say then, "Now that the Temple has been sacked and we can no longer offer sacrifices, God will accept our prayers instead." On the contrary, during the last years the First Temple was standing, with sacrifices still being offered in accordance with the Torah, the Lord refused to hear our prayers for mercy. How much worse, then, would it be once the Temple was destroyed by the anger of the Lord?

As Jews, we must come to grips with the fact that there have been periods of time in which we had no assurance of national atonement because of our sins. Even the Talmud records that for the last forty years before the Second Temple was destroyed, the Lord did not accept the sacrifices offered on the Day of Atonement (see b. Yoma 39b; and see vol. 1, 2.1). How would this make a religious Jewish person feel? And how would a God-fearing Jew feel when the Temple was actually destroyed? While the Temple was standing, there was at least some hope for national atonement, no matter how sinful the people were. But once the Temple was destroyed, it was as if God were closing the door on national grace and mercy. How frightful and traumatic the destruction of the Temple must have been for our people,[158] and how easy it is to see how our leaders would have tried to pick up the pieces somehow, someway, even by grasping at spiritual straws and claiming that prayer would now replace sacrifice. But this couldn't really remove the sense of despair and divine rejection that our people experienced.

Just consider this petition from the traditional morning prayer service, as found in the *Siddur*. It acknowledges that the Temple was destroyed "through our sins" but then asks God to accept prayer in the place of sacrifices, calling on Hosea 14:2, a verse that, rightly translated and interpreted (see above), does not provide even the slightest support for the view that prayer replaces sacrifice. This is the petition, lifted to God in prayer every morning for more than fifteen hundred years by traditional Jews worldwide:

> Master of the Worlds, You commanded us to bring the continual offering at its set time, and that the Kohanim [priests] be at their assigned

service, the Levites on their platform, and the Israelites at their station. But now, through our sins, the Holy Temple is destroyed, the continual offering is discontinued, and we have neither Kohen [priest] at his service, nor Levite on his platform, nor Israelite at his station. But You said, "Let our lips compensate for the bulls" [Hosea 14:2]—therefore may it be Your will, O LORD, our God and the God of our forefathers, that the prayer of our lips be worthy, acceptable and favorable before You, as if we had brought the continual offering at its set time and we had stood at its station.[159]

Can you feel a dimension of futility in this prayer, especially when you realize that it is followed by the recitation of the fifth chapter of the Mishnaic tractate Zevahim, outlining in painstaking detail the specific rulings for the offering of animal sacrifices at the altar? Once again, there is the clear recognition that the Temple's destruction means that something is very wrong, and therefore, there is an uncertain hope in God's willingness to receive his people's prayers in place of sacrifices. Can you sense that there is no assurance of being heard in this prayer?[160] To be honest, many of the prayers found in the Prayerbook send a similar message—sometimes clear, sometimes veiled—that something is amiss in Israel's relationship with God, despite all of his covenantal promises, which also form an integral part of the Prayerbook. Heartfelt pleas for mercy are found on almost every page. Just consider the second to last prayer of the Shemoneh Esreh, praying that our prayers will be heard:

Hear our voice, O LORD our God, pity and be compassionate to us, and accept—with compassion and favor—our prayer, for God who hears prayers and supplications are You. From before Yourself, our King, turn us not away empty-handed, for You hear the prayer of Your people Israel with compassion. Blessed are You, O LORD, Who hears prayer.[161]

Perhaps if you have prayed these prayers, asking God not to turn you away empty-handed, you too have felt a barrier, a breach, a breakdown of some kind between you as a Jew and the God of our forefathers. Perhaps you too have sensed that something was spiritually disjointed, but you have not known what the problem was. Could it be you are sensing that you have no acceptable form of atonement for your sins and that all the prayers in the world cannot take the place of blood atonement? Could it be you recognize that you pray these prayers daily as part of the Jewish people, a people who is still scattered around the world, a people who even with a homeland still has no Temple, a people who still awaits some hint that the Messiah will come—though he was expected so many centuries ago?

I would suggest that you give this topic of sacrifice and atonement some careful consideration. In the objections that follow, we will deal with the issue of the centrality of blood atonement according to the Hebrew Scriptures, the question of how Yeshua's death meets the requirements of an atoning sacrifice, and the question of why, if Yeshua's death paid the price for our sins, some of the prophets seem to anticipate sacrifices in a restored, future Temple. We'll also look at some other relevant issues, including the question of how Gentiles received forgiveness before the days of Jesus.

For now, one thing is clear: Not a single verse in the Hebrew Bible states that the prophets repudiated the sacrificial system or that prayer replaced sacrifice.

3.10. Even if I accept your premise that blood sacrifices are of great importance in the Torah, the fact is that our Hebrew Bible—including the Torah itself—offers other means of atonement, not just the shedding of blood.

> There can be no question that blood atonement is the central and most important form of atonement in the Bible. The blood is essential, foundational, and irreplaceable. Because blood sacrifices form the heart and soul of the biblical system of atonement, both the New Testament and numerous authoritative Rabbinic traditions state that without shedding of blood, there is no atonement. Take away the blood, and the entire biblical system of atonement collapses.

Before we address the question of whether there were several different forms of atonement given by God in the Hebrew Scriptures, let's first consider the central importance of blood atonement throughout those same Scriptures. Then we can examine the accuracy of the New Testament statement in the letter to the Hebrews that "the law requires that nearly everything be cleansed with blood, and without the shedding of blood there is no forgiveness" (Heb. 9:22).

From the very beginning of human history, the Torah records that people offered blood sacrifices to the Lord, either at their own initiative or by divine command. In the Book of Genesis, we read of animal sacrifices being offered to the Lord by Abel, Noah, Abraham, and Jacob. But this, in and of itself, proves nothing, since there is no explicit mention of atonement or forgiveness in conjunction with these offerings, and it would be difficult to prove from these passages that the shedding of blood was *central* to the religion of the patriarchs. Important, yes; central, no.

When we turn to the Book of Exodus, however, the situation begins to change. The shedding of blood—by divine command—becomes quite central. On the eve of Israel's departure from Egypt, it was the blood of the Passover *(pesach)* lamb, put on the two doorposts and lintel of the house, that was a sign to the destroying angel, as the Lord said, *"The blood will be a sign for you* on the houses where you are; and *when I see the blood,* I will pass over you. No destructive plague will touch you when I strike Egypt" (Exod. 12:13). The divine commandment was explicit and detailed:

> Then Moses summoned all the elders of Israel and said to them, "Go at once and select the animals for your families and slaughter the Passover lamb. Take a bunch of hyssop, dip it into the blood in the basin and put some of the blood on the top and on both sides of the doorframe. Not one of you shall go out the door of his house until morning. When the LORD goes through the land to strike down the Egyptians, he will see the blood on the top and sides of the doorframe and will pass over that doorway, and he will not permit the destroyer to enter your houses and strike you down."
>
> Exodus 12:21–23

During this first Passover, only the blood of the sacrificial lamb separated between life and death.

Exodus 24 records another milestone event for the people of Israel, namely, their formal entering into a covenant with God, and that event too was sealed by blood. The Torah records that Moses explained to the people God's commands and requirements and they responded by saying, "Everything the LORD has said we will do" (Exod. 24:3).

> Then [Moses] sent young Israelite men, and they offered burnt offerings and sacrificed young bulls as fellowship offerings to the LORD. Moses took half of the blood and put it in bowls, and the other half he

sprinkled on the altar. Then he took the Book of the Covenant and read it to the people. They responded, "We will do everything the LORD has said; we will obey." Moses then took the blood, sprinkled it on the people and said, "This is the blood of the covenant that the LORD has made with you in accordance with all these words."

Exodus 24:5–8

Moses actually sprinkled the blood on the people, demonstrating in no uncertain terms that this divine covenant had been formalized and finalized by the shedding of blood.[162] Obviously, this ceremony was of great importance, and it would be an error to downplay the key role played by the shedding of blood in the faith of our forefathers. In fact, the Targum of Onkelos, the most important Aramaic translation of the Torah read in the synagogues in the early centuries of this era, added a surprising phrase to Exodus 24:8, which I have emphasized here: "And Moses took the blood and poured it on the altar *as atonement* for the people." How interesting! The Rabbinic traditions reflected in the Targum actually went beyond the text of Scripture by stating that this blood provided atonement for the people. This indicates that the concepts of the shedding of blood and atonement were intimately connected in the minds of the Talmudic rabbis and their predecessors.[163] It's almost as if there was an immediate mental association made between the words *blood* and *atonement,* just as there would be an immediate association between the words *husband* and *wife* or *Michael Jordan* and *basketball.* Blood sacrifices and atonement fit together like a hand in a glove.

So already in Exodus we have two major events connected with the shedding of blood: first, the Passover; second, the ratifying of God's covenant with his people. Therefore, it comes as no surprise when we see that blood was applied *to the priests* and *to the altar* when they were consecrated to the Lord. This was the process: Sacrifices were offered to the Lord to make atonement (see Exod. 29:33), and the blood of those sacrifices was used in the ritual in which the priests and the altar were set apart for divine service. As it is written in Exodus 29:20, "Slaughter [the ram], take some of its blood and put it on the lobes of the right ears of Aaron and his sons, on the thumbs of their right hands, and on the big toes of their right feet. Then sprinkle blood against the altar on all sides."

Why was the application of blood necessary? There are at least two reasons: First, the priests and the altar were directly involved in providing atonement for Israel, and therefore, both were consecrated with blood; second, the blood provided purification and purgation for both the priests and the altar.[164] This underscores yet again how central the blood was in the atonement system.[165]

Continuing in Exodus, the next important text we come to is 30:10, the first reference in the Pentateuch to annual atonement: "Once a year Aaron shall make atonement on [the altar's] horns. This *annual atonement* must be made *with the blood of the atoning sin offering* for the generations to come. It is most holy to the LORD." How striking! The first reference to annual atonement (to take place on Yom Kippur, the Day of Atonement) says nothing about prayer, nothing about good deeds, nothing about fasting, nothing even about repentance, as important and necessary as those things are.[166] Instead, the Torah speaks only of blood. Why? *Because atonement rites are intimately connected to the blood.* Take it away, and you have no atonement.

In fact, at this point it would be useful for us to turn to Leviticus 16, where the laws for the Day of Atonement are set forth in great detail. There we see again that the blood is absolutely central. Speaking of the ceremonies to be performed by the high priest that day, Scripture states:

> He is to take some of the bull's *blood* and with his finger sprinkle it on the front of the atonement cover; then he shall sprinkle some of it with his finger seven times before the atonement cover. He shall then slaughter the goat for the sin offering for the people and take its *blood* behind the curtain and do with it as he did with the bull's *blood:* He shall sprinkle it on the atonement cover and in front of it. In this way he will *make atonement* for the Most Holy Place because of the uncleanness and rebellion of the Israelites, whatever their sins have been. He is to do the same for the Tent of Meeting, which is among them in the midst of their uncleanness. . . . Then he shall come out to the altar that is before the LORD and *make atonement* for it. He shall take some of the bull's *blood* and some of the goat's *blood* and put it on all the horns of the altar. He shall sprinkle some of the *blood* on it with his finger seven times to *cleanse* it and to *consecrate* it from the uncleanness of the Israelites.

> Leviticus 16:14–16, 18–19

So the Holy of Holies, the most sacred place on earth, the specific location where God promised to reveal himself to his people (see Lev. 16:2), was cleansed from Israel's uncleanness by blood, just as the altar and the Tent of Meeting as a whole were cleansed by blood. Everything related to atonement and cleansing had to do with blood.[167]

To reiterate: There was one day ordained by God for the atonement of the people, and central to the rituals and ceremonies of that day was blood. And there was one place where God promised to appear to his people (the Tabernacle/Temple) and one ordained place where they were to bring their sacrifices and offerings (the altar) and both the Tabernacle and altar were cleansed by blood. We dare not downplay the importance of the blood.

Throughout the Book of Leviticus, which is *the* book in the Scriptures dealing with sacrifice and atonement, whenever atonement is mentioned (forty-nine times in all), it is *always* in conjunction with blood sacrifices (for Lev. 5:11–13, see below). And the key text that explains the reason for this is Leviticus 17:11: "For the life of a creature is in the blood, and I have given it to you to make atonement for yourselves on the altar; it is the blood that makes atonement for one's life."[168]

Of course, I am aware that anti-missionaries seek to downplay the importance of Leviticus 17:11, arguing that the context of this verse is the prohibition against consuming blood (see v. 10), and that Leviticus 17:11 is merely explaining *why* eating of blood is prohibited, namely, because it is used to atone. But the anti-missionaries would stress that Leviticus 17:11 in no way states that blood is the main or only way of atonement.[169]

Unfortunately, while Messianic Jews are accused of failing to pay attention to Leviticus 17:11 in context, in reality, some anti-missionaries have actually failed to pay attention to the verse itself. As Rashi explained, "For every creature is dependent on blood, therefore I have given it to you on the altar to atone for the life of man; let life come and atone for the life." In other words, the reason that blood sacrifices played such a central role in the Torah is because they operated on the principle of substitution, i.e., on the principle of life for life. Thus, an ancient midrash on Leviticus 1:2 states: "When you voluntarily offer a *korban olah* [i.e., a burnt offering] and it is slaughtered and its blood sprinkled upon the altar, I consider it as if you have offered your very selves."[170] Similarly, Rabbi J. H. Hertz, commenting on Leviticus 17:11, observed, "The use of blood, representing life, in the rites of atonement symbolized the complete yielding up of the worshipper's life to God, and conveyed the thought that the surrender of a man to the will of God carried with it the assurance of Divine pardon."[171] Similarly, with respect to Leviticus 17:11, Christian Old Testament scholar John E. Hartley noted that the pouring out of the animal's blood is also important. The blood represents the animal's *npš*, "life." The offerer has already identified himself with the animal by laying his hands on the animal's head; with this gesture the offerer recognizes that the death of the animal will commute the penalty for his sin. It needs to be underscored that the sacrificial system loudly proclaims that the penalty of sin is death. Thus the giving of a life *(npš)* on the altar for the life *(npš)* of the offerer upholds justice.[172]

It is therefore no surprise that Leviticus 17:11 was the proof text commonly used by the Talmudic rabbis to indicate that the atoning power of the sacrifices was in the blood. Several different times in the Talmudic literature—in quite authoritative sources, I should note—it is observed that "there is no atonement without the blood," exactly as stated in Hebrews 9:22. In fact, there are leading Jewish scholars (see below) who point out that the author of Hebrews was simply repeating the *universally accepted Jewish view of his day* when he wrote that, according to the Torah, "without the shedding of blood there is no forgiveness."[173] As expressed concisely by New Testament scholar Harold Attridge, these words "constitute a cultic maxim well known in Jewish tradition."[174]

It is in the context of animal sacrifices—specifically, the wording of Leviticus 1:4 ("He is to lay his hand on the head of the burnt offering, and it will be accepted on his behalf to make atonement for him")—that the Talmudic rabbis asked,

> Does the laying on of the hand [on the sacrifice] make atonement for one? Does not atonement come through the blood, as it is said: For it is the blood that maketh atonement by reason of the life! [Lev. 17:11] . . . Does the waving [of the offering] make atonement? Is it not the blood which makes atonement, as it is written, "For it is the blood that maketh atonement by reason of the life" [again, Lev. 17:11]? (b. Yoma 5a, as translated in the *Soncino Talmud*; cf. also the virtually identical wording in b. Zevahim 6a; b. Menahot 93b; Sifra 4:9).[175]

"But," you ask, "isn't the Talmud simply teaching that, *as far as sacrifices are concerned*, their atoning power lies only in the blood? In other words, the Talmud isn't making a statement about atonement in general, nor is it teaching that atonement comes only through the blood. It's simply saying that the atoning power of sacrifices is found in the blood. That's the explanation I heard from my rabbi."

Well, your rabbi was not entirely wrong, since he has explained the immediate context in part. But he has failed to note exactly *why* the rabbis concluded that atonement was found only in the shedding of a sacrificial animal's blood and not in the process of laying one's hand on the sacrifice or in waving it before the Lord. It was because the rabbis knew that "there is no atonement without the blood." In other words, since it was an accepted fact that there was no atonement without the blood (this stock phrase, "there is no atonement without the blood," found repeatedly in the Talmud, is almost proverbial in nature), the rabbis had no trouble concluding that it was the blood—and not any other aspect of the sacrifices—that effected atonement. Thus, Oxford professor Geza Vermes, one of the foremost Jewish scholars of the Dead Sea Scrolls, stated that "according to Jewish theology, there can be no expiation without the shedding of blood: 'ên kapparah 'ella' bedam."[176] Similarly, Professor Baruch Levine, in his commentary on Leviticus for the Jewish Publication Society wrote, "Expiation by means of sacrificial blood-rites is a prerequisite for securing God's forgiveness. As the rabbis expressed it, 'ein kapparah 'ella' be-dam, 'There is no ritual expiation except by means of blood.'"[177]

Again, this is because blood sacrifices operated on the principle of life for life, an innocent sacrificial animal being offered up in place of the guilty sinner. That's why the blood had to be shed.[178] This concept was so ingrained in the Jewish psyche that to this day many Orthodox Jews around the world still offer a blood sacrifice on the eve of Yom Kippur (or in some circles, the eve of Rosh Hashanah), taking a live rooster (for men) or hen (for women) and waving it around their heads three times as they say, "This is my substitute, this is my vicarious offering, this is my atonement [kapparah]. This rooster (or hen) shall meet death, but I shall find a long and pleasant life of peace."[179] They recognize that they still need the blood, and they recognize the principle of substitution, or life for life. Thus, when they take the fowl to slaughter immediately after performing this ceremony, its death is viewed as the replacement and atonement for their own lives.

To further emphasize the vital connection between blood and atonement, let me cite the observations made by the two most important Talmud commentaries (Rashi and Tosafot) to this Rabbinic dictum that "there is no atonement without blood." Rashi states that "the fundamental principle ('iqqar) of atonement is in the blood" (b. Yoma 5a). Tosafot, also discussing the Talmudic statement that there is no atonement without the blood, makes reference to a passage found elsewhere in the Talmud (b. Pesahim 59b) that indicated that the priests had to eat certain specified sacrifices if those offerings were to have their atoning effect.[180] Tosafot then concludes, "But in any case, the fundamental principle [again, *'iqqar*] of atonement doesn't exist without blood" (b. Zevahim 6a).

Of course, I fully recognize that these same rabbis claimed that once the Temple was destroyed, prayer, repentance, and charitable deeds replaced sacrifices (see my discussion, below). However, I am simply responding to your objection that the Torah itself provided alternate forms of atonement, and in the process, I am demonstrating just how irreplaceable the blood actually was. All this is summarized in an important passage in 1 Chronicles, one of the last books of the Old Testament to be written. We read in 1 Chronicles 6:48–49[33–34]:

> [The] Levites were assigned to all the other duties of the tabernacle, the house of God. But Aaron and his descendants were the ones who presented offerings on the altar of burnt offering and on the altar of incense in connection with all that was done in the Most Holy Place, making atonement for Israel, in accordance with all that Moses the servant of God had commanded.

Notice once again: When atonement is mentioned, it is not connected with prayer, repentance, or good deeds, as fundamentally important as all these are, and as essential as they are to our right standing before God. Rather, when atonement and ritual expiation are mentioned, they are connected with sacrifices and offerings. Even the traditional Rabbinic viewpoint recognized that while the Temple was standing, atonement came through blood sacrifices. (My difference with the rabbis would not be over this issue but over the issue of whether prayer and repentance *replaced* sacrifices after the Temple was destroyed; see above, 3.9, and below, 3.13.) Thus, Maimonides wrote in his authoritative Law Code, "At this time, when the Temple is not standing *and we do not have the altar of atonement* [my emphasis], there is nothing but repentance; repentance atones for all transgressions." In teaching this, Maimonides was simply restating the teaching of the Talmud found in b. Berakhoth 55a (among other passages; cf. b. Sukkah 55b; b. Hagigah 27a): "As long as the Temple stood, the altar atoned for Israel. Now a man's table atones for him."[181]

Among biblical scholars, both Jewish and Christian, there is little dispute about this matter: While the Temple was standing, blood sacrifices were the principle and irreplaceable means of atonement for Israel. Discussing the concept of death as an atonement (in other words, a person's own death would serve as final payment for his sins), Professor Ephraim E. Urbach, one of the leading scholars of Rabbinic literature, observed:

> The doctrine of R. Ishmael, R. Judah, and Rabbi that death—even death without repentance—has the power to atone originated only after the Destruction, for with regard to the Temple period it is stated, "And for all other prohibitions ordained in the Torah, be they light or grave . . . premature death and execution by the court, the scapegoat makes atonement" (*M. Shev'uot* i, 6). . . . At the time when the Temple still stood, it was certainly unnecessary and inappropriate to regard death as an atonement.[182]

So Urbach is stating that there was no need to speculate on other forms of atonement while the Temple was still standing, since the sacrifices (including the scapegoat on the Day of Atonement; see below, 3.12) atoned for Israel. This is the consistent position of the Scriptures as well as the consistent position of the Talmud. To quote Urbach again:

> The fasts that multiplied after the Destruction also assumed the character of a surrogate and replacement for the atonement effected by the sacrifices. This fact found concrete expression in the prayer attributed to Rav Sheshet: "Sovereign of the universe, it is known to Thee that when the Temple was in existence, if a man sinned he would bring a sacrifice, of which only the fat and the blood were offered up, and he would be granted atonement. Now I have observed a fast and my own fat and blood have been diminished. May it be Thy will that my diminished fat and blood be accounted as though I had offered them up before Thee on the altar, and do Thou show me favour" [b. Berakhoth 17a].[183]

It was only after the Temple was destroyed that the Talmudic rabbis came up with the concept that God had provided other forms of atonement aside from blood. Once more, we will let Urbach explain:

> The sacrifices only expiated iniquities between man and God, for which it was not in the power of an earthly court to impose punishment. Transgressions that were liable to punishment by a court were not atoned for by sacrifices, and only the penalty brought with it atonement for sin. . . . *When the court's right to impose the death-penalty was abrogated and the Temple was destroyed, involving the abolition of the sacrifices, a sense of despair and the feeling that Israel had been deprived of the possibility of atonement prevailed.* "It once happened that Rabban Johanan b. Zakkai was leaving Jerusalem and R. Joshua was walking behind

him, when the latter saw the Temple in ruins. Said R. Joshua: 'Woe to us that this is in ruins—*the place where the sins of Israel were expiated!*' Rabban Johanan b. Zakkai replied: 'My son, be not grieved, we have a means of atonement that is commensurate with it. Which is this? It is the performance of lovingkindness, as it is said, "For I desire loving kindness and not sacrifice"'" (Hosea vi 6; Urbach is citing Avot d. R. Nathan, Version I, iv, 11a).[184]

As we saw in the previous answer (above, 3.9), this was a tragic—even though well-intended—innovation of the rabbis. Nonetheless, the passage underscores one thing: While the Temple was standing, it was fully understood that blood sacrifices brought atonement, and no one who loved the Torah thought of bypassing those sacrifices or downplaying their vital importance.

J. H. Kurtz, a leading, nineteenth-century Christian scholar of the Old Testament, made similar observations on the sacrificial system:

When the sacrifice of animals is mentioned in the law, *making atonement (lekapper 'alayw)* is nearly always expressly mentioned, and for the most part this alone, as being the purpose, end, and fruit of the sacrifice. It is perfectly obvious, indeed, that there were other ends to be attained—such, for example, as the self-surrender of the sacrifice *to* Jehovah in the burning of the sacrificial gift, and the enjoyment of fellowship *with* Jehovah in the sacrificial meal; but the fact that these ends could not possibly be attained in any other way than by means of expiation, and on the basis of expiation, gave to the latter its incomparable, all-surpassing importance, and its central place in the plan of salvation, the progressive stages of which were symbolically represented in the sacrificial worship.[185]

How then do we explain Leviticus 5:11–13, a Torah law that stated that a poor Israelite who was unable to bring the required sin offering of a lamb, goat, turtledoves, or pigeons could bring instead an offering of fine flour—yet the flour still brought them atonement and was itself considered a sin offering? The answer is really quite simple, as the verses themselves indicate:

If, however, he cannot afford two doves or two young pigeons, he is to bring as an offering for his sin a tenth of an ephah of fine flour for a sin offering. He must not put oil or incense on it, because it is a sin offering. He is to bring it to the priest, who shall take a handful of it as a memorial portion and burn it on the altar on top of the offerings made to the LORD by fire. It is a sin offering. In this way the priest will make atonement for him for any of these sins he has committed, and he will be forgiven. The rest of the offering will belong to the priest, as in the case of the grain offering.

According to verse 12, the priest will "take a handful of it [i.e., the flour] as a memorial portion and burn it *on the altar on top of the offerings* made to the Lord by fire." Then "the priest will make atonement for him" (v. 13). In other words, the priest, in his capacity as mediator for the people, and having mingled the flour with the blood sacrifices that were already on the altar, would make atonement for his fellow Israelite.

Nowhere is it written that "the flour will make atonement" or that "the life of a creature is in the flour." Rather, the whole basis for atonement was in the sacrificial blood on the altar, and through a flour offering, even poor Israelites could participate in the atoning power of the altar. But there is not a single verse in the Bible that would even hint that flour, in and of itself, had any atoning power, and the rabbis never suggested that, in the absence of the Temple, flour could be substituted for sacrifices. Without the atoning altar and its sacrifices, the flour had no power at all.[186]

What then do we make of the references to atonement money in Exodus 30? Let's take a look at the passages in question:

> When you take a census of the Israelites to count them, each one must pay the Lord a ransom for his life at the time he is counted. Then no plague will come on them when you number them. Each one who crosses over to those already counted is to give a half shekel, according to the sanctuary shekel, which weighs twenty gerahs. This half shekel is an offering to the Lord. All who cross over, those twenty years old or more, are to give an offering to the Lord. The rich are not to give more than a half shekel and the poor are not to give less when you make the offering to the Lord to atone for your lives. Receive the atonement money from the Israelites and use it for the service of the Tent of Meeting. It will be a memorial for the Israelites before the Lord, making atonement for your lives.
>
> Exodus 30:12–16

> Then the officers who were over the units of the army—the commanders of thousands and commanders of hundreds—went to Moses and said to him, "Your servants have counted the soldiers under our command, and not one is missing. So we have brought as an offering to the Lord the gold articles each of us acquired—armlets, bracelets, signet rings,

earrings and necklaces—to make atonement for ourselves before the
Lord."

Numbers 31:48–50

Do these texts prove that the Torah ordained other forms of atonement in addition to blood sacrifices, specifically, atonement money?
Not in the least. In fact, modern Jewish scholars have made an excellent case for the fact that these texts had nothing at all to do with
atonement and forgiveness but rather with protection from the wrath
of God.

"How so?" you ask.

I can best explain my point by taking a careful look at both passages, raising only one, basic question: What does the Bible say?

First, we should make note of the fact that these are the only two
places in the entire Tanakh where either the words or the general concept of "atonement money" *(keseph kippurim)* are found. In both of
these passages, something unusual is being discussed, namely, taking a census (i.e., counting the people), something that could be a
dangerous undertaking.[187] As stated in Exodus 30:12, "When you take
a census of the Israelites to count them, each one must pay the Lord
a ransom for his life at the time he is counted. *Then no plague will
come on them when you number them.*" Tragically, when David on his
own initiative counted the people of Israel, a plague did break out
among them (see 2 Samuel 24). This should get our attention, reminding us that the context here is protection from a plague not atonement for sin.

Second, in Exodus 30:11–16, God commands every male Israelite
who was to be counted in the census to pay a *kopher* (ransom) for his
life. Similarly, in Numbers 31:50, having just counted the soldiers
who had gone into battle with Midian (again, they had taken a census), the officers decided to offer some of the spoils to God and thus
to pay a *kopher* for their lives.

What exactly was a *kopher*? According to Exodus 21:29–30, the
owner of a habitually goring ox that killed a man would have to pay
a *kopher* (i.e., a fixed amount of ransom money), rather than be killed
himself. As the text says, "He may redeem his life by paying whatever
is demanded" (Exod. 21:30).[188] For a murderer, however, there could
be no *kopher* (ransom payment; the murderer himself would have to
be put to death; see Num. 35:31–32; see also Ps. 49:8). Overall, *kopher*
is used fourteen times in the Hebrew Scriptures, meaning ransom
(the verses just cited, along with verses such as Isa. 43:3) or bribe,

payoff (cf. 1 Sam. 12:3; Prov. 6:35; Amos 5:12). Never once, however, does it have anything to do with atonement of sin.

"But what's so important about that? After all, the sections we just read from Exodus and Numbers both speak of 'making atonement.' So what if *kopher* itself only means 'ransom'? Really, I don't see your point."

I understand why. You see, *kopher*, "ransom," and *kipper*, "atone," come from the exact same Hebrew root, and in the texts you just referred to, the Hebrew should not be translated *to make atonement for your lives* but *to pay a ransom for your lives*. To reiterate: The texts here have to do with protection from a plague not forgiveness of sins or personal atonement. It is therefore with good reason that religious Jewish leaders and the most respected Jewish authorities on atonement and the root *kipper* have written that the proper interpretation of the phrase in question here is, as stated, "to pay a ransom for your lives" or "to make appeasement." Commenting on Exodus 30:15, the late Chief Rabbi Hertz explains that the phrase rendered "to make atonement for your lives" is "an amplification" of *kopher*, which Hertz defines as "the money paid by one who is guilty of taking human life in circumstances that do not constitute murder."[189] Commenting on Numbers 31:50, Jacob Milgrom states that "the ransom to God was a necessary prophylactic against the onslaught of a plague that could be expected for conducting a census."[190]

Now, what is striking is that Rabbi Shmuel ben Meir (known as Rashbam), the highly respected grandson of Rashi, argued for this very same position more than eight hundred years ago, stating in his widely used Torah commentary that the words often translated here as "atonement *(kippurim)* money" derive their meaning from the fact that the money served as a ransom *(kopher)* for their lives (see his succinct comment to Exod. 30:16). So even leading Rabbinic commentators recognized that the Hebrew root *kipper* in Exodus 30:11–16 and Numbers 31:50 meant "to pay a ransom," while in Leviticus 17:11 it meant "to make atonement." These were two different contexts, and the meaning of the words in each context was different—as recognized by the rabbis.[191]

In fact, we can take this one step further and look at what Rashi, the number one traditional Torah commentator of all time, has to say. Discussing this very Hebrew phrase in Exodus 30:15, Rashi explains it to mean "so that you will not be smitten with a plague because of the census." In other words, *lekapper* here has nothing to do with atonement for sin. This interpretation is confirmed by the main commentaries on Rashi's Torah commentary. With reference to Exodus 30:15, the Siftey Hachamim commentary explains Rashi to mean, "this is not to atone *[lekapper]* for your sins as is the case with the other [biblical usages] of *kapparah,* but the concept is of '*kapparah*' in connection with the census."[192] The Gur Aryeh commentary on Rashi states concisely, "but not atonement *[kapparah]* for sin, since it is already written (Exod. 30:12), 'so that there will be no plague against you.'"

Here, one classical Jewish commentator after another is making it clear that Exodus 30:15 does *not* teach that a monetary offering brought atonement. (Could you imagine the Scriptures stating, "For it is the money that makes expiation for your sins"? That sounds more like a bribe than it sounds like the Bible. Or how about, "There is no atonement without the giving of jewelry"?)

Interestingly enough, Rashi offered an alternative explanation to the verse in question. It is possible, he says, that Exodus 30:15 actually refers to three different monetary offerings, one of which helped pay for the animal sacrifices, specifically stating that it was *the sacrifices which serve to make atonement*. This is not a "Christian" invention. Rashi is only stating what the Bible makes clear: If the concept of atonement (as opposed to only ransom) was actually in view in Exodus 30:11–15, then it must be explained by the fact that the monetary offering went to the Tabernacle to support the priestly ministry there, in particular, the offering up of atoning sacrifices on behalf of the people.[193]

Because there is no reference to blood sacrifices or sin in the context here, Rashi suggests that the root *kipper* must mean "pay a ransom to avert a plague," or else the usage of *kipper* in the sense of atonement must be explained with reference to the blood sacrifices. The monetary offering of the Israelites who were counted in the census would help finance the Tabernacle service, which centered around blood sacrifices.

So unless Rashi's second interpretation is correct—in which case the atoning power of the monetary ransom was in the *blood sacrifices* of the altar—we can safely conclude that there is no connection between either of these narratives and the concept of personal atonement or forgiveness of sins, nor would anyone say, "The money [or jewelry] in and of itself makes atonement." These texts simply demonstrate that the Hebrew root *kipper* can at times refer to paying a ransom or turning away wrath.

This is also the key to understanding Numbers 16:46–48[17:11–13], where, according to some translations, it appears that *incense* made atonement for the people. Actually, stopping a plague—not atoning for sins—was the main issue in the text in Numbers, since a plague had just broken out in the Israelite camp because of the transgression of the leaders, whose incense God refused, consuming them all with fire. As the plague erupted in the camp, Moses gave urgent instructions to Aaron the high priest:

> Take your censer and put incense in it, along with fire from the altar, and hurry to the assembly to make atonement for them. Wrath has come out from the LORD; the plague has started." So Aaron did as Moses said, and ran into the midst of the assembly. The plague had already started among the people, but Aaron offered the incense and made atonement for them. He stood between the living and the dead, and the plague stopped.

Jacob Milgrom states that the verb *kipper*, usually translated to make atonement or expiation, "in this context carries the connotation of 'make appeasement.'" He further explains, "In the cults [i.e., temple-related rituals] of the ancient Near East, incense served to appease and sooth divine wrath," citing examples from ancient Egypt to support his claims.[194] The bottom line is that atonement for sins is not the subject here. The unusual connection between incense and the root *kipper* also struck Rashi, who cited some extremely imaginative midrashim to explain why "the incense prevented the plague":

> **and atone for them.** This secret was given over to him by the angel of death when he went up to heaven that incense holds back the plague . . . as is related in Tractate *Shabbath* (89a).
> **He stood between the dead** . . . He took hold of the angel and held him against his will. The angel said to him, "Allow me to accomplish my mission." He [Aaron] said to him, "Moses commanded me to stop you." He said to him, "I am the messenger of the Omnipresent, and you are the messenger of Moses." He said to him, "Moses does not say anything on his own volition, but only at the bidding of the Almighty. If you do not believe [me], the Holy One, blessed is He, and Moses are at the entrance of the Tent of Meeting; come with me and ask." This is the meaning of the statement, "Aaron returned to Moses" (*Mid. Tanchuma Tetzaveh* 15). Another interpretation: Why with incense? Because the Israelites were slandering and vilifying the incense, saying that it was a deadly poison; through it Nadab and Abihu died; through it two hundred and fifty people were burnt. The Holy One, blessed is He, said,

"You shall see that it will stop the plague, and it is sin that caused their death" [*Mid. Aggadah*. See *Mechilta Beshallach* (*Vayassa* 6:5, *Ber.* 33a)].[195]

Rashbam also explains the use of incense in light of the immediate context, where God rejected the incense offered by Korah and his followers. The point, according to Rashbam, was "to demonstrate to the people that the incense which brings death, if offered by unauthorized persons, brings life if it is offered by lawful priests."[196]

The Talmud also found it necessary to explain how incense could "make atonement," discussing this very text and concluding that it only atoned for gossip, since "if someone brings a word in secret, he will make atonement by a deed in secret" (see b. Zevahim 88a).[197] This, of course, underscores just how difficult it was to connect incense with atonement from a biblical—or even logical—viewpoint.[198] Who for a moment would make a general statement that "incense makes atonement" or would think that once the Temple was destroyed the Jewish people could burn incense for their sins? Is there any reference to this in Jewish tradition, not to mention in the rest of the Scriptures? The very thought of it is as unbelieveable as the notion that either flour, money, or jewelry could make atonement for sin. In all honesty, it seems almost disingenuous when some anti-missionaries claim that the Torah offered alternate forms of atonement other than blood sacrifices, as if blood sacrifices did not form the heart, soul, and very fiber of the entire atonement system, and as if any of the other alleged means, such as flour, could be effective for a moment without blood sacrifices. The Torah is very clear on this.

Was incense closely involved with the sacrificial system? It certainly was, as can easily be seen by reading through Leviticus 16, which outlines the duties of the high priest on the Day of Atonement, as well as by simply noting how often the burning of incense appeared in the context of sacrifices and offerings.[199] But did incense—or flour offerings—have any atoning power when isolated from the blood sacrifices? Certainly not.

"Well," you say, "it seems that you've made a good case so far, especially in light of the Jewish commentaries you've supplied. But what about all the other verses in the Torah that speak of valid atonement without the shedding of blood? How do you respond to them?"

I can't respond to them, because they don't exist! We have exhausted every Torah reference that could possibly be taken to speak of atonement without blood (flour, money, incense), and we have found there is no support for the anti-missionary position.[200]

"But what about the references in other parts of the Hebrew Bible? I know that none of them would contradict the Torah, but they might add something to what the Torah says about atonement."

Actually, the apparent references to atonement without blood in the rest of the Hebrew Scriptures are even less compelling than those in the Torah. Let's look at every text that could be understood as proving that the Tanakh recognized atonement without blood.

Of course, we know that there are many texts in the Hebrew Scriptures that speak of God as a forgiving and merciful God, and most of them do not make mention of blood sacrifices. This is self-evident and is to be expected, since the psalmists and prophets were simply proclaiming truths about the nature of God, not explaining the means and nature of atonement. The Torah had already done that in great detail, and for the most part, in those ritual texts there was no mention of the nature of God. Instead, in these priestly Torah texts the means of expiation are clearly laid out; in the psalms and prophetic books the nature of God is proclaimed, coupled with a call to repent of sin. The two concepts go hand in hand. A holy and compassionate God establishes a national system of atonement and calls his people to repent and be forgiven.[201]

The psalms often praised God for his mercy, sometimes using the root *kipper.* (Note that the following translations are from the NJPSV, so no one can accuse the translators of Christian bias.) "When all manner of sins overwhelm me, it is You who forgive *[kipper]* our iniquities" (Ps. 65:4[3]). "But He, being merciful, forgave *[kipper]* iniquity and would not destroy; He restrained His wrath time and again and did not give full vent to His fury" (Ps. 78:38). "Help us, O God our deliverer, for the sake of the glory of Your name. Save us and forgive *[kipper]* our sin, for the sake of Your name" (Ps. 79:9).

But verses such as these in no way support the view that the Lord ordained means of atonement other than the blood. First, as is recognized by most translators, it is best to render *kipper* here with "forgive," since this is something God is doing, not man.[202] Second, even if someone wanted to argue that *kipper* here should be translated with "atone," none of these texts say for a moment that God forgave his people's sin *without* the Day of Atonement, or without the sacrificial rites, or without blood. Rather, these verses simply reflect the goodness and mercy of our God, who graciously forgives sin and iniquity and who is implored to do it again.[203] They have nothing to do with *God's requirements for his people* relative to atonement and forgiveness. In fact, some of the verses just cited make no reference to repentance either, but that does not prove that the Lord forgave (or forgives) his unrepentant people. Rather, these texts simply describe the gracious acts of God. (For the concept that God has always forgiven sins based on the atoning death of the Messiah, see below, 3.15.)

What about other passages that use the root *kipper* and speak of *people* doing something to effect their atonement, with no reference to blood sacrifices? Most of the verses in question are found in the Book of Isaiah, and interestingly, in almost every case, the New Jewish Publication Society Version does *not* translate these verses with the words *atone* or *expiate*.[204] Why? Because the root also carries the meanings of "purge, wipe away," and the context of the verses calls for a translation with "purge" rather than "atone." I'll compare the NJPSV (remember this is a leading Jewish translation) with the NIV (a leading Christian translation), highlighting the words in question: "Assuredly, by this alone shall Jacob's sin be *purged away;* this is the only price for removing his guilt: that he make all the altar-stones like shattered blocks of chalk—with no sacred post left standing, nor any incense altar" (Isa. 27:9 NJPSV). "By this, then, will Jacob's guilt be *atoned for,* and this will be the full fruitage of the removal of his sin: When he makes all the altar stones to be like chalk stones crushed to pieces, no Asherah poles or incense altars will be left standing" (Isa. 27:9).

Notice here that "purged away" *(yekuppar)* is parallel with "removing," reminding us that Isaiah is not speaking of *atonement* of sin but rather of the *removal* and *purging* of sinful idolatrous practices. Interestingly, the Septuagint, the oldest existing Jewish translation, dating to more than two hundred years before Jesus, rendered *kipper* here with "take away, remove," *not* with "atone" or "expiate." And Abraham Ibn Ezra, the penetrating medieval Bible commentator, explained the usage of *kipper* as follows: "The meaning (of the words) is that the decree (of judgment) will be abolished if they abolish (their) idolatrous worship."

Isaiah's own experience in chapter 6 of his book is also of interest, although it certainly does not substantiate the claim that the Hebrew Scriptures recognized various forms of atonement aside from blood. According to Isaiah 6:5–7, the prophet had an overwhelming, awe-inspiring vision of the Lord sitting enthroned in the Temple. The experience completely unnerved him:

> "Woe to me!" I cried. "I am ruined! For I am a man of unclean lips, and
> I live among a people of unclean lips, and my eyes have seen the King,
> the LORD Almighty." Then one of the seraphs flew to me with a live coal

in his hand, which he had taken with tongs from the altar. With it he
touched my mouth and said, "See, this has touched your lips; your guilt
is taken away and your sin atoned for."

Isaiah 6:5–7

Once again, however, it is the New Jewish Publication Society Version that renders the key verse differently, translating, "Now that this
has touched your lips, your guilt shall depart and your sin be *purged
away*" (Isa. 6:7, emphasis mine). So just as in Isaiah 27:9, this important Jewish translation felt that *kipper* did not mean "atone, expiate"
but rather "purge away," and here too, just as in Isaiah 27:9, *kipper* is
parallel to *sar*, "take away, remove." Of course, it is possible that Isaiah's experience *was* related to atonement for sin, but that presents no
problem at all for our position for at least two reasons: First, the
prophet is cleansed by a burning coal taken from the altar, just as
Aaron took fire from the altar when he offered incense in Numbers
16[17], and just as the flour offering had to be mingled with the sacrifices on the altar; second, it would be without precedent to make a
major doctrine out of the visionary experience of a prophet, especially
when this text would be the one and only example of burning coals
"making atonement." And who would deduce from this that in the
absence of blood sacrifices we should take burning coals to our lips
to effect atonement for our sins? Or could it be that we need to enlist
the help of the seraphim to apply the coal to our lips, since that is how
it happened with Isaiah? Unfortunately, as ludicrous as these sugges-
tions are, Isaiah 6:7 has sometimes been cited by anti-missionaries in
their attempt to prove that there are other forms of biblically sanc-
tioned atonement other than the blood.[205]

The simple fact is that the context makes it clear that Isaiah's visionary experience had to do with the *purging away* of his confessed guilt,
namely, that of being "a man of unclean lips" who lived "among a
people of unclean lips." So the coal from the altar was applied to his
lips, removing his guilt and purging away his sin.[206]

And now for something that may surprise you. We have now examined *all* the relevant verses that allegedly support the position that the
Hebrew Bible sanctions various means of atonement apart from the
shedding of blood. We can safely say, then, that we have demonstrated
conclusively that blood sacrifices were the one, God-ordained means
of atonement in the Hebrew Bible.

Let me leave you with the witness of the Word, spanning the generations and the millennia. The testimony has always been the same.

In the days of Hezekiah, when the First Temple was standing, blood sacrifices made atonement for the nation: "Early the next morning King Hezekiah gathered the city officials together and went up to the temple of the LORD. . . . *The priests then slaughtered the goats and presented their blood on the altar for a sin offering to atone for all Israel,* because the king had ordered the burnt offering and the sin offering for all Israel" (2 Chron. 29:20, 24).

In the days of Nehemiah, when the Second Temple was built, blood sacrifices continued to make atonement for the nation. The priests and Levites pledged:

> "We assume the responsibility for carrying out the commands to give a third of a shekel each year for the service of the house of our God: for the bread set out on the table; for the regular grain offerings and burnt offerings; for the offerings on the Sabbaths, New Moon festivals and appointed feasts; for the holy offerings; *for sin offerings to make atonement for Israel;* and for all the duties of the house of our God."
>
> Nehemiah 10:32–33

Even in what some interpreters believe will be a future Third Temple, as envisioned by Ezekiel (see below, 3.17), blood sacrifices make atonement for the nation:

> You are to give a young bull as a *sin offering* to the priests, who are Levites, of the family of Zadok, who come near to minister before me, declares the Sovereign LORD. You are to take some of its *blood* and put it on the four horns of the altar and on the four corners of the upper ledge and all around the rim, and so purify the altar and *make atonement* for it.
>
> Ezekiel 43:19–20 (see also v. 26)

> Also *one sheep* is to be taken from every flock of two hundred from the well-watered pastures of Israel. *These will be used for the grain offerings, burnt offerings and fellowship offerings to make atonement for the people,* declares the Sovereign LORD. All the people of the land will participate in this special gift for the use of the prince in Israel. It will be the duty of the prince to provide the burnt offerings, grain offerings and drink offerings at the festivals, the New Moons and the Sabbaths— at all the appointed feasts of the house of Israel. *He will provide the sin offerings, grain offerings, burnt offerings and fellowship offerings to make atonement for the house of Israel.*
>
> Ezekiel 45:15–17 (see also v. 20)[207]

The consistent testimony of the Tanakh is indisputable and clear, as summarized by the author of Hebrews: "Without the shedding of blood there is no forgiveness." Any other system of atonement that does not include the blood is not biblical, and any other system of atonement that fails to offer substitutionary atonement (i.e., an innocent sacrificial victim dying on behalf of a guilty sinner) is not able to provide real forgiveness of sins. God established life for life—not money for life, not jewelry for life, not flour for life, not incense for life—as the means of expiation for his people. As the Talmudic rabbis recognized—at least while the Temple stood—"There is no atonement without the blood."

3.11. According to Proverbs 16:6, love and good deeds make atonement. So who needs sacrifices?

> If I were to follow your logic, I could just as easily say, "According to Proverbs 16:6, love and good deeds make atonement, so who needs Yom Kippur (the Day of Atonement)?" That is to say, if atonement can be made between man and God through doing good, then there is no need for suffering and chastisement, no need for prayers and confession, no need even for the Day of Atonement. What Bible-believing Jew would hold to such a view? This points us to the real meaning of this verse, namely, "Through lovingkindness and truth, sin is *wiped away*." In other words, on a practical, person-to-person level, being loyal, loving, and truthful will overcome and eradicate the prior effects of sin. But the verse is not directly related to issues of atonement, purification, and forgiveness in the sight of God, nor is it reasonable to think that the Lord would overthrow countless verses in the Torah with one phrase in Proverbs.

While it is true that both the Bible and Rabbinic Judaism emphasize the importance of acts of kindness and charity along with the need for making restitution, nowhere does the Bible teach that love and good deeds eliminate the need for prayer or confession of sins to God, nor do the Scriptures teach that doing good alone guarantees atonement.[208]

Interestingly, the sages dealt at length with the issue of receiving forgiveness for different levels of transgression. According to a debate recorded in the Mishnah, Talmud, and Mishneh Torah of Maimonides,[209] if someone violates a positive commandment (meaning, "You shall") and repents, he is immediately forgiven (with reference to Jer. 3:22), but if he violates a negative commandment (meaning, "You shall not") and repents, his forgiveness is suspended until the Day of Atonement (the rabbis support this with reference to Lev. 16:30).[210] If he transgresses a commandment punishable by *karet* (literally, "cutting off")[211] or liable to capital punishment by the court and then repents, both his repentance as well as the effects of the Day of Atonement are held in abeyance, and he achieves atonement by means of suffering (*yissurin;* citing Ps. 89:32). In the event, however, that he is guilty of profaning the divine Name, the merits of his repentance, the Day of Atonement, and his chastisements are all suspended (or provide partial atonement), and it is only death that cleanses *(mitah memareqet)* and secures complete atonement.[212]

We see from all this that authoritative Jewish tradition teaches that all the acts of repentance in the world—including acts of love and kindness to one's neighbor—do not guarantee atonement for all sins, nor do these morally commendable acts make void other means of forgiveness instituted by God—in particular the Day of Atonement.

What then does Proverbs 16:6 mean? As explained previously (see above, 3.10), the Hebrew verb *kipper* (used in this verse) does not always mean "atone, expiate."[213] Sometimes it simply means "wipe away, remove, purge," and, for the most part, either the context, the grammar, or both tell us how *kipper* should be translated. In fact, Rashi, commenting on the use of *kipper* in Genesis 32:21 stated that "every time *kapparah* occurs with the words 'guilt' and 'sin' or with the word 'face,' it is to be interpreted as an expression of wiping off or removal."[214] In the verse in question here, *kipper* is used to explain how the wrong effects of sin can be removed or purged—meaning, how the effect of someone's offenses against another person can be wiped away. It is through love and good deeds. This is brought out in the following translations: "By mercy and truth iniquity is purged: and by the fear of the LORD men depart from evil" (KJV). "Guilt is wiped out by loyalty and faith, and the fear of the LORD makes mortals turn from evil" (REB; cf. also the NEB).[215]

Even putting these translations of *kipper* aside, we should remember that the verse we are considering is found in the Book of Proverbs, the most practical, down-to-earth book in the Bible. It is not found in Exodus, Leviticus, or Numbers, books in the Torah that spend considerable time outlining the method and means by which the people of Israel could come into right relationship with God. Rather, this verse comes from a book filled with wise counsel and sage advice for day-to-day living, teaching us how we can live our lives here in the fear of the Lord. It would be unlikely, therefore, to find the doctrine of atonement discussed here, unless it was in the context of "atoning" for sins of man against man. Fritz Maass, a Hebrew and Old Testament scholar, addressed this very point in his article on *kpr*. He wrote:

> "Atonement" is an interpersonal process on three occasions in the OT. Jacob wants to "atone" Esau's countenance with gifts, i.e., to placate or appease (Gen 32:21); Prov teaches that one can "atone for" (= repay) a debt through goodness and faithfulness (*bᵉḥesed weʾᵉmet;* Prov 16:6); and that a wise man can "atone for" (= appease) the king's wrath (16:14); 16:6 could refer to a relationship with God.[216]

So while Maass recognizes the possibility that Proverbs 16:6 could refer to atonement of sins between man and God, he prefers to read it in the context of an "interpersonal process," which certainly suits the context in Proverbs as a whole.[217] It also underscores the fact that ritual atonement, centered around the priests ministering in the Tabernacle/Temple and focused in particular on the Day of Atonement, is virtually never separated from blood sacrifices (see above, 3.10).[218] However, in other contexts that are unrelated to Temple, priesthood, sacrifice, or ritual atonement, *kipper* can be used in different senses. That is the case here in Proverbs, and it would be an error to attempt to expand or amend the Torah's teaching on expiation and atonement with this one line in Proverbs, especially given the fact that this particular line is subject to different interpretations.

To reiterate an important truth that we emphasized previously (see above, 3.9), neither the prophets nor the psalmists nor the author(s) of Proverbs would contradict or negate Moses, and whatever Proverbs 16:6 is saying, it is *not* saying that the sacrifices on the Day of Atonement or the daily sacrificial services were unnecessary or obsolete. As we noted at the outset, you might as well argue that the Day of Atonement itself—even in its traditional Jewish form with the emphasis on prayer, confession, fasting, and repentance without blood sacrifices—is unnecessary, since, according to this objection, love and good deeds are all the atonement we need.

On the contrary, love and good deeds alone have never paid in full for our sins, not in biblical days and not today. Our good deeds could be likened to the good works done by a petty thief sentenced to community service to pay for his crimes, but they could not be likened to a life sentence incurred by a violent, repeat rapist to pay for his crimes. In other words, in no way do love and good deeds satisfy all the claims of justice, be it human justice or divine justice. They do, however, help to clean up the mess that sin creates in our interpersonal relationships. This is what Proverbs is teaching here.[219]

3.12. It's clear that you misunderstand the entire sacrificial system. Sacrifices were for unintentional sins only. Repentance was the only remedy for intentional sins.

We all know that there were different functions for the sacrifices, including ritual purification, thanksgiving, personal consecration, and making of vows, along with atonement for unintentional sins. But the sacrifices on Yom Kippur (the Day of Atonement) provided atonement for both intentional and unintentional sins, something taught emphatically in the Talmud and Law Codes. Scripture is clear on this, and Jewish tradition never questioned it. There was also one particular sacrifice (namely, the 'asham, the guilt offering or reparation offering) that in conjunction with repentance served as atonement for intentional sins (called "transgressions" in the Bible). We should point out too that according to some Rabbinic traditions, repentance could "convert" intentional sins to unintentional sins, hence paving the way for atonement through sacrifice.

Before answering your objection, it's important that I clear up some misconceptions. First, as we have noted previously, Christians and Messianic Jews do not believe for a moment that sacrifices *without* repentance and faith did anyone any good (see vol. 1, 1.11, and above, 3.8–3.9). Second, we do not believe that after every sin an

Israelite had to go to the Temple in Jerusalem (or before that, to the Tabernacle) and offer a sacrifice. Every animal in the land fit for sacrifice would have been slaughtered within days if that were the case, and no one would have had time to do anything except offer sacrifices day and night. Normal life would completely cease if such an impossible scenario existed. Third, we do not believe that God's people can sin freely, then repent and bring a sacrifice, then sin freely again. Rather, as we pointed out in an earlier discussion, we agree with the Talmudic statement that "he who says, I will sin and repent, I will sin and repent, repentance is not vouchsafed to him" (m. Yoma 8:9, and see above, 3.8). As the psalmist expressed it, "If I had cherished sin in my heart, the Lord would not have listened" (Ps. 66:18). Fourth, we believe that for those who continue in willful and defiant sin, there is no forgiveness (we'll come back to this point shortly).

What then was the purpose of sacrifices and offerings in Israel? We must remember that there were different kinds of sacrifices and different functions for those sacrifices in the religious life of our people. Some sacrifices, such as the burnt offerings (Hebrew, 'olah, also known as the whole offering or holocaust), were offered up as symbols of complete dedication and devotion to the Lord.[220] Other sacrifices, such as the todah, were offered in thanksgiving to the Lord, while other sacrifices, such as the sin offering (Hebrew, hatta't), were offered to remove ritual impurity (among other things), and still others, such as the fellowship (or peace) offerings (Hebrew, shelamim), were offered in worshipful communion.

As to differences between the sin and guilt offerings (hatta't and 'asham respectively), Hebrew professor George Buchanan Gray, lecturing in the 1920s, could state, "The precise distinction between the sin-offering and the guilt- or trespass-offering is not altogether clear, and has been much discussed."[221] More recently, however, R. Laird Harris, a Christian biblical scholar and Hebraist, wrote:

> The difference between the sin offering and the guilt offering was in the nature of the sin. The former was for what might be called general sins; the latter for sins that injured other people or detracted from the sacred worship. The guilt offering thus involved not only a sacrifice but also restitution plus a fine of 20 percent (6:5 [5:24 in the Hebrew]). The sins for which the sin offering was prescribed are called "unintentional sins" (4:2), or those done "through ignorance" (KJV). The same expression is used in connection with the guilt offering (5:15).[222]

Or as expressed by Baruch Levine, a leading Jewish authority on atonement and sacrifice:

Chapters 4 and 5 [of Leviticus] contain the laws governing expiatory sacrifices, the purpose of which is to secure atonement and forgiveness from God. These offerings are efficacious only when offenses are inadvertent or unwitting. They do not apply to defiant acts of premeditated crimes. Whenever an individual Israelite, a tribal leader, a priest, or even the chief priest, or the Israelite community at large is guilty of an inadvertent offense or of failing to do what the law requires, expiation through sacrifices is required.[223]

However, under certain circumstances, the 'asham could atone for intentional sins. As Levine noted:

The offenses outlined here [in Lev. 5:20–26, or 6:1–7 in most English translations] were quite definitely intentional! A person misappropriated property or funds entrusted to his safekeeping, or defrauded another, or failed to restore lost property he had located. . . . If, subsequently, the accused came forth on his own and admitted to having lied under oath—thus assuming liability for the unrecovered property—he was given the opportunity to clear himself by making restitution and by paying a fine of 20 percent to the aggrieved party. Having lied under oath, he had also offended God and was obliged to offer an 'asham sacrifice in expiation. . . . God accepts the expiation even of one who swears falsely in His name because the guilty person is willing to make restitution to the victim of his crime.[224]

This observation alone shoots a hole in the anti-missionary teaching that only unintentional sins could be atoned for with blood sacrifices.[225]

"But," you object, "that's hardly sufficient proof. If anything, all you've demonstrated is that for a very small number of specifically enumerated sins, one particular sacrifice brought atonement. What about all the other sins people commit? Where does the Torah say that sacrifices provided atonement?"

The Torah says so explicitly in Leviticus 16, the most important atonement chapter in all of the Pentateuch, the chapter in which the rituals for the Day of Atonement are laid out. However, before turning to Leviticus 16, let me give you an important Talmudic perspective. As noted by the Rabbinic scholar Solomon Schechter in his discussion of sacrifices and atonement,

The continual offering was a communal offering, nor is there in the Bible ascribed to it any atoning power; but there is a marked tendency in Rabbinic literature to bestow on all sacrifices, even such as the burnt-offering and the peace-offering, some sort of atoning power for certain classes of sins, both of commission and omission, for which the Bible ascribes no sacrifice at all.[226]

Thus, the rabbis went *beyond* the Torah in ascribing atoning power for all kinds of sins to all kinds of sacrifices. Again, we see how flawed the anti-missionary position actually is, also exposing that in its zeal to counteract the claims of the New Testament, it will sometimes counteract the claims of Rabbinic Judaism too. And when we read Leviticus 16, we see that the position is not flawed in a minor way. It is fatally flawed. Look carefully at these key verses:

When Aaron has finished making atonement for the Most Holy Place, the Tent of Meeting and the altar, he shall bring forward the live goat [in English, this is commonly known as the "scapegoat"]. He is to lay both hands on the head of the live goat and confess over it all the wickedness and rebellion of the Israelites—all their sins—and put them on the goat's head. He shall send the goat away into the desert in the care of a man appointed for the task. The goat will carry on itself all their sins to a solitary place; and the man shall release it in the desert.

Leviticus 16:20–22

Notice carefully what the text says: The High Priest is to confess over the head of this goat "all the wickedness and rebellion of the Israelites—all their sins"—and "all" means "all." Notice also that the text specifically speaks of the "wickedness" (or "iniquity"; Hebrew, *'awon*) and "rebellion" (Hebrew, *pesha'*, meaning willful transgression) of the Israelites, not merely their unintentional sins.

"But what do the rabbis say about this? What is written in the Talmud?"

With regard to the kinds of sins atoned for by the sacrificial goats of Yom Kippur, the Talmud is even more explicit than the biblical text. Here are two different translations of m. Shevu'ot 1:6, a well-known text in traditional Jewish law:

A. And for a deliberate act of imparting uncleanness to the sanctuary and its Holy Things, a goat [whose blood is sprinkled] inside and the Day of Atonement effect atonement.

B. And for all other transgressions which are in the Torah—
C. the minor or serious, deliberate or inadvertent, those done knowingly or done unknowingly, violating a positive or a negative commandment, those punishable by extirpation *[karet]* and those punishable by death at the hands of the court,
D. the goat which is sent away [Lev. 16:21] effects atonement.[227]

And for uncleanness that occurs in the Temple and to its holy sacrifices through wantonness, [the] goat whose blood is sprinkled within [the Holy of Holies on the Day of Atonement] and the Day of Atonement effect atonement, and for [all] other transgressions [spoken of] in the Law, light or grace, premeditated or inadvertent, aware or unaware, transgressions of *positive commands* or *negative commands*, sin whose penalty is excision or sins punishable by death imposed by the court, the scapegoat makes atonement.[228]

As codified and explained by Maimonides almost one thousand years later (*Laws of Repentance*, 1:2):

Since the goat sent [to Azazeil][229] atones for all of Israel, the High Priest confesses on it as the spokesman for all of Israel, as [Lev. 16:21] states: "He shall confess on it all the sins of the Children of Israel."

The goat sent to Azazeil atones for all the transgressions in the Torah, the severe and the lighter [sins]; those violated intentionally and those transgressed inadvertently; those which [the transgressor] became conscious of and those which he was not conscious of. All are atoned for by the goat sent [to Azazeil].

This applies only if one repents. If one does not repent, the goat only atones for the light [sins].

Which are light sins and which are severe ones? Severe sins are those which are punishable by execution by the court or by premature death *[karet]*. [The violation of] the other prohibitions that are not punishable by premature death are considered light [sins].[230]

Here, then, is a perfectly clear statement from the most authoritative sources of traditional Judaism that the sacrifices offered and the ceremonies performed on the Day of Atonement effected atonement for all kinds of sins, intentional and unintentional, willful and inadvertent. The only question raised by the Rabbinic sources is to what degree repentance was a necessary part of the equation, a question that all Messianic Jews would answer by saying, "Repentance plays a vital part in the equation!" (See below, 3.21.) In this context, Jacob Milgrom notes:

Even the annual purification rite for the sanctuary and nation requires that the high priest confess the deliberate sins of the Israelites (Lev. 16:21), while the latter demonstrate their penitence, not by coming to the Temple—from which deliberate sinners are barred—but by fasting and other acts of self-denial (Lev. 16:29; 23:27–32; Num. 29:7). Thus, contrition for involuntary sin and confession for deliberate sin are indispensable to the atonement produced by the sacrificial system, and they differ in no way from the call to repentance formulated by the prophets.[231]

Returning to the Talmudic discussion, I should also point out to you what the Talmud says about the atoning power of the goat whose blood is sprinkled inside the Most Holy Place. As we read previously in m. Shevu'ot 1:6, "And for uncleanness that occurs in the Temple and to its holy sacrifices through wantonness, [the] goat whose blood is sprinkled within [the Holy of Holies on the Day of Atonement] and the Day of Atonement effect atonement." The Talmud explains this with reference to Leviticus 16:15–16:

> He [i.e., the High Priest] shall then slaughter the goat for the sin offering for the people and take its blood behind the curtain and do with it as he did with the bull's blood: He shall sprinkle it on the atonement cover and in front of it. In this way he will make atonement for the Most Holy Place because of the uncleanness and rebellion of the Israelites, whatever their sins have been. He is to do the same for the Tent of Meeting, which is among them in the midst of their uncleanness.

The rabbis (see b. Shevu'ot 2b; 6b–14a) comment specifically on the words *rebellion* (transgressions in Hebrew) and *sins*, explaining that "transgressions" refers to acts of rebellion—which are certainly intentional—while "sins" refers to inadvertent acts.[232] And it is the goat whose blood is sprinkled in the Most Holy Place that effects atonement for the people, just as the blood of the bull offered up by the High Priest effects atonement for him (m. Shevu'ot 1:7, following Lev. 16:11, "Aaron shall bring the bull for his own sin offering to make atonement for himself and his household, and he is to slaughter the bull for his own sin offering."). Notice also that it is a sin offering that effects atonement for Aaron and the people of Israel, demonstrating that it is not only the guilt offering that effects atonement for willful sins.[233]

Let me also remind you of the prayer of Solomon offered up at the dedication of the Temple (1 Kings 8; 2 Chronicles 6), in which he asked God to forgive his sinning people when they turned to God in repentance and prayed toward the Temple. The Lord promised that he would, in fact, forgive and restore—*because of the sacrifices offered up in the Temple* (see 2 Chron. 7:12–16, and the discussion above, 3.9)—and the text makes clear that inadvertent or unintentional sins were not the only things covered by Solomon's prayer. See, for example, 1 Kings 8:33–36, 46–50; 2 Chronicles 7:14, clearly referring to all kinds of sins and transgressions.

We can also ask why many Orthodox Jews still practice the custom of *kapparos* (or *kapparot*) on the eve of Yom Kippur (or Rosh Hashanah) if sacrifices only atoned for unintentional sins. Why then do they take a live fowl and wave it around their heads while confessing that the fowl is their substitute and payment? As described by Rabbi Abraham Chill:

> A custom that has prevailed in many Jewish communities throughout the world for centuries and which was the cause of a great deal of controversy and apologetics is that of *Kapparot*, the expiatory offering. This ritual, which takes place during the night and early morning preceding Yom Kippur, involves taking a live white fowl, swinging it around one's head while reciting: "This is my atonement; this is my ransom; this is my substitute." As if saying: if on Yom Kippur it is decreed that I must die, then this fowl which will shortly be slaughtered should serve as my substitute."[234]

It's also fair to ask, What kinds of sins do Jews confess every year on Yom Kippur? The answer—known to all who have ever recited the prescribed prayers and confessions for that day—is that Jews confess to almost every imaginable sin on Yom Kippur, leaving almost no stone unturned. Yet, while the Temple was standing, those were the very sins for which atonement was sought through sacrifice, repentance, and fasting. We could also ask, If prayer and repentance replace sacrifices according to Rabbinic teaching, what are they actually replacing if sacrifices were so ineffective?[235] The answer is obvious: The sacrifices were anything but ineffective.

How then should we understand Numbers 15:22–31? These verses seem to teach that sacrifices could be brought to atone for unintentional sins, but for willful, defiant sins no sacrifice was possible. The sinner's guilt would remain on him. Let's look at this passage, allowing some Jewish biblical scholars to explain its meaning:

> Now if you unintentionally fail to keep any of these commands the LORD gave Moses—any of the LORD's commands to you through him,

from the day the LORD gave them and continuing through the generations to come—and if this is done unintentionally without the community being aware of it, then the whole community is to offer a young bull for a burnt offering as an aroma pleasing to the LORD, along with its prescribed grain offering and drink offering, and a male goat for a sin offering. The priest is to make atonement for the whole Israelite community, and they will be forgiven, for it was not intentional and they have brought to the LORD for their wrong an offering made by fire and a sin offering. The whole Israelite community and the aliens living among them will be forgiven, because all the people were involved in the unintentional wrong. But if just one person sins unintentionally, he must bring a year-old female goat for a sin offering. The priest is to make atonement before the LORD for the one who erred by sinning unintentionally, and when atonement has been made for him, he will be forgiven. One and the same law applies to everyone who sins unintentionally, whether he is a native-born Israelite or an alien. But anyone who sins defiantly, whether native-born or alien, blasphemes the LORD, and that person must be cut off from his people. Because he has despised the LORD's word and broken his commands, that person must surely be cut off; his guilt remains on him.[236]

Milgrom explains:

The possibility of sacrificial atonement is explicitly denied to the individual who presumptuously violates God's law (Num. 15:30–31). This, however, does not mean, as many critics aver, that sacrificial atonement is possible only for involuntary wrongdoers. To cite but one exception, the *asham* offering is prescribed for that premeditated crime called by the rabbis *asham gezelot* (Lev. 5:20ff.; Num. 5:5–8). A more correct assertion, then, would be that the priestly system prohibits sacrificial atonement to the unrepentant sinner, for the one who "acts defiantly . . . it is the Lord he reviles" (Num. 15:30). This is an explicit postulate of post-biblical literature: "the *hattat*, the *asham*, and death do not atone except with repentance" (Tosef., Yoma 5:9; cf. Yoma 8:8).[237]

Or as expressed concisely by Rashi, "Only at the time when his iniquity is upon him shall he be cut off, meaning, as long as he has not repented" making reference to b. Sanhedrin 90b, where the Talmud explains that Numbers 15:31 leaves open the possibility that the sinner might still repent. Thus, his guilt remains on him as long as he fails to repent.

Interestingly, there is almost an exact New Testament parallel to this warning in Numbers 15:30–31, and it is found—not surprisingly—in the Letter to the Hebrews:

> If we deliberately keep on sinning after we have received the knowledge of the truth, no sacrifice for sins is left, but only a fearful expectation of judgment and of raging fire that will consume the enemies of God. Anyone who rejected the law of Moses died without mercy on the testimony of two or three witnesses. How much more severely do you think a man deserves to be punished who has trampled the Son of God under foot, who has treated as an unholy thing the blood of the covenant that sanctified him, and who has insulted the Spirit of grace? For we know him who said, "It is mine to avenge; I will repay," and again, "The Lord will judge his people." It is a dreadful thing to fall into the hands of the living God.
>
> Hebrews 10:26–31

The point in both cases is clear: There is no sacrifice, no forgiveness, no atonement for those who commit—and continue in—willful, defiant sin. If they don't turn back in repentance, *nothing* will atone for them. As noted by R. L. Harris with reference to Numbers 15:30–31, "Here the NIV has correctly caught the sense of the unpardonable sin—not one done intentionally, but one done 'defiantly,' i.e., in rebellion, sinning against light (cf. Matt. 12:31–32)."[238] The Hebrew image is quite clear: The sinner transgresses "with a high hand" *(beyad ramah)*—almost challenging God to punish him or hold him to account. But God is not one to be challenged! As Moses reminded the children of Israel, "Know therefore that the LORD your God is God; he is the faithful God, keeping his covenant of love to a thousand generations of those who love him and keep his commands. But those who hate him he will repay to their face by destruction; he will not be slow to repay to their face those who hate him" (Deut. 7:9–10).

But for those who would repent and perform the required Temple service, abundant mercy and pardon was available (see vol. 1, 1.11, and below, 3.21).

Looking back, then, at what we have seen so far, we can say categorically that sacrifices were not for unintentional sins only. The sacrifices on Yom Kippur argue against this position, specific sacrifices (the *'asham* and the *hatta't*) argue against it, other scriptural principles argue against it, the Talmud and Law Codes argue against it, the custom of *kapparot* argues against it, and the concept of repentance offered in conjunction with sacrifices argues against it. But there is something else we should look at briefly, namely, the Rabbinic view that through repentance, intentional sins, even quite deliberate sins, could be converted to unintentional sins, and thus covered through normal atonement rites. Dr. Rich Robinson, a research scholar for Jews for Jesus, has put together some important quotations on this subject. He observes that "according to the sages, repentance could turn an intentional sin into an unintentional sin and so be eligible for sacrifice," offering the following ancient and modern sources in support:

> R. Simeon b. Lakish said: Great is repentance, which converts intentional sins into unintentional ones (b. Yoma 86b; this is the rendering of Milgrom; as rendered in the Soncino edition, it reads: Great is repentance, for because of it premeditated sins are accounted as errors).
>
> This literary image [of the "high hand"; Num. 15:30–31] is most apposite for the brazen sinner who commits his acts in open defiance of the Lord (cf. Job. 38:15). The essence of this sin is that it is committed flauntingly. However, sins performed in secret, even deliberately, can be commuted to the status of inadvertencies by means of repentance.[239]

> . . . I submit that the repentance of the sinner, through his remorse . . . and confession. . . , reduces his intentional sin to an inadvertence, thereby rendering it eligible for sacrificial expiation.[240]

> . . . The early rabbis . . . raise the question of how the high priest's bull is capable of atoning for his deliberate sins, and they reply, "Because he has confessed his brazen and rebellious deeds it is as if they become as unintentional ones before him" (Sipra, Ahare par. 2:4,6; cf. t. Yoma 2:1). Thus it is clear that the Tannaites attribute to repentance—strikingly, in a sacrificial ritual—the power to transform a presumptuous sin against God, punishable by death, into an act of inadvertence, expiable by sacrifice.[241]

Of course, there are other scholars who reject this Rabbinic concept that intentional sins can be "converted" to unintentional sins through repentance, and I am not fully convinced of it myself.[242] I only bring it up because it reflects another problem (from a Rabbinic perspective) with the anti-missionary position regarding sacrifice and atonement.

In any case, I have presented clear, definite scriptural evidence, supported by Rabbinic tradition as well, that the sacrificial system instituted by God for the people of Israel, joined, of course, with repentance, provided atonement for intentional as well as and unintentional sins.

3.13. Even if I accept your arguments about the centrality of blood sacrifices, it only held true while the Temple was standing. The Book of Daniel teaches us that if the Temple has been destroyed and is not functional, prayer replaces sacrifice. In fact, the Book of Ezekiel is even more explicit, telling Jews living in exile—and therefore without any access to the Temple, even if it were standing—that repentance and good works are all God requires.

> You are obviously referring to Ezekiel 18 and 33, where we learn that a wicked man who repents is accepted by God—with no mention of sacrifices—along with Daniel 6:10, where it tells us that Daniel, living in exile, prayed toward the Temple (i.e., facing Jerusalem) three times a day. But the idea that prayer replaces sacrifice is simply not taught in the passages you refer to, nor is it in harmony with other important passages from the Hebrew Scriptures. I also find it interesting that the exiles couldn't wait to return to Jerusalem to rebuild the Temple and offer sacrifices again. They knew how important this was. Further, it is significant that to this day many Orthodox Jews kill a rooster or chicken on the Day of Atonement and offer it as an atoning, substitutionary sacrifice on their behalf. Despite the Rabbinic teaching that prayer has replaced sacrifice, they still feel the need to offer a blood sacrifice on Yom Kippur.

Let's look first at Daniel 6, in which we read that the prophet Daniel, living in exile and faced with a decree from the king not to pray to anyone other than the king himself, continued steadfast, "praying and asking God for help" (Dan. 6:11): "Now when Daniel learned that the decree had been published, he went home to his upstairs room where the windows opened toward Jerusalem. Three times a day he got down on his knees and prayed, giving thanks to his God, just as he had done before" (Dan. 6:10). From this text, some traditional Jews argue that Daniel understood that prayer replaced sacrifice, pointing out that he prayed toward Jerusalem (and therefore, toward the site of the Temple) and that he did this three times daily, in place of the daily Temple sacrifices. But are these claims supported by the text? No.

Daniel 6:10 is telling us one thing and one thing alone: Daniel prayed to God three times a day facing Jerusalem. That's it. It is not teaching some new doctrine (namely, that prayer replaced sacrifices), nor is it establishing a lasting custom for the generations to come (namely, that all Jews should pray three times daily).[243] I could just as well argue that Daniel was praying for the Messiah to come (since he knew that the Messiah would come to Jerusalem), and the fact that he prayed three times a day proved that he believed in the Trinity! The verse doesn't teach this anymore than it teaches that prayer replaces sacrifices when the Temple is not standing. Rather, Daniel 6:10 simply describes Daniel's daily prayer habit, nothing more and nothing less. And it was quite natural for him to face Jerusalem in prayer.[244] Jerusalem represented the earthly center of God's kingdom, the place where kings from David's line sat enthroned, the site of the holy Temple. Plus, judging from some of the recorded prayers of Daniel, he had Jerusalem on his mind. As the learned Old Testament scholar Gleason Archer asked, "To what other direction should Daniel turn than to the Holy City, the place of his heart's desire, the focal point of his hopes and prayers for the progress of the kingdom of God?"[245]

According to Daniel 9:1–2, the prophet was intensely interested in the restoration of Jerusalem: "In the first year of Darius son of Xerxes (a Mede by descent), who was made ruler over the Babylonian kingdom—in the first year of his reign, I, Daniel, understood from the Scriptures, according to the word of the LORD given to Jeremiah the prophet, that *the desolation of Jerusalem* would last seventy years." Therefore, he sought God in prayer and fasting:

> So I turned to the Lord God and pleaded with him in prayer and petition, in fasting, and in sackcloth and ashes. I prayed to the LORD my God and confessed: "O Lord, the great and awesome God, who keeps his covenant of love with all who love him and obey his commands, we have sinned and done wrong. We have been wicked and have rebelled; we have turned away from your commands and laws. We have not listened to your servants the prophets, who spoke in your name to our kings, our princes and our fathers, and to all the people of the land."
>
> Daniel 9:3–6

With great passion and pain, Daniel confessed to the Lord that his judgments were right, acknowledging that the exile and the destruction of Jerusalem (see especially v. 12) were deserved, pleading with God for restoration:

Now, O Lord our God, who brought your people out of Egypt with a mighty hand and who made for yourself a name that endures to this day, we have sinned, we have done wrong. O Lord, in keeping with all your righteous acts, turn away your anger and your wrath from *Jerusalem, your city, your holy hill.* Our sins and the iniquities of our fathers have made *Jerusalem* and your people an object of scorn to all those around us. Now, our God, hear the prayers and petitions of your servant. For your sake, O Lord, look with favor on *your desolate sanctuary.* Give ear, O God, and hear; open your eyes and see the desolation of *the city that bears your Name.* We do not make requests of you because we are righteous, but because of your great mercy. O Lord, listen! O Lord, forgive! O Lord, hear and act! For your sake, O my God, do not delay, because *your city* and your people bear your Name.

Daniel 9:15–19

It is important to notice two things in Daniel's prayer. First, his central focus was Jerusalem. Just look at how he appeals to God on behalf of this city, calling it *your* city, *your* holy hill, the city that bears *your* name, the place of *your* desolate sanctuary. Second, he recognized fully that the Temple was destroyed because of Israel's sins, therefore, "we and our kings, our princes and our fathers are covered with shame because we have sinned against you" (Dan. 9:8):

All Israel has transgressed your law and turned away, refusing to obey you. Therefore the curses and sworn judgments written in the Law of Moses, the servant of God, have been poured out on us, because we have sinned against you. You have fulfilled the words spoken against us and against our rulers by bringing upon us great disaster. *Under the whole heaven nothing has ever been done like what has been done to Jerusalem.* Just as it is written in the Law of Moses, all this disaster has come upon us, yet we have not sought the favor of the LORD our God by turning from our sins and giving attention to your truth. The LORD did not hesitate to bring the disaster upon us, for the LORD our God is righteous in everything he does; yet we have not obeyed him.

Daniel 9:11–14

These passages are indisputably clear: Jerusalem's destruction was an act of divine judgment, "just as it is written in the Law of Moses," and just as the Lord promised Solomon:

If you turn away and forsake the decrees and commands I have given you and go off to serve other gods and worship them, then I will uproot Israel from my land, which I have given them, and will reject this temple I have consecrated for my Name. I will make it a byword and an object of ridicule among all peoples. And though this temple is now so imposing, all who pass by will be appalled and say, "Why has the LORD done such a thing to this land and to this temple?" People will answer, "Because they have forsaken the LORD, the God of their fathers, who brought them out of Egypt, and have embraced other gods, worshiping and serving them—that is why he brought all this disaster on them."

2 Chronicles 7:19–22[246]

These verses declare in no uncertain terms how terrible a judgment the destruction of the Temple would be and how greatly that destruction would convey the depth of the Lord's displeasure with his people. Daniel felt that deeply, and he was stung and embarrassed by his people's rebellion and sin. The Temple had been sacked, the holy city demolished! God was angry with his people, cutting them off from the very place of sacrifice and atonement and exiling them from their city and their land. How shameful this was for the people of the Lord. He did exactly what he told Solomon he would do if Israel's sins became intolerable, rejecting the very Temple—his own Temple—that was built for his fame and renown.

With this in mind, and remembering that Daniel 9 records one of Daniel's own prayers, we see that Daniel 6:10 does not teach that prayer replaces sacrifice when the Temple is not standing. On the contrary, for Daniel the destruction of the Temple meant that as a nation we were under divine judgment, devoid of a place for sacrifices and worship, devoid of a system of atonement. At best, he could hope for mercy from God as an individual, while on a national scale only the restoration of his people to the land coupled with the rebuilding of the Temple would be a sign of divine favor.[247]

This is underscored by Jeremiah 29, a divinely inspired letter written by Jeremiah, who was living in Judah, to the exiles living in Babylon:

This is what the LORD says: "When seventy years are completed for Babylon, I will come to you and fulfill my gracious promise to bring you back to this place. For I know the plans I have for you," declares the LORD, "plans to prosper you and not to harm you, plans to give you hope and a future. Then you will call upon me and come and pray to me, and I will listen to you. You will seek me and find me when you seek me with all your heart. I will be found by you," declares the LORD, "and will bring you back from captivity. I will gather you from all the nations and places where I have banished you," declares the Lord, "and will bring you back to the place from which I carried you into exile."

Jeremiah 29:10–14

God was saying to his people, "After you have paid for your sins in exile, I will have mercy on you and bring you back to this land. *Then* I will show you my favor."

How shocked Daniel would have been if a fellow Jew came up to him in exile and said, "Don't worry about a thing, Daniel. Your prayers take the place of sacrifices. Who needs a Temple anyway? Prayer is much more spiritual." What a contradiction of everything Daniel expressed in prayer and confession as recorded in the Scriptures. And what a contradiction of the actions of the exiles upon their return to Jerusalem. Reinstituting sacrifices was their central concern.

Of course, we know that Solomon asked the Lord to hear the prayers of his exiled people when directed toward Jerusalem. But as we saw in our careful treatment of his prayer (2 Chronicles 6; 1 Kings 8), Solomon's petition was offered to the Lord at the *dedication of the Temple*, at which time the Lord said he would answer Israel's prayers *because of the Temple sacrifices* (2 Chron. 7:12; see above 3.9). But if their sins became too grievous, he would destroy the Temple as a sign of his fierce judgment, exiling his people (2 Chron. 7:19–22, quoted above).[248] And no Temple meant no national atonement. This was a frightful thought.

We can understand, then, why Ezra and his contemporaries had one central goal in returning to Jerusalem from exile: They wanted to rebuild the Temple and offer sacrifices. (See below.) They did not say to themselves, "We have means of atonement and forgiveness other than sacrifices and offerings. In fact, we have means of atonement and forgiveness *better* than sacrifices and offerings. Let's not go back to something as antiquated and unnecessary as blood sacrifices. Let's move forward." Instead, they risked their own lives to rebuild the Temple and restore the place of sacrifices and offerings. Nothing was more important to them.

Even the edict of King Cyrus, who was raised up by God and allowed the Jews to return from exile, indicates how important sacrifices and offerings were in the minds of the people:

This is what Cyrus king of Persia says: "The Lord, the God of heaven, has given me all the kingdoms of the earth and he has appointed me to *build a temple for him* at Jerusalem in Judah. Anyone of his people among you—may his God be with him, and let him go up to Jerusalem in Judah and *build the temple of the LORD,* the God of Israel, the God who is in Jerusalem. And the people of any place where survivors may now be living are to provide him with silver and gold, with goods and livestock, and with freewill offerings for *the temple of God* in Jerusalem."

Ezra 1:2–4

In the first year of King Cyrus, the king issued a decree *concerning the temple of God* in Jerusalem: Let *the temple be rebuilt as a place to present sacrifices,* and let its foundations be laid. It is to be ninety feet high and ninety feet wide, with three courses of large stones and one of timbers. The costs are to be paid by the royal treasury. Also, the gold and silver articles of the house of God, which Nebuchadnezzar took from the temple in Jerusalem and brought to Babylon, are to be returned to their places in *the temple* in Jerusalem; they are to be deposited in *the house of God.*

Ezra 6:3–5

Cyrus, as a tool in the hands of God, allowed the exiles to return for one primary purpose: to rebuild the Temple in Jerusalem. And note well that he fully understood the purpose of the Temple: It was a place to present sacrifices.

How did Ezra and the returning exiles respond? (Remember, these were people who lived *after* the events recorded in the Book of Daniel and after the prophecies of Ezekiel.) This is what these Jews went about doing:

Then the family heads of Judah and Benjamin, and the priests and Levites—everyone whose heart God had moved—prepared to go up and *build the house of the LORD* in Jerusalem. All their neighbors assisted them with articles of silver and gold, with goods and livestock, and with valuable gifts, in addition to all the freewill offerings. . . . When they arrived at the house of the LORD in Jerusalem, some of the heads of the families gave freewill offerings *toward the rebuilding of the house of God* on its site. According to their ability they gave to the treasury for this work 61,000 drachmas of gold, 5,000 minas of silver and 100 priestly garments.

Ezra 1:5–6; 2:68–69

They were so eager to offer sacrifices again that they built the altar before the Temple foundations were laid and began to sacrifice to the Lord. They couldn't wait to do it.

When the seventh month came and the Israelites had settled in their towns, the people assembled as one man in Jerusalem. Then Jeshua son of Jozadak and his fellow priests and Zerubbabel son of Shealtiel and his associates began to build *the altar of the God of Israel to sacrifice burnt offerings on it, in accordance with what is written in the Law of Moses the man of God.* [Notice that the text does not say: They decided not to rebuild the altar for sacrifices, based on the fact that the prophets repudiated sacrifices. No. They knew that the prophets were in harmony with the Torah, fully affirming its commandments.] Despite their fear of the peoples around them, *they built the altar on its foundation and sacrificed burnt offerings on it to the Lord, both the morning and evening sacrifices.* Then in accordance with what is written, they celebrated the Feast of Tabernacles with *the required number of burnt offerings* prescribed for each day. After that, *they presented the regular burnt offerings, the New Moon sacrifices and the sacrifices for all the appointed sacred feasts of the Lord, as well as those brought as freewill offerings to the Lord.* On the first day of the seventh month *they began to offer burnt offerings to the Lord,* though the foundation of the Lord's temple had not yet been laid.

Ezra 3:1–6

Do you see how important it was for them to offer sacrifices to the Lord? Do you see how they longed to be back in Jerusalem, bringing the required daily and festival offerings? To reiterate: They were so eager to do so that the first thing they did was rebuild the altar. Much of the Book of Ezra is devoted to the courageous struggle of these former exiles to rebuild the Temple on its site.

Obviously, these Jews did not have the slightest notion that prayer had replaced sacrifice. Therefore, it is not surprising at all that Rabbinic leaders were distraught when that Second Temple was destroyed about six hundred years later, wondering what they would do for atonement. It took other Rabbinic leaders to inform them that prayer replaced sacrifices (see Avot d'Rabbi Nathan, Version I, iv, 11a, cited above, 3.10, and y. Ta'anit 2:1, 65b, cited above, 3.9). They had never heard of such a thing before!

In fact, six hundred years *after* the time of Daniel, we know that the Jewish leadership hardly thought that sacrifices were unimportant or that prayer could simply be substituted for sacrifices. In fact, a historical testimony noted in the article on "Sacrifices" in the *Encyclopedia Judaica* provides eloquent testimony to just how central the sacrificial system was to our people:

The importance which the Jews attached to sacrifice is evidenced by the fact that they continued to offer the daily *tamid* sacrifice throughout almost the entire period of the siege of Jerusalem [at the end of the war against Rome in 66–70 c.e.]. Despite the hardship and privations of this period and the famine which raged, the Temple service continued until the walls of the city were breached by the Romans on the 17th of Tammuz. The *tamid* sacrifice then had to be discontinued due to the lack of lambs and qualified priests within the Temple precincts (Ta'an. 4:6; Jos., Wars, 6:94). Three weeks later on the Ninth of Av the Temple was destroyed by the Romans and the sacrificial system came to an end.[249]

What a poignant and powerful proof that sacrifices, rather than being downplayed and devalued by the Jewish leadership, were highly esteemed and prized.

As to the claim that Daniel prayed three times a day to coincide with the three daily times of sacrifice, there is one major problem: There were only *two* daily times of sacrifice (see Num. 28:1–8; Ezra 3:4; for references to "the evening sacrifice," see 1 Kings 18:29; Ezra 9:3–5; Ps. 141:2; Dan. 9:21). The correspondence doesn't work because the correspondence isn't there.

Then why did Daniel pray three times daily? I'll answer this question with a question: Why not? We often make reference to doing something "morning, noon, and night," and it is really quite natural to divide the day into three parts. On the other hand, the psalmist spoke of praising God seven times a day (Ps. 119:164), yet we would never think of making a doctrine out of this practice. He also said, "At midnight I rise to give you thanks for your righteous laws" (Ps. 119:62). What sacrifice did this correspond to? What Temple ritual was this replacing? The answer, of course, is self-evident. None at all. In the same way, it is quite a leap of logic—not to mention a theological impossibility based on Daniel's prayer in chapter 9—to claim that Daniel's thrice-daily prayer took the place of the twice-daily Temple sacrifices.

I should also remind you that the last of the Eighteen Benedictions (Shemoneh Esreh), recited daily by traditional Jews, is a prayer for the rebuilding of the Temple. I quoted this earlier (above, 3.9), but it's worth quoting again: "Be favorable, O Lord our God, toward Your people Israel and toward their prayer, and restore the service to the Holy of Holies of Your Temple. The fire-offerings of Israel and their prayer accept with love and favor, and may the service of Your people Israel be favorable to You."

Interestingly, the commentary of Etz Yoseph explains the petition for the restoration of the Temple service as follows: "As we conclude

Shemoneh Esrei, which is our substitute for the Temple's sacrificial service, we ask that the *true* service be restored to the Temple."[250] Even here, in a traditional commentary to the Prayerbook, a commentary accepting the Rabbinic teaching that prayer replaces sacrifice when the Temple is not standing, it is recognized that prayer is not a fully adequate substitute for sacrifices.[251] We can safely say, then, based on God's word to Solomon in 2 Chronicles 7:19–22, based on Daniel's prayer to God in Daniel 9, and based on the actions of Ezra and his colleagues upon their return to Jerusalem, that there is no support for the view that prayer replaced sacrifice during the exile when the Temple was not standing. Even the petition we just cited from the Shemoneh Esrei hints at this.

What about Ezekiel 18 and 33? Those texts seem clear: If a wicked man repents of his sin, God will pronounce him righteous; he will not die for his sins, and his wicked deeds will be forgotten. On the other hand, if a righteous man becomes wicked, all his righteous deeds will be forgotten, and he will die for his sins. The anti-missionary argument is twofold: First, it points out that according to Ezekiel, a person becomes righteous through repentance alone, and there is no mention at all of sacrifices and offerings in either chapter. Second, it claims that these chapters were spoken by the prophet to the Jewish people in exile, and therefore, with no access to the Temple. Thus, according to this argument, the Hebrew Bible made provision for Jews living at any time and in any place who were unable to offer sacrifices for themselves at the Temple.

There are several problems, however, with this line of reasoning. To help shed some light on this, let's step back and put the anti-missionary argument into a proper historical perspective. You see, it's easy from our vantage point twenty-five hundred years later simply to say, "Ezekiel said such and such, and this is how it applies to us today." A better approach would be, "How did Ezekiel's words apply to his contemporaries, how did his words apply to the following generations who received his prophecies as the Word of God, and how do they apply to us today as well?"

You might say, "The Word of God is the Word of God. It's timeless, it's true, and it's always relevant. I don't see where your line of reasoning is going."

Allow me, then, to explain. Let's say I agree with you that Ezekiel prophesied to his fellow exiles who languished in Babylon while the Temple in Jerusalem lay in ruins. (Actually, I *do* agree with this; it is historically accurate.) And let's say that I also agree with you that he was telling his Jewish people how to get right with God without Temple, priesthood, and sacrifices. (I *don't* agree with this.) What happened, then, after the Temple was rebuilt? Did the words of the Lord to Ezekiel become null and void? Or worse yet, did these words encourage Jews *not* to participate in the Day of Atonement, *not* to make pilgrimages to the Temple, *not* to bring sacrifices and offerings, *not* to follow the Torah? The answer, of course, is no on both accounts. Ezekiel's prophetic messages, which became recognized as the Word of God, did not become null and void, nor did they encourage people to disregard the Torah or its system of atonement.

We can also raise another, major objection to your interpretation, similar to that raised with reference to Daniel 6:10, above. It is simply this: If Ezekiel's contemporaries understood his message the way the anti-missionaries do, why then were they so eager to return to Jerusalem and rebuild the Temple? In fact, we can raise a further objection: If Ezekiel was the one chosen by God to bring the revelation that repentance alone was needed when the Temple was not standing, why was he the one also chosen to receive the vision of the future Temple with a restored system of sacrifice and atonement? (For discussion of this Temple vision, see below, 3.17. We will see there that Ezekiel had every reason to expect that the Temple would be built *in his lifetime*.) Now do you understand my point about reading Ezekiel in its proper context, both for his day and for succeeding generations?

"Well then," you ask, "how do you explain away his words? They are clear: God requires repentance not sacrifices."

Actually, I find no reason to "explain away" Ezekiel's words. I agree with what he said; I only disagree with your interpretation of what he said. You see, he was not making a statement about atonement and forgiveness without sacrifices. Rather, he was responding to a widespread misunderstanding that existed among his contemporaries, a misunderstanding that completely undercut individual moral responsibility. According to this view, the parents could sin and escape scot-free, while their children would suffer for the parents' sins:

> The word of the LORD came to me: "What do you people mean by quoting this proverb about the land of Israel: 'The fathers eat sour grapes, and the children's teeth are set on edge'? As surely as I live, declares the Sovereign LORD, you will no longer quote this proverb in Israel. For every living soul belongs to me, the father as well as the son—both alike belong to me. The soul who sins is the one who will die. . . . The son

will not share the guilt of the father, nor will the father share the guilt of the son. The righteousness of the righteous man will be credited to him, and the wickedness of the wicked will be charged against him."

Ezekiel 18:1–4, 20

All of Ezekiel 18 is devoted to this subject, explaining the issue in great detail (see also Jer. 31:29–32).[252] It has nothing to do with atonement.

"But it does," you object. "It teaches that repentance is all that God requires."

Once again, I beg to differ. The text makes no statement about atonement. It simply identifies traits of a righteous person:

He does not eat at the mountain shrines or look to the idols of the house of Israel. He does not defile his neighbor's wife or lie with a woman during her period. He does not oppress anyone, but returns what he took in pledge for a loan. He does not commit robbery but gives his food to the hungry and provides clothing for the naked. He does not lend at usury or take excessive interest. He withholds his hand from doing wrong and judges fairly between man and man. He follows my decrees and faithfully keeps my laws. That man is righteous; he will surely live, declares the Sovereign LORD.

Ezekiel 18:6–9

Who would differ with this description? It is similar to descriptions and exhortations found in the New Testament: Followers of Jesus are called on to repent and to prove their repentance by their actions (e.g., Matt. 4:17; Luke 13:3, 5; Acts 26:20; 2 Cor. 7:10–11; see also Luke 3:7–14); they are expected to demonstrate righteous conduct in thought, word, and deed (e.g., Matt. 5:21–30; Rom. 13:13–14; Eph. 4:17–5:18; 1 John 3:3); they are commanded to turn from everything unclean and defiling, perfecting holiness out of reverence for God (e.g., 2 Cor. 6:14–7:1; 2 Peter 3:10–12). On these things we agree. The teachings of the New Testament are permeated with high and lofty ethical values, often taking the moral requirements of the Hebrew Bible to a deeper level (see vol. 3, 5.21, 5.28).

Ezekiel also identifies the traits of a wicked man: "He eats at the mountain shrines. He defiles his neighbor's wife. He oppresses the poor and needy. He commits robbery. He does not return what he took in pledge. He looks to the idols. He does detestable things. He lends at usury and takes excessive interest" (Ezek. 18:11–13).

This too is similar to New Testament teaching on the traits of the wicked, those who by their deeds prove that they do not belong to God. Paul even spoke of people who "claim to know God, but by their actions they deny him. They are detestable, disobedient and unfit for doing anything good" (Titus 1:16). The New Testament is perfectly clear on this:

Do you not know that the wicked will not inherit the kingdom of God? Do not be deceived: Neither the sexually immoral nor idolaters nor adulterers nor male prostitutes nor homosexual offenders nor thieves nor the greedy nor drunkards nor slanderers nor swindlers will inherit the kingdom of God.

1 Corinthians 6:9–10

No one who lives in him [i.e., God and/or the Messiah] keeps on sinning. No one who continues to sin has either seen him or known him. Dear children, do not let anyone lead you astray. He who does what is right is righteous, just as he is righteous. He who does what is sinful is of the devil, because the devil has been sinning from the beginning. The reason the Son of God appeared was to destroy the devil's work. No one who is born of God will continue to sin, because God's seed remains in him; he cannot go on sinning, because he has been born of God. This is how we know who the children of God are and who the children of the devil are: Anyone who does not do what is right is not a child of God; nor is anyone who does not love his brother.

1 John 3:6–10

God "will give to each person according to what he has done." To those who by persistence in doing good seek glory, honor and immortality, he will give eternal life. But for those who are self-seeking and who reject the truth and follow evil, there will be wrath and anger. There will be trouble and distress for every human being who does evil: first for the Jew, then for the Gentile; but glory, honor and peace for everyone who does good: first for the Jew, then for the Gentile. For God does not show favoritism.

Romans 2:6–11

Now, what if I took these New Testament texts, which are just as explicit as those found in Ezekiel, and claimed they proved that faith in Jesus was not required, that all God wanted was for people to do what was right and just? I would be misrepresenting the facts by using texts to prove something they were not meant to prove.[253] Remember, we saw that Ezekiel's words could not be taken to mean that repentance was all that was required if the Temple was not standing (or not accessible), since: (1) These words would then be meaningless once the Temple was rebuilt, or else, if they retained their meaning, they would stand in direct opposition to the Torah; (2) Ezekiel's contemporaries, men and women who heard these very words, couldn't wait to return to Jerusalem and rebuild the Temple; (3) Ezekiel was the prophet to whom God gave the vision of a future Temple with sacrifices for atonement, a vision in which Israel's sins were dealt with once and for all (again, see below, 3.17).

How then do I reconcile Ezekiel's words with my theology of sacrifice and atonement? I don't reconcile them because they are two sides of the same coin. Just as the New Testament requires faith in God's means of atonement and repentance from evil deeds (see, e.g., Acts 20:21, the words of Paul: "I have declared to both Jews and Greeks that they must turn to God in repentance and have faith in our Lord Jesus"), so also the Hebrew Scriptures require faith in God's means of atonement and repentance from evil deeds. The Torah outlines the former; Ezekiel outlines the latter. The Torah points to repentance as well, but the theme is not spelled out in most sacrifice and atonement contexts;[254] Ezekiel points to a restored Temple with atoning sacrifices (Ezekiel 40–48), but the theme is not present in chapter 18. So it is not a matter of either repentance or atoning sacrifices but a matter of both repentance and atoning sacrifices.

If we wanted to press your argument, we could say that according to Ezekiel 18, Sabbath observance is not important, since the prophet doesn't mention it in chapter 18, nor are any of the holy days—including Passover, Rosh Hashanah, and Yom Kippur—of any importance, since he doesn't mention them in the chapter, nor is prayer of any importance, since he doesn't mention it in the chapter. Would you accept this line of reasoning? Obviously not. Then why do you argue that the chapter teaches Jews in exile how to get right with God without sacrifices and offerings? And why, for that matter, didn't the Lord remind Ezekiel that prayer replaced sacrifices while the Temple was not standing? It was because Ezekiel 18 had nothing to do with the subject of how to receive atonement while living in exile. In fact, some of the language used by Ezekiel—referring to the wicked who "eat at the mountain shrines" (Ezek. 18:6, 11, 15; cf. also 6:13) might best be applied to Jews *living in the land of Israel.*[255]

Further, the anti-missionary interpretation of Ezekiel 18 is unknown to the Talmudic rabbis and medieval Jewish Bible commentators. In other words, it is a recent invention devised with the sole purpose of refuting Messianic Jewish beliefs. There is no record of any prominent rabbi in the past utilizing this text to prove that God provided an alternative method of atonement for his exiled people living without a Temple. This says a great deal, especially when you realize that (1) Traditional Judaism believes that the farther back in time we go, the closer we are to the original revelation at Mount Sinai. Therefore, later generations should not dismiss the accepted beliefs and customs of the earliest generations of sages and teachers. It is also highly unlikely that rabbis today could discover important new interpretations of Scripture that eluded past generations. (2) The "Jewish-Christian" debate has been going on for more than nineteen hundred years, and most objections to Christian interpretations of Messianic prophecies and Christian doctrine are found in the Rabbinic commentaries dating back to the eleventh and twelfth centuries. Therefore, it is all the more striking to discover that this particular argument by the anti-missionaries never occurred to the Jewish scholars of the past.

Let me offer another piece of evidence that Jews around the world have often felt the need for a blood sacrifice at the time of Rosh Hashanah or Yom Kippur, wanting to have *something* die as a substitute for their sins even though the Temple was not standing. As we saw above (3.12), there has been a persistent practice, common to this day, in which Orthodox Jews perform the ceremony of *kapparot* on the eve of either of the holidays just mentioned.

To expand on our previous description of this ceremony, let me quote the *Encyclopedia Judaica:*

> Kapparot: custom in which the sins of a person are symbolically transferred to a fowl. The custom is practiced in certain Orthodox circles on the day before the Day of Atonement (in some congregations also on the day before Rosh Ha-Shanah or on Hoshana Rabba). Psalms 107:10, 14, 17–21, and Job 33:23–24 are recited; then a cock (for a male) or a hen (for a female) is swung around the head three times while the following is pronounced: "This is my substitute, my vicarious offering, my atonement; this cock (or hen) shall meet death, but I shall find a long and pleasant life of peace." The fowl is thought to take on any misfortune which might otherwise befall a person in punishment of his sins. After the ceremony, it is customary to donate the fowl to the poor, except for the intestines which are thrown to the birds. Some rabbis recommended that money, equivalent to the fowl's value, be given instead.[256]

This ceremony becomes even more meaningful when we look at the verses recited from Job: "Yet if there is an angel on his side as a mediator, one out of a thousand, to tell a man what is right for him, to be gracious to him and say, 'Spare him from going down to the pit; *I have found a ransom for him'"* (Job 33:23–24; the Hebrew for ransom is *kopher,* discussed at length above, 3.10). It is interesting that many religious Jews feel the need for a ransom at the time of Yom Kippur. This alone explains why the ceremony of *kapparot* has persisted throughout the centuries, despite the sanctions of some of the leading rabbis. It could also explain why other leading rabbis heartily endorsed it.[257]

Sadly, traditional Judaism has gone on for more than nineteen hundred years without the Temple or God-ordained animal sacrifices, and this is often considered a proof of its strength and vitality. As Rabbi Hertz noted,

> With the cessation of sacrifices, study of the Torah, Prayer and Beneficence definitely take the place of the Temple Service. It is for this reason that the disappearance of the Temple did not in any way cripple Judaism. When the Temple fell, there still remained the Synagogue— with reading and exposition of the Torah, and congregational worship without priest or sacrificial ritual.[258]

We have seen, however, that all these things—study of the Torah, prayer, and beneficence—as noble and important as they are, do not take the place of the Temple service. Therefore, as we have stated repeatedly, either God has left us without a means of atonement or else he has provided it once and for all through the Messiah Jesus. Let me encourage you to search the Scriptures and ask the Lord for grace and help to accept the evidence of the Word. God in his mercy has *not* left us alone. Instead, he has displayed his compassion for all the world to see through the sacrificial death of the Messiah for our sins.

Interestingly, many scholars believe that it was during this very time of exile in Babylon that the teaching of Isaiah's Suffering Servant came to prominence. The concept of a righteous sufferer dying for his people's sins was being planted in the hearts and minds of God's people, as the Lord began to direct them to the one who would bring to fulfillment the system of Old Covenant blood sacrifices by offering up himself. By the time the Second Temple was destroyed in 70 c.e., this righteous servant of the Lord, the Messiah, had already come and done his work, and it was none other than Daniel the prophet who received a divine revelation about final atonement coming to his Jewish people during the days of the Second Temple (see

Dan. 9:24–27, discussed in vol. 1, 2.1, and in more detail, in vol. 3, 4.18–4.21). Daniel and his fellow exiles could only look ahead with hopeful and longing hearts for the fulfillment of that vision. Today, the Jewish people can look back to the one who paid the ransom for our souls.

In a very real sense, then, you could say that every single sin God has ever forgiven, he has forgiven because of his Son, the righteous Messiah, who paid our debt in full, dying in our place and thereby bringing atonement, in keeping with the Rabbinic concept that "the death of the righteous atones" (see below, 3.15). The Temple sacrifices had a certain role to play and a certain effectiveness in bringing ritual purification and temporary atonement to God's people, but they could not utterly cleanse the conscience or transform the inner being, procuring eternal forgiveness of sins. This had to await the death of the Messiah, and if the Jewish people had any hope of obtaining mercy from God during times of exile and divine judgment, it would still be through the Messiah's grace.

And so, before the Messiah's coming, as our people turned to God in contrition, putting their hope in his promise of redemption, he would forgive them based on their repentance and faith. This is what Paul meant when he stated that God announced the gospel in advance to Abraham:

> Consider Abraham: "He believed God, and it was credited to him as righteousness." Understand, then, that those who believe are children of Abraham. The Scripture foresaw that God would justify the Gentiles by faith, and announced the gospel in advance to Abraham: "All nations will be blessed through you." So those who have faith are blessed along with Abraham, the man of faith.
>
> Galatians 3:6–9

The promise of universal blessing coming through Abraham's descendants was the promise of the gospel in "seed" form. Abraham believed the promise, and God pronounced him righteous because of that (Gen. 15:6; see above, 3.7). Thus, in every generation, as God's people embraced his promise and put their trust in that divine pledge, they could be pronounced righteous by faith, until the promise was realized in the Messiah. Now, we look back to the Messiah and put our trust in his work on our behalf, believing God's promise once again. The Temple sacrifices, so central to Israelite religious life, served to instill in our minds—day and night, as it were—the importance of blood atonement and the need for an innocent substitute to die in our place. Therefore, we can see that God has always had one system of atonement and one system alone, namely, substitutionary atonement, life-for-life atonement, blood atonement. Blood sacrifices were always foundational for our people, and they always pointed toward that day when the ideal Substitute would come and lay down his life for us.

3.14. The Book of Jonah shoots down all your arguments about sacrifice and atonement, especially with reference to Gentiles. When Jonah preached, the people repented, and God forgave them—no sacrifice, no blood offering.

> Did you know that traditional Judaism, based on the Torah, teaches that the Temple sacrifices made atonement for the Gentile world? This was part of Israel's call as a priestly nation, and it was Israel's Temple offerings that helped make Gentile repentance acceptable to God.

When God brought our people out of Egypt, he said to them, "You yourselves have seen what I did to Egypt, and how I carried you on eagles' wings and brought you to myself. Now if you obey me fully and keep my covenant, then out of all nations you will be my treasured possession. Although the whole earth is mine, you will be for me a kingdom of priests and a holy nation" (Exod. 19:4–6).

Israel was called to be a priestly nation, and part of that calling included making intercession and atonement for the nations of the world. (Remember, this was an integral part of the priestly calling, therefore, as a *priestly nation,* Israel would make intercession and atonement for the world.) According to this concept, when a Gentile nation repented and turned to God, its repentance would be accepted in conjunction with the sacrifices and prayers offered up by the people of Israel. That's why the prophet Jonah called on the Ninevites to repent of their sins. Offering up sacrifices was Israel's job as a priestly nation.

"Who says so?" you ask.

Actually, the Talmudic rabbis say so. In b. Sukkah 55b (see also Pesikta deRav Kahana, Buber edition, 193b–194a) we read that the seventy bulls that were offered every year during the Feast of Tabernacles (Sukkot; see Num. 29:12–34) "were for the seventy nations," which Rashi explains to mean, "to make atonement for them, so that rain will fall throughout the world."[259] In this context—and in light of the destruction of the Temple by the Romans in 70 c.e.—the Talmud records the words of Rabbi Yohannan: "Woe to the nations who destroyed without knowing what they were destroying. For when the Temple was standing, the altar made atonement for them. But now, who will make atonement for them?" Such a strong statement bears repeating: "When the Temple was standing, the altar made atonement for them." Blood sacrifices were indispensable. (See above, 3.10, for an in-depth discussion of this.)

Now, I recognize that God can have mercy on whom he wants to have mercy and compassion on whom he wants to have compassion (see Exod. 33:19), but he has ordained prayer, atonement rites, repentance, and faith as the means by which his people participate with him in procuring forgiveness and mercy. Thus, he singled out one particular people, the nation of Israel, and called them to conduct the Temple services, celebrating the holy days and offering sacrifices for their own sins and the sins of the world. Ultimately, these sacrifices pointed to the once-and-for-all sacrifice of Yeshua for the sins of the world.[260]

The bottom line is this: All of us have sinned, Jew and Gentile alike, and all of us need a way to come into right standing with God. We will see in the next objection that it was the Messiah who opened the door for all peoples to come into God's presence by shedding his blood on our behalf, completely fulfilling what the sacrificial system could only point to in part.

3.15. Even if I admit that we need blood atonement, I still won't believe in Jesus. God wanted the blood of a goat or a lamb, not a person. He doesn't want human sacrifice!

All of us know that God is not interested in human sacrifice. But are you aware that the Hebrew Scriptures, the Talmud, as well as the New Testament clearly teach that the death of the righteous has atoning power? When the Messiah, the totally righteous one, laid down his life, it was the ultimate act of atonement in human history.

What you are about to read could change your life. But first I want to give you a little background. In 1962, twenty-eight-year-old Don Richardson, with his wife and baby, went as a missionary to the head-hunting Sawis of Irian Jaya, New Guinea. These were tribal people who, for all intents and purposes, were still living in the Stone Age. They had never seen a metal tool, let alone a flashlight. They were intrigued by this young white family who now lived in their midst, and little by little, they accepted the Richardsons.

The missionaries painstakingly learned the language and culture of the Sawi people, patiently sharing with them the good news about the one true God. But the natives were completely insensitive. In fact, when they heard about Judas betraying Jesus, they hooted with joy. Deceit was a virtue in their culture! It seemed that Don Richardson was hitting his head against a brick wall.

Then, after many months of futility, Don experienced a dramatic breakthrough. In order to resolve a conflict between two warring tribes—there was constant strife and violence between the various tribal groups—an ancient custom was followed. The leader of one tribe gave his firstborn son to the other tribe for life. The son was called a "peace child," and the giving of this son brought reconcilia-tion between the two warring factions. Suddenly, Richardson had his opening: "God gave his own Son as a peace child! God gave Jesus to bring about reconciliation between himself and sinful mankind." At last the natives began to understand.

In the years that followed, thousands of these idol-worshiping, murderous people were wonderfully transformed, and Don Richard-son made a discovery: In different religions and cultures throughout the world, God has strategically placed what Richardson calls "redemptive analogies"—examples of spiritual truth that point clearly to the message of the gospel.[261] What Richardson may not have known was this: God has placed these "redemptive analogies" in Judaism more than any other religion or culture, and the most important of all these redemptive analogies found in Judaism is that *the death of the righteous brings atonement to the world.*

Here are the words of a respected Orthodox Jewish historian, Rabbi Berel Wein. How was it that the Jewish people survived the horrors of the massacres in Eastern Europe in the seventeenth century? According to Rabbi Wein:

> Another consideration tinged the Jewish response to the slaughter of its people. It was an old Jewish tradition dating back to Biblical times

that the death of the righteous and innocent served as an expiation for the sins of the nation or the world. The stories of Isaac and of Nadav and Avihu, the prophetic description of Israel as the long-suffering servant of the Lord, the sacrificial service in the Temple—all served to reinforce this basic concept of the death of the righteous as an atonement for the sins of other men.

Jews nurtured this classic idea of death as an atonement, and this attitude towards their own tragedies was their constant companion throughout their turbulent exile. Therefore, the wholly bleak picture of unreasoning slaughter was somewhat relieved by the fact that the innocent did not die in vain and that the betterment of Israel and humankind somehow was advanced by their "stretching their neck to be slaughtered." What is amazing is that this abstract, sophisticated, theological thought should have become so ingrained in the psyche of the people that even the least educated and most simplistic of Jews understood the lesson and acted upon it, giving up precious life in a soaring act of belief and affirmation of the better tomorrow. This spirit of the Jews is truly reflected in the historical chronicle of the time:

"Would the Holy One, Blessed is He, dispense judgment without justice? But we may say that he whom God loves will be chastised. For since the day the Holy Temple was destroyed, the righteous are seized by death for the iniquities of the generation" (*Yeven Metzulah*, end of Chapter 15).[262]

Do you grasp the significance of what you just read? An Orthodox rabbi who most definitely does not believe in Jesus is telling us that according to the Bible and Jewish tradition the death of the righteous serves as an atonement for the sins of other men, "as an expiation for the sins of the nation or the world." And notice carefully the words of the medieval chronicle *Yeven Metzulah:* It was *since the destruction of the Temple* that the righteous were "seized by death for the iniquities of their generation." The connection is clear: Since there are no more sacrifices of atonement, it is the death of the righteous that atones. In similar fashion, the Zohar, the most sacred book of Jewish mysticism, states, "As long as Israel dwelt in the Holy Land, the rituals and the sacrifices they performed [in the Temple] removed all those diseases from the world; now the Messiah removes them from the children of the world (2:212a)."[263] This is not some new doctrine that the "Christian church" created. This is thoroughly Scriptural and quite Jewish. It explains the purpose and meaning of Jesus' death.

Before we look into the Hebrew Bible, however, I want to point out that on several occasions the Talmud itself teaches that "the death of the righteous atones" *(mitatan shel tsaddiqim mekapperet).* In a well-known discussion (b. Mo'ed Qatan 28a), the Talmud asks why the Book of Numbers records the death of Miriam immediately after the section on the red heifer (see Num. 19:1–20:1). The answer is that just as the red heifer atones, so also the death of the righteous atones (see also Rashi to Num. 20:1).[264] And why, the Talmud asks, is the death of Aaron recorded in conjunction with the Torah's reference to the priestly garments (see Num. 20:25–28)? The answer is, just as the garments of the high priest atone (see Exodus 28, especially v. 38), so also the death of the righteous atones. (Some of the Rabbinic texts read "atones for Israel" in all the cases just cited.)

This theme is actually fairly common in Rabbinic literature. Look, for example, at Leviticus Rabbah 20:12, repeated elsewhere verbatim (e.g., y. Yoma 2:1, Pesikta deRav Kahana 26:16): "Rabbi Hiyya Bar Abba said: The sons of Aaron [i.e., Nadab and Abihu] died the first day of Nisan. Why then does the Torah mention their death in conjunction with the Day of Atonement [which occurred on the tenth of Tishrei; see Lev. 16:1]? It is to teach that just as the Day of Atonement atones, so also the death of the righteous atones."[265]

What is the Scriptural support offered for this view? It is 2 Samuel 21:14: "They buried the bones of Saul and his son Jonathan in the tomb of Saul's father Kish, at Zela in Benjamin, and did everything the king commanded. After that, God answered prayer in behalf of the land."

Here is the background to this verse: There had been a famine in the land for three years, causing David to earnestly seek the Lord. God informed him, "It is on account of Saul and his blood-stained house; it is because he put the Gibeonites to death" (2 Sam. 21:1). So in order to appease the Gibeonites, David turned over to them seven of Saul's descendants, whom the Gibeonites killed, leaving their bodies exposed and unburied. Two of the men were sons of Rizpah, Saul's concubine, and she stayed with the corpses day and night, even in soaking rain. When David heard this,

> he went and took the bones of Saul and his son Jonathan from the citizens of Jabesh Gilead. (They had taken them secretly from the public square at Beth Shan, where the Philistines had hung them after they struck Saul down on Gilboa.) David brought the bones of Saul and his son Jonathan from there, and the bones of those who had been killed and exposed were gathered up. They buried the bones of Saul and his son Jonathan in the tomb of Saul's father Kish, at Zela in Benjamin, and did everything the king commanded. *After that, God answered prayer in behalf of the land.*
>
> 2 Samuel 21:12–14

The death of these men appeased the Gibeonites, and then God answered prayer on behalf of the land, from which the Talmud deduces that "the death of the righteous atones." Other Rabbinic sources state that just as the sacrifices and rituals of the Day of Atonement were effective only for those who repented, so also the death of the righteous secured atonement only for those who repented.[266] It seems to me that the "Christian apostles" wrote about this several hundred years earlier, pointing to the truly righteous one, the Messiah, our spotless Lamb.

An interesting passage in the Midrash reads, "Moses said to God, 'Will not the time come when Israel shall have neither Tabernacle nor Temple? What will happen with them then?' The divine reply was, 'I will then take one of their righteous men and keep him as a pledge on their behalf so I may pardon [or atone for] all their sins'" (Exodus Rabbah, Terumah 35:4). We have the same theme stated once again: When there is neither Tabernacle nor Temple, the life and death of the righteous will make atonement, just as we read earlier in *Yeven Metzulah*. The Zohar supports this concept with a citation from Isaiah 53, the Messianic prophecy most widely quoted by Christians and Messianic Jews.

> The children of the world are members of one another, and when the Holy One desires to give healing to the world, He smites one just man amongst them, and for his sake heals all the rest. Whence do we learn this? From the saying, "He was wounded for our transgressions, bruised for our iniquities" [Isa. 53:5], i.e., by the letting of his blood—as when a man bleeds his arm—there was healing for us—for all the members of the body. In general a just person is only smitten in order to procure healing and atonement for a whole generation.[267]

Talk about redemptive analogies! A Christian evangelist couldn't have said it any better. This is the very heart of the gospel message: The Messiah—the holy and righteous servant of the Lord—was smitten for the sins of the world, and through his death we can receive atonement for our sins and healing for our souls. As stated in Midrash Assereth Memrot:

> The Messiah, in order to atone for them both [for Adam and David], will *make his soul a trespass offering,* as it is written next to this, in the Parashah [scriptural passage]. *Behold my servant* [i.e., Isa. 52:13–53:12]: *'shm* [guilt offering], i.e. cabalistically [i.e., using Rabbinic Bible numerics], Menahem son of Ammiel [a title for the Messiah in the Talmud].[268]

The Messiah took our place. We sinned. He died. We were guilty. He was punished. We deserved death. He gave his life. We rejected him. He accepted us. What an incredible message. It's seems far too good to be true. But it *is* true, and it's biblical. It's Jewish too.

Rabbinic scholar Solomon Schechter summarizes the Talmudic teaching that suffering and death atone for sin, with specific reference to the death of the righteous:

> The atonement of suffering and death is not limited to the suffering person. The atoning effect extends to all the generation. This is especially the case with such sufferers as cannot either by reason of their righteous life or by their youth possibly have merited the afflictions which have come upon them. The death of the righteous atones just as well as certain sacrifices [with reference to b. Mo'ed Qatan 28a]. "They are caught (suffer) for the sins of the generation. If there are no righteous, the children of the schools (that is, the innocent young children) are caught for the sins of the generation" [b. Shabbat 32b]. There are also applied to Moses the Scriptural words, "And he bore the sins of many" (Isa. 53 [12]), because of his offering himself as an atonement for Israel's sin with the golden calf, being ready to sacrifice his very soul for Israel when he said, "And if not, blot me, I pray thee, out of thy book (that is, from the Book of the Living), which thou hast written" (Exod. 32 [32] [b. Sotah 14a; b. Berakhoth 32a]). *This readiness to sacrifice oneself for Israel is characteristic of all the great men of Israel, the patriarchs and the Prophets acting in the same way, whilst also some Rabbis would, on certain occasions, exclaim, "Behold, I am the atonement of Israel"* [Mekhilta 2a; m. Negaim 2:1].[269]

I remind you once again: This is the teaching of the Talmud not the New Testament, yet it is this very teaching that demonstrates to us just how biblical and Jewish the doctrine is.

Almost every Jew has learned about the Maccabees, those noble warriors who fought against the oppressive Greek rulers in the second century B.C.E. It is their victory that we celebrate at Hannukah. But how many of us know what the Book of Fourth Maccabees (written by a Jewish author between 100 B.C.E. and 100 C.E.) records about the significance of their deaths? It is written that they prayed, "Cause our chastisement to be an expiation for them. Make my blood their purification and take my soul as a ransom for their souls" (4 Maccabees 6:28–29). Of these righteous martyrs it is recorded: "They have become as a ransom for the sin of our nation, and by the blood of these righteous men and the propitiation of their death, Divine Providence delivered Israel" (4 Maccabees 17:22).

Where did this concept of righteous martyrdom first arise? According to Jewish tradition, it went back to the binding of Isaac. When Abraham was ready to offer his own son as a sacrifice to God, this same Book of Fourth Maccabees states: "Isaac offered himself for the sake of righteousness. . . . Isaac did not shrink when he saw the knife lifted against him by his father's hand" (4 Maccabees 13:12; 16:20).

This was the understanding of the rabbis. They believed that Isaac was a grown man (actually, thirty-seven years old!) when God tested Abraham, commanding him to offer Isaac on Mount Moriah (Genesis 22). Although the biblical account emphasizes the obedience of Abraham, the rabbis also stressed the obedience of Isaac. In fact, there is a midrash that says at the time of creation, when God was about to make man, the angels asked what man's significance was. One of his answers was this: "You shall see a father slay his son, and the son consenting to be slain, to sanctify my Name" (Tanhuma, Vayyera, sec. 18). That was the height of sacrificial service: A father offering up his own son, and the son willingly laying down his life for the glory of God. Yes, I know that sounds like the gospel. In fact, the midrash compares Isaac, who carried on his shoulder the wood for the burnt offering (himself!), to "one who carries his cross on his own shoulder."[270]

And here is something truly fascinating: Although Isaac was *not* sacrificed, the rabbis taught that "Scripture credits Isaac with having died and his ashes having lain upon the altar" (Midrash HaGadol on Genesis 22:19). Yes, "God regards the ashes of Isaac as though they were piled upon the altar" (Sifra, 102c; b. Ta'anit 16a).

But there was a problem here. Geza Vermes, a world-renowned specialist in early Jewish traditions, from whose study on the binding of Isaac we have taken several of the previous references, explains that the rabbis needed to take this a step further because of the Rabbinic view that there was no atonement without the shedding of blood. (For more on this point, see above, 3.10.) So the rabbis needed to teach that Isaac actually shed his blood. And they did! One ancient source, compiled less than two hundred years after the death of Jesus, states, "The Holy One, blessed be He, said to Moses: 'I keep faith to pay the reward of Isaac son of Abraham, who gave one fourth of his blood on the altar'" (Mekhilta d'Rashbi, p. 4; Tanh. Vayerra, sec. 23).[271]

Vermes also notes that the "blood of the Binding of Isaac" is mentioned four times in the early Jewish midrash called the Mekhilta of Rabbi Ishmael. In Exodus 12:13, God promised the Israelites that when he passed through the land to destroy the firstborn sons of the Egyptians, he would pass over the houses of the Israelites who had applied the blood of the Passover lambs to the lintels and doorposts of their houses. The midrash interprets the verse to mean, "'And when I see the blood, I will pass over you'—I see the blood of the Binding of Isaac." God wasn't looking at the blood of the lambs, he was looking at the blood of Isaac.

Vermes even states that

> according to ancient Jewish theology, the atoning efficacy of the *Tamid* offering [the fixed, daily offering], of all the sacrifices in which a lamb was immolated, and perhaps, basically, of all expiatory sacrifice irrespective of the nature of the victim, depended upon the virtue of the Akedah [the binding of Isaac], the self-offering of that Lamb whom God had recognized as the perfect victim of the perfect burnt offering.[272]

In keeping with this, one of the Targums to the Torah puts this prayer in the mouth of Abraham: "Now I pray for mercy before You, O Lord God, that when the children of Isaac come to a time of distress You may remember on their behalf the Binding of Isaac their father, and loose and forgive them their sins and deliver them from all distress."[273] This tradition is reflected in the New Year prayer of the Talmudic Rabbi Bibi bar Abba: "So when the children of Isaac commit sin and do evil, remember on their behalf the Binding of Isaac . . . and full of compassion towards them, be merciful to them."[274]

This same thought is also carried over in a prayer still included in the additional service for the Jewish New Year (Rosh Hashanah), which culminates with the words, "Remember today the Binding of Isaac with mercy to his descendants." We are forgiven through the merit of the sacrifice of Isaac! The rabbis even taught that the final resurrection of the dead would take place "through the merits of Isaac, who offered himself upon the altar" (Pesikta deRav Kahana, 32). Did you have any idea that such traditions existed among our people?

As we noted earlier, Solomon Schechter observed that "some [Talmudic] Rabbis would, on certain occasions, exclaim, 'Behold, I am the atonement of Israel.'" To this day, when a leading rabbi dies, it is quite common for the mourners to say, "May his death serve as an atonement for us!" And in a moving account from the Holocaust, Rabbi Shem Klingberg, known among his followers as the Zaloshitzer Rebbe, was led out to be slaughtered by the Nazis. In a matter of moments, after saying his last prayer, he would be gunned down, but first, he stopped, lifted his eyes to heaven, and cried out in a piercing voice, "Let me be an atonement for Israel!"[275] It is deeply ingrained in Jewish tradition that the death of the righteous atones.

Let me explain the logic behind this fundamental truth, followed by clear biblical support. If someone sins and as a result of that sin experiences difficulty and hardship, we commonly say they are "suffering for their sins" or "paying for their sins." The more serious the sin, the greater the suffering. This concept is found in Leviticus 26:43 and Isaiah 40:1–2:

> For the land will be deserted by them and will enjoy its sabbaths while it lies desolate without them. They will pay for their sins because they rejected my laws and abhorred my decrees.

> Comfort, comfort my people,
>   says your God.
> Speak tenderly to Jerusalem,
>   and proclaim to her
> that her hard service has been completed,
>   that her sin has been paid for,
> that she has received from the LORD's hand
>   double for all her sins.

In light of such verses, it's easy to see how the rabbis arrived at concepts such as "exile atones" (b. Berakhoth 56a; b. Sanhedrin 37b). In other words, because of serious, persistent, corporate sins, the people of Israel would go into exile, and when they had served their time, so to say, they would be regathered to the Land, much like a criminal going to jail for one year, five years, or life without parole, depending on the crime committed. Of course, it is significant that the Hebrew nowhere uses the word *atone* in any of these contexts, since atonement had to do with removing guilt and purifying from sin, not just "paying for it." Still, it's easy to understand this line of thinking, and there certainly is some truth behind it. The rabbis carried it through in great detail.

As we saw previously (above, 3.11), the rabbis taught that for some sins the simple act of repentance was sufficient to secure forgiveness. For other sins, repentance and restitution were required before forgiveness was granted by God. For another class of sins, even after repentance and restitution, forgiveness was suspended until the Day of Atonement. For yet another class of sins, even after repentance, restitution, and the Day of Atonement, forgiveness was suspended until the guilty party passed through a certain amount of suffering.

Finally, for the last class of sins, even after repentance, restitution, the Day of Atonement, and sufferings, forgiveness was suspended until death. In other words, the death of the guilty party served as the final payment for his sins (see b. Yoma 85b; Mishneh Torah, Hilkhot HaTeshuvah 1:4). In fact, according to early Jewish law, before a man was stoned to death for his crimes, he was asked to make public confession, and, the Mishnah teaches, if he does not know how to confess, he is told to say, "Let my death be an atonement for all my transgressions" (m. Sanhedrin 6:2).[276]

Now, let's take this one step further and go directly to the Torah. According to Numbers 25, the children of Israel had committed sin with the Moabites, worshiping their gods and sleeping with their women. The Lord's anger burned against them, and a plague began to spread among the people. "The LORD said to Moses, 'Take all the leaders of these people, kill them and expose them in broad daylight before the LORD, so that the Lord's fierce anger may turn away from Israel'" (Num. 25:4). God would be satisfied with the death of the ringleaders. Their punishment would suffice for the nation.

Then, an Israelite man brought a Moabite woman into his tent in full view of Moses and the people. "When Phinehas son of Eleazar, the son of Aaron, the priest, saw this, he left the assembly, took a spear in his hand and followed the Israelite into the tent. He drove the spear through both of them—through the Israelite and into the woman's body. Then the plague against the Israelites was stopped" (Num. 25:7–8).

The slaying of these representative sinners turned away God's wrath from the people. Here is where the text gets interesting. In light of his actions, the Lord promised Phinehas and his descendants a lasting covenant of peace, "because he was zealous for the honor of his God and *made atonement for the Israelites*" (Num. 25:13). How did he "make atonement for the Israelites"? By putting to death the public, representative sinners. *Their* death was sufficient punishment for the rest.[277]

If death could serve as a payment for an *individual's* specific sin, then, in the case of specific *corporate* sin, the death of the ringleaders could serve as a payment for the specific sins of the community as a whole. But what about the death of the righteous? What if the most righteous leader in the community offered up his own life as a ransom payment? What if he said, "Kill me, but let them go." How much would his death be worth?

When terrorists take a hostage, they take someone of standing and prominence, and that one life serves as a bargaining chip, something we can easily understand in natural terms. How much weight does the life of the Pope carry in the eyes of the Catholic Church? How valuable would the life of a Hasidic Rebbe be to his followers? What if the lives of all the people in a large Catholic or Hasidic community were threatened, and their Pope or Rebbe offered to die in their place? Wouldn't that one life—and death—be considered to be of far greater worth than the lives of even millions of his followers? Without doubt. It would be considered far more significant too.

In God's sight, the lives of his righteous servants have great value, and their deaths carry weight. In fact, there is abundant material to be found in Jewish tradition regarding the "merits of the patriarchs" or the "merits of the righteous,"[278] and there is no life more valuable than that of the Messiah, the perfectly righteous one, and no death more important than his. When he died, his death served as a ransom payment for the sins of the entire world. That was why he came into this world, not to be served, "but to serve, and to give his life as a ransom for many" (Mark 10:45).

At this point you might ask, "But where is that taught in the Hebrew Bible?" We learned earlier (3.10) that the sacrificial system was based on the principle of life for life. An innocent victim took the place of the guilty party. Then, if we make a careful comparison of Numbers 8:12 with Numbers 8:10, 19 we see that *the Levites themselves* served to "make atonement" or "turn away wrath" on behalf of the Israelites. As explained by Jacob Milgrom, one of the foremost experts on the biblical system of atonement, "our text, [Num.] 8:19, would then imply that the Levites are *ransom for Israel,* a lightning rod to attract God's wrath upon themselves whenever an Israelite encroached among the sancta [i.e., the holy place]."[279] What a vivid expression: The Levites served as "a lightning rod to attract God's wrath upon themselves" whenever an Israelite violated the Holy Place.

Turning to Numbers 35, we discover that the death of the high priest had atoning power. The context refers to intentional or unintentional manslaughter. In the case of willful homicide, the murderer had to be put to death, because "bloodshed pollutes the land, and atonement cannot be made for the land on which blood has been shed, except by the blood of the one who shed it" (Num. 35:33).

The only way to remove the pollution of bloodshed was by the blood of the one who first shed it. No other form of atonement was acceptable. But in the case of unintentional homicide, the manslayer would flee to a protected place called a city of refuge, where he would remain for the rest of his life (Num. 35:1–15, 22–25). There was only one thing that could secure his release from the city of refuge: the death of the high priest. "The accused must stay in his city of refuge until the death of the high priest; only after the death of the high priest may he return to his own property" (Num. 35:28).

This is critically important. Blood had been shed unintentionally. Someone was killed, the land was polluted, and the only acceptable ransom payment was the death of the one who killed. But he was not worthy of death. The homicide was accidental. So the innocent manslayer was banished to the city of refuge for life, unless the high priest, the people's representative spiritual leader and the one who interceded for the nation, died. The high priest's death would release him. The death of the high priest would take the place of his own.

The Talmud (m. Makkot 2:6; b. Makkot 11b; see also Leviticus Rabbah 10:6) asks the question: Isn't it the exile of the innocent manslayer [in the city of refuge] that expiates? The answer is no. "It is not the exile that expiates, but the death of the high priest." And Milgrom comments, "As the High Priest atones for Israel's sins through his cultic [i.e., ritual] service in his lifetime (Exod. 28:36; Lev. 16:16, 21), so he atones for homicide through his death."[280]

This theme finds its climax in the Hebrew Scriptures in the portrait of the righteous, Suffering Servant of the Lord in Isaiah 53. There we read these powerful words:

> Surely he took up our infirmities
>   and carried our sorrows,
> yet we considered him stricken by God,
>   smitten by him, and afflicted.
> But he was pierced for our transgressions,
>   he was crushed for our iniquities;
> the punishment that brought us peace was upon him,
>   and by his wounds we are healed.
> We all, like sheep, have gone astray,
>   each of us has turned to his own way;
> and the LORD has laid on him
>   the iniquity of us all.
>
>   Isaiah 53:4–6

Now you understand why so many Jews through the ages have read these verses and suddenly exclaimed, "That's talking about Jesus! He was our righteous Messiah. He died for our sins. His death served as a ransom for our souls. Now I see it. Now I understand."

In the closing verse of Isaiah 53, God promises, "Therefore I will give him a portion among the great, and he will divide the spoils with the strong, because he poured out his life unto death, and was numbered with the transgressors. For he bore the sin of many, and made intercession for the transgressors" (v. 12). The Messiah bore our sins! This is exactly what Peter, known as Shimon Kepha, wrote more than 150 years before the Mishnah was finalized:

> When they hurled their insults at him, he did not retaliate; when he suffered, he made no threats. Instead, he entrusted himself to him who judges justly. He himself bore our sins in his body on the tree, so that we might die to sins and live for righteousness; by his wounds you have been healed. For you were like sheep going astray, but now you have returned to the Shepherd and Overseer of your souls.
>
> 1 Peter 2:23–25

How odd it is that some Jewish interpreters can read these very verses from Isaiah 53 in terms of Israel's hardships and deaths and claim that the sufferings of our people paid for the sins of the nations (an interpretation that is easily refuted; see vol. 3, 4.5–4.17), but when Messianic Jews read Isaiah 53 in terms of the atoning power of the death of the Messiah, these same interpreters say, "The text has nothing to do with paying for anybody's sins."

Others have objected, saying, "Nowhere in Jewish teaching does a sacrifice pay for future sins." But what then is meant by the traditional prayer, "May the death of Rabbi X serve as an atonement for this generation"?[281] Surely that included sins committed by his generation after his death. And what about the Rabbinic tradition concerning the meritorious power of the binding of Isaac, effective for all subsequent generations and even the resurrection of the dead? And what of the words of Rabbi Shimon bar Yohai recorded in the Talmud in b. Sukkah 45b:

> [Because of the troubles I have known], I can free the entire world from punishment from the day on which I was born to this very moment, and were my son, Eliezer with me, it would be from the day on which the world was made to this moment, and were Yotam ben Uzziah [a famous, righteous sufferer] with us, it would be from the day on which the world was made to its very end.[282]

The rabbi's sentiment, to be sure, was noble, his exaggeration beyond belief.

But there *is* one whose perfect life and substitutionary death can free every one of us from the guilt of our sins, satisfying the wrath of God and making complete atonement for us all. The Messiah, the obedient Son, said to his Father, "Let my life be an atonement for them." And God said, "It is enough." "For [the Messiah] died for sins once for all, the righteous for the unrighteous, to bring you to God" (1 Peter 3:18).

As Saul of Tarsus, known around the world as the apostle Paul, explained:

> You see, at just the right time, when we were still powerless, [Messiah] died for the ungodly. Very rarely will anyone die for a righteous man, though for a good man someone might possibly dare to die. But God demonstrates his own love for us in this: While we were still sinners, [Messiah] died for us. Since we have now been justified by his blood, how much more shall we be saved from God's wrath through him! For if, when we were God's enemies, we were reconciled to him through the death of his Son, how much more, having been reconciled, shall we be saved through his life! Not only is this so, but we also rejoice in God through our Lord Jesus [the Messiah], through whom we have now received reconciliation.
>
> Romans 5:6–11

The "Christian gospel" is Jewish! The death of the righteous—the *truly* righteous, the Messiah, the High Priest of Israel and the nations, the Redeemer who pays for our sins—atones.

Now, stop for a moment and take stock of your own life. What if you were to write on individual pieces of paper every sin you ever committed: every lie, every selfish deed, every unclean act, every lustful thought, every angry word, every unkind attitude, every single time you chose not to obey the Lord, every time you had the opportunity to do good and didn't do it, every time you broke one of God's commands, large or small, by commission or omission . . . is there any end to the list? Soon those pieces of paper would become a mountain! And that would reflect only your own sins—in fact, it would reflect only the sins of which you were aware. What about the mountain of my sins? And what about the sins of the rest of the human race? Multiply those mountains six billion times. And that would only cover this generation! What about the countless multitudes who lived here for the thousands of years before us? Our cumulative guilt is staggering.

Who could possibly pay for these mountains and mountains of sins? The Son of God could. The Son of God did! The life and death of the Messiah was of infinite worth in His Father's sight, and his blood makes atonement for us in full. It even seems that the Zohar, in its typical mystical terms, grasped the role of the Messiah in all this. In commenting on a passage just cited, Isaiah 53:5, the Zohar relates:

> The Messiah enters [the Hall of the Sons of Illness] and summons all the diseases and all the pains and all the sufferings of Israel that they should come upon him, and all of them come upon him. And would he not thus bring ease to Israel and take their sufferings upon himself, no man could endure the sufferings Israel has to undergo because they neglected the Torah.[283]

Had not the Messiah taken our place, suffering on our behalf, we would have perished long ago.

Let the truth be told. God did not ultimately want the blood of bulls and lambs, nor did Isaac die for our sins, and all the righteous martyrs and godly priests could never make us truly whole. The Messiah did it, once and for all. The death of the righteous atones. Through him you can make a break with your past, receive the forgiveness of sins, and start with a brand-new slate. Through him your life can be changed. The Messiah took your place. Today can be *your* Day of Atonement if you fully trust in him.

3.16. I can't believe the death of Jesus paid for my sins because the Torah teaches that for blood to be effectual, it had to be poured on the altar in a specific way. This obviously does not refer to Jesus.

> The specific laws in the Torah regarding the sprinkling of the blood on the altar had to do with the sacrifices offered on that altar. In those cases, specific regulations applied. At other times in the Hebrew Scriptures, blood and sacrifices were offered in different ways and in different places. More importantly, there is obviously no connection between the laws for offering animal sacrifices on the altar and the Jewish teaching that "the death of the righteous atones." Therefore, the blood of those righteous martyrs did not have to be poured out on the altar of Jerusalem.

The first time I heard this objection was in a public debate in 1986, and most of the crowd seemed surprised that the objection was even raised. After all, the answer seemed obvious: There were specific laws regarding how the blood of animal sacrifices was to be applied to the altar; the blood of the Messiah pointed to that which the animal's blood only typified. Of course, if Messianic Jews believed in human sacrifice (which we don't), and if the Torah called for human sacrifices and required that the blood of those sacrifices be placed on the altar in a specific way to atone for sins (which it doesn't), then I would agree with your objection. In fact, it would then be fair to ask you, "If Yeshua's blood had been shed on the Temple altar in Jerusalem according to the Torah's requirements, would you then believe in him?"

Naturally, I could point out that at certain times and under certain circumstances, God accepted blood sacrifices that were *not* offered up on the altar in Jerusalem (see, e.g., 2 Sam. 24:17–25 and 1 Kings 18:31–39).[284] This, however, is not the real issue, since (1) the sacrifices prescribed by the Torah *prefigured* the sacrificial death of the Messiah, but the Messiah himself was not to be treated like an actual animal sacrifice (e.g., the priests did not offer him up, nor did they eat his flesh after his death, nor did they remove his entrails); and (2) in keeping with biblical teaching and Jewish tradition, Yeshua willingly offered his life as a righteous martyr making atonement for the sins of the world. Thus, his blood was not poured out on the altar any more than was the blood of religious Jews through the ages whose deaths were considered an atonement for their generation (see above, 3.15).

If you have an argument, it is with the prophet Isaiah, who wrote in 53:10 that the Lord would make his righteous servant an *'asham* (guilt offering).[285] Yet according to your objection, the servant would have had to shed his blood on the altar in Jerusalem if he were really to be a guilt offering. This is, quite obviously, farfetched and misses the point that these were *images* and *types* to be fulfilled, not regulations to be carried out in detail.

The altar blood had to do with altar sacrifices. The blood of the Messiah had to do with the principles typified by those sacrifices.[286] Thus, Hebrews 13:11–12 states, "The high priest carries the blood of animals into the Most Holy Place as a sin offering, but the bodies are burned outside the camp. And so Jesus also suffered outside the city gate to make the people holy through his own blood." Therefore, the Jewish people and the nations of the world have not been left without an atoning sacrifice. The Messiah paid it all, fulfilling the image and purpose of the Torah's system of atonement and shedding his blood on our behalf.

3.17. If the death of Jesus was the fulfillment of the sacrificial system, why do the prophets anticipate sacrifices when the Third Temple is built?

I'm glad you raised this objection, since it has the merit of acknowledging the importance of sacrifices and offerings in the prophetic books (which is the exact opposite of the premise of objection 3.9, above). However, from our current vantage point, it is difficult for us to know exactly what God was speaking through the prophets concerning a future Temple with restored sacrifices. Was the language merely symbolic, with the Temple speaking of God's presence among his people and sacrifices speaking of their worshipful response? Or will the prophecies be literally, not symbolically, fulfilled? In that case, were the prophets speaking of a Temple to be built by the Messiah in the age to come? If so, then we could cite the Rabbinic tradition that in the age to come all sacrifices and offerings will be abolished except for thanksgiving offerings. These sacrifices would then be of a non-atoning character, and therefore would have nothing to do with the once-and-for-all atonement purchased for us by the sacrifice of Jesus the Messiah. In any case, we should use caution in our discussion here, as did the Talmudic rabbis, realizing how difficult it is to clearly interpret some of the key, relevant chapters in the Tanakh.

There are several passages in the prophetic books that appear to anticipate sacrifices in the context of an end-time, Messianic vision—in other words, in passages that Christians would interpret with reference to the *second coming* of Jesus. However, the New Testament seems to indicate that Jesus, through his death and resurrection, made any future sacrifices completely unnecessary:

Unlike the other high priests, he does not need to offer sacrifices day after day, first for his own sins, and then for the sins of the people. He sacrificed for their sins once for all when he offered himself.

Hebrews 7:27

First [the Messiah] said, "Sacrifices and offerings, burnt offerings and sin offerings you did not desire, nor were you pleased with them" (although the law required them to be made). Then he said, "Here I am, I have come to do your will." He sets aside the first to establish the second. And by that will, we have been made holy through the sacrifice of the body of Jesus [the Messiah] once for all.

Hebrews 10:8–10

"That's the whole point," you say. "Since these texts state that Yeshua's death on the cross made future sacrifices unnecessary, why then would God say through his prophets that sacrifices would be restored in a future Messianic Temple? Doesn't that contradict the message of the New Testament? Doesn't that contradict the entire Christian gospel?" Let's see exactly what the prophets had to say.

We will consider first the vision of Ezekiel recorded in the last eight chapters of his book, in which the prophet describes a Temple that was to be built, complete with an altar, sacrifices, and priests. Ezekiel saw the glory of God fill that Temple, the very same glory that years earlier he had seen leave the Temple in Jerusalem, shortly before its destruction (see Ezekiel 10). The Lord gave a wonderful promise:

> Son of man, this is the place of my throne and the place for the soles of my feet. This is where I will live among the Israelites forever. The house of Israel will never again defile my holy name—neither they nor their kings—by their prostitution and the lifeless idols of their kings at their high places. When they placed their threshold next to my threshold and their doorposts beside my doorposts, with only a wall between me and them, they defiled my holy name by their detestable practices. So I destroyed them in my anger. Now let them put away from me their prostitution and the lifeless idols of their kings, and I will live among them forever.

Ezekiel 43:7–9

Ezekiel also received detailed instructions regarding the Temple altar and the restored sacrificial system, including commands to offer sin offerings and guilt offerings, with the blood being used for atonement (see, e.g., Ezek. 42:13; 43:18–21; there are references to making atonement for the altar, the Temple, and the people of Israel; see 43:20, 26; 45:15, 17, 20). Based on these chapters, it would seem clear that Ezekiel, writing by divine inspiration, described a fully functioning Temple where the sins of the people of Israel could be expiated by means of blood sacrifices. How then do I reconcile that description with the verses we just read from Hebrews, pointing to the once-and-for-all nature of Yeshua's sacrificial death?

On the one hand, I believe this portion of Scripture presents potential problems for traditional Jews as well as Messianic Jews, since traditional Judaism teaches that prayer, repentance, and charity replaced the sacrificial system—in fact, as we saw above (3.9; cf. also 3.8, 3.13), anti-missionaries claim that prayer, repentance, and charity were *superior* to sacrifices and were *preferred* by the Lord to sacrifices—yet Ezekiel is telling us that the glorious, end-time Temple will have a restored animal sacrifice system. Based on the anti-missionary logic, this would be a decided step *backward*. On the other hand, the fact that there would be future blood sacrifices offered up for Israel's atonement presents difficulties for Messianic Jews, since it seems to make void the Messiah's atoning death on our behalf. So again we ask, What's the answer?

Before responding directly to that question, let me share with you the comments of leading traditional Jewish authors. Rabbi Dr. S. Fisch, in his compendium of the most important Rabbinic commentaries on Ezekiel, made these telling remarks concerning chapters 40–48:

> These closing chapters present almost insuperable difficulties. They contain discrepancies, contradictions with Pentateuchal laws, and terms which do not occur elsewhere. . . . The Rabbis of the Talmud (Men. 45a) remarked that only the prophet Elijah, who will herald the ultimate redemption, will elucidate these chapters. They added the observation that had it not been for Rabbi Chanina ben Hezekiah, who explained several of these difficulties, the Book of Ezekiel would have been excluded from the Scriptural canon.[287]

Similarly, Rav Dr. Joseph Breuer, writing from a thoroughly Orthodox perspective, introduced these difficult chapters in Ezekiel with the following remarks:

> We will not presume to give a detailed commentary on these passages. We will merely attempt to set down some thoughts they engender, and even that only with the greatest circumspection. Especially when the Prophet deals with Jewish law, we have followed the interpretations of our Sages and Commentators and, in particular, those given by Rashi, even where those clearly pose problems. In many instances we will have to do without a complete explanation. Our reticence is justified by the comment of the Rambam: "The future structure to be built, even though it is written of in Ezekiel, is not interpreted or explained" (Hilkhot Bet

HaBehira, 1:4). Hence, the writings of Ezekiel pertaining to the future Sanctuary are beyond our clear and detailed understanding.[288]

In light of these comments, I think you would agree that it is unwise to build a major theological doctrine from Ezekiel 40–48—especially a doctrine that you would use in an attempt to deny the validity of belief in Yeshua the Messiah. What if the shoe were on the other foot and I were using these chapters to prove to you the necessity of faith in Jesus? You would surely say to me—with ample justification— "This is hardly the place from which you can deduce Messianic proof texts. Maimonides even told us that Ezekiel's Temple vision could not be interpreted from our present, limited vantage point."

Over and again in the Talmud (b. Menahot 45a), as apparent discrepancies are found between Ezekiel's Temple laws and the comparable laws in the Torah, the sages respond with, "Elijah will explain it in the future!" And as mentioned by Rabbi Fisch, it is Chaninah ben Hezekiah who is credited with saving the Book of Ezekiel from being suppressed (Hebrew, *nignaz,* literally, "hidden away"), since the tradition states that he stayed in his attic until he finished expounding these chapters, using three hundred cruises of oil to—literally—keep the midnight oil burning.[289] However, as Rashi explains, because of our sins, all of Chaninah's interpretations have been lost.[290] In the light of such difficulties, how can anyone possibly use these chapters in Ezekiel to prove a major doctrinal point? If traditional Jews struggled to reconcile Ezekiel's words with the words of Moses without much success—leaving most of the problems for Elijah to figure out—why should Messianic Jews be faulted if they don't all agree on one, airtight, dogmatic interpretation of these chapters that is in full and complete harmony with the words of the New Testament?

There is one other major problem that we should note with regard to these chapters: It seems clear that Ezekiel was led to anticipate the building of this Temple *in his lifetime.* Remember, Ezekiel had been in exile for years when the First Temple was destroyed (note Ezek. 33:21–22), and now God was speaking to him about revealing his glory, forgiving his people, and bringing the exiles back to the Land (see Ezek. 39:21–29). It is in this context that the Lord gave Ezekiel the vision of the Temple. In other words, God said that he would have mercy on his people, restore them to the Promised Land, and call them to build a Temple that would be filled with his presence. How then was Ezekiel to know that this vision did not refer to the *Second* Temple (which was, in fact, built by the returning exiles just a few decades later), but rather to a *Third* Temple, which, twenty-five hundred years later, has still not been built?

In addition to this, God actually said to Ezekiel in this vision,

> Son of man, describe the temple to the people of Israel, that they may be ashamed of their sins. Let them consider the plan, and if they are ashamed of all they have done, make known to them the design of the temple—its arrangement, its exits and entrances—its whole design and all its regulations and laws. Write these down before them so that they may be faithful to its design and follow all its regulations.
>
> Ezekiel 43:10–11

Ezekiel was commanded to share with his contemporaries the design of the Temple with a view toward bringing them to repentance in order that they, in turn, could build the Temple according to the divine specifications. We can safely say, then, that things did not turn out as Ezekiel might well have expected.[291]

This difficulty is underscored by the comments of the illustrious Rabbi David Kimchi (Radak), who actually finds proof of the resurrection of the dead in Ezekiel 43:10. Explaining the words "let them measure [NIV, consider] the plan," he writes:

> They will measure the design of the form of the House which you will show them, and they will understand it as a sign that they will yet rebuild the Temple in the future when the Redeemer comes and the dead are resurrected. They will understand it as a sign that those who see this form will be alive when the Temple is rebuilt in the future, and this is proof of the resurrection of the dead.[292]

What an interpretation! Ezekiel will show the Temple plans to his contemporaries who will one day build that very Temple, but that day will not come until the Messianic age—which proves the resurrection of the dead. So instead of the plain and obvious meaning of the text—namely, that the Jews to whom Ezekiel would show the plans would repent and then build the Temple *in their lifetimes*—Radak tells us that the very fact that those same men will build the Temple thousands of years later demonstrates that they will be raised from the dead. What eloquent testimony to the fact that these chapters present problems to all interpreters, Jewish or Christian.

Radak also draws attention to Ezekiel 43:19, where the prophet is told, "*You are* to give a young bull as a sin offering to the priests, who are Levites, of the family of Zadok, who come near to minister before me, declares the Sovereign LORD." (See also the following verses, in which Ezekiel is told, "*You are* to take some of its blood . . . *You are* to take the bull for the sin offering . . . *you are* to offer a male goat without defect for a sin offering . . . *you are* to offer a young bull and a ram from the flock . . . *You are* to offer them before the LORD . . . *you are* to provide a male goat daily for a sin offering." Similar expressions are found in chapters 44–48, where Ezekiel is told how *he* is to perform other Temple functions, allot the land to the tribes of Israel, and divide the city.) As rendered by Rabbi A. J. Rosenberg, the prolific translator of Rabbinic commentaries into English, Radak writes:

> God tells Ezekiel, who is a priest, that he will give the sacrifice to the priests to offer up; but he himself will sprinkle the blood to make the altar fit for atonement. For although Aaron will be there, Ezekiel will be the High Priest, or perhaps Ezekiel will be Aaron's assistant. Accordingly, this verse refers to the future resurrection of the dead. According to the Rabbis, who say that these verses are speaking of the altar of the Second Temple, it is possible that Ezekiel returned from Babylon with the former exiles. However, there is a tradition that Ezekiel was buried in Babylon. Moreover, sacrificial procedures delineated here were not performed by the returnees from the exile, who built the altar before building the Temple (Ezra 3:1ff.).[293]

How fascinating! Traditional Jewish translators actually wonder if some of these verses apply to the Second Temple—based on the most obvious reading of the text, which would make Ezekiel a central figure in the actual building and serving of the Temple. But it is also obvious from reading the text that the promised restoration—which would be glorious and transforming in its effects—did not come to pass either. This really presented some problems, as we learn from Rashi's commentary on Ezekiel 43:11. As explained by Rosenberg:

> Just as Joshua entered the Land in a miraculous manner and vanquished the peoples of Canaan, so should Ezra have entered the Land in such a manner and vanquished its inhabitants. However, since the people had sinned, they did not merit such a conquest. *Rashi* adds that the redemption then would have been permanent and that they would have built this Temple described to Ezekiel. *Rashi* adds that their sin was that they had not truly repented of their previous sins. They had not taken upon themselves to cease sinning. He quotes others who attribute their failure to attain this miraculous conquest to their intermarriage with gentile women in Babylon.[294]

Rashi is stating that Ezekiel's Temple *should have been built* in the days of Ezra—in other words, within decades of Ezekiel's prophetic vision—but because of Israel's sin, it was not.[295] Therefore, the vision had to be postponed until a Third Temple would be built, although that was not what God originally intended, nor could it have been what Ezekiel understood.

Now, in quoting these commentaries at length, I in no way mean to belittle the likes of Rashi and Radak, both of whom were intellectual giants and brilliant scholars of the highest order. Rather, by quoting their remarks, I mean to underscore the interpretive difficulties found in Ezekiel 40–48, as the commentaries of Rashi and Radak illustrate so well. Given the fact, then, that the Talmudic rabbis could only wait for Elijah to come and explain the apparent problems in these chapters, I ask again, "How then can these same chapters be used to argue against the Messiah's once-and-for-all atoning death on the cross?"

"I think I have the answer," you reply. "The *details* may be unclear, but the *principles* are perfectly clear. In the future there will be sin offerings and guilt offerings, and that fact by itself proves that your emphasis on the atoning power of the blood of Jesus is unsupported."

Not at all. First, the sages never said it was just the details that were unclear. Rather, the difficulty of the details made the entire section of Scripture difficult to interpret. If the *specific laws* governing the sacrifices were unclear, how then can we say that the function of *the sacrifices themselves* was clear? Second, other Rabbinic traditions state that in the age to come, all sacrifices will be abolished except for thanksgiving offerings, leaving us to wonder exactly where this Temple visions fits in. (Is the Messianic age separate from the age to come, or are the two one and the same?) Third, it is fair to ask why the people of Israel will need atonement during the Messianic age (according to Radak, meaning the resurrection age), especially in light of the glorious vision of Ezekiel 47–48, where it is prophesied that the whole land will be filled with the glory of the Lord and with healing life. Fourth, as I said before, you would not believe me if I used these chapters to prove a point about Jesus. Instead, you would remind me of the Talmudic teaching that we'll have to wait for Elijah to come and straighten things out.

How then should we interpret these chapters? Obviously, I'm not entirely sure I grasp their full significance either, and it would be foolish to be dogmatic. But let me offer a few thoughts that might be helpful. In fact, let me begin by asking a question: What was God's purpose in calling Israel to build the Tabernacle? It is expressed in Exodus 25:8: "Then have them make a sanctuary [Hebrew, holy place] for me, and *I will dwell among them*." (Note that the verb for "dwell" is *sh-k-n*, from which we get the noun *shekina*, speaking of God's presence in our midst; see above, 3.1–3.2, and note Exod. 29:45.) This was also God's purpose in allowing Solomon to build the Temple: "As for this temple you are building, if you follow my decrees, carry out my regulations and keep all my commands and obey them, I will fulfill through you the promise I gave to David your father. And *I will live among the Israelites* and will not abandon my people Israel" (1 Kings 6:12–13; the Hebrew here is identical to Exod. 25:8; instead of "live" the text should say "dwell").

What is God's central promise in the Temple vision of Ezekiel? "Now let them put away from me their prostitution and the lifeless idols of their kings, and *I will live* [Hebrew, dwell] *among them forever*" (Ezek. 43:9). Once again, we see God's desire: He wants to dwell in the midst of his people. But you may have noticed a pattern in the three cases cited. In each of them, holiness is required. The Lord will not dwell in the midst of sin and spiritual filth. This leads us to another interesting observation on the part of Rashi and Radak. They believed that Ezekiel's vision coincided with the Day of Atonement, namely, the tenth day of the New Year (Hebrew, Rosh Hashanah, occurring in the month of Tishrei), and, following the Talmud (b. Arachin 12a), they claimed that the year he received his vision was actually a jubilee year.[296]

Why was this so important? According to Leviticus 25, the jubilee was to be celebrated every fiftieth year, beginning on the Day of Atonement. During this year, all debts were canceled and all slaves freed. It was the year of release, and according to the Talmud, Ezekiel's Temple vision was given on this particular date because it was the time for the Jewish people to be released from captivity in Babylon. As Radak observed, "Since slaves are released on this date, the Day of Atonement in the Jubilee year, God chose this time to show the prophet Israel's emergence from exile and the building plan of the future Temple, indicating that he would forgive Israel and no longer remember their sins."[297] This is highly significant, since it would mean that *three* themes of great importance were all intertwined here: (1) the theme of the Temple and God's dwelling among his repentant people; (2) the theme of atonement, because of the Temple sacrifices and the timing of the vision on the Day of Atonement; and (3) the theme of the release of God's people from captivity.

The problem is that the vision fell far short of fulfillment. Exiles did return, but not all of them, and the return was hardly glorious; the Temple was rebuilt, but it lacked the glory of Solomon's Temple (see vol. 1, 2.1), and it was not built according to Ezekiel's specifications; and Ezekiel never got to be a part of it.

What then do we make of all this? Could it be that Ezekiel, being a priest, spoke of things to come in the only language he had available? In other words, could it be that the vision is completely symbolic?

"Why do you suggest that?" you ask.

That's a fair question. I suggest it because of the problems mentioned above, namely, the many apparent contradictions between Ezekiel's vision and the Torah coupled with the fact that the promise to Ezekiel was not fulfilled in his lifetime, although the text seemed to indicate that he would be part of its fulfillment. We must ask then, Is there more to this than meets the eye? Perhaps the Scripture passage was never meant to be literally fulfilled.

Consider also that the prophets who spoke of Israel's return from exile (Jeremiah and Isaiah) or who spoke of the Second Temple being built (Haggai and Zechariah) described events so glorious that they could only be described as a new creation and a second exodus (see vol. 3, 4.5). But none of this panned out the way the prophets described, even though they made it clear that the glory of the Second Temple would be greater than the glory of the First Temple and that final atonement for Israel would be made during the days of that Temple (see vol. 1, 2.1). What happened?

I'll answer that in a moment, but first let's examine the possibility that Ezekiel's vision is filled with symbolic meaning and may not be intended to be interpreted literally. In other words, we're not waiting for Elijah to come and explain the details because it's not certain that the details were ever meant to be implemented. Rather, this vision was God's way of saying to his servant, "I will forgive my people, wipe away their sins, and bring my glory in their midst again. See it, taste it, touch it. It will surely happen!"

Ezekiel the priest was shown a vision of future glory, and for him, nothing could be more glorious than a restored Temple. And for a priest like Ezekiel, nothing could more certainly speak of purification and atonement than blood sacrifices. Nothing could convey a greater sense of promise that God would again favor his people than a vision such as this. (This is similar to the traditional Jewish notion that heaven will be something like an endless yeshiva on high. For a rabbi, what could be more wonderful?) Let me also remind you of the Rabbinic comments we just cited regarding the timing of the vision, namely, that "God chose this time to show the prophet Israel's emergence from exile and the building plan of the future Temple, indicating that he would forgive Israel and no longer remember their sins."

This brings us back to the theme of the prophesied return from exile and rebuilding of the Second Temple. Either the words of the prophets were not fulfilled because the Bible is not true (not an option for a traditional Jew or for me); or the words of the prophets were not fulfilled because of Israel's sins, a solution sometimes suggested by the rabbis (in which case God's detailed, specific, prophesied timetable goes out the window, again not an option for me and hardly one acceptable for a traditional Jew, despite the Rabbinic traditions); or God fulfilled his promises through the coming of the Messiah into the world (which makes sense in light of dozens of other Scripture passages).

What do I mean by "God fulfilled his promises through the coming of the Messiah into the world"? The answer is simple: The purpose God had for sending the Messiah into the world was that God might dwell in our midst forever. In fact, just as the Pharisees downplayed the importance of the Temple in Jerusalem by emphasizing the importance of the local synagogue and the individual Jewish home, the followers of Jesus pointed to a different kind of Temple, a spiritual Temple, a Temple made up of redeemed Jews and Gentiles, a Temple suitable for God.[298] Here are some New Testament descriptions of the people of God functioning as the Temple of God. He now dwells in us! "In him [namely, Jesus] the whole building is joined together and rises to become a holy temple in the Lord. And in him you too are being built together to become a dwelling in which God lives by his Spirit" (Eph. 2:21–22). "Don't you know that you yourselves are God's temple and that God's Spirit lives in you? If anyone destroys God's temple, God will destroy him; for God's temple is sacred, and you are that temple" (1 Cor. 3:16–17).

It is a Temple requiring holiness:

> What agreement is there between the temple of God and idols? For we are the temple of the living God. As God has said: "I will live with them and walk among them, and I will be their God, and they will be my people. Therefore come out from them and be separate, says the Lord. Touch no unclean thing, and I will receive you. I will be a Father to you, and you will be my sons and daughters, says the Lord Almighty." Since we have these promises, dear friends, let us purify ourselves from

everything that contaminates body and spirit, perfecting holiness out
of reverence for God.

2 Corinthians 6:16–7:1

It is a Temple in which we now offer spiritual sacrifices to the Lord,
beginning with the offering of our own lives: "Therefore, I urge you,
brothers, in view of God's mercy, to offer your bodies as living sacrifices, holy and pleasing to God—this is your spiritual act of worship"
(Rom. 12:1). "As you come to him, the living Stone—rejected by men
but chosen by God and precious to him—you also, like living stones,
are being built into a spiritual house to be a holy priesthood, offering spiritual sacrifices acceptable to God through Jesus [the Mes-
siah]" (1 Peter 2:4–5). "Through Jesus, therefore, let us continually
offer to God a sacrifice of praise—the fruit of lips that confess his
name. And do not forget to do good and to share with others, for with
such sacrifices God is pleased" (Heb. 13:15–16).

The point I am making is this: Ezekiel was given a vision of a soon-
to-be-built Temple in which the glory of God would dwell in the midst
of a purified people, yet the details of this vision make it questionable as to whether it would be *literally* fulfilled. Rather, it was God's
way of assuring his prophet that restoration and redemption were
near at hand, that the captives were about to be released, and that
atonement and forgiveness of sins would be provided. Through the
atoning death of our great High Priest, Yeshua the Messiah, Ezekiel's
vision has been set on the road to complete (spiritual) fulfillment,
and the Temple of God is now being built with living stones—with
Jews and Gentiles cleansed and purified with the Messiah's blood.

At the end of this transition age (see vol. 1, 2.1), Ezekiel's vision,
along with the rest of the prophecies of the Tanakh, will reach complete fulfillment. Take away the Messiah, however, and there is neither partial fulfillment, nor is there gradual fulfillment, nor is there
any hope of fulfillment ever coming. It would have been proven long
ago that the prophets were liars or dreamers, since they made it clear
that certain key events, including a divine visitation and final atonement, had to occur before that Temple's destruction in 70 c.e. (see
again vol. 1, 2.1 for details). In light of the New Testament's teaching
that the Lord is now building a worldwide spiritual Temple, it is certainly interesting that there has been no earthly Temple almost this
entire time. Do you see the significance of this?

There is something else worth considering, namely, the language
used elsewhere by Ezekiel and the prophets. Although they were

divinely inspired, they spoke in the language that they had, and so, when Ezekiel wanted to describe his own people living without defenses, peaceful and unsuspecting, he spoke of them living in "unwalled" villages (Ezek. 38:11).[299] Today we would speak of them living in "unarmed" cities. Similarly, when Zechariah described an end-time invasion of Israel, he spoke of armies coming on horses and mules (Zech. 12:4; 14:15). Today we would speak of troops coming in tanks, flying in jets, and launching scud missiles.

How then would the Spirit, communicating through Ezekiel, speak of God providing atonement for his people, of him dwelling in our midst, of the provision of forgiveness and reconciliation, of freedom from slavery and oppression? Could it be that he would do so through a glorious Temple vision, complete with sacrifices, offerings, and priests? I think that this is a possibility worthy of consideration.[300]

If, however, there will be a literal Temple built when the Messiah returns—a possibility we must consider, since we stated from the outset that we can't be dogmatic about this—and if there will be literal sacrifices offered for atonement on the Temple altar, this still does not make void Yeshua's sacrifice on our behalf. In fact, many biblical scholars—evangelical Christians and Messianic Jews—fully expect that this Temple will be built by Yeshua himself.[301] Further, one of their strongest arguments is that no such Temple was ever built and that there are differences between the Mosaic regulations and those given to Ezekiel, proving that this will be a millennial Temple built according to a new Torah. After all, in the new age, is it unthinkable— even to a traditional Jew—that there will be changes in the Torah? A new age would actually *necessitate* changes, since the Torah was made for Israel in this world, not the world to come.[302]

"I don't understand," you protest. "How can there be future animal sacrifices without such sacrifices constituting a denial of the Christian faith?"

The answer has to do with the nature and function of the sacrifices. That is to say, the sacrifices offered up according to the Torah—in other words, the sacrifices *anticipating* and *pointing toward* Yeshua's sacrifice for our sins (see vol. 3, 4.1)—were primarily related to the cleansing of outward defilement or the temporary (at best, annual) pronouncement of forgiveness, whereas the atoning death of Jesus actually transforms our natures. As expressed in the letter to the Hebrews:

> When [the Messiah] came as high priest of the good things that are already here, he went through the greater and more perfect tabernacle

that is not manmade, that is to say, not a part of this creation. He did not enter by means of the blood of goats and calves; but he entered the Most Holy Place [i.e., in heaven] once for all by his own blood, having obtained eternal redemption. The blood of goats and bulls and the ashes of a heifer sprinkled on those who are ceremonially unclean sanctify them so that they are outwardly clean. How much more, then, will the blood of [Messiah], who through the eternal Spirit offered himself unblemished to God, cleanse our consciences from acts that lead to death, so that we may serve the living God!

Hebrews 9:11–14

Just as sacrifices were offered for forty years after Yeshua's death and resurrection—and Messianic Jews apparently participated in some of those sacrificial rites (see Acts 21:17–26)—it could be that sacrifices will be offered in a future Temple, without being in conflict with the atonement provided for us in Jesus. They could even point *back* to his atoning death, just as the Torah sacrifices pointed toward it. In this way, the sacrifices would be memorial in nature, just as the regular reenactment of Yeshua's final Passover meal— known as communion or the Eucharist in Christian circles—serves as a constant reminder of his sacrifice for us: "While they were eating, Jesus took bread, gave thanks and broke it, and gave it to his disciples, saying, 'Take and eat; this is my body.' Then he took the cup, gave thanks and offered it to them, saying, 'Drink from it, all of you. This is my blood of the covenant, which is poured out for many for the forgiveness of sins'" (Matt. 26:26–28). "For whenever you eat this bread and drink this cup, you proclaim the Lord's death until he comes" (1 Cor. 11:26; the words of Paul to followers of Jesus in Corinth).

Just as the Lord's Supper serves as a memorial to his death, so also could animal sacrifices serve as a memorial to "the Lamb of God, who takes away the sin of the world" (John 1:29). In this regard, Ralph Alexander, a Christian biblical scholar, summarizes his view of the purpose of the sacrificial system in Ezekiel's vision:

The sacrificial system will be used as picture lessons to demonstrate the need for holiness in the consecration and purifying of the temple and the altar. They will be visual reminders of man's sinfulness and his need for redemption while at the same time being pictorial memorials of the finished and completed sacrifice of the Messiah who provided atonement for mankind once and for all. The pictures of a holy life and the need for continual commitment to the Messiah's lordship will be demonstrated in the regular burnt offerings. Thanksgiving to God will be visually expressed in the fellowship offerings. In addition, the sacrifices will provide food for the millennial priests even as it did for the Mosaic priests (44:29–31).[303]

May I raise one more question, however, that might put a different slant on all this? Should we really expect the restoration of animal sacrifices? Let me share with you the comments of Chief Rabbi Hertz, although he was coming from a slightly different angle on this:

> The Rabbis, however, hoped that with the progress of time, human conduct would advance to higher standards, so that there would no longer be any need for expiatory sacrifices. Only the feeling of gratitude to God would remain. "In the Messianic era, all offerings will cease, except the thanksgiving offering, which will continue forever" [For the source of this last quote, see below.].[304]

From this point of view, then, it would seem that the restoration of animal sacrifices would be a decided step *backward*, not forward, and it would also seem to be out of keeping with the concept of a glorious Messianic era. This was to be the age of once-and-for-all forgiveness and complete, undefiled righteousness. What need is there for sacrifices of atonement?

"Well, then," you ask, "how do you explain all the other prophecies about sacrifices in the Third Temple? It's one thing to point to the difficulty of interpreting Ezekiel's vision; it's another thing to ignore all the other prophecies."

Actually, out of all the prophets whose words were recorded in Scripture, four others make mention of future sacrifices, namely, Isaiah, Zechariah, Malachi, and Jeremiah. But there are three things that are highly significant about the relevant passages. (1) Only Jeremiah speaks of the Jewish people offering sacrifices in the future, while the others speak of Gentiles worshiping the God of Israel with offerings. (2) None of them speak of atonement or forgiveness of sin in the context of sacrifices and offerings. (3) The references to future sacrifices and offerings in Isaiah, Zechariah, and Malachi take up a total of *three* verses. They are hardly major subjects in these prophetic books.

The one brief reference in Zechariah occurs in the context of the nations of the world coming to worship in Jerusalem after Israel's final victory:

Then the survivors from all the nations that have attacked Jerusalem will go up year after year to worship the King, the LORD Almighty, and to celebrate the Feast of Tabernacles. . . . On that day HOLY TO THE LORD will be inscribed on the bells of the horses, and the cooking pots in the LORD's house will be like the sacred bowls in front of the altar. Every pot in Jerusalem and Judah will be holy to the LORD Almighty, and *all who come to sacrifice* will take some of the pots and cook in them. And on that day there will no longer be a Canaanite in the house of the LORD Almighty.

Zechariah 14:16, 20–21

At most, if read literally, these verses say that sacrifices will be offered by the nations every year during the Feast of Tabernacles, but the sacrifices could be thanksgiving offerings just as well as they could be atonement offerings. And notice the horses! A literal reading presents some problems here too, since it is quite a long trip by horseback from New Zealand or Alaska to Jerusalem. It could be, instead, that the phrase "come to sacrifice" is a metaphor for "come to worship," just as the statement that "there will no longer be a Canaanite in the house of the LORD Almighty" probably represents "anyone who is morally or spiritually unclean—anyone who is not included among the chosen people of God (cf. Isa. 35:8; Ezek. 43:7; 44:9; Rev. 21:27)."[305] This would then tie in with the word of the Lord given to Malachi in the days of the Second Temple:

"Oh, that one of you would shut the temple doors, so that you would not light useless fires on my altar! I am not pleased with you," says the LORD Almighty, "and I will accept no offering from your hands. My name will be great among the nations, from the rising to the setting of the sun. In every place *incense and pure offerings will be brought to my name*, because my name will be great among the nations," says the LORD Almighty.

Malachi 1:10–11

Thus, it could well be that the day will come when the nations of the world will literally burn incense and bring pure offerings to the Lord. It is also possible, however, that verses such as these are to be interpreted metaphorically—with incense and offerings representing prayer and worship—especially in light of the fact that it says this will happen *in every place*, not just in a future Temple in Jerusalem. In any case, there is no reference to a need for future atonement, but only a reference to the universal adoration of the Lord. This is also the theme in the relevant passage in Isaiah: "So the LORD will make himself known to the Egyptians, and in that day they will acknowledge the LORD. They will worship with sacrifices and grain offerings; they will make vows to the LORD and keep them" (Isa. 19:21). Once again, these sacrifices and offerings are expressions of thanksgiving and worship from Gentile nations, and once again, the context makes no mention of atonement. No honest reader can use this passage to question the once-and-for-all nature of the Messiah's atoning death.[306]

Looking now at the key texts in Jeremiah, we find two principle passages that could be understood with reference to sacrifices that will be offered *in the future* by the people of Israel. Note, however, that the first prophecy (in Jeremiah 17) was delivered *before* the destruction of the First Temple, and therefore, it is possible that it was never fulfilled:

> But if you are careful to obey me, declares the LORD, and bring no load through the gates of this city on the Sabbath, but keep the Sabbath day holy by not doing any work on it, then kings who sit on David's throne will come through the gates of this city with their officials. They and their officials will come riding in chariots and on horses, accompanied by the men of Judah and those living in Jerusalem, and this city will be inhabited forever. People will come from the towns of Judah and the villages around Jerusalem, from the territory of Benjamin and the western foothills, from the hill country and the Negev, bringing burnt offerings and sacrifices, grain offerings, incense and thank offerings to the house of the LORD.
>
> Jeremiah 17:24–26

We could easily argue that God offered the people of Judah an opportunity to repent, but they failed to heed his call and missed their chance to receive the promised blessing. This is certainly a fair reading of the text.

The other key prophecy, found in Jeremiah 33, was delivered *after* the destruction of the Temple and promised a restored city and a restored sacrificial system. It is very possible that this prophecy was actually fulfilled in the days of the Second Temple:

> This is what the LORD says: "You say about this place, 'It is a desolate waste, without men or animals.' Yet in the towns of Judah and the streets of Jerusalem that are deserted, inhabited by neither men nor animals, there will be heard once more the sounds of joy and gladness, the voices of bride and bridegroom, and the voices of those who bring

thank offerings to the house of the LORD, saying, 'Give thanks to the LORD Almighty, for the LORD is good; his love endures forever.' For I will restore the fortunes of the land as they were before," says the LORD.

Jeremiah 33:10–11

Again, a fair and honest reading of both of these passages does not necessarily imply or require a future Third Temple and a restored sacrificial system in the coming age. On the other hand, should it be argued that the prophecy in Jeremiah 17 *will* be fulfilled one day and that the prophecy in Jeremiah 33 did not yet come to pass in its fullness, we still have no problem. Just look carefully at the texts. They make explicit reference to burnt offerings, thank offerings, and grain offerings, but they make no mention of sin offerings or guilt offerings. This is significant. In fact, the second prophecy is the proof text that supports the Rabbinic teaching cited above by Rabbi Hertz, namely, that in the age to come, all offerings will be abolished except the thanksgiving offerings.

> R. Phinehas, R. Levi, and R. Johanan, in the name of R. Menahem of Galilee, said: In the time to come all other sacrifices will cease, but the sacrifice of thanksgiving will not cease. All other prayers will cease, but thanksgiving will not cease. As it is written (Jeremiah 33), ". . . the voice of joy and the voice of gladness" (Leviticus Rabbah, 9:7; see also Midrash Psalms 56:4, with reference to Neh. 12:40).[307]

Of course, Jeremiah also mentions Jewish worshipers coming to Jerusalem on chariots and horses—no buses, cars, or planes—and we could still ask whether the passage is simply a picture of joyful celebration, a prophetic symbol of complete restoration. Even if it does indicate that one day sacrifices and offerings will be restored, however, it makes no mention of offerings for atonement or purification, which is highly significant.

To review the evidence, a few prophetic passages indicate the possibility of a future Temple with a restored sacrificial system. However, (1) the only passage making any reference to atonement (Ezekiel 43 and 45) is part of a section so difficult to understand that the Talmudic rabbis said only Elijah could interpret it, while later rabbis (such as Maimonides) said that the prophecies could not be adequately interpreted at this time; (2) the other passages, totaling only a few verses, could refer to past events (such as Jeremiah 33) or to future events (such as Zechariah 14), but none of the passages make any reference to sacrifices for atonement or forgiveness. Rather, specific reference is made to incense, burnt offerings, and thanksgiving offerings, and most of the passages refer to Gentiles, not Jews, bringing these offerings.

What then do we say to the objection presented here, namely, that prophecies of a future, restored Temple with sacrifices contradict the New Testament teaching that the Messiah's death provided once-and-for-all atonement? We say that there is no conclusive evidence to support the objection, and we find nothing in these texts that makes us question the finality, power, and efficacy of Yeshua's atoning death for the sins of the world.

3.18. The Christian concept of salvation is contrary to the Hebrew Bible and Jewish tradition. Jews don't need saving.

> It seems to me you misunderstand the biblical concept of salvation, be it "Christian" or "Jewish." You probably think of salvation in the Hebrew Bible in terms of earthly deliverance and preservation, whereas you understand salvation in the New Testament in spiritual terms, referring only to the salvation of the soul. Actually, the concept of salvation in the Tanakh and in the new covenant Scriptures is comprehensive, dealing with spirit, soul, and body, both in this world and the world to come—in other words, salvation from sin and its effects. In that sense, all human beings, sinful as we are, need saving.

We will discuss the question of original sin and the fall of man below (3.20). For now, let's do our best to answer two questions: (1) What is the biblical concept of salvation? (2) Do Jews need to be saved?

Throughout the Hebrew Scriptures, the Lord is praised for saving his people Israel, and over and over again, his people cry out to him for salvation. For the most part, however, the salvation spoken of seems to be earthly. For example, the Tanakh recounts how God saved his people from the Egyptians (see Exod. 14:30, "That day the LORD saved [Hebrew, y-sh-'] Israel from the hands of the Egyptians, and Israel saw the Egyptians lying dead on the shore"). Just as he saved Israel from Egypt, so he saved them again and again throughout the centuries (e.g., Pss. 28:9; 107:13, 19, all with *y-sh-'*). In light of these great, past acts of salvation, the psalmist cried out to the Lord to save him from his own, present enemies (e.g., Ps. 18:27[28]).

When we turn to the New Testament, however, the emphasis seems to have shifted from earthly salvation to heavenly salvation, in other words, from physical deliverance to spiritual deliverance. As the famous slogan says, "Jesus saves!"—meaning he saves people from sin and hell (see Heb. 7:25). But is there really a great difference between the Old Testament and New Testament concepts of salvation? In reality there is not.

We need to understand first that Israel's conflicts with the nations were part of a larger cosmic battle, a fight for the supremacy of Yahweh above all other gods, a war for spiritual rule. And so, after the Lord saved Israel from the hand of the Egyptians, his people sang in praise, "Who among the gods is like you, O LORD? Who is like you—majestic in holiness, awesome in glory, working wonders?" (Exod. 15:11). There was no one like the Lord!

Notice here that God's reign over the *earth* is connected with his holiness, the spiritual and the physical being interrelated. His rule is absolute, over all hostile forces, be they the chaotic forces of nature or the rebellious forces of the nations. Psalm 74 expresses this even more clearly:

> But you, O God, are my king from of old;
> you bring salvation upon the earth.
> It was you who split open the sea by your power;
> you broke the heads of the monster in the waters.
> It was you who crushed the heads of Leviathan
> and gave him as food to the creatures of the desert.
> It was you who opened up springs and streams;
> you dried up the ever flowing rivers.
> The day is yours, and yours also the night;
> you established the sun and moon.
> It was you who set all the boundaries of the earth;
> you made both summer and winter.

> Psalm 74:12–17

In light of the Lord's triumph over all hostile powers, natural and supernatural, the psalmist makes an appeal: "Remember how the enemy has mocked you, O LORD, how foolish people have reviled your name" (Ps. 74:18). Consider also Psalm 93, in which the unruly forces of nature are pictured as subject to the reign of God:

> The LORD reigns, he is robed in majesty;
>   the LORD is robed in majesty
>   and is armed with strength.
> The world is firmly established;
>   it cannot be moved.
> Your throne was established long ago;
>   you are from all eternity.
> The seas have lifted up, O LORD,
>   the seas have lifted up their voice;
>   the seas have lifted up their pounding waves.
> Mightier than the thunder of the great waters,
>   mightier than the breakers of the sea—
>   the LORD on high is mighty.
> Your statutes stand firm;
>   holiness adorns your house
>   for endless days, O LORD.

As expressed by Professor Willem VanGemeren in his fine commentary on Psalms:

> The Lord established his kingship on earth when he created the "world" (*tebel;* cf. 24:1). The doctrine of God the Creator stands in stark contrast to the pagan teachings on chaos, primordial forces, and random happenings. Yahweh is the Creator-God. He has "established" *(tikkon)* the world, and it will not reel and totter under the duress of hostile forces (10:6; 104:5), because Yahweh has established his rule over it. The nations may rage against his rule, but it will not fall (2:1–4; 46:6). His throne is "established" *(nakon* v. 6, from *kun* as is *tikkon* above). Yahweh is "from all eternity" (90:2), but his rule over earth has a historical dimension ("long ago"; cf. Isa 44:8; 45:21; 48:3, 5, 7–8). Therefore the psalmist associates the "throne" as established when Creation took place.[308]

Now let's turn to Psalm 97, taking note of several important truths as we read: (1) God's reign is based on righteousness and justice; (2) he brings judgment on the false gods (idols) and on those who continue to worship them; (3) he calls his own people to hate evil; and (4) he delivers his godly people from the wicked.

> The LORD reigns, let the earth be glad;
>   let the distant shores rejoice.
> Clouds and thick darkness surround him;
>   righteousness and justice are the foundation of his throne.

Fire goes before him
> and consumes his foes on every side.
His lightning lights up the world;
> the earth sees and trembles.
The mountains melt like wax before the LORD,
> before the Lord of all the earth.
The heavens proclaim his righteousness,
> and all the peoples see his glory.
All who worship images are put to shame,
> those who boast in idols—
> worship him, all you gods!
Zion hears and rejoices
> and the villages of Judah are glad
> because of your judgments, O LORD.
For you, O LORD, are the Most High over all the earth;
> you are exalted far above all gods.
Let those who love the LORD hate evil,
> for he guards the lives of his faithful ones
> and delivers them from the hand of the wicked.
Light is shed upon the righteous
> and joy on the upright in heart.
Rejoice in the LORD, you who are righteous,
> and praise his holy name.

The point I am making here is simply this: Israel's deliverance from hostile forces (normally in the form of sinful nations) and the psalmist's deliverance from hostile forces (normally in the form of human enemies, sickness, sin, or demonic attack) were not simply a matter of physical, earthly salvation. Rather, these saving, delivering acts of God were part of a larger spiritual picture of God's reign over nature and of his reign over all competing spiritual powers. Just read Psalm 18, where David's deliverance is viewed as a mighty triumph of God over evil men as well as over the forces of death and destruction:

For the director of music. Of David the servant of the LORD. He sang to the LORD the words of this song when the LORD delivered him from the hand of all his enemies and from the hand of Saul. He said:

I love you, O LORD, my strength.
The LORD is my rock, my fortress and my deliverer;
> my God is my rock, in whom I take refuge.
> He is my shield and the horn of my salvation, my stronghold.
I call to the LORD, who is worthy of praise,
> and I am saved from my enemies.

The cords of death entangled me;
   the torrents of destruction overwhelmed me.
The cords of the grave coiled around me;
   the snares of death confronted me.
In my distress I called to the LORD;
   I cried to my God for help.
From his temple he heard my voice;
   my cry came before him, into his ears.
The earth trembled and quaked,
   and the foundations of the mountains shook;
   they trembled because he was angry. . . .
He reached down from on high and took hold of me;
   he drew me out of deep waters.
He rescued me from my powerful enemy,
   from my foes, who were too strong for me.
They confronted me in the day of my disaster,
   but the LORD was my support.
He brought me out into a spacious place;
   he rescued me because he delighted in me.

Psalm 18:1–7[8], 16–19[17–20]

Why did God grant this glorious and gracious deliverance? It was because David lived a righteous life, keeping the commands of the Lord and walking blamelessly before him (see vv. 20–24[21–25]).

"But that's my point," you say. "God's salvation of his people was purely earthly. It had nothing to do with heaven or hell."[309]

That's where I beg to differ. *Nothing* that God did on behalf of his people was purely earthly. That's the lesson we learn in these psalms, which are representative samples of similar texts throughout the Hebrew Bible. Israel's earthly life was part of a larger drama, a drama involving visible beings (i.e., humans) and invisible beings (i.e., God, angels, Satan). This drama was being played out here in this world, but it was not merely a worldly drama any more than the Book of Job was merely a worldly drama. Rather, Job, like Israel, was caught between a battle of good versus evil, of God versus Satan, with heavenly witnesses (the angels, called "sons of God" in Job) and earthly witnesses (Job's wife and friends) looking on and at times participating.

The ultimate challenge was this: Would Israel as a nation (or Job or David or Jeremiah, etc., as individuals) maintain a right relationship with the Lord, gaining his favor and obtaining his reward, or would hostile forces, both visible and invisible, triumph over the people of

God, seducing them into sin, wearing them out, and bringing them into bondage? Could God deliver and keep his own, or would the forces of darkness dominate the day? Would righteousness triumph in hearts and lives, or would iniquity and evil win? Really, "salvation" was far more than a limited, earthbound, worldly concept. In fact, it often tied in directly with salvation from sin, be it Israel's own sin (or the psalmist's own sin), or the sinful attacks of the nations (or Satan).

In this way, the Old Testament concept of salvation ties in directly with the New Testament concept of salvation: The Messiah had come, and with him, the kingdom (or reign) of God. This was the beginning of the Messianic era, meaning that God's Spirit was arriving in power, driving back hostile forces and setting captives free. And because this era was described in the Hebrew Bible, Jesus the Messiah quoted passages from the Jewish Scriptures that outlined the purpose of his mission:[310]

> He went to Nazareth, where he had been brought up, and on the Sabbath day he went into the synagogue, as was his custom. And he stood up to read. The scroll of the prophet Isaiah was handed to him. Unrolling it, he found the place where it is written:
>> "The Spirit of the Lord is on me,
>>> because he has anointed me
>>> to preach good news to the poor.
>> He has sent me to proclaim freedom for the prisoners
>>> and recovery of sight for the blind,
>> to release the oppressed,
>>> to proclaim the year of the Lord's favor."
> Then he rolled up the scroll, gave it back to the attendant and sat down. The eyes of everyone in the synagogue were fastened on him, and he began by saying to them, "Today this scripture is fulfilled in your hearing."
>
> Luke 4:16–21

As I stated earlier, the biblical concept of salvation is comprehensive, affecting spirit, soul, and body, and this comprehensive salvation reaches its fullest expression in the New Testament.

"So you're saying that the New Testament doesn't just emphasize spiritual salvation?"

Exactly. In fact, if we focus on the primary word for "save" in the New Testament, the Greek term *sozo*, this will become perfectly clear.[311] We can basically define *sozo* as "to rescue, save, deliver, preserve from danger," including saving, delivering, or preserving from death, sin, sickness, demons, hell, peril, and so on. The usage is quite inclusive. Interestingly enough, in the space of just two chapters in the Gospel of Luke, *sozo* is used in four different contexts: In Luke 7:50 it is used with reference to being *saved from sin* (see 7:36–50), in 8:36 with reference to being *saved from demons* (see 8:26–39), in 8:48 with reference to being *saved from sickness* (see 8:43–48), and in 8:50 with reference to being *saved from death* (see 8:49).[312] Jesus is a Savior (Greek, *soter*) who forgives, delivers, heals, and resurrects, both temporally and eternally. This is in full harmony with the Hebrew Scriptures: The Lord was the Savior, Deliverer, and Healer of his people.[313]

"That's fine," you reply, "but you still haven't addressed the issue of salvation from hell. Where is that taught in the Tanakh? There still seems to be quite a contrast between the Hebrew Bible and the New Testament, regardless of your points so far."

The issue is not one of contrast but of progress. The Old Testament shows the beginning of the journey; the New Testament takes us the rest of the way. What is touched on in the Tanakh—namely, the eternal destiny of men and women—is spelled out clearly in the New Testament.[314] It was the Jewish prophet Daniel, writing roughly one thousand years after Moses and approximately five hundred years after David, who brought the clearest message about heaven and hell in the Hebrew Bible, explaining that "multitudes who sleep in the dust of the earth will awake: some to everlasting life, others to shame and everlasting contempt" (Dan. 12:2). Then, in the centuries between Daniel and Yeshua, Jewish writings reflected much more interest in the afterlife, and by the time Yeshua came into the world, the Pharisees had a strongly developed view about the world to come. The Talmud, compiled in the following centuries, is filled with discussions about these issues.[315] In fact, one of the things that distinguished the Sadducees from the other Jewish groups of the day was their *denial* of a future resurrection.

What the Tanakh merely hinted at and touched on and what Jewish traditions wrote about and debated was fully illuminated in the New Testament. In the words of Paul, Jesus "brought life and immortality to light through the gospel" (2 Tim. 1:10). He revealed what was previously hidden and made clear that which was unclear in the past. And so the salvation and deliverance spoken of in the New Testament develops the concept of salvation and deliverance spoken of in the Tanakh: Whereas the psalmist spoke primarily of being rescued from the jaws of death, the New Testament speaks of being rescued from the jaws of death *and* hell.[316] The Tanakh spoke primarily (but not exclusively) about how our actions and beliefs affect us in this world. The New Testament speaks primarily (but not exclusively) about how our actions and beliefs affect us in the world to come. But this is not a question of either-or; rather, it is a question of emphasis, a question of both-and.[317]

Both traditions, Old Testament and New Testament, stress the importance of right living, of faith in the one true God, of repentance, of obedience. The former puts its primary emphasis on reward and punishment in this world while certainly not ignoring the world to come; the latter puts its primary emphasis on reward and punishment in the world to come while certainly not ignoring this world. So we can answer the first of our two questions by saying that the biblical concept of salvation is a deliverance from present and future judgment, present and future hostile forces, and present and future sin. In this life, the deliverance is partial and temporary; in the life to come, it is total and eternal. If you'll read through the Scriptures from beginning to end—both Tanakh and New Testament—keeping an open mind and a searching heart, you'll find that it really is *one* Bible, *one* revelation, *one* truth.

What about the second question: Do Jews need saving? Obviously, based on the evidence we have just presented, the answer is a resounding yes. Do all human beings, including Jews, have the power to resist some temptations and say no to certain sins? Of course! Every day all of us make moral choices, and even a rapist may choose not to kill his victim—tempted as he may be to do so—while a liar may occasionally feel compelled to tell the truth. We see this established already in the Book of Genesis, where God tells Cain that sin—here the sin of envy and murder—is lurking at the door, and Cain must master it (Gen. 4:7). As Rashi explains, "If you want to, you can overcome it." But it is one thing to overcome a particular sin. It is another to be free from the grip of sin in general. As Proverbs expressed it, "Who can say, 'I have kept my heart pure; I am clean and without sin'"? (Prov. 20:9). Or as the psalmist pleaded, "Do not bring your servant into judgment, for no one living is righteous before you" (Ps. 143:2).

Yes, the Lord knows our nature all too well (see below, 3.21, for more on this), and through the prophet Jeremiah he said, "The heart is deceitful above all things and beyond cure. Who can understand it?" (Jer. 17:9). We don't even know our own hearts! And because of our sins, we are totally dependent on the mercy of God: "If you, O Lord, kept a record of sins, O Lord, who could stand? But with you there is forgiveness; therefore you are feared" (Ps. 130:3–4). Without his forgiveness, we would be utterly lost.

Considering, then, that all of the verses we just cited—from Proverbs, Psalms, and Jeremiah—are taken from our own Hebrew Scriptures, the conclusion is unavoidable: Jews need saving. Sadly, as noted in volume 1, throughout our history we have fallen short, often suffering the fierce wrath of God in judgment. To this very day, we continue to fall short (see vol. 1, 1.10, 1.16; and note also below, 3.21). Does it mean nothing that for almost two millennia, most of our people have been in exile outside of the Land? Is there no significance to the fact that the Temple has been in ruins for more than nineteen hundred years? Surely this speaks to us about our sin, both past and present.

On a more individual level—I speak to you as a fellow Jew—when Dr. Baruch Goldstein gunned down dozens of praying Muslims in Hebron, we realized that we too had our murderous terrorists. When Prime Minister Rabin was assassinated by a fellow Israeli, the entire country was in shock: "We thought we were different!" When we see the great city of Tel Aviv today infested with prostitutes, drugs, and pornography, we realize that we are just as sinful as any other people. When Sabbath means going to the beach for thousands of Israelis and when the high holy days mean happy holidays for thousands of others, we realize that we are just as worldly and careless as sinful Israel was in the Scriptures. When most American Jews are secular, we understand that the idols of materialism have gripped us as much as they have gripped anyone. And when a top religious leader in Israel (Aryeh Deiri) is convicted of crimes of fraud and deceit, then defended by the Sephardic Chief Rabbi (Ovadiah Yoseph) as doing nothing in violation of Rabbinic law and is still hailed by his political party (Shas), we realize that hypocrisy is rife in our midst too.

The bad news, then, is that Jews need saving as much as anyone else. The good news is that God has provided for our full salvation through Messiah Yeshua, the Savior of Jew and Gentile alike: "As the Scripture says, 'Anyone who trusts in him will never be put to shame' [Isa. 28:16]. For there is no difference between Jew and Gentile—the same Lord is Lord of all and richly blesses all who call on him, for, 'Everyone who calls on the name of the Lord will be saved'" [Joel 2:32] (Rom. 10:11–13).

How fitting it is that Paul, in making this statement about salvation to believers in Rome, saw fit to use two quotations from the Hebrew Bible (Isaiah and Joel). It made perfect sense to him, and I hope that now it makes perfect sense to you.

3.19. Jewish people don't need a middleman.

> It all depends on what you mean by "middleman." If you mean no Jew could ever pray to God without a go-between acting on his or her behalf, I agree with you: We don't need a middleman. If you mean that any individual Jew (or the entire nation) could come into God's presence at any time without a divinely ordained agent first going to God on his or her behalf, I disagree with you. When God gave us the Torah, he told us in no uncertain terms that only the descendants of Aaron (i.e., the priests) could enter the Most Holy Place or perform the annual atonement rituals. We were completely dependent on them, along with the Levites who assisted them in their work. So in a general sense, any Jew can cry out to God at any time and plead for mercy; in a specific sense, without priestly atonement and intercession, no Jew has direct access to God.

We don't need to spend a great deal of time on this objection since it all comes down to how we define "middleman." Still, I am aware of the perception some Jews have about the role of Jesus as a mediator between man and God. They view his role as if he were a secretary with an office outside the boss's door, and you have to go through him to get clearance to enter. Actually, the teaching of the New Testament would be closer to this: The boss's door is closed and locked shut. Jesus opens the door and provides the way for us to enter. Or to take the image even further, Jesus himself *is* the door. That's how we should understand the following verses in which Yeshua stated plainly, "I am the way and the truth and the life. No one comes to the Father except through me" (John 14:6). "I tell you the truth, the man who does not enter the sheep pen by the gate, but climbs in by some other way, is a thief and a robber. . . . I tell you the truth, I am the gate for the sheep" (John 10:1, 7).

It is the death and resurrection of the Messiah that has opened the door of heaven for all of us, Jew and Gentile alike. Through him, our sins are forgiven and we can approach God's holy throne with confidence and boldness. We have direct access to the Lord himself. It is in this sense that Jesus is the mediator between God and man: He "gave himself as a ransom for all men" (see 1 Tim. 2:5–6). That's why the New Testament letter to the Messianic Jews exclaims:

Therefore, brothers, since we have confidence to enter the Most Holy Place by the blood of Jesus, by a new and living way opened for us through the curtain, that is, his body, and since we have a great priest over the house of God, let us draw near to God with a sincere heart in full assurance of faith, having our hearts sprinkled to cleanse us from a guilty conscience and having our bodies washed with pure water.

Hebrews 10:19–22

You see, out of all the peoples living on the earth two thousand years ago, it would have been the Jewish people who would have best understood their need for a middleman—someone to approach God on their behalf, someone to help them deal with their sins, someone to procure favor and blessing for them. God-fearing Jews knew full well their spiritual limitations: Only the priests and Levites could perform the Temple functions, and only the high priest could enter the Most Holy Place—the place where God revealed himself (see Lev. 16:2)—and that only once a year. Even then the high priest could only enter with sacrificial blood.

When Uzziah, a godly Judean king, went into the Temple and offered incense, he was smitten with leprosy. He had encroached on the holy, doing something forbidden to all but the priests:

But after Uzziah became powerful, his pride led to his downfall. He was unfaithful to the LORD his God, and entered the temple of the LORD to burn incense on the altar of incense. Azariah the priest with eighty other courageous priests of the LORD followed him in. They confronted him and said, "It is not right for you, Uzziah, to burn incense to the LORD. That is for the priests, the descendants of Aaron, who have been consecrated to burn incense. Leave the sanctuary, for you have been unfaithful; and you will not be honored by the LORD God."

2 Chronicles 26:16–18

Not even kings had direct access into the Temple. Note also that the Bible states it was Uzziah's pride that led to his downfall. He thought he had as much right to enter the Temple and perform priestly service as anyone. God thought otherwise. Uzziah needed a middleman too. In fact, the very turban worn by the high priest enabled him to "bear the guilt involved in the sacred gifts the Israelites consecrate, whatever their gifts may be. It will be on [the high priest's] forehead continually so that they will be acceptable to the LORD" (Exod. 28:38). From this we learn that not even Israel's gifts and offerings would be acceptable to God without the ministry of the high priest. Yeshua is now our great High Priest, making our gifts and offerings acceptable to God. (For more on this, see vol. 3, 4.1.)

You should also remember that God gave Israel prophets to communicate his will to the people. When he spoke directly and audibly to the nation (on Mount Sinai), they were terrified and begged him to stop: "When the people saw the thunder and lightning and heard the trumpet and saw the mountain in smoke, they trembled with fear. They stayed at a distance and said to Moses, 'Speak to us yourself and we will listen. But do not have God speak to us or we will die'" (Exod. 20:18–19). This, then, was the main reason God raised up prophets for his people:

> The LORD your God will raise up for you a prophet like me from among your own brothers. You must listen to him. For this is what you asked of the LORD your God at Horeb on the day of the assembly when you said, "Let us not hear the voice of the LORD our God nor see this great fire anymore, or we will die." The LORD said to me [i.e., Moses]: "What they say is good. I will raise up for them a prophet like you from among their brothers; I will put my words in his mouth, and he will tell them everything I command him."
>
> Deuteronomy 18:15–18

We see then that the Jewish people needed prophets to communicate God's will to them and priests to make atonement on their behalf, and both prophet and priest were often called on to make intercession for the people. Without this intercession, divine judgment would fall.[318] A middleman was sorely needed.

Interestingly, most religious Jews still rely heavily on a middleman, but now he is not called a priest or a prophet but rather a rabbi. It is the rabbi—especially the leading sage in each generation—who tells the community what God requires and interprets the Torah for them. In many ways, he is seen as God's representative, speaking with all the authority that his learning has earned him. In fact, if I were to question a traditional Jew about the validity of his rabbi's interpretation or ruling, he would tell me in response, "Who am I to differ with what my rabbi says?" Not only so, but that rabbi would rely heavily on the rulings and interpretations of *his* rabbi, who in turn leaned heavily on the rulings and interpretations of *his* rabbi—all the way back to the rulings and interpretations of the medieval Law Codes and commentaries, and before that, to the rulings and interpretations of the post-Talmudic sages, and before that, to the rulings and interpretations of the Talmudic rabbis themselves. Jewish tradition actually teaches that it was the Rabbinic leaders who received the inspiration the prophets once had.[319]

The rabbi functions as a middleman in another way as well, and that is in the area of prayer. Many religious Jews—especially Hasidim—believe that the rabbi's prayer carries special weight with God, while nonreligious Jews sometimes send prayer requests to religious Jews living in Jerusalem, asking them to put their requests in the Wailing Wall and say a prayer for them.

The bottom line is that Jews, as human beings, need someone to help them come into right relationship with God and stay in right relationship with God. In biblical times, the main, God-appointed agent was the high priest, and, as we stated, he was the only one who was allowed access into the Most Holy Place in the earthly Tabernacle and Temple. While any Israelite could bring an offering to God, the high priest's work was essential, ultimately enabling that Israelite's offering to be received.

Through the Messiah our High Priest, we have been brought into an entirely different relationship with God, since Jesus has actually opened the door to the Most Holy Place in heaven itself—the very throne room of God—and granted us *direct access* into that holy presence through his blood. That's the kind of middleman we need. Without him, we are shut out, and the door is locked and bolted. With him, it is open wide.

3.20. Jews don't believe in original sin or a fall of man. We do not believe the human race is totally sinful.

There may be some confusion with our terms. Messianic Jews and Christians believe we have fallen from the ideal state in which we were created, and now moral corruption is an inescapable part of our nature. We do not believe that people are totally and exclusively sinful, incapable of doing or choosing anything good. Rather, we believe that *by nature* we are hopelessly *prone to sin* and thoroughly *entangled with sin.* It is because Adam fell—and we must remember that Adam is the father of the human race according to the Torah—that there are murders, rapes, thefts, and criminal acts committed every moment of every day. Because of Adam's fall, we kill one another in war, imprison and torture one another for our own cruel purposes, and even commit genocide. We spend millions of dollars annually on every type of sexual perversion—including pedophilia—while we waste millions more on addictive and destructive drugs. And even the best of us admit to our moral failures, doing things we wish we wouldn't do—in fact, we judge others for doing these very things—and being ashamed of our thoughts, words, or deeds. We are, tragically, a fallen race.

Before we look at the evidence in the Hebrew Scriptures, let me explain what we mean by "original sin" and "the fall." We do not believe that human beings can never do anything good, nor do we believe that all people are always and only evil. On the contrary, we recognize many noble and admirable qualities in countless individuals, and we do not believe that even the most wicked person is devoid of at least some positive, moral qualities. Rather, we believe that as Adam went, so we have gone, and thus our race is a fallen race and we sin "by nature."[320]

According to the Torah, God created the human race to be perfect, giving us a free will capable of choosing complete obedience. In the beginning, it was not our nature to sin; we were not inherently corrupt. When the parents of our race chose to disobey, however, their act produced a catastrophic chain reaction, and sin is now "in our blood," just as the HIV virus is often found in the blood of a child born to someone suffering from AIDS.

No one has to teach a child to disobey, lie, or act selfishly. It comes all too naturally. In fact, it is fairly common for us to criticize the parents of other children we know—"I would *never* raise my child like that"—until we have our own kids! As a parent, haven't you often asked yourself, "Where did my son (or daughter) ever learn such behavior?" The fact is, they didn't have to "learn" such behavior. It came naturally! It won't do to blame their behavior on the "bad kids" your "good kid" hung out with, since the parents of the "bad kids" say the same thing about *your* child. Plus, most of the bad habits our children *did* pick up were picked up from us parents, and we picked those things up from *our* parents, who picked them up from *their* parents. . . . Something is wrong with the human race.

Isn't it strange that the things we "naturally" seem to like and enjoy the most tend to be the very things that are bad for us? Who ever overindulges on brussels sprouts? It is all too easy to overeat, over-sleep, or become addicted to one fleshly lust or another, while it takes determination and resolve to live a disciplined life. Something seems fundamentally amiss.

Just as it takes very little effort to sail with the wind but plenty of effort to sail against it, so also it takes almost no effort to do what is wrong but plenty of effort to do what is right. Do you need to discipline yourself to eat sweets? Do you need to push yourself to have lustful thoughts? Do you find it necessary to strive to be lazy? Is it difficult for you to be selfish? There is no denying the fact that our nature tends to do wrong.

Let's consider this from a different perspective. When you imagine what heaven will be like, do you think there will be murder there? How about hatred? Anger? Greed? Bitterness? Selfishness? Impurity? Cursing? Lying? Will you need a guard dog to protect your premises or a handgun to ward off burglars? Will there be large prisons there to house the criminals? Will you live in constant fear and dread? Of course not, otherwise heaven—by anyone's definition—would not be heaven. And that's the point.

The Torah teaches us in Genesis that everything God created was good. In fact, when God completed the creation of our world, he pronounced it *tov me'od*, "Very good." (Even if you differ with me here and don't take these chapters literally, you cannot escape from the overall teaching that emerges: The Lord called the work of his hands "very good.") Just a few chapters later, we find shame, fear, duplicity, and denial, followed by jealousy, murder (the firstborn son of Adam and Eve kills his own brother), pervasive corruption, and every kind of evil, to the point that God decides to wipe out the entire human race, with the exception of Noah and his family. Adam and Eve, the progenitors of our race, were the pinnacle of God's handiwork; the first child born to them after they disobeyed God (they had no children before that time) became a murderer, guilty of fratricide.

Something horrible happened in between Genesis 1, when God pronounced everything "very good," and chapter 4, when Cain killed Abel. We call this—with good reason—the fall of man, and it explains why children kill their own parents and parents abuse their own children; why some women sell their bodies for shameful purposes and why some men rape women without shame; why each country must have trained armies and—if possible—nuclear arsenals to protect itself from its neighbors; and why in the twentieth century in sophisticated countries such as America and South Africa there could still be widespread racial prejudice and injustice, while in civilized Europe there could be a Nazi Holocaust and a Bosnian ethnic cleansing. The fall of man also explains why there is sickness and disease in the world, why babies are born handicapped, why the earth produces weeds and thorns, and why animals eat one another to live. That is not the way God intended things to be.

In the beginning of human history, there was a fall, and we have not gotten better since. We cannot extricate ourselves from our nature. As the Lord said through the prophet Jeremiah, "Can the Ethiopian change his skin or the leopard its spots? Neither can you do good who are accustomed to doing evil" (Jer. 13:23).

Consider the fact that the twentieth century was the worst in recorded history in terms of national atrocities, murders, and wars.[321] And no sooner is a new technology discovered than it is being used for a destructive purpose—either a hi-tech weapon of war designed to kill a large number of individuals, or a new tool for sexual exploitation and bondage, such as those found on the Internet. Something is innately wrong with our race! When we see a sign that says, "Don't touch!" we want to touch. Isn't this true?

Common sense tells us that God did not make us intrinsically evil or else he would not have been so grieved over our actions, nor would he have found it necessary to destroy us before we destroyed ourselves (see Gen. 6:1–12).[322] And remember, it was so-called "normal" people who either actively or passively participated in the horrors of the Holocaust, the Cambodian genocide, the murderous Communist purges, and the horrors in Rwanda. People did things they never dreamed they would do. Have you—even in ways that are much less shocking or obvious?

Ask the most religious or moral person you know if he or she has had secret thoughts or desires that would embarrass them if they were made known. (You could ask yourself this same question too.) How many times have you done something good only to recognize that you were miserably tainted by pride and self-righteousness even in the very act of doing that good deed or performing that noble service? The fact is, that's human nature—a nature that is fatally flawed and terribly tainted. To quote again from the Book of Jeremiah, "The heart is deceitful above all things and beyond cure. Who can understand it?" (Jer. 17:9).

You might ask, "How then do you explain our noble qualities? Why is it that we often resist temptation and actually improve ourselves morally?" The answer is simple: We are created in God's image, and we have a divinely given conscience that seeks to move us away from evil and in the direction of good. But the divine image within us has been contaminated, corrupted, and marred. Look at what the Bible says in Genesis 5:1, 3: "This is the written account of Adam's line. When God created man, he made him *in the likeness of God*. . . . When Adam had lived 130 years, he had a son *in his own likeness, in his own image;* and he named him Seth."

God made Adam in his own, perfect image, but Adam—after his disobedience and fall—produced offspring in *his* own, imperfect image. The image of God our Father has been corrupted through the image of our father Adam to the point that, by nature, we are more the children of Adam than we are the children of God.

The reason we often strive to do good, engage in sacrificial, charitable acts, and feel guilty when we sin is because there is still a moral light within us (see John 1:4), something we call the conscience, the "shell" of the divine image in which we were created. God's Spirit is also working with us to convict us and turn us back, and if we have been exposed to Scripture, God's Word is also calling us to reform our ways. There is a battle going on in our souls, unless, of course, we have given up the fight.

The problem is that no matter how much we try, we cannot really eradicate moral corruption from our lives. If the human race had ten billion years for self-improvement, it would never reach its goal. No matter how hard we try on our own to live up to God's standards, we will still fall hopelessly short.

To give yourself a simple test, consider that the first and greatest commandment is to love God with all your heart and soul and strength and the second is to love your neighbor as yourself, then try to live out these commandments twenty-four hours a day. Or take an honest, hard look at Yeshua's moral teaching in Matthew 5–7 and see how you measure up to the Messiah's standards. (He explained that if you simply look at someone lustfully you have committed adultery in you heart, while harboring hatred makes you a murderer in your heart.) You might find yourself undone after reading these words. You might also want to experiment on yourself by trying to rid your character of "little" sins such as envy, pride, and greed. You'll be amazed to see just how binding sin is.

Let me remind you of the testimony of Scripture. We already mentioned that in Noah's day, out of the entire population of the world, only eight people were spared.[323] This is absolutely overwhelming. But there is something even more overwhelming: The reason that

God has not sent another flood to destroy the world again is *not* because we have become better. No, it is because we are the same. This is what God said immediately after the flood, "Never again will I doom the earth because of man, since the devisings of man's mind are evil from his youth; nor will I ever again destroy every living being, as I have done" (Gen. 8:21 NJPSV).

The Bible is telling us that if God were to destroy the world because of our wickedness, he would have to do it continually! And note that it was not some fundamentalist Christian preacher who stated that "the devisings [Hebrew, *yetser*] of man's mind are evil from his youth." This is the "diagnosis" of our spiritual condition as given by the Lord and as recorded in our Torah. Tragically, this was the condition of mankind before the flood (see Gen. 6:5), and our condition remained unchanged after the flood.[324] This speaks volumes. Even severe judgment cannot eradicate our sinful roots.

Moving ahead in our history as recorded in Scripture, within days of receiving the Ten Commandments on Mount Sinai, we broke the very first commandment (not to worship idols), and of the entire generation that came out of Egypt in the exodus, only two people entered the land of Canaan. (This too is worthy of some serious reflection.)

Our first king, Saul, was an apostate. His successor, David, our greatest king, committed adultery and murder, while his son Solomon, our wisest king, fell into gross idolatry and almost unimaginable polygamy (seven hundred wives and three hundred concubines). Yet the days of David and Solomon are considered the golden age of our history! One generation later, Israel and Judah split into the northern and southern kingdoms, and within 250 hundred years, the northern kingdom of Israel—*all* of whose kings were evil—was scattered and destroyed, a state in which it remains to this day. As for the southern kingdom of Judah, it was destroyed and exiled 150 years after the downfall of the northern tribes. Why? Because of pervasive, universal sin.[325]

Just consider the words of the prophets. In Jeremiah 5:1, the Lord said to his faithful prophet, "Go up and down the streets of Jerusalem, look around and consider, search through her squares. If you can find but one person who deals honestly and seeks the truth, I will forgive this city." But Jeremiah could not find even one godly person!

In this same period of time the Lord said to Ezekiel, "I looked for a man among them who would build up the wall and stand before me in the gap on behalf of the land so I would not have to destroy it, but I found none. So I will pour out my wrath on them and consume them with my fiery anger, bringing down on their own heads all they have done, declares the Sovereign LORD" (Ezek. 22:30–31).

I appeal to you to accept the testimony of our prophets: God destroyed Jerusalem in 586 B.C.E. because our people as a whole—both nationally and individually—turned away from him. There was scarcely a righteous person among us! Then, after five centuries of restoration in the Land (with plenty of foreign occupation because of our persistent sin), both the Temple and the city of Jerusalem were destroyed again (this took place in 70 C.E.). To this day, more than nineteen hundred years later, the Temple has not been rebuilt.

Even now, as we witness the ongoing miracle of the rebirth of the State of Israel, our moral problems still persist. Nothing has really changed. Most Israelis, practically speaking, are atheists and materialists, while drug use, alcoholism, pornography, and even prostitution are rampant in the "Holy Land." And every female soldier serving in the Israeli army is allowed two free abortions!

As for the very religious Jews, the ultra-Orthodox, they are not always so orthodox. Prominent leaders among them have been caught in political and monetary scandals (not to mention some not-so-hidden sexual scandals as well), while they have been known to use strong-armed intimidation tactics on their religious and theological opponents.[326]

Something is fundamentally wrong with our people, even though God has paid more attention to us and given us more opportunities to do right than any other people on earth. The sad verdict is inescapable: We too suffer from that universal condition called a sinful nature. Jews are smitten with it just as much as Gentiles are. All of us need divine help.

To repeat what I have been saying, if human beings are not fallen, why can't the Palestinians and Israelis simply forgive, forget, and embrace one another in trust? Or here in America, why can't the White Supremacists and the Black Muslims form a coalition of brotherhood? And why do most criminals get out of prison only to go back to their crimes?

Maybe now you can better understand the words of the Tanakh. David states, "Surely I was sinful at birth, sinful from the time my mother conceived me" (Ps. 51:5), while Isaiah 53:6 says, "We all, like sheep, have gone astray, each of us has turned to his own way." Similarly, Proverbs 20:9 asks, "Who can say, 'I have kept my heart pure; I am clean and without sin?'" and Ecclesiastes 7:20 declares, "There is not a righteous man on earth who does what is right and never sins."[327] From the least to the greatest, we all fall short.[328]

Of course, it is possible to point to outstandingly moral individuals, such as the Chafetz Chayyim in Judaism or Mahatma Ghandi in Hinduism. But these seeming exceptions actually prove the rule of the pervasive nature of human sin.

"Really?" you say. "How so?"

Let me answer your question with three questions of my own: (1) Why do men like this *stand out* in their generation? Why are such individuals so rare? It is because we are a sinful lot. And even someone like Mahatma Ghandi had the fatal flaw of being a devoted idol worshiper, something that Judaism forbids for Gentiles too. (2) What do these people say about themselves? Aren't they far more critical of themselves—and certainly far less impressed with themselves—than their admirers are? (3) Would the saintliest rabbi say that he had no need of atonement? Would he say he could stand before God without pleading for mercy? Then how much less can the "average Jew" trust in his or her own righteousness? Let me say it again: We all fall short.

Speaking of "falling" short, there are also some interesting traditional Jewish teachings about the fall of man. Thus the *Encyclopedia of Jewish Religion*, summarizing the major teachings on the subject, simply states that

> through the sin of its first ancestors, the whole human race "fell" from bliss and grace. Christian theology holds this "original sin" to have involved mankind in an inherent and congenital sinfulness and depravity from which only a special Divine act can "save" them. The rabbis generally held that all men die because of Adam's sin (a divergent view is expressed by R. Ammi in *Shab.* 55a) but did not teach a doctrine of original sin. There is, however, a view that the serpent transmitted to Eve a blemish [by copulation] which she passed on to all her descendants. At Mt. Sinai the Israelites were restored to man's original state of perfection, but this was undone again by the sin of the golden calf.[329]

Some midrashic traditions picture Adam as a massive and glorious being whose face outshone the sun and who could stride the earth in just a few steps—until he sinned.[330] Other mystical traditions teach that all human souls were in Adam's soul. Thus, when he fell, the entire human race fell with him. Related to this is the mystical teaching of Rabbi Isaac Luria that "all Israel form a mysterious single body, consisting of Adam's soul,"[331] and in this vein the *Encyclopedia of Hasidism* states that in Lurianic Kabbalah (i.e., Jewish mysticism based on Luria's teaching), the exile of Israel and the Shekhina (i.e., the divine Presence) were "interpreted as a consequence of the disaster that overtook the world at the time of Adam's sin."[332] Thus, "as a result of original sin *(ḥet kadmon)* evil entered the world, with disastrous consequences not only for the whole of creation but also for the sphere of Divine being, and the entire process of history is seen as a struggle to restore the fallen world to its pristine perfection."[333] That is part of our very own Jewish traditions.

Abraham Cohen, in his widely used compendium *Everyman's Talmud,* makes reference to a fascinating account in the Talmud (b. Erubin 13b), stating that for

> two and a half years the School of Shammai and the School of Hillel were divided on the following point: The latter maintained that it had been better if man had never been created; while the former maintained that it is better he was created. The count was taken and the majority decided that it would have been better if he had not been created; but since he has been created, let him investigate his (past) actions. Another version is: Let him examine his (present) actions.[334]

According to Cohen, "At the root of the discussion was the agreed opinion that man is essentially a sinful creature who is bound during his lifetime to do many deeds which earn for him the condemnation of God." The question Cohen raises has to do with "whether the Talmud teaches the doctrine of original sin, viz., whether the human being has inherited the guilt incurred by his first parents and in consequence is essentially corrupt in nature."[335]

As to whether human beings "inherit sin"—implying, then, that we are not responsible for the sins we commit—Cohen answers with an emphatic no. However, Cohen states that according to the Talmudic rabbis, man "may be burdened by the consequences of the wrongdoings of his forefathers," explaining more fully that "the Rabbis subscribed to the view that the sin in the Garden of Eden had repercussions on all subsequent generations." He notes, "It was the direct cause of death which is the fate of every creature. In the same way [the Rabbis] believed that the sin of the Golden Calf left its taint and affected the destinies of mankind ever since. 'There is no generation in which there is not an ounce from the sin of the Golden Calf' (p. Ta'anit 68c)."[336]

Also relevant to our discussion is the traditional Jewish teaching that man has a higher and lower nature, a good inclination and an evil inclination.[337] The problem is that all too often the evil inclination wins out![338] In fact, it was the great Jewish thinker Paul who offered a penetrating insight on the depth of our depravity. He wrote, "You, therefore, have no excuse, you who pass judgment on someone else, for at whatever point you judge the other, you are condemning yourself, because you who pass judgment do the same things" (Rom. 2:1). Our very condemnation of evil in others helps to pronounce condemnation on us!

We claim that we are pretty good people, even moral and righteous, judging others as guilty sinners and transgressors. The problem is we do the very same things they do—except we justify those things in our own lives while condemning them in the lives of others.

It is true, of course, that Judaism calls on its own sinning people to reform their ways and become moral and upright through adhering to the Law of God. And it is certain that many Jews *do* make some kind of turnaround through Torah observance, just as it is true that many others make some kind of change through adherence to a system of religious or moral teaching. But let's be candid. Many of the changes are cosmetic in nature. After all, how many terrorists, murderers, sexual perverts, and social degenerates have been transformed through Jewish tradition?

Of course, this is not the fault of traditional Judaism. It's the fault of the human race. We need God to reach down and save us from our sins. That's why Jesus the Messiah came into this world, and that's why one of his followers could explain to a community of Jewish believers that "he is able to save completely those who come to God through him, because he always lives to intercede for them" (Heb. 7:25). Countless millions can attest to the truth of this verse.

I would encourage you once again to look inside yourself and see who you really are. Perhaps you can relate to this New Testament description of unholy human nature in contrast with the holy law of God:

> We know that the law is spiritual; but I am unspiritual, sold as a slave to sin. I do not understand what I do. For what I want to do I do not do, but what I hate I do. And if I do what I do not want to do, I agree that the law is good. As it is, it is no longer I myself who do it, but it is sin living in me. I know that nothing good lives in me, that is, in my sinful nature. For I have the desire to do what is good, but I cannot carry it out. For what I do is not the good I want to do; no, the evil I do not want to do—this I keep on doing. Now if I do what I do not want to do, it is no longer I who do it, but it is sin living in me that does it. So I find this law at work: When I want to do good, evil is right there with me.
>
> Romans 7:14–21

There is only one way out of this condition, only one way to gain a new heart, only one way to experience true freedom from guilt and gain the power to lead a new life, and that way is a person called Jesus the Messiah.[339] When we put our faith in him and ask God to forgive our sins through his death on our behalf, we too die to the things that once enslaved us, overcoming sin through him. And while we will not experience total perfection in this world, at times struggling with the "old nature," we can already begin to experience a foretaste of the wonderful, holy liberty we will enjoy forever.

This is what Jesus meant when he said to the Jewish men who had put their faith in him: "If you hold to my teaching, you are really my disciples. Then you will know the truth, and the truth will set you free" (John 8:31–32). The choice is yours. Each of us can deny that we are by nature slaves to sin—although that very denial might well be another manifestation of our pride and self-will—or the truth can set us free.

3.21. Jews don't need to repent.

> On the contrary, repentance is one of Judaism's foundations. That's why our own traditional literature—from the Talmud to the Prayerbook to Maimonides to contemporary Jewish thinkers—is filled with teaching on repentance and prayers of repentance. Jews sin like everybody else, and therefore, Jews—just like other human beings—need to repent. That's why our traditional literature puts such an emphasis on repentance.

If someone hadn't told me this was an objection, I never would have believed it. Judaism has always emphasized the importance of repentance (Hebrew, *teshuvah*), to the point that it could even be *overemphasized* in the previous objections (see above, 3.9, 3.12). Here's a small sampling of the rich Jewish teaching on the importance of repentance:

• The Talmudic traditions state, "Great is repentance, for it brings healing to the world" (b. Berakhoth 32a); "Great is repentance, for it reaches the Throne of Glory; . . . for it brings redemption; . . . for it lengthens a man's life" (b. Yoma 86a); "Better an hour of repentance and good deeds in this world than a whole lifetime in the world to come" (m. Avot 4:17); "Repentance is more valuable than sacrifices"

(Pesikta Rabbati 45); "Repentance is greater than prayer" (Tanna deBe Eliyahu Zuta 7).[340]

• Moses Maimonides devoted an entire section of his Law Code (called the Mishneh Torah) to the subject of repentance, teaching emphatically that without repentance there could be no forgiveness and giving detailed instructions on what true repentance is and is not.[341] So great is the power of repentance that he wrote, "Even a person who was wicked his whole life and repented in his final moments will not be reminded of any aspect of his wickedness as [Ezek. 33:12] states 'the wickedness of the evil one will not cause him to stumble on the day he repents his wickedness.'"[342]

• One of the Eighteen Benedictions[343] recited daily by traditional Jews is a specific request for help to repent: "Bring us back, our Father, to Your Torah, and bring us near, our King, to Your service, and cause us to return in complete repentance before You. Blessed are You, O LORD, who desires repentance." A religious Jew prays this prayer thousands of times in his or her lifetime.

• Some of the greatest Jewish minds of this century (such as Rav Soloveitchik, the founder of Yeshiva University, and Abraham Isaac Kook, Israel's first chief rabbi) devoted years to teaching and preaching about the doctrine of repentance, while standard works such as Solomon Schechter's *Aspects of Rabbinic Theology* devoted lengthy sections to the subject.[344] Therefore, it is not surprising that it was a Hasidic rabbi who said, "If I had the choice, I would rather not die. Because in the World-to-Come there are no Days of Awe [referring to the ten days from Rosh Hashanah to Yom Kippur], and what can a person's soul do without the Day of Atonement? What is the point of living without repentance?"[345] And Schechter can point to a well-known Rabbinic tradition regarding Manasseh, the most wicked king in Judah's history who repented and received forgiveness (see vol. 1, 1.11): "Thus, if a man would tell thee that God receives not penitents, behold Manasseh, the son of Hezekiah, he will bear evidence that no creature in the world ever committed before me so many wicked deeds as he did, yet in the moment of repentance I received him."[346]

• A secular Jew who becomes traditional is called a *ba'al teshuva*, literally, "a master of repentance." In fact, the recent book of Rabbi Adin Steinsaltz written to help newly observant Jews is simply called *Teshuvah*.[347] And penitent Jews are accorded the highest respect, as the Talmud states, "Where the repentant stand, not even the completely righteous can stand" (b. Berakhoth 34b).

• In a recent comparative religious study on the subject of repentance, the contributing scholar on Hinduism freely admitted that repentance is generally not viewed as foundational to Hinduism (or other Eastern religions, for that matter), while the Jewish contributor could write,

> For Judaism the conception of repentance—regretting sin, determining not to repeat it, seeking forgiveness for it—defines the key to the moral life. No single component of the human condition takes higher priority in establishing the right relationship with God, and none bears more profound implication for this-worldly attitudes and actions. The entire course of a human life, filled as it is with the natural propensity to sin, that is, rebel against God, but comprised also by the compelled requirement of confronting God's response (punishment for sin) takes its direction—finds its critical turning—at the act of repentance, the first step in the regeneration of the human condition as it was meant to be.[348]

That certainly underscores the foundational importance of repentance in Judaism, doesn't it?

Should you need any further proof that Jews need to repent, and should you need to see firsthand just how many Jews recognize their need to repent, I would suggest you go to a religious Jewish bookstore a few weeks before Rosh Hashanah and Yom Kippur and look at how the books on repentance sell like hotcakes. During this season, Jews become acutely aware of their need to repent as they consider their deeds in light of God's judgment.[349] This emphasis on the foundational importance of repentance is simply the logical continuation of the biblical call to turn from sin and get right with God. In fact, the message of the prophets of Israel can be summed up with one word: Repent![350]

Sadly enough, we Jews, having been given the great privilege of receiving the Torah, have failed to distinguish ourselves by our national obedience to God's laws. To the contrary, we have often distinguished ourselves as being especially obstinate, and so, of all peoples, repentance has been crucial—and precious—to us. As expressed by the late chief rabbi of the British Empire, J. H. Hertz, "The Rabbis proclaim the cardinal importance, well nigh the omnipotence, of Repentance in the spiritual life of man."[351]

3.22. Jews don't believe in a divine Messiah.

> Judaism has never had one, official, universally accepted set of beliefs concerning the Messiah, but it is true that

> traditional Jewish teaching does not speak unequivocally
> of a divine Messiah. However, Jewish tradition often
> describes a highly exalted Messiah as well as a preexistent
> Messiah, so much so that Jewish scholars have sometimes
> spoken of the "semi-divine" or "quasi-divine" nature of the
> Messiah according to these traditions. More importantly,
> the Hebrew Bible itself speaks of the Messiah's divine
> nature, and that must be the deciding factor in what we as
> Jews do and do not believe.

I was once involved in a panel debate featuring three Messianic Jewish leaders and three rabbis. One of the rabbis, who was ultra-Orthodox, stated emphatically that for thirty-five hundred years Judaism
has had only one set of beliefs concerning the Messiah. Unfortunately,
not only was his chronology wrong (there was no such thing as
"Judaism" thirty-five hundred years ago, nor was there even such a
thing as a Jew), but his statement concerning the unity of Jewish belief
in the Messiah was wrong as well. A more accurate statement would
have been that for more than two thousand years Judaism has had
many different beliefs concerning the Messiah. Jewish writings, such
as the Psalms of Solomon, the Similitudes of Enoch, Fourth Ezra, and
the Sybilline Oracles, written between 200 B.C.E. and 100 C.E., contain
different Messianic beliefs than those found in the Dead Sea Scrolls,
also written during the same approximate period of time. And the early
Rabbinic writings, dating from 200 to 600 of this era, contain many
beliefs not reflected in any of the writings just mentioned.

John Collins, a widely respected specialist in apocalyptic literature, notes that rather than thinking of first-century C.E. Jewish belief
in either an earthly Messiah or a heavenly Messiah, "we should think
of a spectrum of messianic expectation, ranging from the earthly messiah of the *Psalms of Solomon* and several Dead Sea Scrolls, through
the transcendent messiah of *4 Ezra* to the heavenly figure of the *Similitudes of Enoch.*"[352]

"But that's where you are missing the point," you say. "Most of
those writings do not reflect mainstream Judaism. It is the Talmud
alone that is authoritative for Jews, and the Talmud is clear concerning the person and work of the Messiah."

Not so. First, as I explained previously (see vol. 1, introduction),
the beliefs reflected in these varied writings from the second century
B.C.E. to the first century C.E. were just as "Jewish" as those reflected
later in the Talmud. It is just that Pharisaic Judaism (which devel-

oped into Talmudic Judaism) survived the destruction of the Temple and became dominant, leaving the other beliefs as mere historic curiosities.[353] Second, and more importantly, the Talmud in no way provides a definitive or categorical description of the Messiah. Just study the famous (and quite lengthy) Messianic discussion in b. Sanhedrin 96b–99a. You will find there a few common beliefs (e.g., the Messiah is referred to as the son of David) in the midst of dozens of other beliefs, traditions, and interpretations intermingled with a great deal of speculation. And much of what is recorded there is mutually contradictory! Add to this the other Messianic passages in the Talmud and Midrash (and there are quite a few of these), and what emerges is a picture that is anything but clear. (For a sampling of these varied texts, see below, 3.23–3.24.)

To illustrate the point, in the tenth century of this era—about four hundred years after the close of the Talmud—the Jewish community in Pumbeditha (in Babylon) asked one of the leading Rabbinic scholars of the day, Rav Hai Gaon, to clarify for them the details of what they should believe about the Messiah. This means that almost one thousand years after the time of Jesus and almost eight hundred years after the writing of the Mishnah these religious Jews were not exactly sure of the details of what they should believe concerning the Messiah. That's because their beliefs were based on the Talmud, which does *not* present systematic discussion and final rulings about most topics it covers, making it necessary for succeeding generations to codify and clarify what the Talmud actually says. In the case of the Messiah, the Talmud is especially vague, since this was more a matter of belief than of legal practice, and the Talmud was more concerned with legal rulings than with sets of beliefs.

Writing a few decades before Hai Gaon, an even more prominent scholar, Rav Sa'adiah Gaon, also addressed the question of the Messiah. He explained that there would actually be *two* Messiahs, the Messiah son of Joseph (mentioned explicitly in the Talmud in b. Sukkah 52a), who was associated with a time of victory mixed with hardship and calamity, and the Messiah son of David, who would establish God's kingdom on the earth. However, if the Jewish people would be God-fearing and obedient, it was possible that there would be only one Messiah, the son of David, and no Messiah son of Joseph, meaning less suffering for Israel.[354] J. I. Schochet provides a useful summary:

> Quite significantly, R. Saadia Gaon (one of the few to elaborate on the role of Mashiach ben Yossef) notes that the sequence is not definite but

contingent! Mashiach ben Yossef will *not* have to appear before Mashiach ben David, nor will the activities attributed to him or his death have to occur. All depends on the spiritual condition of the Jewish people at the time the redemption is to take place.[355]

More than two hundred years later, Moses Maimonides offered a more definitive description of the characteristics of the Messiah. Writing in his authoritative code of law called the Mishneh Torah, Maimonides made mention only of the Messiah son of David, with no reference at all to a Messiah son of Joseph. And because the Mishneh Torah carries so much weight in traditional Judaism, this description of the Messiah is often viewed as the only Jewish belief on this topic. But that is hardly the case, for Jewish tradition is filled with rich and varied teachings on the Messiah and Messianic age.[356] Simply comparing the Talmudic discussion in Sanhedrin with the teaching of Sa'adiah Gaon and the code of Maimonides—not to mention the many traditions found in the midrashic and mystical literature—indicates that Jewish tradition is anything but narrowly uniform with regard to the Messiah.

For that very reason, it is often misleading to say, "Jews don't believe in a divine Messiah, or a suffering Messiah, or that the Messiah will come twice." According to which text? According to which Jewish expression? According to which rabbi or legal authority?

"But didn't you admit at the outset that *no* traditional Jewish teaching speaks directly of a divine Messiah? I fail to see the point of your discussion here."

The point is simply this: Some Jewish teachings describe a highly exalted or preexistent Messiah, while others point to a more earthly, suffering leader. Some teachings speak of the Messiah coming in the clouds of heaven, others speak of him tending to his wounds outside the gates of Rome. Which tradition do we follow? Some Rabbinic teachings refer to one Messiah, others to two Messiahs; still other teachings picture a Messiah who is a warring king, while another set of teachings pictures a Messiah who is primarily a teacher of the law. Again I ask, "Which tradition do we follow?" Jewish Messianic belief is more diverse than you may realize, especially when it comes to the Messiah's sufferings and the timing or sequence of his mission on earth.[357]

With regard to the divinity of the Messiah, it is true there is not one traditional Jewish source that speaks of his divine nature, but there are certainly important sources that speak of his supernatural qualities to the point that scholars have described these aspects of the traditional Jewish Messiah as "semi-divine."[358] This is important, since it would have been logical for Jewish tradition to completely downplay the Messiah's exalted nature in light of New Testament texts that spoke of his divinity (see above, 3.1–3.4). Could it be, then, that texts from the Tanakh pointing toward the Messiah's divinity made it impossible for Rabbinic Judaism to reject this completely? And could it be that the protracted longing of our people for a Messiah who would deliver us from our enemies caused us to look for a more and more exalted figure? Such questions are matters reserved for further research and speculation. What is sure is this: The Hebrew Bible lays the foundation for our belief in a divine Messiah, while a number of Jewish traditions recognize that the Messiah would have certain supernatural qualities. Let's take a look at some of the key texts, beginning with traditional Jewish literature and ending with the Tanakh. (In light of our lengthy discussions on the divine nature of Jesus the Messiah at the beginning of this volume, our treatment here will be limited.)

Because this traditional literature is so vast—it is rightly called the sea of the Talmud—and because it is possible to find a totally obscure, almost unknown text to support virtually any position, we will focus instead on one widely quoted Rabbinic tradition, namely, the midrash to Isaiah 52:13. The Scripture verse reads, "See, my servant will act wisely; he will be raised and lifted up and highly exalted." This is explained in the midrash as follows:

> *Who art thou, O great mountain?* (Zech. iv. 7.) This refers to the King Messiah. And why does he call him "the great mountain?" because he is greater than the patriarchs, as it is said, "My servant shall be high, and lifted up, and lofty exceedingly"—he will be higher than Abraham, who says, "I raise *high* my hands unto the Lord" (Gen. xiv. 22); lifted up above Moses, to whom it is said, "*Lift it* up into thy bosom" (Num. xi. 12); loftier than the ministering angels, of whom it is written, "Their wheels were *lofty* and terrible" (Ez. i. 18). And out of whom does he come forth? Out of David (Yalqut Shim'oni 2:571).[359]

Why did the midrash attribute such prominence to the Messiah here, based on Isaiah 52:13? It could be that elsewhere in Isaiah such terms of exaltation (raised, lifted up, highly exalted) were rightly applied only to God. In fact, you could argue that nowhere in the entire Book of Isaiah is anyone—including the Lord himself—

described in such exalted terms, and so it was only natural that this would catch the attention of the midrashic preachers and writers.[360] What is more interesting than this, however, is the *commentary* on this midrash by leading traditional scholars. Rabbi Don Yitshaq Abravanel, the illustrious Spanish Bible commentator and philosopher, helps put this in context.[361] Noting that the midrash explains Isaiah 52:13 with reference to "the King Messiah," Abravanel states:

> It is extremely difficult to understand how any child of man can be exalted above Moses, of whom the Law bears witness, saying, "No prophet ever arose in Israel like him" (Deut. xxxiv. 10); still more so, then, how any one "born of woman" can assume a position higher than the angels, whose substance admits of nothing above it except the substance of the First Cause: from the latter expression, in fact, Christian teachers have attempted to establish their doctrine of the Divinity of the Messiah.[362]

Now, what is especially noteworthy is that even though Abravanel interpreted Isaiah 52:13–53:12 with reference to the people of Israel, he still felt obligated to explain the midrash to Isaiah 52:13 for two reasons: first, because it carried the strong weight of tradition; and second, "lest otherwise the heretics come and shelter themselves beneath it."[363]

But it is not just "the heretics" who have interpreted this midrash with regard to the Messiah's exalted nature. Some traditional Jewish commentators have not been far behind.[364] Just look at what Rabbi Moshe Ibn Crispin (fourteenth century) wrote about the Messiah's exaltation above the angels:

> *Exceedingly* above the ministering angels, because that same comprehensive intelligence will approach [God] more nearly than theirs. For it is an exceedingly high privilege, that one whose nature is compound and material should attain to a grade of intelligence more nearly Divine than that which belongs to the incorporeal; and so it is said of him that "his strength is greater than that of the ministering angels," because these have no impediment in the exercise of their intellect, whereas that which is compound is continually impeded in consequence of material element in its nature. Accordingly the grade of his intelligence being such as this, he is said to be "lofty exceedingly," and his strength to be "greater than the angels."
> . . . And when this "servant of the Lord" is born, from the day when he comes to years of discretion, he will continue to be marked by the possession of intelligence enabling him to acquire from God what it is

impossible for any to acquire until he reaches that height whither none
of the sons of men, except him, have ever ascended.[365]

When you couple descriptions such as these with other traditions
that speak of the Messiah's preexistence (or the preexistence of his
name; see b. Pesahim 54a; Nedarim 39b)[366] or his coming in the clouds
of heaven (b. Sanhedrin 96b–97a), it is easy to see that there are, in
fact, Jewish traditions that recognize the exalted, superhuman, and
even semi-divine stature of the Messiah. As we also pointed out at the
beginning of this answer, there are also important, religious Jewish
texts dating to the last centuries B.C.E. and the first centuries C.E. that
speak of a heavenly Messiah. However, because they are not part of
the main body of Rabbinic literature, most traditional Jews are
unaware of their content. John Collins offers this analysis of some of
these texts:

> In Jewish writings the emphasis on the heavenly character of the sav-
> ior king appears in texts of the first century CE, especially in the period
> after the failure of the first revolt against Rome and the destruction of
> the Temple *(4 Ezra, Sib[ylline] Or[acles] 5)*. We may suspect, then, that
> it reflects a certain disillusionment with messiahs of human, earthly
> origin. The disillusionment was not complete, as can be seen from the
> messianic revolts of the early second century. Also the hope for a heav-
> enly deliverer, under God, is attested in the early apocalyptic literature,
> notably Daniel 7, and the heavenly messiah of the *Similitudes [of Enoch]*
> is likely to be older than 70 CE. What we find in the writings of the first
> century CE, however, is a tendency to combine traditions about a
> Davidic messiah with the expectation of a heavenly savior. There was,
> then, some flexibility in the use of messianic traditions in this period.
> Daniel's "one like a son of man" could be understood either as a purely
> heavenly figure (in the *Similitudes*) or as a messiah who operates on
> earth to restore Israel *(4 Ezra)*. Danielic imagery could be applied to
> the Davidic messiah to give him a more heavenly, transcendent char-
> acter than is apparent in other sources.[367]

And this brings us back to several key biblical texts. We saw above
(3.3) that the Midrash to Psalm 2:7—in which the Davidic king (i.e.,
King Messiah, according to Rabbi Yudan) is called God's son—joined
several key Scripture passages together, interpreting them with reference to the Lord's anointed one. The verses were (1) Exodus 4:22,
in which God calls Israel his firstborn son, meaning that just as Israel
was God's son so also the king was God's son; (2) Isaiah 52:13,

"Behold, my servant will act wisely," and Isaiah 42:1, "Here is my servant, whom I uphold, my chosen one in whom I delight,"[368] equating the king with the servant of the Lord; (3) Psalm 110:1, "The LORD said to my lord, 'Sit at my right hand,'" a verse quoted by Jesus himself to demonstrate that as Messiah he was more than just David's son, since David in this psalm called him "my lord"; and (4) Daniel 7:13, "In my vision at night I looked, and there before me was one like a son of man, coming with the clouds of heaven," another verse applied by Jesus to his own Messianic mission.

Putting this Rabbinic compilation of Scripture together, we see that the exalted figure coming in the clouds of heaven is none other than the Davidic king, the Son of God. And this leads us back to Daniel 7:13–14, verses we cited in our earlier discussion (above, 3.3), but verses worth looking at again, especially given the fact that both the Talmud and key medieval commentators refer them to the Messiah.[369] Daniel wrote:

> In my vision at night I looked, and there before me was one like a son of man, coming with the clouds of heaven. He approached the Ancient of Days and was led into his presence. He was given authority, glory and sovereign power; all peoples, nations and men of every language worshiped him. His dominion is an everlasting dominion that will not pass away, and his kingdom is one that will never be destroyed.
>
> Daniel 7:13–14

Do these verses, as applied to the Messiah, conclusively prove his divinity? This is certainly debatable, but the fact that he comes with the clouds of heaven and receives worldwide obeisance makes it clear that he is not merely a human![370] In fact, there is a fascinating account in the Talmud concerning the interpretation of Daniel 7:9–10, the verses leading up to vv. 13–14, which we just quoted. Looking first at the Scripture verses in question, we read more of Daniel's visionary account (I have emphasized the phrase that caught the attention of the Talmudic rabbis):

> As I looked,
> *thrones were set in place,*
>   and the Ancient of Days took his seat.
> His clothing was as white as snow;
>   the hair of his head was white like wool.
> His throne was flaming with fire,
>   and its wheels were all ablaze.

> A river of fire was flowing,
>   coming out from before him.
> Thousands upon thousands attended him;
>   ten thousand times ten thousand stood before him.
> The court was seated,
>   and the books were opened.
>
> Daniel 7:9–10

According to the Talmud, there was a debate between some of the leading sages concerning the meaning of "thrones" in the plural:

> One verse says: *His throne was fiery flames* and another verse says: *Until thrones were placed; and one that was the Ancient of Days did sit* [both of these citations come from Dan. 7:9]! There is no contradiction: One [throne] for Him and one for David [meaning the Messiah]. As it has been taught: One [throne] for Him and one for David [meaning the Messiah]. These are the words of R. Akiva. R. Yosi the Galilean said to him: Akiva! How long will you treat the divine presence [Hebrew, *shekinah*] as profane! Rather, one [throne] for justice and one for grace. Did he accept this explanation from him or did he not accept it? Come and hear: One for justice and one for grace; these are the words of R. Akiva (b. Hagigah 14a; note that in the ensuing discussion R. Elazar ben Azariah rejects *both* interpretations, claiming that one throne is for sitting, the other for a footstool!).

Could it be that Rabbi Akiva's first interpretation was correct and that there was a throne for the Ancient of Days and a throne for his Messiah? This certainly makes much better sense in context, hinting once again at the more-than-human status of the Messiah. We saw also in our lengthy discussion of the "Son of God" question (above, 3.3) that both Isaiah 9:6[5] and Psalm 45:7[8] clearly point toward the divine nature of the Messiah. In fact, Cambridge scholar William Horbury pointed out that the Septuagint, significant as the oldest written example of Jewish interpretation of Scripture, had an interesting translation of Isaiah 9:6[5]. He noted that the "Hebrew which can be translated 'wonderful counsellor, mighty god' (9. 5) and presents the royal child as 'a kind of demi-god' ([in the words of] G. Buchanan Gray)[371] is rendered by 'angel of great counsel' (9. 6 [Septuagint] *megalēs boulēs angelos*)."[372] So the Septuagint translated one of the names of this Davidic king—which the Targum understood to be the Messiah—as the "angel of great counsel," while the Hebrew itself actually called him "mighty God," "a kind of demi-god" according to a scholarly Bible commentator.[373] As for Psalm 110:1, where, according to one ancient Jewish interpretation, David calls the Messiah his Lord, readers of the New Testament will recall Yeshua's words to the religious leadership. He asked them:

> "What do you think about the [Messiah]? Whose son is he?" "The son of David," they replied. He said to them, "How is it then that David, speaking by the Spirit, calls him 'Lord'? For he says, "'The Lord said to my Lord: "Sit at my right hand until I put your enemies under your feet."' If then David calls him 'Lord,' how can he be his son?"
>
> Matthew 22:42–45

So then, the Messiah is David's son, but the Messiah is also greater than David.[374]

In light of all this, I submit to you something wonderful and profound: Through the Messiah, God himself has reached out to us, committing himself totally to our redemption and salvation. And as we will see in our next answer, through the Messiah he has fully identified with us in our suffering and pain. As you carefully and prayerfully consider the evidence, you will understand that Yeshua alone fulfills the Messianic expectations of the prophets of Israel and that he alone fulfills the Messianic dream.[375] We could hope for no greater Messiah.

Sadly, in our own day thousands of zealous, devoted Jews continue to proclaim that their deceased Grand Rabbi, Menachem Mendel Schneerson, the Rebbe, is actually King Messiah (see also below, 3.23, and n. 405). But it does not stop there. As Rabbi Dan Cohn-Sherbok observes:

> Some followers of the Rebbe have even gone so far as to use incarnational terminology in describing his mission. [The incarnation, as you may recall from our discussion above, 3.2, refers to God taking on human form. Now the Rebbe's followers are applying incarnational terminology to *him*.] During his lifetime, the *Rebbe* was referred to as the "Essence of the Infinite"; today some Lubavicher Hasidim [i.e., some of the Rebbe's disciples] talk of him as "Master of the Universe."[376]

Not surprisingly, such claims have brought sharp rebukes from non-Hasidic (but quite Orthodox) Jews, especially in Israel. In fact, in response to the claims of the Lubavitchers (known as Chabad), followers of Rav Eliezer Schach, an active leader well into his nineties, posted a large billboard in Hebrew reading:

A SHOCKING REVELATION
In the words of Chabad themselves:
The Rebbe Is the Messiah
and Even the Creator of the World Himself

As described by Samuel Heilman, beneath these words "was reproduced the masthead of the Lubavitcher newsletter . . . and the following paragraph from an article in it, circled and enlarged:

> . . . the Messiah at the time of redemption will be revealed to all people to be made not of flesh and blood, not even flesh and blood like our great teacher Moses, but rather to be the Holy One, blessed be He, himself!

"Juxtaposed to this was another quotation: 'Soon indeed His Holiness, our master, teacher and rabbi, May He Live for Many Good Days, Amen—the King, the Messiah, in all his glory and grandeur will reveal himself.'

"Were the Lubavitchers saying their rabbi was the Messiah, even God Himself? Careful readers would see in the Hebrew letters for 'indeed' . . .—(English: M-M-Š)—the initials of the Lubavitcher Rebbe's name. To opponents like Rabbi Schach even this was appalling. 'THIS PAINS US VERY MUCH!' the poster concluded in giant letters. 'But we cannot close our eyes to the facts.'"[377]

It is ironic, of course, that these Hasidic Jews, who so vehemently reject Yeshua and find the New Testament teaching on the incarnation offensive, can speak of their deceased leader as "Master of the Universe" and point to his alleged divine nature. They implicitly recognize some aspects of the Messiah's divinity, but they have pinned those aspects on the wrong candidate. Jesus alone fits the bill and fulfills the description. He is our divine Messiah, the ideal righteous King, the one whose death is powerful enough to pay for the sins of the entire world (see above, 3.15).

3.23. Jews don't believe in a suffering Messiah.

That is not true. From the Talmud until our own day, important Jewish traditions have acknowledged the Messiah's sufferings. In addition, many Jews believe in *two* messiahs, a triumphant reigning king called Messiah ben

David, and a suffering warrior called Messiah ben Joseph. More importantly, the Hebrew Scriptures speak clearly of the Messiah's sufferings. In fact, it is because our Bible describes the Messiah as a *priest* as well as a king that he had to suffer on our behalf, fulfilling his priestly role. To miss this is to miss an essential part of the Messiah's work.

There are many rich, beautiful, and theologically moving traditions in Jewish literature about the sufferings of the Messiah. In fact, the learned Jewish scholar Raphael Patai devoted an entire chapter to the subject in his unparalleled collection titled *The Messiah Texts*.[378] More than fifty years earlier, Gustaf Dalman, a Christian scholar of Judaica whose reference works are used by Jewish scholars to this day, devoted an entire volume to the subject of the suffering Messiah in Jewish tradition.[379] Further, the texts that describe the Messiah's suffering are not obscure, little-known texts representing the views and opinions of peripheral Jewish groups. Rather, they are found in the most important branches of Rabbinic literature, including the Talmud, the midrashic writings, and the medieval and modern commentaries on the Bible. Some of these traditions speak of the sufferings of the Messiah son of David (or Messiah ben David), *the* Messiah whose coming religious Jews pray for daily. Other traditions speak of the sufferings of the Messiah son of Joseph (Messiah ben Joseph), the immediate forerunner of Messiah ben David according to some traditions (see above, 3.22, and below, 3.24, for more on this).

Patai makes this startling statement regarding the Messiah's sufferings:

> The sufferings Israel must face in the days of the Messiah are temporary and transitory. They will last, according to the Talmudic view . . . seven years; a later Aggada . . . reduces this period to a mere forty-five days. The Messiah himself, on the other hand, must spend his entire life, from the moment of his creation until the time of his advent many centuries or even millennia later, in a state of constant and acute suffering.[380]

Summarizing the key Rabbinic teachings on the sufferings and afflictions of the Messiah, Patai writes:

> Despised and afflicted with unhealing wounds, he sits in the gates of Great Rome and winds and unwinds the bandages of his festering sores; as a Midrash expresses it, "pains have adopted him." According

to one of the most moving, and at the same time psychologically most meaningful, of all Messiah legends, God, when He created the Messiah, gave him the choice of whether or not to accept the sufferings for the sins of Israel. And the Messiah answered: "I accept it with joy, so that not a single soul of Israel should perish." . . . In the later, Zoharic [i.e., mystical] formulation of this legend, the Messiah himself summons all the diseases, pains, and sufferings of Israel to come upon him, in order thus to ease the anguish of Israel, which otherwise would be unbearable.[381]

Jewish tradition is filled with moving references to a suffering Messiah. Let's look first at the traditions relative to Messiah ben Joseph (also called Messiah ben Ephraim in some texts). According to the Talmud (b. Sukkah 52a), this Messiah would perform many mighty acts of valor for his Jewish people before dying in the great war that would precede the reign of Messiah ben David. In fact, Zechariah 12:10 ("They will look on me, the one they have pierced"), quoted with reference to the death of Yeshua in the New Testament, is applied to Messiah ben Joseph in this Talmudic text (for further discussion of Zech. 12:10, see vol. 3, 4.31). The Talmud also goes on to say that God would hear the prayer of Messiah ben David and would raise Messiah ben Joseph from the dead.[382]

Later Jewish traditions expanded on the sufferings of Messiah ben Joseph. This midrash, describing one of the houses in heavenly paradise, is typical:

. . . there sit Messiah ben David and Elijah and Messiah ben Ephraim. And there is a canopy of incense trees as in the Sanctuary which Moses made in the desert. And all its vessels and pillars are of silver, its covering is gold, its seat is purple. And in it is Messiah ben David who loves Jerusalem. Elijah of blessed memory takes hold of his head, places it in his lap and holds it, and says to him, "Endure the sufferings and the sentence your Master who makes you suffer because of the sin of Israel." And thus it is written: *He was wounded because of our transgressions, he was crushed because of our iniquities* (Isa. 53:5)—until the time when the end comes.

And every Monday and Thursday, and every Sabbath and holiday, the Fathers of the World [i.e. Abraham, Isaac, and Jacob] and Moses and Aaron, David and Solomon, and the prophets, and the pious come and visit him, and weep with him. And he weeps with them. And they give him thanks and say to him: "Endure the sentence of your Master, for the end is near to come, and the chains which are on your neck will be broken, and you will go into freedom."[383]

Were you aware that such texts existed in Jewish literature? Judaism *does* believe in a suffering Messiah. In fact, Christian readers will immediately be struck by two parallels between this midrashic description of the sufferings of Messiah ben Ephraim and the very real sufferings of Jesus the Messiah: (1) Both are said to suffer for the sins of their people, Messiah ben Ephraim enduring pain and affliction while waiting to be revealed to Israel, Messiah Yeshua enduring mockery, savage flogging, and crucifixion at the very moment that most of Israel was rejecting him. (2) The sufferings of both are explained with reference to Isaiah 53, the biblical text most frequently cited by followers of Jesus in order to prove that the Hebrew Scriptures did, in fact, point directly to him. Yet here the midrash applies this text to Messiah ben Ephraim, exactly as the Zohar did with reference to the Messiah's sufferings: "In the hour in which they [i.e. the souls of the righteous sufferers] tell the Messiah about the sufferings of Israel in exile, and [about] the sinful among them who seek not the knowledge of their Master, the Messiah lifts up his voice and weeps over those sinful among them. This is what is written, He was wounded because of our transgressions, he was crushed because of our iniquities (Isa. 53:5)."[384]

There is also an extraordinary comment about the atoning power of the death of Messiah ben Joseph made by Moshe Alshekh, the influential sixteenth-century rabbi, in his commentary to Zechariah 12:10:

> I will yet do a third thing, and that is, that "they shall look unto me," for they shall lift up their eyes unto me in perfect repentance, when they see him whom they pierced, that is, Messiah, the Son of Joseph; for our Rabbis, of blessed memory, have said that he will take upon himself all the guilt of Israel, and shall then be slain in the war to make atonement in such manner that it shall be accounted as if Israel had pierced him, for on account of their sin he has died; and, therefore, in order that it may be reckoned to them as a perfect atonement, they will repent and look to the blessed One, saying that there is none beside him to forgive those that mourn on account of him who died for their sin: this is the meaning of "They shall look upon me."[385]

As for Messiah ben David, despite the fact that Maimonides made no mention of any kind of Messianic sufferings for him (referred to above, 3.22), there are many important traditional texts that do speak of the sufferings of Messiah ben David. Here are some key texts.

In the well-known Talmudic passage summarized by Patai (see above), Rabbi Yehoshua ben Levi found Elijah the prophet sitting in a cave and asked him when the Messiah would come. When Elijah replied, "Go, ask him himself," Rabbi Yehoshua asked, "And where does he sit?" Elijah then explained that he sat at the entrance of the city, further clarifying that the Messiah had these distinctive marks: ". . . he sits among the poor who suffer of diseases, and while all of them unwind and rewind [the bandages of all their wounds] at once, he unwinds and rewinds them one by one, for he says, 'Should I be summoned, there must be no delay' (b. Sanhedrin 98a)."[386]

How this conveys the heart of the Messiah, eager and ready to be revealed to his people, yet suffering with them in pain and sickness. The account concludes with this poignant narrative. Rabbi Yehoshua went and found the Messiah, asking him, "When will the Master [meaning the Messiah] come?" The Messiah answered, "Today," a reply that Rabbi Yehoshua found dishonest, later saying to Elijah, "The Messiah lied to me, for he said, 'Today I shall come,' and he did not come." Elijah said, "This is what he told you: *'Today, if you but hearken to his voice'* (Ps. 95:7)."[387]

The Schottenstein Talmud, an extensive and highly valuable Orthodox commentary being published by Artscroll-Mesorah, offers this striking commentary on the passage:

> They [namely, those sitting with Messiah] were afflicted with *tzaraas*—a disease whose symptoms include discolored patches on the skin (see *Leviticus* ch. 13). The Messiah himself is likewise afflicted, as stated in *Isaiah* (53:4): . . . *Indeed, it was our diseases that he bore and our pains that he endured, whereas we considered him plagued* (i.e. suffering *tzaraas* [see 98b, note 39], *smitten by God, and afflicted*. This verse teaches that the diseases that the people ought to have suffered because of their sins are borne instead by the Messiah [with reference to the leading Rabbinic commentaries].[388]

In 1998, while lecturing to a small group of Ph.D. students at a leading Christian seminary, I had occasion to study this very Talmudic text. As I read and translated with these students, I was suddenly overcome with emotion, barely managing to hold back the tears. Somehow this legendary text became real to me, and I was struck by the Messiah's longing to be revealed, his carefulness to be ready at any moment, and the frustration on the part of my Jewish people that "today" had not yet come. How natural it was for me to think back to the pain Yeshua bore when our people did not recognize him, when they could have had their "today" almost two thousand years ago (see

Luke 19:41–44, and my discussion in vol. 1, 2.1). How quickly my mind went to the long and difficult centuries our people have endured, proclaiming daily their faith in the Messiah's imminent coming, still waiting, still hoping. (In the classic words articulated by Maimonides in the Thirteen Principles of Faith and recited daily by traditional Jews, "I believe in the coming of the Messiah, and even if he tarry, yet I will wait for him every day, expecting him to come." See further vol. 3, 4.2.) And how my thoughts went to our Messiah, waiting even now with eager anticipation, ready to return to earth with the blast of the ram's horn. These traditional Jewish texts strike a deep chord in me—and perhaps in you as well. But there's more to learn about the suffering Messiah in traditional Judaism. Let's keep reading.

We have pointed out that portions from Isaiah 52:13–53:12, the famous passage describing the sufferings of the servant of the Lord, were applied to the sufferings of the Messiah in some Rabbinic sources. In this regard, Patai noted that "the Messiah becomes heir to the Suffering Servant of God, who figures prominently in the prophecies of Deutero-Isaiah" (i.e., Isaiah 40–55).[389] Yet this passage was frequently quoted in the New Testament with regard to Jesus. You would have thought that this fact alone would have discouraged the rabbis from using it to refer to the Messiah. After all, if Isaiah 53 is a Messianic text, then Jesus, better than any other candidate, fits the bill. (For in-depth discussion of Isaiah 53, see vol. 3, 4.5–4.17.) Yet some Talmudic rabbis believed this text referred to the Messiah, as did some medieval mystics.

It would be fair to ask, however, whether any of the major Jewish commentators on the Bible actually read Isaiah 52:13–53:12 with regard to the Messiah, since it is one thing for a Talmudic midrash to cite an isolated verse from this section and apply it to the Messiah. After all, Talmudic citations are not meant to be precise interpretations of the biblical text but are often based on free associations and wordplays. It is another thing, however, for a traditional Jewish commentator to apply the text to the Messiah, especially given the missionary activity of the church through the ages, along with the history of "Christian" anti-Semitism (see vol. 1, 2.4–2.9). And yet there were key commentators that *did* apply Isaiah 52:13–53:12 to the Messiah (meaning Messiah son of David), with specific reference to his sufferings.[390]

I am especially familiar with these interpretations due to an unusual event that took place when holding a live radio debate with anti-missionary Rabbi Tovia Singer in May of 1991. As we were discussing Isaiah 53, Rabbi Singer stated that not one traditional Jewish Bible commentary interpreted the passage with reference to Messiah son of David. I differed with him emphatically, stating that several traditional commentaries did, in fact, say that Isaiah 53 referred to the Messiah. To this Rabbi Singer gave me a challenge: If he could prove me wrong, would I become a traditional Jew? "Yes," I responded (since I was sure I was right in my position), asking him in return, "Would you become a Messianic Jew if I could prove you wrong?" To this he in turn responded, "Yes." Right then and there, we shook hands on it. And he was wrong indeed! In fact, we got on the air again a few weeks later (together with the host and moderator, Messianic Jewish leader Sid Roth), and Rabbi Singer explained that what he meant to say was that no traditional Jewish commentary applied Isaiah 53 to the *death* of the Messiah son of David—a subject that had never come up once in our previous discussion.

Of course, Sid and I released Rabbi Singer from his promise (I never expected him to become a believer in Jesus just because he made a mistake in the middle of a live debate), but an unforgettable lesson was learned: Even traditional Jewish commentators referred Isaiah 53 to *the* Messiah, meaning Messiah son of David.[391]

What then were some of the commentaries to which I referred?[392] Most prominently, I pointed to Moses ben Nachman (called Nachmanides or the Ramban), one of the greatest of all medieval Jewish scholars and famed for his Barcelona debate with the Catholic Jew Pablo Christiani (see vol. 1, 2.12). He claimed that Isaiah spoke of "the Messiah, the son of David . . . [who] will never be conquered or perish by the hands of his enemies."[393] In spite of this victorious description of the Messiah, however, Nachmanides also spoke of his suffering:

> *Yet he carried our sicknesses* [Isa. 53:4], being himself sick and distressed for the transgressions which should have caused sickness and distress in us, and bearing the pains which we ought to have experienced. *But we*, when we saw him weakened and prostrate, *thought* that he was *stricken, smitten of God. . . . The chastisement of our peace* was *upon him*—for God will correct him *and by his stripes we were healed*—because the stripes by which he is vexed and distressed will heal us: God will pardon us for his righteousness, and we shall be healed both from our own transgressions and from the iniquities of our fathers. . . .
>
>   *He was oppressed and he was afflicted* [v. 7]: for when he first comes, "meek and riding upon an ass" [Zech. 9:9], the oppressors and officers

of every city will come to him, and afflict him with revilings and insults, reproaching both him and the God in whose name he appears.[394]

Quite strangely, when interpreting the verses that speak clearly of the Messianic servant's death, Nachmanides goes out of his way to avoid the obvious fact that the servant did, indeed, die. Instead, he attempts to explain that the Messiah was *willing* to die, that he *expected* to die, that it would be *reported* that he was cut off from the land of the living, and that evil Israelites, together with wicked Gentiles, would *devise* all kinds of deaths for him.[395] Thus Nachmanides still claims that "there is, however, no mention made in the Parashah [i.e., portion of Scripture] that the Messiah would be delivered into the hands of those who hated him, or that he would be slain, or hung upon a tree; but that he should see seed and have long life, and that his kingdom should be high and exalted among the nations, and that mighty kings should be to him for spoil."[396]

It would have been much truer to the text to speak plainly of the Messiah's death, explaining the references to his seeing offspring and having long life in terms of his resurrection.[397] Still, it is fascinating to see how a rabbi of Nachmanides's stature found it appropriate to read Isaiah 53 as a prophecy of Messiah son of David, describing his sufferings as well as his exaltation.

Other significant commentators interpreting this key passage with reference to the sufferings of Messiah son of David include Rabbi Moshe Kohen Ibn Crispin (or Ibn Krispin), who first described the highly exalted nature of the Messiah (following a famous midrash to Isaiah 52:13; see above, 3.22) and then spoke of his sufferings in great detail, explaining that he would share Israel's "subjugation and distress" and be "exceedingly afflicted":

> . . . his grief will be such that the colour of his countenance will be changed from that of a man, and pangs and sicknesses will seize upon him . . . and all the chastisements which come upon him in consequence of his grief will be for our sakes, and not from any deficiency or sin on his part which might bring punishment in their train, because he is perfect, in the completeness of perfection, as Isaiah says (xi. 2 f.).[398]

Commenting on some of the central verses, Ibn Crispin writes:

> *A man of pains and known to sickness*, i.e., possessed of pains and destined to sicknesses; so all that see him will say of him. They will also, it continues, on account of his loathsome appearance, be *like men hid-*

ing their faces from him: they will not be able to look at him, because of his disfigurement. And even we, who before were longing to see him, when we see what he is like, *shall despise him* till we no longer *esteem him,* i.e., we shall cease to think of him as a Redeemer able to redeem us and fight our battles because of all the effects which we see produced by his weakness.

. . . it will be as though he had borne all the sickness and chastisements which fall upon us. . . . Or, perhaps . . . from his pity and prayers for us he will atone for our transgressions: *and our pains he hath borne,* viz., as a burden upon himself . . . i.e., all the weight of our pains he will carry, being himself pained exceedingly by them. *And we esteemed him stricken, smitten of God, and afflicted.* We shall not believe that there could be any man ready to endure such pain and grief as would disfigure his countenance, even for his children, much less for his people: it will seem a certain truth to us that such terrible sufferings must have come upon him as a penalty for his own many shortcomings and errors.[399]

Much more could be quoted, along with selections from the commentary of Rabbi Mosheh El-Sheikh (or Alshekh), who claimed that "our Rabbis with one voice accept and affirm the opinion that the prophet is speaking of the King Messiah," also referring to a midrash that stated that "of all the sufferings which entered into the world, one third was for David and the fathers, one for the generation in exile, and one for the King Messiah."[400]

In our own day, Isaiah 53 was applied directly to Menachem Schneerson, hailed as Messiah ben David by his devoted followers worldwide, with specific reference to his suffering. Thus, when Rabbi Schneerson (known simply as the Rebbe, in keeping with Hasidic tradition) suffered a stroke in 1992 and could not speak, his followers pointed to Isaiah 53:7, "He was oppressed and afflicted, yet he did not open his mouth; he was led like a lamb to the slaughter, and as a sheep before her shearers is silent, so he did not open his mouth." When his paralyzed condition showed little or no improvement, they pointed to other verses in Isaiah 53 that speak of the sickness of the servant of the Lord. The Rebbe became sick, they claimed, so that we might be healed! When he died in 1994 at the age of ninety-two, some of his most loyal disciples proclaimed in writing that his death was an atonement for us, in keeping with the traditional teaching that the death of the righteous atones (see above, 3.15)—and then they began to pray fervently and wait expectantly for his resurrection and/or return.[401]

If I didn't see and hear and read these things for myself, it would be difficult to believe them, seeing that they form such an exact parallel to the suffering and death of Yeshua (as atonement for our sins), along with his resurrection (thank God, Yeshua really did rise from the dead!), and his awaited return. Yet the traditional Jewish teaching of a suffering Messiah was so ingrained in the Jewish psyche that the suffering and death of the Rebbe was seen by his followers in wholly Messianic terms—in spite of the fact that they had to use a favorite text of "Christian missionaries" (namely, Isaiah 53) in very "Christian" ways. As Patai observes:

> There can be little doubt that psychologically the Suffering Messiah is but a projection and personification of Suffering Israel. . . . Similarly, the Leper Messiah and the Beggar Messiah [spoken of in the Talmud] . . . are but variants on the theme of Suffering Israel personified in the Suffering Messiah figure. And it is undoubtedly true in the psychological sense that, as the Zohar states, the acceptance of Israel's sufferings by the Messiah (read: their projection onto the Messiah) eases that suffering which otherwise could not be endured.[402]

The final text we will read actually gives the fullest and most detailed description of the Messiah's sufferings found anywhere in the major Rabbinic sources. I refer to chapters 34, 36, and 37 of the important eighth- to ninth-century midrash known as Pesikta Rabbati. In fact, the descriptions of the Messiah's sufferings found there are possibly stronger than anything found in the New Testament.[403] Some scholars, basing their position on the fact that the Messiah is called Ephraim in these chapters, believe that the reference is to Messiah ben Joseph. Others, however, point out that he is referred to as "My righteous Messiah," which would normally be taken to mean Messiah ben David. Thus, Rabbi Schochet notes that "the term Ephraim, though, may relate here to collective Israel, thus referring to Mashiach ben David."[404] In any event, what we have before us is indisputable: a Rabbinic text prized by traditional Jews and outlining in graphic detail the vicarious sufferings of the Messiah. Here are selections from Pesikta Rabbati chapter 36 as translated by Patai:

> They said: In the septenary [i.e., seven-year period] in which the Son of David comes they will bring iron beams and put them upon his neck until his body bends and he cries and weeps, and his voice rises up into the Heights, and he says before Him: "Master of the World! How much can my strength suffer? How much my spirit? How much my soul? And how much my limbs? Am I not but flesh and blood? . . ."

In that hour the Holy One, blessed be He, says to him: "Ephraim, My True Messiah, you have already accepted [this suffering] from the six days of Creation. Now your suffering shall be like My suffering. For ever since the day on which wicked Nebuchadnezzar came up and destroyed My Temple and burnt My sanctuary, and I exiled My children among the nations of the world, by your life and the life of your head, I have not sat on My Throne. And if you do not believe, see the dew that is upon my head. . . ."

In that hour he says before Him: "Master of the World! Now my mind is at rest, for it is sufficient for the servant to be like his Master!"[405]

The Fathers of the World [Abraham, Isaac, and Jacob] will in the future rise up in the month of Nissan and will speak to him: "Ephraim, our True Messiah! Even though we are your fathers, you are greater than we, for you suffered because of the sins of our children, and cruel punishments have come upon you the likes of which have not come upon the early and the later generations, and you were put to ridicule and held in contempt by the nations of the world because of Israel, and you sat in darkness and blackness and your eyes saw no light, and your skin cleft to your bones, and your body dried out was like wood, and your eyes grew dim from fasting, and your strength became like a potsherd. All this because of the sins of our children. Do you want that our children should enjoy the happiness that the Holy One, blessed be He, allotted to Israel, or perhaps, because of the great sufferings that have come upon you on their account, and because they imprisoned you in the jailhouse, your mind is not reconciled with them?"

And the Messiah answers them: "Fathers of the World! Everything I did, I did only for you and for your children, and for your honor and for the honor of your children, so that they should enjoy this happiness the Holy One, blessed be He, has allotted to Israel."

Then the Fathers fo the World say to him: "Ephraim, our True Messiah, let your mind be at ease, for you put at ease our minds and the mind of your Creator!"[406]

Amazingly, one key passage cited in the Pesikta with reference to the Messiah's afflictions is Psalm 22, the psalm of the righteous sufferer, a psalm well known among Christians because it is applied to Jesus in the New Testament—although anti-missionaries are quick to point out that it is *not* a Messianic psalm (see vol. 3, 4.24). Yet here it is applied to the Messiah in Pesikta Rabbati.[407] Notice also how the Messiah here willingly suffers because of (or for the sake of) the sins of his people, having to endure rejection, scorn, and mockery—and after that, he is highly exalted. I assure you: If you gave these passages to Christian preachers, they would have plenty of sermon material!

What makes this all the more interesting is that we could have easily expected some Jewish leaders to try to expunge all references to the Messiah's sufferings from the traditional literature, since Christians claimed that according to the Hebrew Scriptures the Messiah *had* to suffer and die. But the fact that there are so many texts that speak of these sufferings in the Talmud, the midrashic collections, the mystical literature, and the Bible commentators reminds us that Judaism does indeed believe in a suffering Messiah. It is too scriptural to deny! However, Messianic Jews would be quick to point out that there is a distinct redemptive reason for these sufferings. They are part of God's gracious help on our behalf and part of the priestly ministry of the Messiah. He reached out to us, becoming like us in our weakness and laying down his life as an atoning sacrifice on our behalf. As we stated in our discussion of the Holocaust (vol. 1, 2.10), Jesus the Messiah is the best-known Jew of all time, yet he was beaten, flogged, humiliated, and nailed to a cross. He is a Messiah with whom we can identify—and who can identify with us—a suffering Messiah who brings life, deliverance, and lasting victory to all who put their trust in him.

The midrash we just cited contains powerful words spoken by the Messiah to Abraham, Isaac, and Jacob: "Fathers of the World! Everything I did, I did only for you and for your children, and for your honor and for the honor of your children, so that they should enjoy this happiness the Holy One, blessed be He, has allotted to Israel." But there is something more powerful than this: Messiah Jesus *really did* suffer and die for the sins of Israel and the world, rising in power and ascending to heaven, where he sits enthroned until the time of his return. All that he did, he did for us! I pray that through his pains, you will find the happiness and peace with God that he has purchased and provided. In the words of Simon bar Jonah, one of Messiah's first followers and a man who witnessed Yeshua's life and death and then saw him after his resurrection,

[Messiah] suffered for you, leaving you an example, that you should follow in his steps. "He committed no sin, and no deceit was found in his mouth." When they hurled their insults at him, he did not retaliate; when he suffered, he made no threats. Instead, he entrusted himself to him who judges justly. He himself bore our sins in his body on the tree, so that we might die to sins and live for righteousness; by his wounds you have been healed. For you were like sheep going astray, but now you have returned to the Shepherd and Overseer of your souls.

1 Peter 2:21–25

3.24. Jews don't believe the Messiah will come twice.

Judaism actually has many different traditions about the coming of the Messiah, including beliefs that there are *two* messiahs who will each come *once,* as well as beliefs that there is a *potential* Messiah present in *each* generation. Scripture and history teach us that there will be *one* Messiah who will come *twice.*

You probably feel that the notion of a "second coming" is a cop-out, a clever excuse as to why Jesus didn't do everything he was supposed to do according to the traditional Jewish view of the Messiah. It's as if Christians are saying, "Just give him one more chance! He'll get it right the next time."[408] Actually, as we have emphasized repeatedly (vol. 1, 2.1; see also vol. 3, 4.30, 4.32), Jesus did everything the Messiah was required to do before the Second Temple was destroyed, he is doing everything the Messiah is presently required to do, and when he returns, he will finish his Messianic task, right on schedule.

In contrast with this biblical position of *one Messiah* fulfilling a wide range of prophecies, first by being born as a man on the earth, then coming with divine power from heaven, traditional Judaism has developed at least three different options (see above, 3.22–3.23): (1) There will be *two* Messiahs, one who will suffer and die and one who will rule and reign.[409] (2) There are *different possible scenarios* for the Messiah's coming, depending on our behavior. If we are righteous, he will come with the clouds; if we are sinful, he will come on a donkey. (3) There is a *potential Messiah* in every generation, and it is up to us to recognize him and become worthy of him. More recently, some of the followers of the Lubavitcher Rebbe, Menachem Schneerson, have developed a fourth option: The Messiah (= Rabbi Schneerson) will be resurrected and then will return and reign as king.[410]

The Schottenstein Talmud, reflecting Orthodox Jewish views, explains the traditional belief about the presence of a potential Messiah in each generation. At the same time, however, it demonstrates how difficult it is to square this teaching with some important Talmudic texts. Commenting on the famous account of Rabbi Yehoshua ben Levi's encounter with the Messiah—almost two thousand years ago (see above, 3.23)—the Schottenstein Talmud explains:

The Midrash states that the Messiah was born when the Temple was destroyed and was subsequently taken to Gan Eden [i.e., the Garden of Eden, or heavenly Paradise]. . . .

This should not be understood to mean that the Messiah is not a natural-born human being. Rather, in every generation since the destruction of the Temple there has lived a person of outstanding piety, ready to be invested with the spirit of the Messiah when the time for the redemption comes. As was the case with Moses, this person will not know that he is destined to be the Messiah, until the time is ready.[411]

All this speculation, however, is unnecessary. The Bible speaks of only one Messiah, from the line of David yet greater than David, a king and yet a priest, first suffering and dying for the sins of Israel and the world, then returning in triumph and judgment. In contrast with Rabbinic speculation, there is no need to create a second Messiah descended from a different tribe, a Messiah whom the Hebrew Scriptures do not know at all. And there is no need to create an either-or scenario (coming in the clouds or riding on a donkey), since the Tanakh speaks of both-and (first riding on a donkey, then coming in the clouds).[412] There is also no need to ask who the alleged potential Messiah is for each generation, since there were specific requirements for the Messiah (including when and where he would be born; see vol. 3, 4.32–4.33), and if he did not come at the appointed time and place, then all the believing in the world cannot make him into the Messiah.

Of course, it is often said that it is anathema for Jews to believe that the Messiah has already come, yet as we have seen, many traditional Jews actually believe that every generation has had a potential Messiah. Thus, following the traditional Jewish logic here, *many* Messiahs have already come but none of them were recognized since none of the previous generations proved worthy enough to merit the Messiah. Traditional Judaism, then, would recognize many *possible* Messiahs who have already come but no *actual* Messiah who has come.

May I suggest another approach? What if Yeshua—the one and only Messiah—came at the time expected by the prophets, but his generation was not worthy of receiving him, leading to his rejection, suffering, and death.[413] All this, however, was known in advance by God, who foresaw and foreordained the Messiah's death as an atoning sacrifice for the world.[414] Therefore, what mankind meant for evil, God meant for good. At the end of this age, when my Jewish people recognize Jesus as Messiah and call on him to return, they will prove themselves worthy of him, and he will joyfully come again in the clouds of heaven, just as Daniel wrote, and establish his kingdom in Jerusalem. Doesn't this make more sense than the traditional Jewish view?

Let me go one step farther: This not only makes more sense, it has a striking parallel in the Torah. Do you remember the story of Joseph and his brothers, the sons of Jacob? Joseph was called by God to be the leader among his siblings, but they hated him and sold him into slavery in Egypt. While Joseph was in Egypt, languishing in prison, God set in motion a plan that led to seven years of severe famine. How does Scripture describe these events? "He called down famine on the land and destroyed all their supplies of food; and he sent a man before them—Joseph, sold as a slave" (Ps. 105:16–17). What a statement! Joseph's brothers maliciously sold him into slavery in Egypt, but the Bible says that *God* sent Joseph there. This is exactly what Joseph said to his brothers many years later: "God sent me ahead of you to preserve for you a remnant on earth and to save your lives by a great deliverance. So then, it was not you who sent me here, but God. He made me father to Pharaoh, lord of his entire household and ruler of all Egypt" (Gen. 45:7–8). Of course, it is true that the brothers bore the responsibility for their sins, but it is equally true that God himself was orchestrating the events, having a higher purpose—the saving of many lives—through it all.

Yet there's more to the story (and the parallel between Joseph and Jesus). Joseph was the viceroy to the Pharaoh when his brothers first came to Egypt to buy grain, but they didn't recognize him. He hardly resembled the seventeen-year-old they had sold into slavery. He was esteemed and venerated by the Egyptians, he spoke Egyptian, and he wore Egyptian garb. Foreigners honored him; his own family didn't even know who he was. (Need I point out the parallel with Yeshua here?) But when the brothers returned the second time to Egypt, Joseph revealed himself to them. Anyone who has read this entire story in Genesis (chapters 37, 39–47) will agree that it is one of the most moving accounts ever written. What intrigue, what suspense, what emotion!

After Jacob died, the brothers of Joseph became afraid that he would retaliate against them because of their cruelty toward him as a teenager. But Joseph responded, "You intended to harm me, but God intended it for good to accomplish what is now being done, the saving of many lives" (Gen. 50:20). This same picture applies to our relationship as Jews with Yeshua.[415]

The first time around, Joseph's brothers didn't recognize him, but the second time he made himself known to them. It was the same Joseph, but he was rejected before he was accepted. (The same thing happened to Moses; see Exodus 2–5.) First he suffered abasement, then he was exalted. First he was esteemed by the Gentiles, then he was honored by his own flesh and blood. And so it will be with Jesus, the Jewish Messiah, and his brothers, the Jewish people. We will recognize him in the end, but we will be held accountable for rejecting him until that time. And while Messianic Jews eagerly await the time when our people as a whole will turn back to God in repentance and put their trust in his Messiah, we encourage each and every individual Jew to make that choice today.

There are not two Messiahs, nor is there a potential Messiah in every generation. There is one Messiah who came once—right on schedule—and in the fullness of time he will come again. With all my heart, I pray that you will acknowledge him today so that you can welcome him when he returns.

3.25. Judaism is a healthy religion. Jews don't see the world as intrinsically evil or denounce marriage or call for self-renunciation. Christians, on the other hand, see the world as evil, advocate celibacy, and say, "Deny yourself, take up your cross, and suffer."

This is an exaggerated and inaccurate statement. Traditional Jews see this world as the corridor to the world to come but stress the importance of life in this world. As for Christians, while stressing the importance of the world to come, they have been responsible for the building of more hospitals, the feeding of more hungry people, and the establishment of more educational institutions than adherents of all other religions of the world combined. The difference between the two is not one of substance but of emphasis. So the real question is, Which emphasis makes more sense? If this life is only a passing shadow (as Psalm 90 teaches), and if we are only pilgrims and strangers here (as Jacob and David said), isn't it logical to live out our few days here in the light of eternity? If we are on this earth for seventy or eighty years and then we enter eternity—either under God's favor or God's judgment—doesn't it make sense to give serious thought to the world to come, making sure

> we are ready to enter our eternal home? Also, both Judaism and Christianity recognize the sinful *tendencies* of the human race; Christianity just puts greater emphasis on subduing those tendencies, calling on its adherents to "put to death the harmful desires of the sinful nature." Finally, Jesus emphasized that we are not here primarily for ourselves but for God and for others, not to be served but to serve. God's kingdom is advanced through suffering and sacrifice, and that too is part of our calling as mature followers of the Messiah.

In order to respond fairly to your objection, I'll divide my answer into three parts: First, we'll consider what the Tanakh, the New Testament, and the Rabbinic writings say about this world and the world to come. Second, we'll look at how these viewpoints have played themselves out in Christianity and Judaism. Third, we'll ask if the New Testament approach to life makes sense in the light of eternity.

There is no question at all that the *primary* emphasis in the Hebrew Scriptures was on this world rather than on the world to come, but that was mainly because God *gradually* revealed the truth about the resurrection of the dead and the world to come.[416] In other words, even though it appears the patriarchs believed in some kind of life after death, we still have to admit that the Torah was not explicit about any of the details.[417] For this reason, groups such as the Sadducees, basing their beliefs only on the Torah, incorrectly denied that there would be a resurrection of the dead. (See Yeshua's refutation of this in Matt. 22:23–33.) However, by the time of Daniel, the revelation was clear: "Multitudes who sleep in the dust of the earth will awake: some to everlasting life, others to shame and everlasting contempt. Those who are wise will shine like the brightness of the heavens, and those who lead many to righteousness, like the stars for ever and ever" (Dan. 12:2–3).

Still, in spite of this gradual revelation of the world to come in the Hebrew Bible, there was a clear understanding that this life was fleeting at best. The patriarch Jacob, as an old man, said to Pharaoh, "The years of my pilgrimage are a hundred and thirty. My years have been few and difficult, and they do not equal the years of the pilgrimage of my fathers" (Gen. 47:9). The psalmist David, a man who literally lived in a king's palace, said, "We are aliens and strangers in your sight, as were all our forefathers. Our days on earth are like a shadow, without hope" (1 Chron. 29:15). According to Psalm 90 (identified as a psalm of Moses in the superscription), "The length of our days is seventy years—or eighty, if we have the strength; yet their span is but trouble and sorrow, for they quickly pass, and we fly away" (v. 10). Psalm 103 contains similar language: "As for man, his days are like grass, he flourishes like a flower of the field; the wind blows over it and it is gone, and its place remembers it no more" (vv. 15–16). Isaiah 40:6–8 sums it up well: "A voice says, 'Cry out.' And I said, 'What shall I cry?' 'All men are like grass, and all their glory is like the flowers of the field. The grass withers and the flowers fall, because the breath of the LORD blows on them. Surely the people are grass. The grass withers and the flowers fall, but the word of our God stands forever.'"

The New Testament uses almost identical descriptions: Peter exhorted the believers to live their lives on this earth "as strangers" (1 Peter 1:17), while Paul—in the midst of suffering and persecution for his faith in the Messiah—could write that "we fix our eyes not on what is seen, but on what is unseen. For what is seen is temporary, but what is unseen is eternal" (2 Cor. 4:18). The language of Jacob (James) is also reminiscent of the language of the Tanakh: "Now listen, you who say, 'Today or tomorrow we will go to this or that city, spend a year there, carry on business and make money.' Why, you do not even know what will happen tomorrow. What is your life? You are a mist that appears for a little while and then vanishes. Instead, you ought to say, 'If it is the Lord's will, we will live and do this or that'" (James 4:13–15).

Rabbinic Judaism also has much to say about the fleeting nature of this life and the importance of belief in the afterlife. According to Rabbi Simcha Paull Raphael, "teachings on life after death have always been part and parcel of the Jewish spiritual legacy."[418] While acknowledging that "Judaism does value life, here and now, over and above a future death and eternal life," he is careful to point out that "this does not imply there is no Jewish belief in afterlife" (13). Rather, "there exists a profound and extensive legacy of Jewish teachings on the afterlife. Over the course of four millennia, Judaism evolved and promulgated a multifaceted philosophy of postmortem survival, with doctrines comparable to those found in the great religions of the world" (14). In fact, Rabbi Raphael argues that many Jews today do *not* believe in an afterlife because of modern secular and rationalistic thinking, historic persecution from the church (which thereby caused Jews to react strongly against the church's beliefs in heaven and hell), and the tragedy of the Holocaust, among other factors. Rabbi Dan Cohn-Sherbok can also state that "as with Heaven, Jewish sources contain extensive and elaborate descriptions of Hell."[419]

"But how do these beliefs play themselves out?" you ask. "Rabbinic Judaism didn't produce nuns who never married or monks who whipped themselves for their sins. Christianity is filled with such unhealthy practices, and they all flow from Jesus' command that his followers must deny themselves."

Let me first respond to the beginning of your question, namely, How do these beliefs play themselves out in Christianity and Judaism? No doubt, there have been many extreme, other-worldly Christians throughout the centuries, and I have no reason to deny this fact. There have been men such as Simon Stylites (c. 390–459), who lived for years perched atop a pillar fifty feet high (and greatly impacted his generation at the same time), or others, almost too many to name, who lived for years in caves.[420] And to this day, Roman Catholicism forbids its priests or nuns to marry, following the example of Paul (see also his teaching in 1 Corinthians 7, discussed below).

But is this what Jesus and Paul intended? Are you aware that the other apostles were married and that Paul's celibacy was the exception (see 1 Cor. 9:5)? Are you aware that Paul *expected* leaders in the church to be married with children? (See 1 Tim. 3:1–5; Titus 1:6; he even asks the question in 1 Tim. 3:5, "If anyone does not know how to manage his own family, how can he take care of God's church?") In fact, he warned of false teachings that would infiltrate the community of believers, speaking of "hypocritical liars, whose consciences have been seared as with a hot iron," people whose teachings had been inspired by deceiving spirits and demons (1 Tim. 4:1–2). What strong words he used! And what were the teachings he considered so dangerous? You can read Paul's words for yourself: "They forbid people to marry and order them to abstain from certain foods, which God created to be received with thanksgiving by those who believe and who know the truth. For everything God created is good, and nothing is to be rejected if it is received with thanksgiving, because it is consecrated by the word of God and prayer" (1 Tim. 4:3–5).

Here Paul is *warning* believers not to follow those who forbid to marry and command people to abstain from certain foods that God created for us to eat and enjoy.[421] And it was Paul who penned some of the most beautiful teaching about marriage—as well as true, godly love—in the ancient world (see Eph. 5:22–32; 1 Corinthians 13). Why then did he encourage the Corinthian believers not to marry? This would seem to be in stark contrast to the Rabbinic dictum that man is not complete until he marries (b. Yebamot 67a; cf. also b. Yebamot

62b), and to the first commandment given—"Be fruitful and multiply"—which could not be fulfilled without marriage.[422]

Actually, Paul made this "anti-marriage" statement only one time—in contrast with his teachings on husbands, wives, and children, which are found in a number of his letters (e.g., Eph. 5:22–6:4; Col. 3:18–21; Titus 2:1–6)—and it was simply stated as a preference. There was also a specific context to his teaching, namely, what he called "the present crisis" (1 Cor. 7:26), apparently a reference to the distresses and troubles the Corinthians were experiencing. At such a time, it's much easier to be single than to be married with children.[423] That's why God commanded Jeremiah not to marry or have children his entire life:

> Then the word of the LORD came to me: "You must not marry and have sons or daughters in this place." For this is what the LORD says about the sons and daughters born in this land and about the women who are their mothers and the men who are their fathers: "They will die of deadly diseases. They will not be mourned or buried but will be like refuse lying on the ground. They will perish by sword and famine, and their dead bodies will become food for the birds of the air and the beasts of the earth."
>
> Jeremiah 16:1–4

Who wants to get married and have a family if that will be their fate?

Paul also added another dimension to his discussion with the Corinthians about marriage:

> I would like you to be free from concern. An unmarried man is concerned about the Lord's affairs—how he can please the Lord. But a married man is concerned about the affairs of this world—how he can please his wife—and his interests are divided. An unmarried woman or virgin is concerned about the Lord's affairs: Her aim is to be devoted to the Lord in both body and spirit. But a married woman is concerned about the affairs of this world—how she can please her husband. I am saying this for your own good, not to restrict you, but that you may live in a right way in undivided devotion to the Lord.
>
> 1 Corinthians 7:32–35

How true this is! Still, Paul fully realized that even in the present crisis the Corinthians were experiencing, and even in light of his practical teaching about single-minded devotion to the Lord, many of those he was writing to would not have the ability or calling to remain single. So he stated clearly that if they got married they were not sinning (1 Cor. 7:36). Unfortunately, his words to the Corinthians have been quoted out of context.[424]

I should also point out to you the unusual example of Ben Azzai, a Talmudic rabbi who never married because his only love was for the Torah (b. Yebamot 63b). This kind of love—for God, for the Messiah, for a dying world—has prompted Christians through the years to choose a celibate life, undistracted by the cares of this world and unhindered by a family, given completely over to the service of God and man, often in perilous, life-threatening situations. In what sense is this wrong, unscriptural, or unhealthy?

Having said this, however, I need to emphasize to you that the *overwhelmingly vast majority* of Jesus' followers around the world embrace marriage for themselves as a God-given, wonderful institution, recognizing the importance of children and family. As it is written in the New Testament, "Marriage should be honored by all" (Heb. 13:4). In fact, you could say that Christians basically follow Jeremiah's words to the Jewish exiles living in Babylon. Having informed them that their captivity would last seventy years, he gave the following counsel:

> Build houses and settle down; plant gardens and eat what they produce. Marry and have sons and daughters; find wives for your sons and give your daughters in marriage, so that they too may have sons and daughters. Increase in number there; do not decrease. Also, seek the peace and prosperity of the city to which I have carried you into exile. Pray to the LORD for it, because if it prospers, you too will prosper.
>
> Jeremiah 29:5–7

This is essentially how followers of Jesus have lived throughout the centuries. We understand that we are living in exile from the Promised Land (heaven) but that we will be here in this world for some time. Therefore, we seek to live out our seventy to eighty years on earth as practically as we can.

But it doesn't stop there. Followers of Jesus take his words very seriously when he refers to us as the light of the world and the salt of the earth (Matt. 5:13–16), exhorting us to "let your light shine before men, that they may see your good deeds and praise your Father in heaven" (v. 16). That is why the church has always led the way in humanitarian efforts around the world. As pointed out by D. James Kennedy and Jerry Newcombe in their book *What If Jesus Had Never Been Born?*, the positive contributions made by Christianity throughout the centuries include hospitals; universities; literacy and education for the masses; capitalism and free-enterprise; representative government; the separation of political powers; civil liberties; the abolition of slavery, both in antiquity and in more modern times; pioneering developments in modern science; the elevation of women; benevolence and charity; the good Samaritan ethic; higher standards of justice; the elevation of the common man; the condemnation of sexual perversions; high regard for human life; the civilizing of many violent, primitive cultures; the codifying and setting to writing of many of the world's languages; greater development of art and music; countless changed lives transformed from liabilities into assets to society because of the gospel.[425]

Consider the following:

- The church has taken the lead in providing health care and emergency help to those in need. How do you think groups such as the Red Cross and the Salvation Army got their names?[426]
- Christian charitable organizations such as World Vision and World Relief are among the first to provide food and practical help in famine-stricken areas, while Christian families actively help in caring for refugees.[427]
- It is Christian money and Christian effort that have enabled tens of thousands of Jews from impoverished countries to return to the land of Israel.[428]
- American universities such as Harvard, Yale, and Princeton, along with British universities such as Oxford and Cambridge, were all founded by and for Christians, while universities such as Wheaton—which remains Christian today—were founded along slave escape routes.
- We actually have a name for the industrious business practices of Christians, namely, the Protestant work ethic.
- Missionaries worldwide have taught uneducated peoples to read and write, instructing them also in proper nutrition and hygiene.
- It was the Christian political leader William Wilberforce who successfully fought to abolish slavery in England, helping to pave the way for its subsequent demise in the United Statest.[429]
- Christians lead the pro-life movement, arguing that even life in the womb is sacred to God and ought not to be snuffed out.[430]
- Some of the world's greatest composers, such as Bach and Handel (just think of Handel's *Messiah*), were Christians, while it

was a Benedictine monk who developed the do-re-mi-fa-so-la-ti system for memorizing the notes c-d-e-f-g-a-b.

- Christian, biblical themes have inspired some of the world's greatest works of art, including the works of Michelangelo and Raphael.
- Tribes who used to be cannibals and headhunters have become civilized and peace-loving through hearing the gospel. In fact, it was the gospel that tamed the ferocious, marauding Vikings.[431]
- It is especially through the efforts of Christian Bible translators that we now have hundreds of languages in written form, enabling formerly illiterate peoples to become educated (not to mention enabling them to read the Word of God in their native tongue).
- In the inner cities of America, it is the church that is most active in feeding the poor, setting up homeless shelters, and caring for wayward children.

I would encourage you to step back and consider the far-reaching, positive effects of Christianity on the world. They have hardly been unhealthy. And by caring for the sick, building hospitals, feeding the poor, fighting for the rights of the unborn, Christians clearly affirm the value of life in this world. And who fights for traditional family values in America more than Bible-believing Christians? Of course, you could say that religious Jews are also pro-family and pro-life, active in charity and engaged in good works, and I would agree with you here.[432] But *that* subject is not being debated right now. Our discussion has to do with the practical outworking of the teachings of the New Testament in this world—and it is undeniable that these teachings have produced an overwhelming amount of good fruit in society.[433] In fact, to illustrate the extent to which Christianity is known as the religion of good works, the Dalai Lama, the most important religious leader in Buddhism today, recently "urged his own monks to emulate 'my Christian brothers and sisters' in transforming Buddhist compassion into concrete acts of social service."[434] Even Buddhists recognize the compassionate, humanitarian actions of the church.

It may also surprise you to know that far from always hindering scientific development, the church throughout the centuries has often fostered it. Kennedy and Newcombe, drawing on the work of Dr. Henry Morris, list the following "outstanding Bible-believing scientists who *founded* the following branches of science":

antiseptic surgery	Joseph Lister
bacteriology	Louis Pasteur
calculus	Isaac Newton
celestial mechanics	Johannes Kepler
chemistry	Robert Boyle
comparative anatomy	Georges Culver
computer science	Charles Babbage
dimensional analysis	Lord Rayleigh
dynamics	Isaac Newton
electronics	John Ambrose Fleming
electrodynamics	James Clerk Maxwell
electromagnetics	Michael Faraday
energetics	Lord Kelvin
entomology of living insects	Henri Fabre
field theory	Michael Faraday
fluid mechanics	George Stokes
galactic astronomy	Sir William Herschel
gas dynamics	Robert Boyle
genetics	Gregor Mendel
glacial geology	Louis Agassiz
gynecology	James Simpson
hydrography	Matthew Maury
hydrostatics	Blaise Pascal
ichthyology	Louis Agassiz
isotopic chemistry	William Ramsey
model analysis	Lord Rayleigh
natural history	John Ray
non-Euclidean geometry	Bernard Riemann
oceanography	Matthew Maury
optical mineralogy	David Brewster

And this is just a sampling.[435]

Regarding medicine and health care, while working on my book *Israel's Divine Healer*, I was struck by the impact that Jesus and his followers have had on that aspect of compassionate, applied science. I wrote there that

as far as the impact of Christianity on the medical profession is concerned, [Dr.] J. W. Provonsha has argued that Jesus, and not Hippocrates, should be viewed as the "Father of Medicine," since Jesus "was more often engaged in acts of healing than in almost anything

else . . . [and it] was the humble Galilean who more than any other figure in history bequeathed to the healing arts their essential meaning
and spirit."[436] And, while [medical scholars] D. J. Guthrie and P. Rhodes
could point out that, "It is sometimes stated that the early Christian
Church had an adverse effect upon medical progress," their conclusion
is that "the infinite care and nursing bestowed under Christian aus-
pices must outweigh any intolerance shown toward medicine in the
early days."[437] Moreover, in the opinion of [medical historian H. E.]
Sigerist, "It remained for Christianity to introduce the most revolu-
tionary and decisive change in the attitude of society toward the sick.
Christianity came into the world as the religion of healing, as the joyful Gospel of the Redeemer and of Redemption. It addressed itself to
the disinherited, to the sick and afflicted and promised them healing,
a restoration both spiritual and physical." Thus, "It became the duty of
the Christian to attend to the poor and the sick of the community."[438]

In this regard, I also quoted the words of Korean physician D. J.
Seel:

> Early in my manhood I said I could not be a physician unless I were
> first a disciple of Jesus Christ. . . . *Jesus healed.* It follows that the gospel
> of Jesus cannot be complete without that compassionate ministry. Jesus
> demonstrated that our God is compassionate, that He is moved by
> human suffering. And therefore Christ's disciples must seek to be
> instruments of healing, in one or more of the various avenues available
> for medical ministry. Christian medicine must be above all else an
> exhibit, a demonstration, of the character of God.[439]

Such quotes and illustrations could be reproduced endlessly, but
the lesson from all this is clear: The gospel of Jesus has had a wonderfully positive influence on life *in this world,* and looking around
the globe today, it is nations with a true Christian legacy that have
the best track record of providing rights for all—minorities, people
of different religious faiths, women—whereas countries ruled by
Islam or godless Communism are the most repressive.[440] Even in
Israel, to the extent that the ultra-Orthodox Jews gain political power,
they are bent on restricting the religious freedom of other Jews.[441]

This last observation leads to me another point. As I said earlier,
I agree with you that traditional Jews are actively involved in various
good deeds and acts of charity, and I recognize that the nation of
Israel is known for its humanitarian acts around the world. But it
seems to me that the more religious a Jew becomes, the less practical influence he or she has on this world. In other words, it seems

that those Jews who have made the greatest impact on society (such as Dr. Jonas Salk, who discovered the polio vaccine, or Albert Einstein the scientist) or who are known for their art or music (such as Marc Chagall the painter, or Itzhak Perlman the virtuoso violinist) were not observant in the traditional Jewish sense. Can you imagine a deeply religious Jewish man practicing violin for ten hours a day when he could be studying Talmud instead? Of course, I know there are Orthodox Jewish scientists and Orthodox Jewish doctors and Orthodox Jewish professors and Orthodox Jewish musicians. On the other hand, I know that the most Orthodox Jews—called *haredim* in Israel—care almost nothing about developing life in this world, unless it pertains to bringing Jews into a Talmudic lifestyle. Where is the "this-worldliness" among the very Orthodox? And what normally happens to traditional Judaism outside of a cloistered environment? It assimilates. These are issues to consider as well.

Regardless of how much you agree with my last points about traditional Judaism and this world, you cannot deny the truth of my points about the outworking of the teachings of the New Testament on the world as a whole: They have greatly enhanced and enriched the quality of our lives here.

The fact is, however, we are only passing through this world, and that brings us to our last question, namely, Does the New Testament approach to life make sense in the light of eternity? The answer, to anyone who believes in the resurrection of the dead, can only be yes.

To help us build on a sound biblical foundation, let's consider some parallels between the Hebrew Scriptures and the New Testament concerning our orientation toward this world: Both affirm that every good thing comes from God (Ps. 84:11; James 1:17) and that he richly gives us these things to enjoy (Eccles. 5:19; 1 Tim. 6:17). Both, however, also warn us about the danger of forgetting the Lord in the midst of earthly abundance (Deut. 8:1–20; Luke 12:13–21; Rev. 3:17), recognizing the peril of putting our trust in riches (Prov. 23:5; 27:23–27; Luke 16:13–31; 1 Tim. 6:3–10, 17–19), and cautioning us to beware of covetousness (Exod. 20:17; Col. 3:5; Heb. 13:5). Both also encourage us to be circumspect in our time here on earth, numbering our days (Ps. 90:12; Eph. 5:15–16) and considering the certainty of our death (Eccles. 3:1–2; Heb. 9:27). In light of this, it is not surprising that even in the Hebrew Bible it is written, "It is better to go to a house of mourning than to go to a house of feasting, for death is the destiny of every man; the living should take this to heart" (Eccles. 7:2).

Now, it is true that all of the Scriptures, both Tanakh and New Testament, recognize the importance of this world in and of itself. Jesus even said, "I have come that they [namely, God's people] may have life, and have it to the full" (John 10:10). However, in light of eternity—fully revealed in the New Testament—we can say that this world is especially important because it prepares us for the world to come. Again, to use the Rabbinic phrase, this world is only the corridor to the world to come (see m. Avot 4:16).[442] And we dare not be carnally minded like Esau, who sold his birthright because he was hungry and wanted a piece of bread (Gen. 25:29–34; Heb. 12:16–17). How he lived to regret his decision! He forfeited lifelong blessing because of a momentary lust for food—just like many of us. We forfeit God's eternal blessing in the world to come because we just have to satisfy our earthly lusts. This makes no sense at all. (If you agree with me here, then you are in agreement with the perspective of the New Testament.)

You can consider this world as the place of preparation. A young woman who is about to go on an important date with her fiancé spends a great deal of time putting on the right clothes, doing her hair, and making sure she looks her best. Why? Because the dressing room is important? Hardly! It is because her fiancé is important, because her night out is important. So also, we have a "date" to stand before God one day, and then, hopefully, to spend the rest of "forever" with him. This is our time to get ready.

I recently came across the *Humanist Manifesto II* (published in 1973), well known for its overt stance against traditional religion. It states, "Promises of immortal salvation or fear of eternal damnation are both illusory and harmful. They distract humans from present concerns, from self actualization, and from rectifying social injustices."[443] Is this the position you espouse? Then your problem is not only with Christianity but with Judaism as well, since the secular humanist philosophy articulated by the *Manifesto* flies in the face of mainstream religious beliefs. Eternal bliss and eternal misery are weighty subjects indeed (see below, 3.27), and the fact that all of us have only one of two fates—eternal blessing in the presence of God or eternal destruction shut out from his presence—should influence the way we live every day of our lives. That is the viewpoint of the New Testament.

But there is more. The New Testament makes it clear that this world is a battleground, and that as followers of the Messiah we must lay our lives down to help save a dying world. It is a call to spiritual warfare—that is, to be soldiers in God's spiritual army (Eph. 6:10–18;

2 Tim. 2:3; see also Psalm 144)—a call to deny ourselves, die to the grip of sin, and glorify God by life or by death (Matt. 16:24; Luke 9:23; Rom. 6:1–23; Phil. 1:20–21). You might look at it like this: Religious Jews have died in every century for *kiddush hashem*, meaning, for the sanctification of God's name, believing that by standing firm for what they believe, they will honor God and ultimately save their people from assimilation. They live and die for a principle. In the same way, followers of Jesus have made a commitment to give themselves for people who are lost without God, knowing that it could cost them their own lives. We are here not to be served but to serve, following in Yeshua's footsteps (Matt. 20:17–28; Phil. 2:5–11).

Of course, Jews attempt to make everything in this world sacred and holy; Christians see the world itself as God's beautiful creation while viewing *the world system* as utterly corrupt (see 2 Cor. 4:3–4; 1 John 2:15–17; 5:19). Therefore, Christians do not share Judaism's optimism about the possibility of making this world sacred and holy. Instead, they possess a determination to do whatever is necessary to relieve suffering in the present while preparing people for the world to come. In doing so, they ennoble human life and human death. (This is not to say that Jews have failed to ennoble human life and death; it is only to say that Christians most certainly have.)

In fact, as Paul wrote more than nineteen hundred years ago, death has now lost its sting (see 1 Cor. 15:51–58).[444] Because of this, even martyrdom has become sacred. In the words of missionary Jim Elliot, martyred by the Auca Indians of Ecuador in 1956, "He is no fool who gives what he cannot keep to gain what he cannot lose." This world is fleeting and fading away; the world to come is eternal. That's why Nate Saint, Elliot's colleague and fellow martyr, could say, "People who do not know the Lord ask why in the world we waste our lives as missionaries. They forget they too are expending their lives and when the bubble has burst they will have nothing of eternal significance to show for the years they have wasted."[445] I for one want to have something to show for my years in this world, something that will endure, something that will make sense in the light of eternity, something that will bring joy to the heart of my Father God.

The fact is that God's kingdom has always been advanced through suffering and sacrifice, and so we deny ourselves for the good of a dying world. Through laying down our lives, we bring life to millions who would otherwise have lived and died without God and without hope. In my opinion, that makes all the sense in the world, and I can think of no better way to spend the few short years I have here—even one hundred years pass in a moment—than in giving myself selflessly to further the purposes of God. What do you think?

3.26. Christianity calls on its followers to exhibit unnatural emotions and feelings such as love for their enemies. This is contrary to the Torah as well as human nature.

> Could it be that what you call "unnatural emotions and feelings" are actually lower, more base human attitudes, while the ethical behavior that Jesus requires from his followers actually reflects higher, loftier, spiritual attitudes? Maybe not everything that is "natural" is good and not everything that is "unnatural" is bad. Could it be that the Messiah calls us to a higher and better life? Could it be that through his gracious help he enables us to put to death our earthly, carnal tendencies and more fully reflect the divine image in which we were created? I would suggest to you that this represents a decided step *up* for the human race, a fruit of the Messiah's work on our behalf.

Traditional Judaism teaches that there are two tendencies (or inclinations) in man, the *yetser hara'* (the evil inclination) and the *yetser hatov* (the good inclination). The godly man must sublimate the evil inclination and cultivate the good inclination. The question is, Which inclination is "natural"? Is it natural to lose one's temper, or is it natural to have a long fuse? Is it natural for a young man to have immoral fantasies, or is it natural for him to be pure and self-controlled? Which kind of behavior is natural? And if our very nature is corrupt, should we be content with doing that which comes naturally, or should we cry out to God for help and do that which comes supernaturally?

The New Testament speaks of the outward self and the inward self, the flesh and the spirit, acknowledging the decided human tendency to do evil and to give in to carnal desires. At the same time it promises transformation through faith in Jesus the Messiah. In light of that promise, Jesus called on his followers to say no to the sinful desires of the flesh and to cultivate the holy ways of the Spirit. That's what he meant when he said that we must "deny ourselves" (for other aspects of this, see immediately above, 3.25). Therefore, when the self wants to hold a grudge, or take revenge, or satisfy a lust, or get puffed up with pride, or be contentious, or lash out in anger, or rail against God, Jesus calls us to deny that "self"—even if it feels unnatural at first. The wonderful reality is that with discipline, denying our sinful desires and taking the higher, spiritual road can become natural.

"But doesn't the Hebrew Bible teach us to take vengeance on our enemies? How can Jesus tell us that we must forgive them? It's not natural, and it's not right to do this."

May I answer your question with a few questions of my own? Isn't it better to forgive one's enemies than it is to harbor hatred toward them? Isn't it better to overcome evil with good than it is to fight evil with evil or, worse still, to be overcome by evil?

"But what about the Scriptures? You didn't address the point that what Jesus taught and what the Torah taught are two, distinctly different things."

Let's take a look at Scripture, examining in particular the question of taking vengeance on our enemies. It is true that God sometimes called the nation of Israel to inflict just punishments on their enemies. So, for example, he instructed them never to forget what the Amalekites did to them after their liberation from Egypt, expressly commanding them, "When the LORD your God gives you rest from all the enemies around you in the land he is giving you to possess as an inheritance, you shall blot out the memory of Amalek from under heaven. Do not forget!" (Deut. 25:19; note also Numbers 31). But would anyone take this as a personal directive today? Would anyone say, "Because God commanded the Israelites to kill all the Canaanites—men, women, children, and livestock—he must be commanding me to kill all the irreligious in my community"? Hardly!

On the contrary, throughout Scripture, God instructed his people to act kindly to their enemies, not to carry a grudge against them, and to leave vengeance to him. In the Torah it is written:

> If you come across your enemy's ox or donkey wandering off, be sure to take it back to him. If you see the donkey of someone who hates you fallen down under its load, do not leave it there; be sure you help him with it.
>
> Exodus 23:4–5

> Do not hate your brother in your heart. Rebuke your neighbor frankly so you will not share in his guilt. Do not seek revenge or bear a grudge against one of your people, but love your neighbor as yourself. I am the LORD.
>
> Leviticus 19:17–18

> It is mine to avenge [says God]; I will repay.
>   In due time their foot will slip;
> their day of disaster is near
>   and their doom rushes upon them.
>
> Deuteronomy 32:35

In similar fashion, Proverbs clearly teaches it is wrong to hold vengeful and hateful attitudes toward our enemies, giving these clear directives: "If your enemy is hungry, give him food to eat; if he is thirsty, give him water to drink. In doing this, you will heap burning coals on his head, and the LORD will reward you" (Prov. 25:21–22).[446] In fact, even if God is actually judging our enemies, Proverbs warns us not to gloat or rejoice over this: "Do not gloat when your enemy falls; when he stumbles, do not let your heart rejoice, or the LORD will see and disapprove and turn his wrath away from him" (Prov. 24:17–18). It was the ungodly who acted with hate and vengeance, while the godly repaid evil with good. As the psalmist wrote:

> Ruthless witnesses come forward;
>   they question me on things I know nothing about.
> They repay me evil for good
>   and leave my soul forlorn.
> Yet when they were ill, I put on sackcloth
>   and humbled myself with fasting.
> When my prayers returned to me unanswered,
>   I went about mourning
>   as though for my friend or brother.
> I bowed my head in grief
>   as though weeping for my mother.
> But when I stumbled, they gathered in glee;
>   attackers gathered against me when I was unaware.
>   They slandered me without ceasing.
> Like the ungodly they maliciously mocked;
>   they gnashed their teeth at me.
>
> Psalm 35:11–16

Interestingly, when Paul wanted to make a strong ethical point in his teachings, as a Jew well-versed in the Hebrew Bible he drew on some of the very texts we just quoted:

> Do not repay anyone evil for evil. Be careful to do what is right in the eyes of everybody. If it is possible, as far as it depends on you, live at peace with everyone. Do not take revenge, my friends, but leave room

for God's wrath, for it is written: "It is mine to avenge; I will repay,"
says the Lord. On the contrary: "If your enemy is hungry, feed him; if
he is thirsty, give him something to drink. In doing this, you will heap
burning coals on his head." Do not be overcome by evil, but overcome
evil with good.

> Romans 12:17–21, quoting Deuteronomy 32:35; Proverbs 25:21–22

Do you disagree with these words? Don't they simply call us to take
the higher road—or, really, the highest road? Think for a moment
about Yeshua being nailed to the cross. Would you have more admi-
ration for him if he cursed his crucifiers in the harshest possible terms,
damning them to eternal torments and wishing evil on their descendants, or would you find him to be more admirable if he said, "Father,
forgive them, for they do not know what they are doing" (Luke 23:34)?
It would certainly be "natural" for an innocent man being crucified
to lash out in anger at those nailing him to the cross, bitterly denouncing those who wrongly accused him as well. But how supernatural—
and beautiful—it is to forgive those very people. That's exactly what
Jesus did, and that's exactly what he calls us to do: "But I tell you who
hear me: Love your enemies, do good to those who hate you, bless
those who curse you, pray for those who mistreat you" (Luke 6:27–28).
While we were yet sinners the Messiah died for us (Rom. 5:6), and it
is this unconditional love that sets the pattern for our behavior: "Bear
with each other and forgive whatever grievances you may have against
one another. *Forgive as the Lord forgave you*" (Col. 3:13; see also Matt.
18:21–35).

I would submit to you that the New Testament simply calls on
believers to take the high ground in disputes and conflicts, and in
doing so it builds on the teachings and examples found in the Tanakh.
And while the lofty ideals of Jesus the Messiah can be quite challenging for us human beings, with his help we can live them out.
Those of us who have taken Yeshua at his word have found that his
way is best, bringing release from wrong, destructive attitudes and
fostering holy, pure attitudes that are in keeping with God's heavenly
kingdom and that will find their full expression there.

Of course, if we were God we would have a perfect sense of right
and wrong, never losing our tempers and never having a bad attitude.
Our anger would be perfect, our sense of justice unerring, our actions
toward our enemies completely upright. The fact is, however, we are
not God; consequently, our attitudes and actions are often tainted
and polluted. So let's leave vengeance and personal retribution to the

Lord, concentrating instead on perfecting the qualities of mercy, compassion, kindness, and goodness.[447] How thrilling it is when these become second nature to us. How thrilling it is to take the high road, even if it means taking the low road in the eyes of man (see, e.g., 1 Cor. 6:1–7). If we have God's approval, that's all we need.

3.27. The only thing that keeps many people in the Christian faith—including Jews—is a fear of hell.

> Of the thousands of followers of Jesus whom I know around the world—both Jews and Gentiles—I cannot think of one who continues to follow Jesus *primarily* because of a fear of hell, let alone *only* because of a fear of hell. We follow him because we love him and recognize him to be our Messiah. Having said this, there is no question that from a biblical perspective (i.e., Torah, Prophets, Writings, New Testament) a healthy fear of the Lord and a recognition that he is the ultimate Judge provides an added incentive to holy living. So our primary motivation for following the Lord is love; a second motivation is to spend eternity with him in his kingdom; a third motivation is to escape the judgment of hell.

The greatest motivation for service is love. Think of how it drives people to sacrifice. A soldier will fight to the death out of love for his country. A mother will run into a burning house to rescue her children. A husband will lay down his life to save his wife from death. Is there anything love will not do? And love produces love! In the context of our discussion here, God's love for us produces a response of love for him. How could we not love him, serve him, and give our all to him and for him? He gave his Son for us! That's why John could write, "We love because he first loved us" (1 John 4:19). His love awakened love in us.

The New Testament is clear on this. We love God and we love one another because of the love he has shown us:

Dear friends, let us love one another, for love comes from God. Everyone who loves has been born of God and knows God. Whoever does not love does not know God, because God is love. This is how God showed his love among us: He sent his one and only Son into the world that we might live through him. This is love: not that we loved God, but that he loved us and sent his Son as an atoning sacrifice for our sins. Dear friends, since God so loved us, we also ought to love one another.

1 John 4:7–11

This is how we know what love is: Jesus [the Messiah] laid down his life for us. And we ought to lay down our lives for our brothers.

1 John 3:16

[Jesus said:] My command is this: Love each other as I have loved you. Greater love has no one than this, that he lay down his life for his friends.

John 15:12–13

It is a gospel principle that he who is forgiven much loves much (see Luke 7:36–50). How much, then, should we love God? He has forgiven all our sins through the death of his Son:

You see, at just the right time, when we were still powerless, [Messiah] died for the ungodly. Very rarely will anyone die for a righteous man, though for a good man someone might possibly dare to die. But God demonstrates his own love for us in this: While we were still sinners, [Messiah] died for us. Since we have now been justified by his blood, how much more shall we be saved from God's wrath through him! For if, when we were God's enemies, we were reconciled to him through the death of his Son, how much more, having been reconciled, shall we be saved through his life!

Romans 5:6–10

That's why Peter could write to his fellow believers, "Though you have not seen him, you love him; and even though you do not see him now, you believe in him and are filled with an inexpressible and glorious joy" (1 Peter 1:8). And that's why Paul could say of his own experience, "But whatever was to my profit I now consider loss for the sake of [Messiah]. What is more, I consider everything a loss compared to the surpassing greatness of knowing [Messiah] Jesus my Lord, for whose sake I have lost all things. I consider them rubbish, that I may gain [Messiah]" (Phil. 3:7–8).

Jesus likened this experience to "treasure hidden in a field. When a man found it, he hid it again, and then in his joy went and sold all he had and bought that field" (Matt. 13:44). He also likened it to "a merchant looking for fine pearls. When he found one of great value, he went away and sold everything he had and bought it" (Matt.

13:45–46). How often do Christians say that Jesus is the pearl of great price?[448] And how many hymns and choruses sung in churches and by Messianic congregations joyfully proclaim our loving response to God's grace toward us? I could write about this almost without end.

There is, however, another side to the story, and that is the fear of the Lord. It is also an important theme. A yachtsman goes out in his boat because he loves boating, but he stays in the boat because he doesn't want to drown. A healthy fear should not be despised. According to the Hebrew Bible, the fear of the Lord is the beginning of wisdom and knowledge (Job 28:28; Ps. 111:10; Prov. 1:7; 9:10), an antidote to sin (Exod. 20:20; Prov. 16:6), the key to long life and blessing (Ps. 34:11–22; Prov. 10:27; 14:27), and a rich treasure (Isa. 33:6). In fact, the author of Ecclesiastes summarized things by saying, "Now all has been heard; here is the conclusion of the matter: Fear God and keep his commandments, for this is the whole duty of man" (12:13). Why? "For God will bring every deed into judgment, including every hidden thing, whether it is good or evil" (Eccles. 12:14).

Similar themes are found in the New Testament as well (see, e.g., Matt. 10:28; Acts 9:31; Heb. 12:28–29; 1 Peter 1:17), and Paul could even say, "Since, then, we know what it is to fear the Lord, we try to persuade men" (2 Cor. 5:11). Why? "For we must all appear before the judgment seat of [Messiah], that each one may receive what is due him for the things done while in the body, whether good or bad" (2 Cor. 5:10). Shades of Ecclesiastes and the Hebrew Scriptures!

You see, it is true that God's people are *primarily* motivated to serve him out of love not fear.[449] But it is also true that he has always warned us of the consequences of disobedience. In fact, the lengthy passages in the Torah warning us of the consequences of breaking the Lord's covenant (see Leviticus 26 and Deuteronomy 28) are more graphic—not to mention far more comprehensive and detailed—than any warnings found in the New Testament. But the entire Bible contains warnings. Moses warned, the prophets warned, the wisdom writers warned, Yeshua warned, his emissaries warned. What else would we expect? Sometimes we need a sharp word of rebuke. Sometimes we need a spiritual slap in the face. Sometimes we need a divine reminder of the awful consequences of sin. I'm glad Jesus said:

> If your hand or your foot causes you to sin, cut it off and throw it away. It is better for you to enter life maimed or crippled than to have two

hands or two feet and be thrown into eternal fire. And if your eye causes
you to sin, gouge it out and throw it away. It is better for you to enter
life with one eye than to have two eyes and be thrown into the fire of
hell.

Matthew 18:8–9

There are many incentives to holiness. What is wrong with this? It's
a good thing to want to escape hell and damnation.[450]

In all candor, I could lodge this objection against Judaism as well.
In fact, I could make a much stronger case for the fear motivation in
traditional Judaism as opposed to the fear motivation in Messianic
Judaism. The image that is always fresh on the mind of followers of
Jesus is that of our Messiah dying on the cross on our behalf, as
explained in John 3:16, perhaps the most famous verse in the entire
Bible: "For God so loved the world that he gave his one and only Son,
that whoever believes in him shall not perish but have eternal life."
In contrast with this, the image that most strongly presents itself to
the Jewish mind—or at least one of the most common images—is that
of God giving the Ten Commandments on Mount Sinai. And according to a well-known midrash, God picked up Mount Sinai and held
it threateningly over the head of his people Israel, asking them
whether or not they would accept his covenant. Not surprisingly, they
replied, "Everything the Lord has said we will do" (Exod. 24:3; see
also 24:7).[451] Who then is serving out of love and who is serving out
of fear?

I also find it ironic that anti-missionaries claim Messianic Jews
won't deny Jesus because they are afraid they will be sent to hell for
denying him, but these same anti-missionaries will then tell Messianic
Jews that we are guilty of idolatry and are in danger of falling under
the fiery judgment of God. One ultra-Orthodox rabbi whom I met at
Stony Brook University in the mid-1980s told me that if he and I were
living in biblical times, I would have been brought before the Sanhedrin and burning metal would have been poured down my throat!
The bottom line is that I love God far too much to let fear tactics turn
me away from serving him and honoring his Messiah with all my
heart and soul. I honestly believe that if you knew the Lord the way
I know him, you couldn't help but love him too.

Let me leave you with a personal invitation from Yeshua himself,
the Good Shepherd who gave his life for the sheep (John 10:10–15),
the Savior of the world who invites us to become his friends (John
15:14–15). Only in him will we find satisfaction and rest.

If anyone is thirsty, let him come to me and drink. Whoever believes in me, as the Scripture has said, streams of living water will flow from within him. . . . Whoever drinks the water I give him will never thirst. Indeed, the water I give him will become in him a spring of water welling up to eternal life. . . . I am the bread of life. He who comes to me will never go hungry, and he who believes in me will never be thirsty.

John 7:37–38; 4:14; 6:35

With all that is within me, I urge you to come home to our Messiah and eat and drink with him. There is still room at his table. And even if following him costs you everything, you will never look back with remorse. As expressed by the saintly Robert Murray M'Cheyne 150 years ago, "There is nothing that you can possibly need but you will find it in Him." And that is why missionary Henry Martyn, despite losing everything and sacrificing his life to reach the Muslim world with the message of Messiah's love, could also write, "With Thee, O my God, is no disappointment. I shall never have to regret that I have loved Thee too well."

3.28. I find much beauty in the teachings of Jesus, and I think there are some good arguments in favor of Christianity. But I find it impossible to believe in a religion that condemns all people to hell—including many moral, good, kind, and sensitive people, not to mention countless millions of religious Jews, Muslims, Hindus, and Buddhists—simply because they don't believe in Jesus. I can't follow a religion whose God tortures people in flames forever for not believing in someone they never even heard of.

To be honest with you, I don't follow that religion either, nor would I be able to put my trust in a God like that. Only one thing really matters: Is there a place called hell, and is there a judgment after death? If so, what is hell like, and who deserves to go there? What about you? Do you deserve heaven or hell? Also, we can argue endlessly about the afterlife, something which neither of us has experienced firsthand. But does your view of sin, judgment, and God agree with the current state of the world, a world filled with suffering and tragedy, and does it line up with the historical experience of our people? What followers of Jesus believe is this: All of us have sinned and broken God's commandments, resulting in untold tragedy for the human race. In his mercy, God sent his Son, the Messiah, into the world to take our place and pay for our sins. He is our hope and our salvation. If we reject him, we remain lost in this world and we will be lost in the world to come. As to the exact nature of the sufferings of hell, Scripture does not speak with scientific precision, but the Tanakh, the New Testament, and even the Rabbinic literature give us some frightful descriptions. As for those who never heard about Jesus, God will be their judge, not you and not me.

Have you read this volume through in its entirety? Then you know that we have provided reasonable, logically argued, biblically based answers to some of the weightiest Jewish objections to belief in Jesus. You have seen that the New Testament teaching on the nature of God and the divinity of the Messiah is in harmony with the Hebrew Scriptures; that blood sacrifices, joined with repentance, were the heart and soul of the Torah's system of atonement; and that Yeshua, in keeping with a lofty Jewish concept, brought atonement to the world through his death. Perhaps you have lowered your defenses and are honestly willing to consider the claims for the messiahship of Jesus. Still, there is one thing bothering you, and that is the picture of millions of good, religious people burning forever in hell just because they didn't know about Jesus.

Let me encourage you simply to consider what we know for a fact: This world is filled with sin, and as a result, it is filled with suffering. This is *not* the way God created things. All the sickness in the world, all the pain, the war, the hatred, the cruelty, the fear—all of it is due to sin. If the human race had not sinned at the beginning of time and if we had not continued to sin in every generation, none of this would be here. The world would literally be a perfect paradise. Yet we have forsaken God and worshiped and served other gods and other things in his place, and we have paid a terrible price for our disobedience and folly. So if this is the effect of sin in this world, what will its effect be on the world to come? Or to phrase the question differently, What are the eternal consequences of rejecting God?

Think of wicked, ungodly sinners who hurt and destroyed many innocent people but who seem to live full, healthy lives themselves. They somehow manage to avoid the penalties of human courts and even God's court during their earthly years. When do they get punished? Or what about people who knew God but then scorned and rejected him, suffering very few visible consequences in their lives? When do they face judgment? Can you agree with me that there will be at least *some* people who will deserve punishment in the world to come and that God will be a righteous and fair judge? If so, then the words of Yeshua should make sense to you. "For a time is coming when all who are in their graves will hear [God's] voice and come out—those who have done good will rise to live, and those who have done evil will rise to be condemned" (John 5:28–29).

"But," you say, "according to Christian beliefs, many *good* people will be condemned to hell! How do you square that with Jesus' words?"

Actually, you may have a skewed idea of what Christianity really is. (I would encourage you to look again at 3.27, immediately above, as well as vol. 1, 2.4–2.9.) Perhaps it would be better for you to think of the Messianic Jewish faith of the New Testament, the faith that was sent on a worldwide mission almost two thousand years ago to bring the good news about the one true God and his Messiah to every nation and people. It is a faith offering salvation and forgiveness to everyone, regardless of what sins they have committed, regardless of how they have lived, regardless of what their background has been. As Jesus said to his eleven Jewish emissaries (called "apostles"), "This is what is written: The [Messiah] will suffer and rise from the dead on the third day, and repentance and forgiveness of sins will be preached in his name to all nations, beginning at Jerusalem. You are witnesses of these things" (Luke 24:46–48). "Go into all the world and preach the good news to all creation. Whoever believes and is baptized will be saved, but whoever does not believe will be condemned" (Mark 16:15).

This is the ultimate religion of mercy, the supreme expression of the love of God, the loftiest example of compassion that the world has ever seen. This is how the New Testament (possibly in Yeshua's own words) explains it:

> For God so loved the world that he gave his one and only Son, that whoever believes in him shall not perish but have eternal life. For God did not send his Son into the world to condemn the world, but to save the world through him. Whoever believes in him is not condemned, but

whoever does not believe stands condemned already because he has not believed in the name of God's one and only Son. This is the verdict: Light has come into the world, but men loved darkness instead of light because their deeds were evil. Everyone who does evil hates the light, and will not come into the light for fear that his deeds will be exposed. But whoever lives by the truth comes into the light, so that it may be seen plainly that what he has done has been done through God.

John 3:16–21[452]

You see, without the mercy of God, none of us is good enough to merit eternal life or to enter his kingdom. The best of us fall short (see above, 3.20). And to be perfectly honest, most of us have not sought his mercy on our own. This world has occupied most of our attention. The worries of life, the love of material things, the lusts of the flesh, the sins of covetousness and greed, our endless pursuit of pleasure and fame, the desire for earthly security, the craving of knowledge—the list is virtually endless—all these things have squeezed God out of most of our lives. As Jews (or Gentiles) we have hardly put the most important things first, and we have failed miserably to love the Lord with all our heart, soul, and strength—the first and greatest commandment according to the Hebrew Scriptures, the ancient rabbis, and the New Testament. And throughout the world, people have created other gods in his place, gods of wood and stone, gods who engage in violence and immorality, gods of terror and fear, gods that in no way represent the one true God. For the most part, even when we have sought him, we have done it our way, causing more harm than good.

But in God's infinite love, he sought us. He sent the Messiah—the only one who ever lived without sin, the one who was a man just like us, but the one who was also more than man, expressing the very image of God in the flesh, the spotless, innocent Lamb, the Messiah—to die for our sins. Yeshua paid it all, carrying on his shoulders the accumulated guilt of the entire human race and shedding his blood to make us holy. What love! What unexpected mercy! What an expression of the heavenly Father's heart, broken with pain over a sinning, dying world. And it is this great love that constrains the Messiah's followers to go throughout the world—often at the cost of their own lives—to tell everyone the wonderful news about Jesus. They proclaim a message of amnesty and pardon through Yeshua's atoning death. They proclaim a message of reconciliation. As Saul of Tarsus (known as the apostle Paul) expressed it:

All this is from God, who reconciled us to himself through [Messiah] and gave us the ministry of reconciliation: that God was reconciling the world to himself in [Messiah], not counting men's sins against them. And he has committed to us the message of reconciliation. We are therefore [Messiah's] ambassadors, as though God were making his appeal through us. We implore you on [Messiah's] behalf: Be reconciled to God. God made him who had no sin to be sin [or a sin offering] for us, so that in him we might become the righteousness of God.

2 Corinthians 5:18–21

The gospel message is simple: Be reconciled to God. Come into a right relationship with your creator. He has reached out to you through his Son. It is Yeshua the Messiah who does what even the best and most beautiful of our Jewish traditions cannot do. It is Jesus the Savior of the world who does what no other religion can do. He purchases our pardon, secures our right standing with God, and provides us with a new heart. That's why those of us who know him feel so compelled to share these wonderful truths whenever we can. That's why we are willing to sacrifice almost anything to let the world know just what God has done. That's why we pray and fast for our friends and loved ones to come to know the Lord. (Perhaps you are reading this book right now because someone has been praying for you. Perhaps God is actively working in your life to draw you to himself. If you sense that he is speaking to you, you would do well to listen to his voice. Don't refuse his voice of love. Don't scorn his offer of forgiveness, his offer to wipe your slate clean and give you a new start, free and clear.)

Rather than allow your mind to be confused with endless speculation, consider these simple facts: The Hebrew Scriptures, the Rabbinic writings, and the New Testament all warn us of coming judgment, sometimes speaking of its eternal duration (see above, 3.27). Whatever this place of judgment (called hell) holds in store, you don't want to go there. Through Jesus the Messiah, your sins can be forgiven and your heart cleansed, and you can now live a brand-new life in obedience to God. You don't have to perish. You don't have to be judged guilty on that day. And rather then wondering about the fate of those who never heard about Jesus (we addressed this subject at length in vol. 1, 1.10), consider once again these words that Yeshua spoke to his emissaries: "Go into all the world and preach the good news to all creation. Whoever believes and is baptized will be saved, but whoever does not believe will be condemned" (Mark 16:15–16).

It is the responsibility of his followers to take the message to everyone; it is the responsibility of those who hear to repent and believe. You, therefore, are not responsible for those who have never heard, and neither you nor I are their judges. What you are responsible for is responding to the message for yourself: Will you accept God's love expressed to you through Messiah's death on your behalf, or will you take your chances and try to merit heaven on your own?

We know that most people in this world are not living godly, holy lives. Therefore, the warning of Jesus makes a great deal of sense: "Enter through the narrow gate. For wide is the gate and broad is the road that leads to destruction, and many enter through it. But small is the gate and narrow the road that leads to life, and only a few find it" (Matt. 7:13–14). Which gate lies ahead of you? Which road are you on? The road to destruction is broad and wide; the road to life is narrow. Which way are you going? If you were called to stand before God in judgment this very hour (as I write this very sentence, Yom Kippur—the Day of Atonement—is at hand), how would you fare? If the righteous, all-seeing Judge began to weigh your deeds in the balance, examining your motives, calling you to account for both sins of omission as well as sins of commission, how would you stand? God has a perfect memory, and he sees through all our flimsy excuses.

But there is good news. (Yes, the message of the New Testament really is good news.) The Messiah took our place in judgment, in keeping with a traditional Jewish concept expressed in the Zohar: "The children of the world are members of one another, and when the Holy One desires to give healing to the world, He smites one just man amongst them, and for his sake heals all the rest" (see above, 3.15). You can be healed. You can be delivered from the guilt and dominance of sin. You can become a new creation in the Messiah. That's the power and beauty of the new covenant, as God said through Jeremiah: "For I will forgive their wickedness and will remember their sins no more" (Jer. 31:34; see also Heb. 8:12; 10:17). Why carry your sins all the way to the judgment seat of almighty God, risking his wrath and punishment? Today you can stand before his mercy seat. Yeshua, our merciful and faithful High Priest, has made atonement for us. Read these words, written to Jewish believers in Jesus twenty centuries ago, with an open and prayerful heart:

> Therefore, since we have a great high priest who has gone through the heavens, Jesus the Son of God, let us hold firmly to the faith we profess. For we do not have a high priest who is unable to sympathize with

our weaknesses, but we have one who has been tempted in every way, just as we are—yet was without sin. Let us then approach the throne of grace with confidence, so that we may receive mercy and find grace to help us in our time of need.

Hebrews 4:14–16

If you are convinced that Yeshua is, in fact, our promised Messiah, and if you understand that he calls you to surrender your life to the will of our heavenly Father, I encourage you to stop right now and call out to God from a sincere and honest heart. You might want to pray a prayer similar to this: "God, I recognize that I have sinned in your sight, deserving your righteous judgment. I make no excuses for my sins. I consider myself guilty as charged. But I believe that Yeshua the Messiah died in my place and rose from the dead, purchasing my complete forgiveness. And so, almighty God, I ask you to wash me clean, to forgive me and receive me, to give me a brand-new heart, and to make me your child. Be my Father and my God. I repent of my sins, and I put my faith in your Son, receiving him today as my Lord. Lead me and guide me through this life, and then accept me into your eternal kingdom. Amen."

If you prayed that prayer in sincerity, know that God himself heard you, and it is he who has promised that everyone who calls on his name will be saved (Joel 2:32[3:4]; Rom. 10:13). You have taken the first step toward living a brand-new life. It is to you that Jesus says, "If you hold to my teaching, you are really my disciples. Then you will know the truth, and the truth will set you free" (John 8:31–32). I would encourage you to tell someone you know who truly believes in our Messiah (perhaps the person who gave you this book) that you too have come to faith and that you are committed to living for God and following his Word.[453]

If you are not yet ready to call out to God for forgiveness, if you are still wrestling with doubts and questions or still battling with the call to repent of your sins, I encourage you to continue seeking him for guidance, to continue praying and studying, and to come to grips with the ugliness of sin. God has promised that those who seek him with all their hearts will find him (Deut. 4:29; Jer. 29:13). And God doesn't lie. It is my fervent hope that you will find *no good reason* to reject Jesus and *every good reason* to receive him as your Messiah and master and friend. As Moses said to our people many years ago, "This day I call heaven and earth as witnesses against you that I have set before you life and death, blessings and curses. Now choose life, so that you and your children may live and that you may love the LORD your God, listen to his voice, and hold fast to him" (Deut. 30:19–20). I echo his voice and urge you as well: Choose life!

The final book of the Bible ends with a glorious picture of the heavenly city, the new Jerusalem, a place of rest, of peace, of joy, a place where we serve and enjoy God forever:

> Then I saw a new heaven and a new earth, for the first heaven and the first earth had passed away, and there was no longer any sea. I saw the Holy City, the new Jerusalem, coming down out of heaven from God, prepared as a bride beautifully dressed for her husband. And I heard a loud voice from the throne saying, "Now the dwelling of God is with men, and he will live with them. They will be his people, and God himself will be with them and be their God. He will wipe every tear from their eyes. There will be no more death or mourning or crying or pain, for the old order of things has passed away."
>
> Revelation 21:1–4

That city will be my eternal home. I pray it will be your home too, regardless of what it may cost you in this world, regardless of the opposition you may face along the way. Inheriting eternal life will be worth it all.

How do you enter the Holy City of God? Yeshua himself is the way.

Notes

Part 3 Theological Objections

1. Cited by A. Lukyn Williams, *A Manual of Christian Evidences for Jewish People* (New York: Macmillan, 1919), 1:95.

2. Jack Cottrell, *God the Redeemer* (Joplin, Mo.: College Press, 1987), 135.

3. Robert Crossley, cited in ibid., 136.

4. According to S. Daniel Breslauer, "The central concept in Jewish theology is monotheism." However, he immediately adds, "Affirming God's unity and oneness is more than a numerical claim. Monotheism claims that God is unique, that the divine transcends all experienced pluralities." See "God: Jewish View," in *A Dictionary of the Jewish-Christian Dialogue*, ed. Leon Klenicki and Geoffrey Wigoder (New York: Paulist Press, 1984), 73. For Breslauer's explanation of Judaism's problems with the Trinity, see below, n. 14.

5. Similar to this is the statement of Charles Spurgeon, one of the most dynamic preachers of the nineteenth century: "As well might a gnat seek to drink in the ocean, as a finite creature to comprehend the Eternal God."

6. Gerald Sigal, *The Jew and the Christian Missionary: A Jewish Response to Missionary Christianity* (Hoboken, N.J.: Ktav, 1981), 126–27, cites verses such as Exod. 9:7; 2 Sam. 13:30; 17:12, 22; Eccles. 4:8, all of which, he claims, use *'echad* in the sense of "absolute one." So, e.g., when 2 Samuel 13:30 states, "Absalom has slain all the king's sons, and there is not one of them left," Sigal finds support for his contention that, "the word 'one' used in these verses means an absolute one and is synonymous with the word *yaḥid*, 'the only one,' 'alone.'" To the contrary, as already stated, *'echad* simply means "one" just as our English word means "one," with nothing further implied, being the simple and logical word to use (in either English or Hebrew) in any of Sigal's examples. In fact, it is quite easy to expose the fallacious nature of Sigal's argument. To apply his logic to the English language, we could deduce from the sentence, "All the other couples left, and just one couple remained," that the remaining couple was an absolute unity! Also, it can be argued, that Ecclesiasties 4:8, "There is one, and he has not a second; yea, he has neither son nor brother," which Sigal finds to be of "special interest," actually militates *against* his position, since *'echad* here requires two further modifying clauses to indicate that it was speaking of only one individual. But the worst is still to come. Without telling us how he knows this, Sigal states, "It is in this sense [i.e., "the only one, alone"], with even greater refinement, that *'echad* is used in Deuteronomy 6:4: 'Hear, O Israel, the Lord our God, the Lord is One.' Here, *'echad* is used as a single, absolute, unqualified one." Says who? How does Sigal know that

'echad has *that* meaning here—and "with even greater refinement"—and not that of compound unity? This is a classic example of circular reasoning: reading one's doctrine into the text and then pointing to that text to prove the doctrine!

7. See, e.g., these additional examples: Genesis 1:5 (evening and morning make up one day, here meaning the first day); Genesis 1:9 (all the waters of the earth are gathered to one place); Genesis 41:25–26 (Pharaoh's two dreams are actually one); Exodus 24:3 (all the people answered with one voice).

8. Cf. the comments of the contemporary Jewish biblical scholar Moshe Weinfeld to Deuteronomy 6:4–25 (*Deuteronomy 1–11*, Anchor Bible [New York: Doubleday, 1991], 328–57). On the meaning of 'echad in Deuteronomy 6:4, he notes, "the connotation of 'one' here is not solely unity but also aloneness" (337), with reference to 1 Chronicles 29:1 ("the word 'one [*'echad]*' implies exclusiveness"), also commenting that in ancient Near Eastern and Greek literature, "oneness in reference to a god involves aloneness" (338). In Ugaritic (a sister language to biblical Hebrew), *'hd* can be used to mean alone; cf., e.g., *KTU* 1.4:VII:49, with *'hdy* ("I alone"); see also the usage of *ahadun/wahidun* in the Koran (6:19, with the formula, "Say: He is a unique/only [*wahidun]* God," repeated frequently in the Koran) and note especially Sura 112:1 (cf. also 39:4 and elsewhere), "Say: He is Allah, the One!" (this is the rendering of Mohammed Marmaduke Pickthall, *The Meaning of the Glorious Koran* [New York: Mentor, n.d.], 454); Rudi Paret's German translation (*Der Koran: Übersetzung von Rudi Paret* [Stuttgart: W. Kohlhammer, 1980], 439), has, "Sag: Er ist Gott, ein Einziger" (i.e., "Say: He is God, an Only One" which is then explained in the rest of the Sura: He doesn't beget; he wasn't begotten; and there is no one comparable to him.) The translation of Abdullah Yusuf Ali reads, "He is God, the One and Only" (*The Meaning of the Glorious Qur'an* [Cairo: Dar Al-Kitab Al-Masri, n.d.], 1807), which is identical to the rendering of Deuteronomy 6:4 in *The Complete ArtScroll Siddur*, translated with an anthologized commentary by Rabbi Nosson Scherman (Brooklyn: Mesorah, 1987), 91, "Hear O Israel: HASHEM is our God, HASHEM, the One and Only." For further discussion of Israelite monotheism (and/or monolatry) in its ancient Near Eastern context, see Michael L. Brown, *Israel's Divine Healer*, Studies in Old Testament Biblical Theology (Grand Rapids: Zondervan, 1995), 67–78.

9. For further linguistic support for this position, see A. B. Ehrlich, *Mikra Ki-Pheshuto* (New York: Ktav, 1969), 1:322, with reference to Joshua 22:20 (speaking of Achan): "He was not the only one [Hebrew, *'echad]* who died for his sin." Ehrlich, who was a brilliant Hebrew scholar, explained the usage of 'echad in Deuteronomy 6:4 with reference to "other gods that were not the god of Israel," noting that the intent of the verse is not "to say to you that the Lord is an absolute unity in himself, since in those days, every god was an absolute unity and there was no division in their unity, and our forefathers who received the Torah had no doubt for themselves concerning the matter that their God was an absolute unity." See further the comments of the Jewish biblical scholar Jeffrey H. Tigay, *Deuteronomy*, The JPS Torah Commentary (Philadelphia: Jewish Publication Society, 1996), 76, to Deuteronomy 6:4: "This is not a declaration of monotheism, meaning that there is only one God. That point was made in 4:35 and 39, which state that 'YHVH alone is God.' . . . This understanding of the Shema as describing a relationship with God, rather than His nature, has the support of Zechariah 14:9."

10. It is worth repeating here that even if someone wanted to argue that the emphasis in the Shema is that the Lord our God is 'echad (in the sense of "one" and not "alone"), we have seen clearly that this would still tell us nothing about his essential

nature (absolute unity vs. compound unity vs. tri-unity, etc.). When Jesus quotes the words of the Shema (see below), he also says, "Hear, O Israel, the Lord our God, the Lord is one" (Mark 12:29), meaning that the Lord is our one and only God. But, in context, Jesus was certainly not entering into a discussion here about the essential nature of his heavenly Father!

11. Weinfeld, *Deuteronomy 1–11*, 330, 337–38. This declaration could also mean that there is only one YHWH as opposed to the many different "Baals," who were worshiped throughout the ancient Near Eastern world (*ba'al* means "lord" in the sense of "master"), such as Baal Hadad, Baal Berit, Baal Peor, Baal Zebub. But there was only Yahweh! See further J. C. De Moor and M. J. Mulder, "*ba'al*," in *Theological Dictionary of the Old Testament*, ed. H.-J. Fabry and H. Ringgren, trans. John T. Willis (Grand Rapids: Eerdmans, 1985), 2:181–200; Judith M. Hadley, "Baal: Theology," in *The New International Dictionary of Old Testament Theology and Exegesis*, ed. Willem VanGemeren (Grand Rapids: Zondervan, 1997; henceforth cited as *NIDOTTE*), 4:422–28.

12. This is the Rabbinic explanation of how the people of Israel became worthy of reciting the Shema. The alleged response of Jacob, *barukh shem kavod malkhuto le'olam va'ed*, is, of course, the refrain that follows the Shema in the traditional liturgy.

13. As we have emphasized above, even if the common, traditional interpretation of the Shema is followed stating that the Lord is "one," the question still remains, "What does the word 'one' (*'echad*) mean?"

14. These quotes are taken almost verbatim from Simon Herman, "Sefirot," in *The Encyclopedia of Hasidism*, ed. Tzvi M. Rabinowicz (Northvale, N.J.: Aronson, 1996), 436–37. According to Breslauer, however, "The great heresy feared by the mystics . . . is 'cutting off the roots,' separating these attributes from the hidden divine source and giving them an independent status. Their divine aspect lies in their identification with God's secret unity, not in their clear distinctive and individual manifestations. . . . Jews, emphasizing the paradox of monotheism, have refused to give independent status to God's attributes of Creator, Redeemer, and Sustainer. They find in Christian claims of a Trinity just the 'cutting off of the roots' which Judaism defines as heresy" ("God: Jewish View," 74, 76). A better way to understand Christian views of the Trinity, however, would be to speak of the total interrelatedness and essential oneness—with clear distinctions—of the tree (including its roots, trunk, and branches). As expressed by Christian theologian Jack Cotrell, "The traditional trinitarian view is that God is one in nature/essence/being/substance." As to God being three in one, Cottrell explains, "when we say that God is three persons in one essence, we are saying that he is three centers of consciousness sharing one divine essence" (*God the Redeemer*, 154, 159). For a useful study, see Millard J. Erickson, *God in Three Persons* (Grand Rapids: Baker, 1995).

15. Quoted in Risto Santala, *The Messiah in the Old Testament in the Light of the Rabbinical Writings*, trans. William Kinnaird (Jerusalem: Keren Ahvah Meshihit, 1992), 121.

16. Still, the Talmud asks, what is the significance of these plural forms? Part of the answer given is that "the Holy One, blessed be He, does nothing without first consulting His household above" with reference to Daniel 4:17. For translation of this text (b. Sanhedrin 38b) and related texts, see H. N. Bilalik and Y. H. Ravnitzky, eds., *The Book of Legends: Sefer Ha-Aggadah*, trans. W. G. Braude (New York: Schocken, 1992), 517–21 (here, 519–20, #124).

17. See, e.g., 2 Kings 1:3, where Baal Zebub is called "the god [Hebrew, *'elohim*] of Ekron." Note that in the Akkadian dialect attested in Tell El-Amarna, Egypt, the Pharaoh, who was considered divine, is literally called "my gods"; cf. also Rykle Borger,

Assyrisch-babylonische Zeichenliste, Ergänzungsheft zur 1. Auflage (AOAT 33) (Kevelaer/Neukirchen-Vluyn: Butzon & Bercker/Neukirchener, 1981), 417, who cites evidence that the Sumero-Akkadian plural form *dingir-meš* (meaning "gods") can also have a singular meaning.

18. There are other interesting examples, e.g., the word for "face" is the plural form *panim;* the word for compassion is the plural form *rahamim* (from a root related to "womb"); for discussion of these plural forms, see *Gesenius' Hebrew Grammar,* ed. and enlarged by E. Kautzsch, trans. A. E. Cowley (Oxford: Clarendon, 1910), 463, sec. 145.3.

19. For summaries of recent scholarly discussion, see the Genesis commentaries of Gordon Wenham, Victor P. Hamilton, Claus Westermann, and Nahum Sarna.

20. Ephraim E. Urbach, *The Sages: Their Concepts and Beliefs,* trans. Israel Abrahams (Cambridge: Harvard, 1987), 26, refers to the Talmudic view that "the belief in One God is the principle creed, and whoever negates it is called *kofer ba'Iqqar* [one who denies the primary principle of the faith]." According to Aryeh Kaplan, *The Real Messiah? A Jewish Response to Missionaries* (New York: Orthodox Union/National Conference of Synagogue Youth, 1985), 21, "Christianity negates the fundamentals of Jewish faith, and one who accepts it rejects the very essence of Judaism. Even if he continues to keep all the rituals, it is the same as if he abandoned Judaism completely. The Talmud teaches us, 'Whoever accepts idolatry, denies the entire Torah.'"

21. Aryeh Kaplan states, "Worship of any three-part god by a Jew is nothing less than a form of idolatry. . . . The three-part God of Christianity is not the G-d of Judaism. Therefore, in the Jewish view, Christianity may very well be a variation of idolatry" (*The Real Messiah?*, 15). Our present discussion has exposed the erroneous nature of Kaplan's statement, in particular his notion of a "three-part god."

22. A similar prophecy is found in Zephaniah 3:9: "For then I will make the peoples of pure speech, so that they all invoke the LORD by name and serve him with one accord" (NJPSV) (*shechem 'echad,* literally, one shoulder).

23. According to New Testament scholar Murray Harris, *Jesus as God* (Grand Rapids: Baker, 1992), 294–95, 1 Corinthians 8:5–6 could well be Paul's reformulation of the Shema (note especially the phrase *eis kyrios,* one Lord, in the light of the Septuagint's rendering of Deut. 6:4). He notes tellingly, "It would seem that Paul never relinquished his inherited Jewish monotheism but reformulated it so as to include Christ within the Godhead. In light of other monotheistic statements scattered throughout the NT, it is safe to assume that no NT writer regarded the surrender of monotheism as the corollary of belief in the essential deity of Christ" (295). See also the observations of Israeli scholar Pinchas Lapide in idem and Jurgen Moltmann, *Jewish Monotheism and Christian Trinitarian Doctrine,* trans. Leonard Swidler (Philadelphia: Fortress, 1981), 39, cited in Harris, n. 77. For additional monotheistic statements by Paul in the New Testament, see Romans 3:30; Ephesians 4:6.

24. For a useful compilation of Rabbinic sources, see Urbach, *The Sages,* 37–65, "The *Shekhinah*—The Presence of God in the World"; see further the classic article of G. F. Moore, "Intermediaries in Jewish Theology—Memra, Shekinah, Metatron," *Harvard Theological Review* 15 (1922): 41–85, with recent strictures, however, from Margaret Barker in her important—and controversial—study *The Great Angel: A Study of Israel's Second God* (London: SPCK, 1992), 134–61; note also Michael E. Lodahl, *Shekhinah/Spirit: Divine Presence in Jewish and Christian Religion* (New York: Paulist Press, 1995).

25. David Goldstein, *"Shekhinah," Encyclopedia of Hasidism,* 455.

26. Murray Harris also notes the difficulties in understanding that arise simply because of the English language. For example, if I ask a Christian, "Is Jesus God?" does that mean, "Is he the Trinity?" or, "Is he the same as the Father?" or, "Is he Yahweh?" or, "Is he the Second Person of the Trinity?" What if I ask instead, "Is Jesus divine?" Are these two different questions, or have I simply clarified the question? This is similar to asking, "Is the Shekhina divine?" instead of, "Is the Shekhina God?" It is possible that a rabbi would say yes to the first question and no to the second. Again, this is not as simple as some people would want us to think. In mystical Jewish circles, one thinks of the designation R. Isaac Luria as "the divine Rabbi Isaac" *(ha'elohi rabbi yishaq)*, clearly meaning "God-like" and indicating the semantic range of the Hebrew words *'elohim* and *'elohi.*

27. I am indebted to Professor Harris for pointing out the significance of Revelation 22:1–4 to me.

28. See Bilalik and Ravnitzky, *Book of Legends,* 519, #120

29. G. A. F. Knight, *A Biblical Approach to the Doctrine of the Trinity, Scottish Journal of Theology, Occasional Papers,* no. 1 (Edinburgh and London: Oliver and Boyd, 1953), 14–15. See idem, *Christ the Center* (Grand Rapids: Eerdmans, 1999).

30. Robert Hayward, *Divine Name and Presence: The Memra* (Totowa, N.J.: Allanheld, Osmun, 1981), 147, 149, states that, *"Memra* is God's *'HYH* [i.e., "I am," based on Exod. 3:14], His name for himself expounded in terms of His past and future presence in Creation and Redemption," observing that Memra "was surely one of the most profound and wonderful of the scribal meditations on the Name of the God of Israel." For critical interaction with some of Hayward's work, cf. the works of Bruce Chilton, cited below, n. 34.

31. Cf. *Yeyn HaTob,* 1:351, which simply notes here (as it does elsewhere in similar contexts), "to remove personification *[hagshamah],"* i.e., of the Deity; cf. the discussion of Ezra Zion Melammed, *Bible Commentators* (Jerusalem: Magnes, 1978), cited below, n. 42.

32. Santala, *Messiah in the Old Testament,* 90–91 (with the spelling normalized from "Mimra" to "Memra"); I have used his examples as given on 89–90; see further Hayward, *Divine Name and Presence,* and cf. the lengthy discussion below, n. 34.

33. "Logos," in R. J. Werblowsky and G. Wigoder, eds., *The Oxford Dictionary of Jewish Religion* (New York: Oxford, 1997; henceforth cited as *ODJR*), 423.

34. Larry W. Hurtado, *One God, One Lord* (Philadelphia: Fortress, 1988), 45. Compare the discussion there with Sigal's analysis of Philo's *logos* in *The Jew and the Christian Missionary,* 145–50. According to Sigal, "The Christian doctrine of the Logos, 'Word,' has its origins in the writings of Philo," claiming that "Philo judaizes his idea by identifying the Reason of the Greek philosophers (*Logos* in Greek means both 'word' and 'reason') with the Aramaic term *memra'* ('the Word')" (145–46). He concludes that "Philo's Logos is nevertheless alien to Judaism" (149). Suffice it to say that some of Sigal's discussion would come as a surprise to both Jewish and Christian scholars of Philo. For a more balanced assessment, see George R. Beasley-Murray, *John,* Word Biblical Commentary (Waco: Word, 1987), 4–10; and David H. Johnson, "Logos," in *Dictionary of Jesus and the Gospels,* ed. Joel B. Green and Scot McKnight (Downers Grove, Ill.: InterVarsity Press, 1992), 481–82 (the entire article runs from 481–84). See further David Winston, *Logos and Mystical Theology* (Cincinnati: Hebrew Union College, 1985); James D. G. Dunn, *Christology in the Making,* 2d ed. (Grand Rapids: Eerdmans, 1989), especially 213–50. Of particular value in this context is the study of Bruce Chilton, a specialist in Targumic literature and New Testament studies. See "Typolo-

gies of Memra and the Fourth Gospel," in his *Judaic Approaches to the Gospels* (Atlanta: Scholars, 1994), 177–201 (with bibliography of recent studies on 177). Chilton writes, "Within the study of the fourth Gospel, commentators in recent years have largely dismissed the hypothesis that *memra* might be a precedent for the usage of *logos*. That dismissal, however, is produced by a misconception of both terms. . . . The present argument holds that the Targumic theologoumenon of the *memra* as God's activity of commanding has influenced the sense of *logos* in the fourth Gospel, and that logos in that Gospel is not fundamentally a christological term, as contemporary discussion has assumed" (185–86). See also Bruce Chilton, "Recent and Prospective Discussion of *mêmra*," in *Judaic Approaches to the Gospels*, 271–304. Barker, *The Great Angel*, cites the work of earlier scholars (including J. W. Etheridge, B. F. Westcott, and Alfred Edersheim) in full support of the connection between the Targumic Memra and John's Logos (see 137), also listing ten important parallels between Philo's Logos and the Targums' Memra. Both were identified as the Name of the Lord; man was said to be created in the image of both the Logos and the Memra; both were pictured as the viceroy of a great King; both were identified with the Angel of YHWH who guided Israel in the desert; both were depicted as heavenly judge; both were mediators between man and God; both performed high priestly functions; both were the agents of creation; both were involved in God's covenant with Israel; both were pictured as speaking from between the cherubim (see 146–47). Barker notes interestingly, "The monotheism of mainstream rabbinic Judaism which is now reflected in the Targums may not have been the Judaism of the people to whom they were originally addressed. The fact that Memra is opaque to us, even though originally intended as a translation and clarification, must stand as a warning" (147). For a comprehensive listing of occurrences of *memra'* in all extant Targums to the Torah (aside from Onkelos), broken down by category, see Chilton, "Recent and Prospective Discussion of *memra'*," 296–304. See further Chilton, "Eight Theses on the Use of Targums in Interpreting the New Testament," in *Judaic Approaches to the Gospels*, 305–15, for some important concerns regarding the use and misuse of the Targums in New Testament study. For speculations on the variations in usage of *memra* between the so-called Palestinian Targums and those thought to be Babylonian Targums, see Barker, *The Great Angel*, 141–59, with reference also to the observations of Jacob Neusner, perhaps the most influential scholar of early Judaica in this generation, on the incarnation of God in Babylonian Judaism: "It is the representation of God as a human being who walks and talks, cares and acts, a God who not only makes general rules but also by personal choice transcends them and who therefore exhibits a particular personality" (from his study *The Incarnation of God: The Character of Divinity in Formative Judaism* [Philadelphia: Fortress, 1988], 21, cited in Barker, ibid., 158–59). Barker also finds Neusner's reasoning for this development intriguing: "Neusner recognized that this direct encounter had been part of the original expression of the Scriptures and argued with a great deal of evidence that when the writers of this period 'began to represent God as personality . . . they *reentered* the realm of discourse about God that Scripture had originally laid out' [28, her emphasis]. He hints at the reason for abandoning the older ways. When the earlier Talmud, the Jerusalem Talmud, had been formed within the Palestinian community it had addressed the threat posed by Christianity in the fourth century AD, and, since, Christianity had its own way of reading the Old Testament, a '*Judaic response took the form of a counterpart exegesis*' [107, her emphasis]. The Jewish sages adapted Scripture to their new needs. . . . [Jewish] Scholars in Babylon, however, were under no such pressures: 'Consequently, it was in the Bavli [the Babylonian Talmud] in particular that God became Man'" (159). Note, however, that these comments should not be construed to imply in any way that Neusner accepts Christian views of the incarnation; rather, they simply indicate how the language of the Hebrew Scriptures, in which God is often portrayed in human terms, has been applied in various streams of Rabbinic Judaism, as well as in the New Testament.

35. Hurtado, *One God, One Lord*, 45.

36. "Early Christianity took up the notion of Logos and in the *Gospel of John* (1:1) the Logos as an eternal, divine principle is said to have been made flesh in the person of Jesus" ("Logos," *ODJR*, 423). Since this concept became so important in developing "Christian" theology, it is speculated that this could have "contributed to the disappearance of *logos* speculations, together with the whole Philonic tradition, from Jewish thought. [Note in this context that the term '*memra*' of the Lord,' so common in the Targums, is not found once in the Talmuds.] In kabbalistic literature concepts similar to that of *logos* reappear in the doctrine of Sephirot" (ibid.). Margaret Barker notes that the Jewish theologian Kaufman Kohler "suggested that the rabbis abandoned the personified Memra because of the Christians." See his *Jewish Theology Systematically and Historically Considered* (New York: n.p., 1918), 199, n. 3, cited in, Barker, *The Great Angel*, 160, n. 10.

37. For caveats against making these divine personifications into independent, semi-divine entities, see Hurtado, *One God, One Lord*, 46–48.

38. R. E. Brown, cited in Fritz Rienecker and Cleon Rogers, *A Linguistic Key to the Greek New Testament* (Grand Rapids: Zondervan, 1982), 219.

39. Commenting on Colossians 2:9, N. T. Wright, *Colossians and Philemon*, Tyndale New Testament Commentary (Downers Grove, Ill.: InterVarsity Press, 1986), 103, observes that "Christ is not a second, different Deity: he is the embodiment and full expression of the one God of Abraham, Isaac, and Jacob."

40. G. R. Beasley-Murray, *John*, 2; cf. the rendering of Eugene H. Peterson in *The Message:* "No one has ever seen God, not so much as a glimpse. This one-of-a-kind God-expression, who exists at the very heart of the Father, has made him plain as day."

41. See the Talmudic commentaries on the dictum that "whoever translates a verse literally [Hebrew, *ketsurato*, according to its form], is a liar and whoever adds to it reproaches and blasphemes [God]" (b. Qiddushin 49a) as compared to the statement that "a scripture never departs from its plain sense *[peshuto]*" (b. Shabbat 63a). Note the application of the first principle in Midrash HaGadol (cited by Barker, *The Great Angel*, 143, following G. H. Box and Raphael Patai) in the context of the nature of God: "R. Eliezer said: 'He who translates a verse literally is a liar. He who adds to it commits blasphemy. For instance, if he translated [Exod. 24:10] *And they saw* the God of Israel, he spoke an untruth; for the Holy One . . . sees, but is not seen. But if he translated, *And they saw the Glory of the Shekhinah of the God of Israel* [which is the rendering of Targum Neofiti and Targum Pseudo-Jonathan], he commits blasphemy; for he makes three (a trinity) viz., Glory, Shekinah, and God.'"

42. There are many other examples in which the Targum replaced "God," or "the Lord" with "the glory of the Lord"; see, e.g., Genesis 28:16 (the Hebrew says, "Surely the Lord is in this place"; the Targum reads, "Surely the glory of the Lord abides in this place"); Genesis 17:22 ("And God went up from Abraham," is replaced with, "And the glory of the Lord went up from Abraham"); Leviticus 9:4 ("For today the Lord will appear to you," is changed to, "For this day the glory of the Lord will be revealed to you"). For more examples, see Melammed, *Bible Commentators*, 162.

43. See further Barker, *The Great Angel*. On a more popular level, see also Robert Leo Odom, *Israel's Angel Extraordinary* (Bronx, N.Y.: Israelite Heritage Institute, 1985).

44. See also the Targum to 1 Kings 8:27, in the context of Solomon's prayer at the dedication of the Temple. The Hebrew reads, "But will God really dwell on the earth?", changed in the Targum to, "But is the Lord really willing for his Shekhinah to dwell among men?" Note also God's response in 9:3: "I have consecrated this temple, which you have built, by putting my Name there forever. My eyes and my heart will always be there," which becomes in the Targum, ". . . I have sanctified this house which you built for my Shekhinah to abide there forever, and my Shekhinah will abide in it with my will being done there always."

45. Nahum Sarna, *Genesis,* The JPS Torah Commentary (Philadelphia: Jewish Publication Society, 1989), 383 (Excursus 10, Angelology).

46. Ibid., 383–84.

47. Here is one more Targumic example of the degree to which the *Shekhina* took the place of God himself. The Hebrew for 2 Kings 1:3 reads (see also v. 6), "Is it because there is no God in Israel that you are going off to consult Baal-Zebub, the god of Ekron?", while the Targum says, "Is there not a God whose Shekhinah abides in Israel that you go to inquire of Baal Zebub, the idol of Ekron?"

48. Rabbi Adin Steinsaltz, *The Talmud: The Steinsaltz Edition,* vol. 6, *Tractate Bava Metzia, Part VI* (New York: Random House, 1992), 159.

49. Commenting on Genesis 18:22, "The men turned away and went toward Sodom, but Abraham remained standing before the Lord," W. Gunther Plaut, the Reform Jewish rabbi and biblical scholar, notes simply, "In this verse 'the men' are clearly distinguished from God." See idem, ed., *The Torah: A Modern Commentary* (New York: Union of American Hebrew Congregations, 1985), 128.

50. On the words "they ate" in Genesis 18:8, Plaut notes, "Traditional interpreters experience great difficulties here. If the three are divine messengers, why do they eat? According to the Midrash, they merely appeared to eat. According to Rashi, they pretended out of courtesy. The text of course is oblivious of later Jewish dietary laws that forbade serving milk and meat at the same meal" (ibid., 122).

51. This is also the reason for Miriam's virginal conception of Yeshua, since the Son of God could not be born in the normal human way, otherwise he would have been only a normal human. See further vol. 3, 5.9–11.

52. See n. 24, above, for references.

53. Rabinowicz, *Encyclopedia of Hasidism,* 454.

54. For discussion of some of these terms and the theological debates surrounding them, see R. P. C. Hanson, *The Search for the Christian Doctrine of God* (Edinburgh: T & T Clark, 1988).

55. The Hebrew of this verse is perfectly clear, but I have intentionally followed the traditional Jewish translation of the Judaica Press Complete Tanakh so that no one would think I was trying to impose a "Christian" translation on the verse. With specific reference to this verse, Harris Lenowitz, professor of Hebrew at the University of Utah, notes, "A quasi-divine nature is established, in the preexilic period, for the messiah to possess forever or for as long as those biblical texts remain potent." See his important work, *The Jewish Messiahs: From the Galilee to Crown Heights* (New York: Oxford, 1998), 11.

56. Cf. Rashi to Psalm 2:7; for further references to the historical background of Psalm 2, see the commentaries of H.-J. Krauss; Peter C. Craigie; A. A. Anderson; and Franz Delitzsch.

57. The view of G. Buchanan Gray, "'King': The References to the 'King' in the Psalter, in their Bearing on Questions of Date and Messianic Belief," *Jewish Quarterly Review* 7 (1895): 658–86, that *yelidtika* here, as well as *yullad* in Psalm 87:4–6, "is simply a metaphor for 'brought into existence'" overly downplays the force of *y-l-d* in Psalm 2. Saul Levin, *The Father of Joshua-Jesus* (Binghamton, N.Y.: State University of New York, 1978), 178, while referring to Psalm 2:7 as "the only verse in the Old Testament where the LORD uses the vocabulary of ordinary reproduction," argues that "the context within that very verse shows this is the language of adoption, addressed to one already alive." While Gray claims that a reference to actual begetting in Psalm 2 would have required a different verbal form (namely, *holadtika*, especially with regard to the male role; see Levin, *The Father*, 178, n. 4), *yalad* is frequently used in this sense as well (according to some lexicons, as many as twenty-two times in the Hebrew Bible; cf. the genealogical formulae in Genesis 5 and 10). Rashi explains Psalm 2:7 to mean that at his coronation the Davidic king would be called God's son (over the people of Israel, who were corporately called God's son in Exod. 4:22), a view similar to Levin's. However, Hebrew *yalad* means "bear, bring forth, beget," not simply designate someone "son."

58. I have drawn some of these points from a still unpublished paper I delivered at the 1988 annual conference of the Society of Biblical Literature, entitled, "*gîlû bir'adâ* and *nass̆equ bar* (Ps. 2:11b–12a): Toward a Satisfactory Solution." See also vol. 3, 4.22.

59. Key verbs would include *'avad* (serve; worship); *hishtahavah* (do obeisance to; bow down before); *yadah* (praise); Aramaic *pelah* (worship).

60. There are at least two instances in Rabbinic literature in which this verse, removed from its context, is explicitly understood to mean, "Your throne, O God, is for ever and ever," and is cited to prove that God's throne is eternal; see *Otsar HaMidrashim, Hekhalot,* sec. 3; *Shnei Luhot HaBerit, Sefer Bamidbar-Devarim, Parashat Shofetim, Torah Ohr, 2.* This provides eloquent testimony to the fact that I have stressed in my discussion, namely, that no one would ever question the obvious and proper translation of this verse had it been in a different context.

61. For a thorough discussion of the translation issues dealing with Psalm 45:6[7], quoted also in Hebrews 1:8, see Murray J. Harris, "The Translation of *Elohim* in Psalm 45:7–8," *Tyndale Bulletin* 35 (1984): 65–89; idem, "The Translation and Significance of *ho theos* in Hebrews 1:8–9," *Tyndale Bulletin* 36 (1985): 129–62. The rendering of Mitchell Dahood, *Psalms 1–50,* Anchor Bible (Garden City, N.Y.: Doubleday, 1966), 269, "The eternal and everlasting God has enthroned you!" has found little or no scholarly support (rightly so). The NJPSV, in contrast to the 1917 JPS version (cf. Metsudat David), renders, "Your divine throne is everlasting," with reference to 1 Chronicles 29:23, a verse cited by Ibn Ezra in his commentary to Psalm 45:6[7], where he interprets the phrase in question to mean, "Your throne is the throne of God." Rashi (along with an anonymous interpretation cited by Ibn Ezra, with support from Exod. 22:27), finds a lesser meaning for *'elohim,* namely, "prince, judge" with reference to Exodus 7:1. Rosenberg's English translation of Rashi accordingly renders *'elohim* with "judge" (Rabbi A. J. Rosenberg, *The Judaica Press Complete Tanach with Rashi,* CD ROM [Brooklyn, N.Y.: Davka Corporation and Judaica Press, 1999]. Note also that *'elohim* does not mean "judge" at Exodus 7:1, contrary to Rashi, as indicated also by the usage of *navi'*, prophet, in the same verse, and as recognized by most English translations; cf. the NIV's, "Then the LORD said to Moses, 'See, I have made you like God to Pharaoh, and your brother Aaron will be your prophet.'") All this underscores the difficulty this phrase in Psalm 45 presents for translators and interpreters, especially those coming from a traditional Jewish background.

62. H.-J. Kraus, a leading German Old Testament scholar, notes that "the deification of the king in the ancient Near East can be documented in the greatest variety of examples" (*Psalms 1–59*, trans. H. C. Oswald [Minneapolis: Augsburg, 1988], 455). He translates Psalm 45:6[7] as, "Your throne, O divine one, (stands) forever and ever." According to John J. Collins, one of the top Dead Sea Scrolls scholars in the world, "Already in the Hebrew Bible there were intimations of divinity in some of the royal psalms, most obviously Ps. 45:6[7], where the king is addressed as *'elohim.*" See his important study *The Scepter and the Star: The Messiahs of the Dead Sea Scrolls and Other Ancient Literature* (New York: Doubleday, 1995), 208.

63. Note 1 Samuel 28:13, in which the NRSV correctly renders *'elohim* as "divine being"; contrast the Septuagint, Vulgate, AV, and RSV.

64. A related Jewish concept is that in every generation there is a potential Messiah who *could* be revealed should Israel prove worthy (see also b. Sanhedrin 94a, which states that God wanted to make Hezekiah the Messiah, but he fell short). Thus, in theory, *certain* Messianic prophecies *could have been fulfilled* in the prophet's generation, but, in fact, will *not* be fulfilled until *the* Messiah is finally revealed. See below, 3.24.

65. The JPSV of 1917 simply transliterates the Hebrew; the NJPSV renders, "The Mighty God is planning grace; the Eternal Father, a peaceable ruler," a novel, yet grammatically possible interpretation, but one that somehow escaped Jewish rabbis, translators, and interpreters until a few years ago, pointing out just how novel—and too ingenious?—a rendering it is.

66. According to Midrash Bereshit 97:6 and Midrash Ruth 7:5, these verses speak of the six qualities of Hezekiah; see also Pesikta Rabbati 46:4, which refers these titles to Hezekiah; cf. also *Otsar Midrashim, Yaakov Avinu*, sec. 6.

67. See also *Otsar Midrashim, Rabbeinu HaKadosh*, sec. 7.

68. Ibn Ezra's interpretation here also counters the argument that in the Bible names such as Jeremiah (meaning Yahweh is exalted), or Isaiah (Yahweh is salvation), or Jehoshaphat (Yahweh is judge) tell us about God, not the people themselves, and so names such as Mighty God refer to Yahweh, not the child. Such an argument, however, does not work for several reasons: (1) In the Bible, many names *are* reflective of the person himself; Solomon was given the name Yedidiah (beloved of Yahweh) because the Lord loved him, and Yaakov (Jacob) received his name because he grasped the heel (*'ekev*) of his brother; (2) It is one thing to call someone Raphael, meaning "God healed"; it is another thing to call someone Mighty God!; (3) Even the Targum recognizes that the king here is called Sar Shalom (Prince of Peace) because there would be peace in *his* days. Without doubt, the titles are descriptive of the child, not God.

69. In Michael Friedländer's English translation of Ibn Ezra's commentary on Isaiah, *The Commentary of Ibn Ezra on Isaiah* (New York: Feldheim, n.d. [the original edition was published in 1873]), 52, he renders *'el gibbor* as "mighty chief," a completely forced rendering but a necessary one in light of Ibn Ezra's application of the verse to Hezekiah.

70. See vol. 3, 5.9; and cf. Oskar Skarsaune, *The Incarnation: Myth or Fact?*, trans. Trygve R. Skarsten (St. Louis: Concordia, 1991).

71. There is a striking parallel to this verse in the Dead Sea Scrolls (remember, the Scrolls are Jewish not Christian documents), written in the decades immediately before Jesus. In the so-called "Son of God" text (4Q246), it is written of a Messianic figure: "Son of God he shall be called, and they will name him Son of the Most High. . . . The sword will cease from the earth, and all cities will pay him homage." For discussion,

see Collins, *The Scepter and the Star,* 155. For other possible Son of God texts, see ibid., 164–65; for general discussion with references, see ibid., 154–72.

72. Regardless of what interpretation you put on this verse, I am using it here as a starting point for discussion. For the difficulties it presented to a traditional Jewish commentator writing last century, see *Malbim on Mishley,* abridged and adapted in English by Rabbi Charles Wengrov (New York: Feldheim, 1982), 300–301: "The five parts of the verse denote a series of questions on the creation of the universe" in the last of which "the questioner asks about the First Cause and its emanation, the primary Intellect, which two of the classical philosophers called Father and Son." According to Christian Old Testament scholar Allen P. Ross, "Proverbs," *Expositor's Bible Commentary* (Grand Rapids: Zondervan, 1979; henceforth cited as *EBC*), 5:1019–1020, "The parallel reference to 'son' was identified as Israel in the Midrash or in other places as the demiurge [according to Gnostic beliefs, the first emanation of God, kind of a diminished deity], the Logos, or a simple poetic parallelism for 'his name.' Christian interpreters have seen here a reference to the Son of God (a subtle anticipation of the full revelation in the NT)." According to Rashi, the words "what is his name and what is the name of his son," mean, "If you say that there already was one like him, tell me what his son's name is, i.e., what family is descended from him, and we will know who he is" (Rosenberg translation).

73. C. G. Montefiore and H. Loewe, *A Rabbinic Anthology* (New York: Schocken, 1974), 7, notes that, "I have not come across any passage [in Rabbinic literature] which seriously tackles the Christian conception of the Trinity, or which attempts to show that a Unity, which is a simple and pure Unity, is a higher or truer conception of the divine nature than a Unity of a Trinity or than a Trinity in a Unity. Where the Rabbis reply to the *minim* (heretics, sectaries, and sometimes Christians), they always represent these *minim* as believing in many gods. In other words, the doctrine of the Trinity (if that is referred to) is construed to mean Tritheism, which indeed was, and perhaps still is, its vulgar corruption. Hence the 'replies' are to-day of no particular interest, being somewhat obvious and commonplace."

74. According to a top Jewish scholar of Semitics, E. A. Speiser, "Heb. *ru'ah* means primarily 'wind, breeze,' secondarily 'breath,' and thus ultimately 'spirit.' But the last connotation is more concrete than abstract" (*Genesis,* Anchor Bible [Garden City, N.Y.: Doubleday, 1962], 5, note a to Gen. 1:2).

75. First Corinthians 2:11 says: "For who among men knows the thoughts of a man except the man's spirit within him? In the same way no one knows the thoughts of God except the Spirit of God."

76. The NJPSV, the most important, contemporary Jewish version of the Bible, translates the beginning of verse 33 as, "because they rebelled against him," as if "His Spirit" was only a synonym for "Him." The same is done in Micah 2:7. Unfortunately, these renderings do not advance our understanding of these texts.

77. Alan Unterman, "Ru'ah Ha-Kodesh," *Encyclopedia Judaica* (henceforth cited as *EJ*), CD ROM edition (Israel: Judaica Multimedia, 1997), 14:364–67, recognizes the difficulty of this usage, noting, "A more problematical use of the term *Ru'ah ha-Kodesh* is when it is in some way hypostatized, or used as a synonym for God." However, the significance of such usage is downplayed: "This hypostatization is essentially the product of free play of imagery, and does not have the connotations of *Ru'ah ha-Kodesh* as an entity separate from God. Neither are there any overtones of the *Ru'ah ha-Kodesh* somehow forming part of the Godhead, as is found in the Christian concept of the Holy Ghost. . . . Sometimes it is used merely as a synonym for God, and at others it refers to the

power of prophecy through divine inspiration." If such statements could be made about the Rabbinic citations, I wonder if similar conclusions could be reached regarding the New Testament material. According to H. Loewe, *Rabbinic Anthology*, 7, with reference to Pesikta Rabbati 12a (where God speaks to the Holy Spirit), "It would, however, be quite inaccurate and illegitimate to use a clearly rhetorical passage like the above as an argument for the separate existence of the Holy Spirit" (see also ibid., 677, n. 50). But is the issue really one of "separate existence" as much as it is a matter of certain distinctions between God, generally speaking, and the Holy Spirit, in particular?

78. The Rabbinic midrash even finds a play on words here: Egypt said, "Lest [Hebrew, *pen*] they will spread out"; the Holy Spirit said, "So [Hebrew, *ken*] they will spread out." See Rashi to Exodus 1:12.

79. See Louis Ginzberg, *The Legends of the Jews*, trans. Henrietta Szold (Philadelphia: The Jewish Publication Society of America, 1928), 6:402. The source of the midrash is Sepher HaKaneh (which is Sepher HaPeli'ah) 36a.

80. William G. Braude, the respected translator of classic Rabbinic literature, compares Romans 8:26–27 to this passage, claiming that in Romans 8, "the holy spirit, as it were, personifying Israel, prays to God on Israel's behalf" (*The Legends of the Jews*, 195, n. 2, with credit for this suggestion to Brother Caedmon Holmes of the Abbey of St. Gregory the Great in Portsmouth, R.I.). Although it is extremely unlikely that the Holy Spirit in Romans 8:26–27 personifies Israel, there is no question that there are striking parallels between the New Testament portrayal of the Holy Spirit and that of the Rabbinic literature, as will be emphasized below.

81. The Aramaic word used here for "defense counsel" is borrowed from the Greek *synegoros*. In the New Testament, the Holy Spirit is called the Counselor, from the Greek *parakletos*. These concepts are closely related, although the Rabbinic images here go beyond anything found in the New Testament as far as making the Holy Spirit into a separate, personal entity.

82. As noted above, n. 77, in the well-known eighth- and ninth-century midrash, Pesikta Rabbati 12a, God is depicted as speaking to the Holy Spirit.

83. If the New Testament teaching on the Holy Spirit was deemed offensive, un-Jewish, and unbiblical by the Rabbinic authorities in the first five centuries of this era, why is identical imagery used in their writings? It is common knowledge that as Christian doctrine developed and certain Messianic proof texts were used by Christian apologists the rabbis intentionally distanced themselves from those views and interpretations, even polemicizing against them. (Note also the fact, mentioned above, that the important Targumic concept of the "Word of the Lord" in the Targums—so similar to the New Testament concept of the divine Word—is completely lacking from all Talmudic literature.) Why then were the rabbis so free to speak of the Holy Spirit in terms that so closely parallel the New Testament usage? Could it be that no conflict was perceived between the two? Could it be that the conscious reaction *against* the Christian teaching arose much later, as both sides became more fixed—and somewhat unbiblical—in their doctrines? Was the Rabbinic reaction directed against the (incorrect) view that Christians believed that the Holy Spirit was one of three gods whom they worshiped? (See the comment of H. Loewe, above, n. 73.)

84. Sa'adiah Gaon, in his classic work *Emunot veDe'ot* ("Beliefs and Opinions"), chapter 8, follows Talmudic teaching that points to Joel's prophecy as a sign of the Messianic age: All the Israelites would then be able to prophesy! As Sa'adiah taught: "And all the desolate land will be settled until no desolate place will be left in it. Then the light of the *Shekhina* will shine on the Temple until the luminaries will be dimmed

by its light . . . so that those who do not know the way to the Temple will go toward that light, because it will be from heaven to earth. Then prophecy will spread in our people until even our children and our servants will prophesy. . . . Until if one of the Children of Israel will go to one of the lands and will say that 'I am of Israel,' they will say to him, 'Tell us what will be tomorrow?' or, 'What was yesterday?' of the things which were secret among them. And when he tells them, it will be clear to them that he is from Israel" (as rendered by Raphael Patai, *The Messiah Texts* [Detroit: Wayne State Univ., 1979], 319).

85. In Leviticus 26:12, God promised obedient Israel, "I will walk among you and be your God, and you will be my people." How does this happen? By His Spirit! Ezekiel 37:27 said that in the future, God's dwelling place will be among His people. For the present, this takes place through the Holy Spirit: "In him [i.e., Jesus] the whole building [meaning the community of all believers] is joined together and rises to become a holy temple in the Lord. And in him you too [meaning Gentiles along with Jews] are being built together to become a dwelling in which God lives by his Spirit" (Eph. 2:21–22). Because God's people are all over the earth and not localized in one place, his dwelling place is not limited to one particular structure or building. Rather, by the Holy Spirit, all believers jointly become the Temple in which the Lord dwells.

86. Sigal, *The Jew and the Christian Missionary*, 260–61, with absolutely no supporting evidence, simply denies the fact that Christians, by the power of the Spirit, can obtain miracles from God through faith. Referring to Mark 16:16–18 and 1 Corinthians 12:4–31, Sigal writes, "But can the Christian actually perform these miraculous deeds? No, of course not! . . . What is the reason for the Christian inability to fulfill the words of Jesus? Obviously, Christians cannot perform these miraculous deeds because Jesus' claims have no validity." Would Sigal then except the validity of Jesus' claims if he was confronted by bona fide, supernatural, God-glorifying miracles performed in the name of Jesus? For a recent compendium of testimonies compiled by the Assemblies of God, see Ralph W. Harris, *Acts Today: Signs and Wonders of the Holy Spirit* (Springfield, Mo.: Gospel Publishing House, 1995). See also David C. Lewis, *Healing: Fiction, Fantasy or Fact?* (London: Hodder & Stoughton, 1989).

87. For a discussion of the concept of the Shekhina (the manifest presence of God), often connected with the Holy Spirit in Rabbinic literature, see above, 3.1–2.

88. Scherman, *ArtScroll Siddur*, 108, "Davidic Reign." It is also ironic that anti-missionaries object to the idea of the Messiah being divine (see above, 3.2–3.3) and then turn around and object to a non-divine Messiah being the savior, since God alone is the Savior! On the necessity of the Messiah being divine in order to pay for the sins of the world, see Wayne Grudem, *Systematic Theology* (Grand Rapids: Zondervan, 1994), 578.

89. For Messianic Jewish reflections on Romans 10:9–10, see Joseph Shulam with Hilary Le Cornu, *A Commentary on the Jewish Roots of Romans* (Baltimore: Messianic Jewish Publishers, 1998), 350–51. According to David H. Stern, *Jewish New Testament Commentary* (Baltimore: Jewish New Testament Publications, 1992), 401, "To *acknowledge . . . that Yeshua is Adon* [Hebrew for Lord] implies committing oneself to obeying him (1:5); this is the meaning of *'kurios'* [Greek for Lord] at Mt 7:21–23."

90. For similar teachings throughout the New Testament, see, e.g., Matt. 5:13–16; 25:31–46; Acts 20:35; Heb. 13:16. Note that even the fine linen with which believers will be clothed in the heavenly city is described in Revelation 19:8 as representing "their righteousnesses" (meaning, their righteous acts).

91. Although some Jewish traditions, as reflected in the NJPSV, translate the Hebrew word *tsedaqah* as "merit" or "credit" (see also Deut. 6:25 in the NJPSV), there are valid

reasons for rejecting this rendering in favor of the more common translation of the word, namely, "righteousness." For the meaning and usage of *tsedaqah*, see A. Ho, *Sedeq and Sedaqah in the Hebrew Bible*, American University Studies, series 7, Theology and Religion 78 (New York: Lang, 1991). Note, however, that both the basic meaning and the complementary nature of verses such as Genesis 15:6 and Deuteronomy 6:25 remain the same, whether one translates with "righteousness" or "merit." Cf. also Rashi, who uses both the words merit *(zekhut)* and righteousness *(tsedaqah)* in explaining how God regarded Abraham's faith.

92. According to a well-known—but striking—statement in the Jerusalem Talmud (Hagigah 1:7), God is depicted as saying, "Would that my people abandoned me but kept my Torah," the rationale being that if they kept the Torah, the leaven in the Torah would bring them back to God in the end. From another perspective, Reform Jewish scholar Eugene B. Borowitz, *Liberal Judaism* (New York: Union of American Hebrew Congregations, 1984), 129, actually raises the question, "Must a Good Jew Believe in God?" He states that his assertion, namely, that there is "nothing more fundamental to being a good Jew than belief in God," is "the most controversial one I shall make." To explain his point, he asks, "Shall we indeed say that Israelis who have risked their lives for their people but are atheists are not good Jews? Shall we demean the Jewish status of many who, though unbelievers, have worked devotedly to upbuild Jewish life here and overseas? By what right do I assert that such people are not good Jews? Surely there are other views of a good Jew which do not involve believing in God or, if they do, do not make it the basis of everything else in Jewish life." From a biblical perspective, I heartily affirm the assertion of Borowitz that "nothing [is] more fundamental to being a good Jew than belief in God," and find it in no way "controversial."

93. See 3.9 for documentation regarding how much of the Torah deals with sacrifices.

94. Based on this verse, Rashi notes tellingly that according to the Torah, *this one sin* was the reason that Moses and Aaron could not enter the Promised Land. How serious it is when we fail to trust the Lord! Nachmanides (Ramban) points out that the sin of Moses and Aaron is elsewhere described by the Lord in the strongest possible terms: "but you acted treacherously against me" (Deut. 32:51); "you rebelled against my command" (Num. 27:12). Note, however, that his possible suggestion to change the meaning of *lo' he'emantem bi* to "you didn't strengthen the Israelites to sanctify me" is both forced and unnecessary. His longer explanation is more to the point: They were guilty of failing to believe in the name of the Lord, and it is through faith that the miracle is performed.

95. There is an extensive body of traditional Jewish literature that has been built on the 613 comandments (Hebrew, *taryag mitzvot*); for a convenient summary, see Noah Aminoah and Yosef Nitzan, *Torah: The Oral Tradition*, trans. Haim Schacter and Larry Moscovitz (n.p.: World Zionist Organization, n.d.), 47–52 (with reference to Sefer Mitzvot Gadol, Sefer Mitzvot Katan, and Sefer Hachinuch, some of which are now available in English). More recently, see Abraham Chill, *The Mitzvot: The Commandments and Their Rationale* (Jerusalem: Keter Books, 1974), and note *The Concise Book of Mitzvoth: The Commandments Which Can Be Observed Today*, compiled by The Chafetz Chayim, adaptation and notes by Charles Wengrov (New York: Feldheim, 1990).

96. Paul also cites Habakkuk 2:4 in Galatians 3:11: "Clearly no one is justified before God by the law, because, 'The righteous will live by faith.'" For a discussion of this verse in context, see the commentaries of Ronald K. Y. Fung, Richard Longenecker, Hans Dieter Betz, and J. Louis Martyn; cf. also Ben Witherington, *Grace in Galatia: A Commentary on Paul's Letter to the Galatians* (Grand Rapids: Eerdmans, 1998).

97. Note, however, that such a translation would make little or no sense in the Talmudic discourse just cited in Makkot, and it is therefore with good reason that most
English translations of Makkot translate Habakkuk 2:4 as, "The righteous will live by
his faith." As noted by Shulam and Le Cornu, *Romans*, 359, n. 15, with specific reference to b. Makkot 24a and b. Sanhedrin 43b, "Inheriting 'life' is therefore based not
only on the righteousness of observing the commandments but on faithfulness."

98. Note also that Hebrews 11, the great "faith" chapter in the New Testament, contains a litany of heroic acts of obedience. People of faith act!

99. For the main creeds, see the standard work of Philip Schaff, ed., *The Creeds of
Christendom* (Grand Rapids: Baker, 1996); note that there is no record of major creeds
in the church until the fourth century, therefore, almost three hundred years after the
death and resurrection of Yeshua.

100. For our discussion of the Shema, see above, 3.1, and note also the reference
to Urbach, *The Sages*, above, n. 20.

101. For background to Maimonides' Thirteen Principles of Faith, see, concisely,
ODJR, 691–92. For an explanation of Judaism based on the Thirteen Principles, see
Louis Jacobs, *We Have Reason to Believe: Some Aspects of Jewish Theology Examined
in the Light of Jewish Thought* (London: Valentin, Mitchell, 1965); Mosheh Max, *I
Believe: An Exposition of Maimonides' Thirteen Principles of Faith and Their Imple-
mentation in Jewish Life* (Jerusalem: Feldheim, 1973).

102. See vol. 1, 1.5.

103. On this passage, see C. Thomas Rhyne, *Faith Establishes the Law* (Chico, Calif.:
Scholars, 1981), and see the bibliography to 5.29 in vol. 3.

104. See Midrash Tehillim, Perek 119, Siman 64, my translation.

105. See m. Yoma 8:9; note also Pesikta Rabbati 44a. In a similar vein, the New
Testament makes reference to the need to prove one's repentance by one's deeds; see,
e.g., Matt. 3:8; Acts 26:20. Note also 2 Cor. 7:10–11; James 2:17. For a related New Testament text, see Matt. 21:28–32.

106. For the importance of sacrifices and offerings in the worship of God, note Ezra
4:1–2: "When the enemies of Judah and Benjamin heard that the exiles were building
a temple for the LORD, the God of Israel, they came to Zerubbabel and to the heads of
the families and said, 'Let us help you build because, like you, *we seek your God and
have been sacrificing to him*' since the time of Esarhaddon king of Assyria, who brought
us here.'" That was simply the way of the ancient world. Note also Judg. 6:17–24;
13:1–21. Michael E. Stone, a professor at Hebrew University, believes that even after
the destruction of the Temple by Nebuchadnezzar, "Some sacrificial cult was probably maintained in Jerusalem" (cf. Jer. 41:5–6). He also makes reference to the well-
known fact that some of the Jews in exile erected Temples and offered sacrifices in the
locations where they took up residence (the best attested case being that of the Jews
in Elephantine in Upper Egypt). See his article "Reactions to Destruction of the Second Temple: Theology, Perception and Conversion," *Journal for the Study of Judaism*
12 (1981): 194–204 (here, 194–95). I express my appreciation to my friend Dr. Phil
Miller, head librarian at Hebrew Union College and Jewish Institute of Religion, New
York, for xeroxing and faxing this article to me on two days' notice. His staff also helped
me track down a key reference in volume 1.

107. As a point of comparison, note that there are a total of forty-seven references
to the Sabbath in the entire Torah, whereas there are thirty-two references alone to
sacrifices as a sweet-smelling aroma, and the overall number of references to sacrifices in the first five books dwarfs the total number of references to the Sabbath.

108. Yeshua also did this in his role as our great High Priest; see again below, 3.15, and note further vol. 3, 4.1.

109. Rabbi Tovia Singer, from his web site, www.outreachjudaism.org/sin.html.

110. I should note that liberal biblical scholars (both Jewish and Christian) have sometimes argued that the prophets did, in fact, reject the sacrificial cult, even arguing that the prophetic literature *preceded* the Torah, which is seen to be a later, priestly retrojection. This was the classic and influential view of Julius Wellhausen, *Prolegomena to the History of Ancient Israel* (Gloucester, Mass.: Peter Smith, 1973), adapted by many in the following decades, although largely abandoned in recent years. Cf. Robert P. Gordon, ed., *The Place Is Too Small for Us: The Israelite Prophets in Recent Scholarship* (Winona Lake, Ind.: Eisenbrauns, 1995), 9–12.

111. For the Rabbinic usage of Hosea 6:6 to prove that charitable deeds replaced sacrifice, see below, 3.10. Of course, if this was Hosea's intent or meaning, it is strange to think that he would have written these categorical words on behalf of the Lord while the Temple in Jerusalem was still standing and completely accessible to his fellow Israelites living in the North. And what place, then, would this verse have once it was received as Scripture and read by Jews living in the land of Israel while the Second Temple was standing?

112. William L. Holladay, *Jeremiah 1,* Hermeneia (Philadelphia: Fortress, 1986), 261, notes that "Roland de Vaux [the Catholic biblical scholar] has wisely pointed out that the passages in question no more condemn the cult than Isa 1:15 suggests a condemnation of prayer; the problem is the formalism of exterior worship without any corresponding interior disposition (compare Isa 29:13)," with reference to de Vaux's *Ancient Israel: Its Life and Institutions* (New York: McGraw Hill, 1961), 454–55.

113. For a discussion of the authorship and editing of Psalm 51, see Willem Van-Gemeren, "Psalms," *EBC,* 5:384.

114. For a discussion of the Hebrew here, especially as quoted in Hebrews 10:5, see vol. 3, 5.5.

115. There are, of course, several ways to interpret the Hebrew text here, and some have argued that the prepositional phrase "about me" *('alay)* can also mean "to my debit." For an older but still insightful discussion, see Franz Delitzsch, in *Commentary on the Old Testament, Psalms,* C. F. Keil and idem, trans. Francis Bolton (Grand Rapids: Eerdmans, 1973), 2:39–40.

116. We will discuss the Rabbinic interpretation of this passage below, in relation to Jeremiah 7:21–23 and Amos 5:21–27; see also Midrash Ha-Chafetz to Leviticus 1:2, cited below, 3.10.

117. The Greek *latreia* is the equivalent of the Hebrew *'avodah,* "rite, act of divine service," found, e.g., in Exodus 12:25–26; 13:5.

118. "'*rb III,*" *NIDOTTE,* 3:522.

119. Anyone familiar with the New Testament will know that similar rebukes are found throughout the teachings of Jesus, Paul, and the apostles: All the praying, confessing, and sacrificing in the world is of no value whatsoever when it proceeds from a hypocritical heart.

120. This is even attested by the names containing divine elements discovered in inscriptions from Northern Israel. As noted by John Bright, *History of Israel,* 3d ed. (Philadelphia: Westminster, 1981), 260, "It is significant that the Samaria Ostraca yield almost as many names compounded with 'Ba'al' as with 'Yahweh.'"

121. Shalom M. Paul, *Amos,* Hermeneia (Philadelphia: Fortress, 1991), 192.

122. See Charles Lee Feinberg, "Jeremiah," *EBC*, 6:431, with reference to Rabbi Dr. H. Freedman, whose comments are cited in our text, below.

123. I have revised the NIV translation to bring out the force of the traditional Jewish argument; the NIV had added the word *just* to bring out its understanding of the passage, hence, "For when I brought your forefathers out of Egypt and spoke to them, I did not *just* give them commands about burnt offerings and sacrifices, but I gave them this command" (my emphasis). This interpretation, however, is not widely followed.

124. Aaron Rothkoff, "Sacrifices," *EJ* (CD ROM), 14:599–615.

125. If you read Anson F. Rainey's remarks carefully, you would have realized that some liberal scholars believe that prophets such as Jeremiah and Amos were unaware of the teaching in the Torah that connected sacrifices and offerings with the exodus from Egypt and the wilderness wanderings. This is because these scholars believe that those portions of the Torah that record such events were written later, after the days of these prophets. Of course, Orthodox Jews and Evangelical Christians completely reject this view based on their belief in the inspiration of the Torah, along with the internal evidence of the biblical writings themselves.

126. Dr. J. H. Hertz, *The Pentateuch and Haftorahs*, 2d ed. (London: Soncino, 1975), 439.

127. Ibid., his emphasis.

128. Abraham Joshua Heschel, *The Prophets* (New York: Harper & Row, 1962), 1:196–97. Heschel also states tellingly, "How supremely certain ancient man was that sacrifice was what the gods most desired may be deduced from the fact that fathers did not hesitate to slaughter their own children on the altar. When Mesha, the king of the Moabites, was hard-pressed in war, he sacrificed his own son, who would have reigned as his successor, for a burnt-offering upon the wall (II Kings 3:27)" (ibid., 196).

129. Ibid., 196–97.

130. This is basically the view of Rashi, Radak, Ibn Ezra, and Metsudat David. See also their comments to Amos 5:25.

131. This is the view reflected in the NIV. See above, n. 120.

132. Cf. also Hertz, *Pentateuch and Haftorahs*, 439. See further ibid., 561: "The Prophets were orators, and made occasional use of hyperbole, in order to drive home upon the conscience of their hearers a vital aspect of truth which those hearers were ignoring. And when they were confronted by the pernicious belief that God desired nothing but sacrifice, and saw sacrifice being held to excuse iniquity, heartlessness, and impurity—they gave expression to their burning indignation in the impassioned language of vehement emotion" (with specific reference to Jer. 7:22).

133. This is basically the view of Jacob Milgrom, a leading Jewish authority on sacrifice and atonement, in his article, "Concerning Jeremiah's Repudiation of Sacrifice," *ZAW* 89 (1977): 273–75. He has been followed by several recent Jeremiah commentators, including William Holladay (Hermeneia) and Peter C. Craigie (with Page H. Kelley and Joel F. Drinkard Jr., Word Biblical Commentary).

134. Feinberg, "Jeremiah," 431–32 (commenting on Jer. 7:23–26): "Actually, God had not spoken at Sinai of sacrifices but only of obedience (v.23)—and this even before the law was given (Exod. 19:3–6). Jeremiah's words show that he had in mind in v. 23 the giving of the Ten Commandments. Among these were no directions for sacrifices; they dealt solely with spiritual and moral matters. The OT order was first obedience and worship of God and then institution of sacrifices (cf. Ps 51:16–19). In Judah, as Jeremiah shows, the whole sacrificial system was invalidated on the ground that it was

not carried out in true faith (v.24). Obedience always was and would be the dominant consideration."

135. Holladay, *Jeremiah*, 56, his emphasis.

136. Cf. the pointed comments of Hertz, *Pentateuch and Haftorahs*, 561: "God would not be the God of Holiness if He did not 'hate' and 'despise' sacrifices, hymns, and songs of praise on the part of unholy and dishonourable worshippers. But there is no intimation that sacrifice, prayer and praise will continue to be 'hated', if the worshippers cast away their vile and oppressive deeds." In this connection, Hertz cites the Scottish biblical scholar W. L. Baxter, who observed that "there was use, a seemly and beneficial use, of sacrifice, but there was also abuse, a vile and God-dishonouring abuse. The Prophets made war upon the latter, but it does not follow that they objected to the former." Note also that some translations, such as the NIV, join Amos 5:25 with the following verses, changing the meaning of the entire passage. So, e.g., the New Living Translation renders Amos 5:25–27 as, "'Was it to me you were bringing sacrifices and offerings during the forty years in the wilderness, Israel? No, your real interest was in your pagan gods—Sakkuth your king god and Kaiwan your star god—the images you yourselves made. So I will send you into exile, to a land east of Damascus,' says the LORD, whose name is God Almighty." The meaning, then, changes completely. This interpretation of the text can be dated back to John Calvin in the sixteenth century and was championed last century by C. F. Keil, a leading Lutheran Old Testament scholar.

137. Hertz, *Pentateuch and Haftorahs*, 561, here, commenting on Isaiah 1:4, 11–17. Note again the harmony of Hertz's interpretation with what we have been emphasizing throughout our answer to this objection: "If this is to be taken as an absolute condemnation by Isaiah of all sacrifice, then that absolute condemnation must also include Sabbaths and Festivals; solemn Assemblies, *i.e.*, public gatherings for worship, and the appearing before the LORD in the Temple: for all these are classed by him with 'blood of bullocks' and 'fat of fed beasts'. But, of course, to Isaiah, prayers and Sabbaths and solemn assemblies and Temple were noble and sacred institutions, indispensable to religious life, and it was only their intolerable *abuse* which he condemned. The same things applies to his view of sacrifices."

138. There is another problem with this view, namely, it is really not true to the biblical text. In other words, if the prophets and psalmists really meant to say that prayer could or should replace sacrifice, then their true ideas would have been contrary to Torah. If they really didn't mean to say that prayer could or should replace sacrifice, then how can their texts be called on to support that very position? What right do we have to use someone's figurative speech (or hyperbole) to prove our literal point? For a realistic statement of how the Rabbinic view developed, see these brief remarks in the article on "Atonement" in the *ODJR*, 78: "With the destruction of the Temple and the automatic abolition of the sacrificial system, these and similar verses [i.e., from the prophetic books] formed the basis of the doctrine of the existence of alternatives to the sacrificial system."

139. See Rabbi Tovia Singer's web site: www.outreachjudaism.org/sin.html.

140. See Robert Gordis, "The Text and Meaning of Hosea XIV 3," *Vetus Testamentum* 5 (1955): 88–90, reprinted in idem, *The Word and the Book* (New York: Ktav, 1976), 347–49; see also Menahem Mansoor, *Revue de Qumran* 3 (1961): 391–92. (Mansoor authored a widely used biblical Hebrew grammar; Gordis was a highly respected biblical scholar at the Jewish Theological Seminary.)

141. The careful reader will notice that that is the identical reading of Hebrews 13:15, "the fruit of our lips." In fact, this reading is so natural that Hebrew scholar Douglas Stuart, in his commentary on Hosea, simply translates with "we will fully repay the fruit of our lips," without even providing a textual comment! See his *Hosea–Jonah*, Word Biblical Commentary (Dallas: Word, 1987), 210–13. This would be an example of what Semitic scholars refer to as "the enclitic *mem*," referring to the well-attested phenomenon in which the Hebrew letter *m* at the end of a word is grammatically superfluous; on this cf. the seminal study of Horace D. Hummel, "Enclitic *Mem* in Early Northwest Semitic," *Journal of Biblical Literature* 76 (1957): 85–107; and note the more recent works cited in Bruce K. Waltke and M. O'Connor, *An Introduction to Biblical Hebrew Syntax* (Winona Lake, Ind.: Eisenbrauns, 1990), 159, n. 45. Thus, Gordis, among many others, would read the Hebrew consonants *prym* as *peri-m* ("fruit" followed by the letter *mem*; Mansoor simply moves the *mem* to the beginning of the next word—a reading that is entirely possible—producing *peri misepatenu*, also meaning, "fruit from our lips"). According to Francis Anderson and David Noel Freedman, both renowned Hebrew and biblical scholars, the *mem* of the Hebrew text here "is an unassailable example of the enclitic particle" (*Hosea*, Anchor Bible [New York: Doubleday, 1980], 645).

142. See Gordis (ibid., 347), who states, "The difficulties of the traditional interpretation of MT [i.e., the Masoretic Text] are patent," also making the important grammatical observation that the accusative of the verb rendered "to pay" *(shillem)* "generally represents the debt or obligation being discharged [with reference to Exod. 21:36; 20:12; 22:5; 2 Kings 4:7; 1 Sam. 12:6; Joel 2:25; Prov. 19:17], not the object of payment [with reference only to "the legal phraseology of the Covenant Code," citing Exod. 21:37[36]; 22:3ff.]. Most frequently by far the verb governs *neder* 'vow' in the accusative [with reference to Deut. 23:22; 2 Sam. 15:7; Isa. 19:21; Nahum 1:15; Pss. 22:26; 50:14; 61:9; 65:2; 116:14, 18; Prov. 7:14; Job 22:26; Eccles. 5:3, among others]." He thus interprets the phrase in question to mean, "We shall pay the fruit of our lips, i.e., we shall fulfill our vows to God," understanding the final *mem* of *parim* to be enclitic (see immediately above, n. 141, for enclitic *mem*). A. B. Ehrlich, *Mikra*, 3:393, after explaining the grammatical usage (with reference to the unusual phrase *goyyim tsarayw* in Num. 24:8), states that "paying bulls" refers to "the words of our lips, as if to say, We will act in accordance with everything we confess to you." So, rather than understanding the text to mean that prayer replaces sacrifice, Ehrlich is saying that the image of sacrifice explains Hosea's idiom.

143. According to the footnote in the New Jewish Publication Society Version, the meaning of the Hebrew for this verse is uncertain, despite the fact that virtually all of the major, medieval Jewish commentators (including Rashi, Ibn Ezra, Radak) interpret it in keeping with the tentative translation offered by the NJPSV, reading, "Instead of bulls we will pay [the offering of] our lips." The fact that the bracketed words—which are not found in the original—have to be supplied underscores the difficulty of the Hebrew text. The Stone edition of the Tanakh renders Hosea 14:3[2] as, "Take words with you and return to HASHEM; say to Him, 'May You forgive all iniquity and accept good [intentions], and let our lips substitute for bulls.'" But where does *shillem* ever mean "substitute"?

144. It should also be pointed out that even Rabbi Singer's interpretation of Hosea 3:4–5 is defective, since he emphatically states that the prophecy described a state in Israel's history in which there would be no animal sacrificial system, and hence no possibility of blood atonement, whereas the prophecy says far more than that—and

really, says something different than that. As Douglas Stuart noted, Hosea spoke of the removal of objects of worship accepted by God (e.g., sacrifice) as well as objects of worship outlawed by God (e.g., pillar; see Deut. 16:22, in which some translations refer to a sacred stone; and teraphim, also known as household gods). Thus, Stuart states, "The sacrificial system and the ephod were orthodox. The pillar and the teraphim were abominably pagan. Israel, in its syncretism, had mixed the holy with the forbidden—had adulterated its religion. So, orthodox and heterodox features *alike* would now be taken away. Neither leadership, nor worship, nor divination would any longer be available to Israel's citizens" (*Hosea–Jonah*, 67). In light of this observation, it is clear that Hosea 3 does not show the people of Israel "how they are to replace the sacrificial system during their protracted exile" (as claimed by Rabbi Singer).

145. "Atonement," *EJ* (CD ROM), 3:830–31, citing y. Ta'anit 2:1, 65b; see further Pesikta deRav Kahana 191a, cited in part in Montefiore and Loewe, *Rabbinic Anthology*, #868.

146. For the benefit of those who are not familiar with the texts quoted by Rabbi Singer, I should point out some of the more glaring errors: He makes reference to Solomon's "startling prophetic message," calling it his "inauguration sermon," whereas it was simply a prayer to God. (This makes quite a difference!) Worse still, he states, "There was no mention of a cross or a dead messiah in King Solomon's prophetic message" whereas there was no mention of *any* Messiah, living or dead, in Solomon's prayer. As for the lack of reference to a cross, why *should* there have been a reference to the cross in Solomon's prayer?

147. Interestingly, there was another Rabbinic view concerning means of atonement during times such as those described by Hosea, times when there was neither Temple nor sacrifice. It was the teaching that the death of the righteous made atonement! According to the midrash, "Moses said to God, 'Will not the time come when Israel shall have neither Tabernacle nor Temple? What will happen with them then?' The divine reply was, 'I will then take one of their righteous men and keep him as a pledge on their behalf so I may pardon all their sins'" (Exodus Rabbah, Terumah 35:4, discussed below, 3.15). As stated in the medieval chronicle Yeven Metsulah, ". . . since the day the Holy Temple was destroyed, the righteous are seized by death for the iniquities of the generation" (cited in full below, 3.15).

148. I have basically followed the rendering of *ArtScroll Siddur*, 111, substituting Lord for Hashem here and elsewhere. For further discussion of this petition, see below, 3.13.

149. Scherman, *ArtScroll Siddur*, 33. A closely related petition is, "May it be Your will, O Lord, our God and the God of our forefathers, that this recital be worthy and acceptable, and favorable before You as if we had offered the continual offering in its set time, in its place, and according to its requirement" (ibid., 35).

150. Ibid., 32, my emphasis.

151. Notice how Temple prayer and sacrifice are *joined together* in Isaiah 56:6–7: "And foreigners who bind themselves to the Lord to serve him, to love the name of the Lord, and to worship him, all who keep the Sabbath without desecrating it and who hold fast to my covenant—these I will bring to my holy mountain and give them joy in my house of prayer. Their burnt offerings and sacrifices will be accepted on my altar; for my house will be called a house of prayer for all nations."

152. If you read carefully the verses to which Rabbi Singer referred, namely, 1 Kings 8:46–50 (2 Chron. 3:26–40), you will see that there is not a hint of the Temple being destroyed. Rather, those exiled (apparently not the entire population) will repent and

pray towards that very Temple, and as they do, God will forgive them. Again, the reason is obvious: They mix their prayers of repentance with the sacrifices being offered on their behalf (prayers, which, according to the later Talmudic rabbis, were efficacious in their atoning power), and God hears and forgives.

153. According to Rabbi Dan Cohn-Sherbok, *The Jewish Messiah* (Edinburgh: T & T Clark, 1997), 43, with reference to the destruction of the Second Temple, "Once the Temple had been destroyed and the Jewish people driven out of their homeland, the nation was bereft. In their despair the ancient Israelites longed for a kingly figure who would deliver them from exile and rebuild their holy city." Thus, in Rabbi Cohn-Sherbok's eyes, the destruction of the Second Temple helped pave the way for a deeper Messianic hope among the Jewish people.

154. For expressions of mercy after God's temporary rejection of his people, see verses such as Isaiah 54:7–10: "'For a brief moment I abandoned you, but with deep compassion I will bring you back. In a surge of anger I hid my face from you for a moment, but with everlasting kindness I will have compassion on you,' says the LORD your Redeemer. 'To me this is like the days of Noah, when I swore that the waters of Noah would never again cover the earth. So now I have sworn not to be angry with you, never to rebuke you again. Though the mountains be shaken and the hills be removed, yet my unfailing love for you will not be shaken nor my covenant of peace be removed,' says the LORD, who has compassion on you." For a strong, Messianic Jewish affirmation of God's eternal, immutable covenant with his people Israel, see Michael L. Brown, *Our Hands Are Stained with Blood: The Tragic Story of the "Church" and the Jewish People* (Shippensburg, Pa.: Destiny Image, 1992), 117–53.

155. This would have been similar to the people of Judah saying to Isaiah, "God has said he will not accept our prayers because our hands are covered with blood. So we'll give tithes instead, and God will accept that." On the contrary, God would not accept tithes any more than prayers or sacrifices or praises or fasts—unless they were accompanied by repentance. In the same way, since the destruction of the Temple was an act of judgment by God, it would be ludicrous to say, "We cannot offer sacrifices because the Temple is in ruins as judgment on our sins. So we'll offer prayers instead!"

156. For the question of how Jews received atonement during the Babylonian exile, see below, 3.13, and n. 247.

157. As rendered by Rabbi Rosenberg. The commentary of Gur Aryeh to Rashi here is illuminating.

158. According to Jacob Neusner, *First-Century Judaism in Crisis*, augmented edition (New York: Ktav, 1982), 24–25, speaking with reference to the destruction of the Second Temple, "No generation in the history of Jewry has been so roundly, universally condemned by posterity as that of Yohanan ben Zakkai. Christianity remembered, in the tradition of the Church, that Jesus wept over the city and said a bitter, sorrowing sentence [making reference to Matt. 23:37–39]. . . . So for twenty centuries, Jerusalem was seen through the eye of Christian faith as a faithless city, killing prophets, and therefore desolated by the righteous act of a wrathful God. But Jews said no less. From the time of the destruction they prayed, 'On account of our sins we have been exiled from our land. . . .' It is not a great step from 'our sins,' to 'the sins of the generation in which the Temple was destroyed.' It is not a difficult conclusion, and not a few have reached it. The Temple was destroyed mainly because of the sins of the Jews of that time, particularly 'causeless hatred.' Whether the sins were those specified by Christians or by Talmudic rabbis hardly matters. This was supposed to be a sinning generation." Neusner, for his part, states, "It was *not* a sinning generation, but one

deeply faithful to the covenant and to the Scripture that set forth its terms, perhaps more so than many who have since condemned it." See also Stone, "Reactions to Destructions of the Second Temple," 196: "If the documents of the Second Temple age that deal with these destructions and desecrations are examined, it becomes apparent that theodicy became the central issue. Israel's suffering was thought to be the result of sin; a punishment inflicted by God who covenanted with the nation. Israel's fate was seen as bound to Israel's action and God's justice." He states further, "The profound impact of such destructions is appreciable only in light of the central role of Jerusalem, the Temple and the High Priesthood in the whole of Jewish life in the Second Temple period" (198). See also the relevant chapters in Doron Mendels, *The Rise and Fall of Jewish Nationalism* (Grand Rapids: Eerdmans, 1992).

159. Scherman, *ArtScroll Siddur*, 41, 43.

160. Contrast this with the assurance that followers of Yeshua have through his atoning sacrifice: "Therefore, brothers, since we have confidence to enter the Most Holy Place by the blood of Jesus, by a new and living way opened for us through the curtain, that is, his body, and since we have a great priest over the house of God, let us draw near to God with a sincere heart in full assurance of faith, having our hearts sprinkled to cleanse us from a guilty conscience and having our bodies washed with pure water. Let us hold unswervingly to the hope we profess, for he who promised is faithful" (Heb. 10:19–23).

161. *ArtScroll Siddur*, 109, 111.

162. See passages such as Genesis 15 for the important role played by blood sacrifices in covenant making.

163. On the dating and origin of Targum Onkelos, see Philip S. Alexander, "Targum, Targumim," in *The Anchor Bible Dictionary*, ed. David Noel Freedman (New York: Doubleday, 1992), 6:320–31 (specifically, 321–22).

164. You might wonder why the Most Holy Place, altar, and Tent of Meeting needed "atonement" (or purgation, purification) because of Israel's uncleanness and rebellion. How could inanimate objects need "atonement"? First, you must remember that the root *kipper* can mean both atone, expiate as well as purge, purify; second, you can think of these holy places and holy items, which were situated right in the middle of the Israelite people, much like a nonsmoker in a room filled with smokers. The nonsmoker gets polluted by the smoke of the others, even smelling like smoke after leaving the room, to the point that the nonsmoker's clothes need to be "purged" from the smell of smoke. In the same way, Israel's sins polluted God's holy place and holy altar; see Baruch A. Levine, *In the Presence of the Lord: A Study of the Cult and Some Cultic Terms in Ancient Israel* (Leiden: Brill, 1974), and contrast with Averbeck, *"kpr,"* NIDOTTE, 2:699–702. According to Rashi (to Ezek. 43:20, the command to purify the altar and make it fit for atonement), "You shall 'wipe' it of its ordinariness to initiate it into sanctity, so that it will be fit for [providing] atonement from then on." See Rabbi A. J. Rosenberg, *Ezekiel*, vol. 2, The Judaica Books of the Prophets (New York: Judaica Press, 1991), 387.

165. As explained by Milgrom, ". . . sin is a miasma which wherever committed is attracted to the sanctuary. There it adheres and accumulates until God will no longer abide in it. Hence, it is forever incumbent upon Israel, through the indispensable medium of its priesthood, to purge the sanctuary regularly of its impurities lest God abandon it and the people to their doom" (Milgrom, "Kipper," *EJ* [CD ROM], 10:1039–44)—and this purging could not be accomplished without blood!

166. For the essential role played by repentance in the Bible (Old Testament and New Testament), as well as in later Rabbinic tradition, see vol. 1, 1.11, and below, 3.21.

167. I will discuss the important role of the so-called scapegoat, which was not slaughtered on the Day of Atonement but rather was sent away to carry Israel's sins into the wilderness, below, 3.12. I would note here, however, that ancient Jewish traditions indicate that the goat *was* in fact killed on Yom Kippur (according to the traditions, by driving it off a cliff), apparently to insure that it would not return to the camp and that it would, in fact, die shortly after having Israel's sins symbolically transferred to it.

168. For other possible translations, which do not affect our discussion, see the commentaries of Jacob Milgrom, Baruch Levine, John E. Hartley, Erhard S. Gerstenberger, and Gordon F. Wenham, along with the comments of Richard Averbeck, cited below, n. 171.

169. As stated by Rabbi Tovia Singer, "In the immediate context of Leviticus 17:11 we find that the Torah is speaking of the prohibition of eating blood, not the subject of sin and atonement. The Torah discusses blood atonement in this verse only as a byproduct of its central theme. This crucial message is lost when missionaries quote Leviticus 17:11 alone, without the surrounding texts as its proper background. . . . Leviticus 17:10–11 is therefore declaring two principles about blood: 1) you may not eat it 2) amongst all the various rituals associated with the sin sacrifice, such as the laying of the hands on the animal, slaughtering, collecting, carrying, sprinkling, placing of the animal on the altar, it is only the sprinkling the blood on the altar that brings about the atonement. [I should point out that Rabbi Singer's second point here is without scriptural foundation; rather, it reflects Talmudic comments on Leviticus 1:4, which I will discuss below. In other words, Leviticus 17:11 is *not* explaining that "amongst all the various rituals associated with the sin sacrifice . . . it is only the sprinkling the blood on the altar that brings about the atonement."] You therefore may not eat the blood. *This verse does not state or imply that one cannot have atonement for sin without a blood sacrifice.* Such a message would contradict all of the Jewish scriptures which clearly outline two other methods of atonement more pleasing to God than a sacrifice—heartfelt repentance and charity." (As posted on his web site [see above, n. 109].) I should note here that almost every paragraph on this particular web page is fraught with errors, some of them quite glaring. All the major points made by Rabbi Singer are refuted in the objections here dealing with atonement (3.9–3.17). As we carefully study every relevant verse in the Hebrew Scriptures, we will see just how exaggerated and misleading his comments are that *"all of the Jewish scriptures . . . clearly outline* two other methods of atonement more pleasing to God than a sacrifice" (my emphasis). I would encourage the careful reader to remember Rabbi Singer's claims and examine them against the evidence presented from the text of the Hebrew Bible itself.

170. Midrash Ha-Chafetz to Leviticus 1:2, cited in *Torah Shelemah* 25:17 and by Joshua Berman, *The Temple: Its Symbolism and Meaning Then and Now* (Northvale, N.J.: Jason Aronson, 1995), 126.

171. Hertz, *Pentateuch and Haftorahs,* 487. In his careful study of *kipper,* Prof. Richard E. Averbeck, an Old Testament scholar who is also an expert in Sumerian literature, explains the significance of Leviticus 17:11 as follows: "Blood atonement is mentioned in Lev 17:11 as the rationale for draining the blood from the domesticated animal before eating the meat. The point is not that the blood atones for killing the animal [contra Milgrom] but, instead, that if one was going to utilize the blood for

anything, its only proper use was to make atonement on the altar of the Lord. To eat the blood would be to eat not only the flesh of the animal but to eat the animal's *nepeš* [life, soul], which the Creator of all *nepeš* (Gen 1:20–21, 24, 30; 2:7, 19) had long ago reserved for himself (Gen 9:3–5) and now assigned to the purpose of atonement alone (Lev 17:11–14)." See his article on *"kpr," NIDOTTE*, 2:689–709 (here, 695). As noted correctly by Erhard S. Gerstenberger, *Leviticus*, Old Testament Library, trans. Douglas W. Stott (Louisville: Westminster John Knox, 1996), "The assertion 'the life of the body is in the blood' (v. 11) or 'the life of the every body is its blood' (twice in v. 14) would not have been emphasized three times for no reason at all. . . . But how is atonement through blood to take place? . . . The background to these blood rites apparently involves legal considerations. Life forfeited through guilt—namely, that of the offerer—is redeemed from the warranted punishment through the presentation of the life of another" (240–42; and see ibid. for important anthropological perspectives on the significance of blood in various cultures).

172. John E. Hartley, *Leviticus*, Word Biblical Commentary (Dallas: Word, 1992), 65. Hartley, following D. J. McCarthy (*Journal of Biblical Literature* 88 [1969]: 166–76), also points out "that attaching such significance to blood is unique to Israel among the cults [i.e., Temple rituals] of the Middle East, indicating that the handling of the blood was assigned special significance because of Israel's unique theological outlook" (ibid.).

173. Quite oddly, Rabbi Tovia Singer claims that Hebrews 9:22 could be a "stunning mistranslation" of Leviticus 17:11, basing his claim on the fact that Christian study Bibles generally cross reference Hebrews 9:22 with Leviticus 17:11. But as anyone using a study Bible knows, a cross reference between the Old Testament and New Testament does not mean that the New Testament author was necessarily quoting the Old Testament author. It simply means that one verse provides support or background for the other verse. In the case in point here, there is no translation involved at all (this is really self-evident), anymore than there is a quotation (or "stunning misquotation") of Leviticus 17:11 in the Talmudic texts just cited. Rather, Leviticus 17:11 provides the biblical support for the statement penned in Hebrews 9:22, which simply reflects the common Jewish view of the day that "there is no atonement without the blood." Note also that the root *kipper* (in the Rabbinic phrase just quoted, the noun *kapparah*) sometimes overlaps with verbs meaning "forgive, pardon" explaining why Hebrews states that "without the shedding of blood there is no forgiveness [literally, remission]"; cf. Jeremiah 18:23 (where *kipper* is rendered by the NJPSV as "pardon"), along with the verses from Psalms, cited below.

174. Harold W. Attridge, *The Epistle to the Hebrews*, Hermeneia (Philadelphia: Fortress, 1989), 258.

175. Jacob Neusner, in his American translation, renders the key words as "atonement is only through the blood."

176. Geza Vermes, "Redemption and Genesis xxii: The Binding of Isaac and the Sacrifice of Jesus," in his *Scripture and Tradition in Judaism*, Studia Post-Biblica 4 (Leiden: E. J. Brill, 1961), 193–227 (here, 205), with reference to b. Yoma 5a. Interestingly, Vermes adds, "The antiquity of this talmudic rule is attested by the Epistle to the Hebrews ix. 22: *xoris haimatekxusias ou ginetai aphesis*, 'without the shedding of blood there is no remission'" (ibid., 205, n. 4).

177. Hartley, *Leviticus*, 23, with reference also to b. Yoma 5a. Although I have assembled these references on my own, I was interested to see that the Talmudic quotes, together with the citation from Baruch Levine, were also cited in a Jews for Jesus web

site refuting the erroneous position of Rabbi Tovia Singer. See www.jews-for-jesus.org/CASE/BIBLICAL/Sin.html.

178. According to the *EJ* article "Sacrifices," "The surrender of a living thing was a major factor in nearly every kind of sacrificial ritual; that life was being forfeited was signified by the extraction of animal's blood: 'For the life of the flesh is in the blood; and I have given it for you upon the altar to make atonement for your souls; for it is the blood that makes atonement, by reason of the life [that is in it]' (Lev. 17:11). The people were therefore forbidden to eat the blood (Lev. 17:10; also Gen. 9:4; Lev. 3:17; 7:26; Deut. 12:16, 23; 15:23), since life belonged only to God."

179. We will make reference to this ceremony again below, 3.13.

180. See Exodus 29:33, cited above; this verse, however, which we just cited above, refers only to the sacrifices offered in the ceremony of the consecration of the priests.

181. According to Rashi (see b. Hagigah 27a), "a man's table atones for him" means, "in the entertaining of guests." With due respect to Rashi and the Talmud, it is only fair to point out that there is absolutely no biblical support for this concept. The Torah doesn't even hint at such a thing.

182. Urbach, *The Sages*, 432, 434. For a discussion of this very important passage cited here from the Mishnah, see below, 3.12.

183. Urbach, *The Sages*, 433–34.

184. Ibid., 433–34, my emphasis.

185. J. H. Kurtz, *Offerings, Sacrifices and Worship in the Old Testament*, trans. James Martin (Peabody, Mass.: Hendrickson, 1998), 66, his emphasis.

186. In this vein, 1 Samuel 3:14 states that the guilt of the high priest Eli's house will "never be atoned for by sacrifice or offering" (the Hebrew term for offering here referred primarily to flour). How unthinkable it would be to read, "The guilt of Eli's house will never be atoned for by flour"! Rather, the only atoning efficacy of the flour offerings was in their being joined with the blood sacrifices on the altar.

187. Nahum Sarna, *Exodus*, The JPS Torah Commentary (Philadelphia: The Jewish Publication Society, 1991), 196, notes simply, "the idea seems to be that a census places the lives of those counted in jeopardy."

188. Sarna, ibid., notes concisely, "Hebrew *kofer* is a monetary payment made in lieu of a physical penalty incurred."

189. Hertz, *Pentateuch and Haftorahs*, 352. Hertz explains the ransom payment both here and in Numbers 31 with reference to warfare, suggesting that the Israelite men were being numbered for war, at which time they would potentially be involved in the taking of life, but not murder (for which, as noted above, no *kopher* was acceptable). Thus, Hertz, following the German biblical scholar Benno Jacob, states that, "The soldier who is ready to march into battle is in the eyes of Heaven a potential taker of life, though not a deliberate murderer. Hence he requires a 'ransom for life.'"

190. Milgrom, *Numbers*, 264, with further reference to Excursus 19, "Levitical 'Kippur'" and Excursus 2, "The Census and Its Totals."

191. The only thing in common between the two contexts is the concept of substitution: In Exodus 30 and Numbers 31, monetary payment is made to avert wrath; in Leviticus 17:11, the blood of sacrifices is put on the altar to procure atonement. For another view that links these two contexts more closely, see Levine, *In the Presence of the Lord*, 67. See further the discussion in Averbeck, *"kpr,"* 695.

192. This is repeated verbatim in the commentary of Mizrachi; see also Be'er BaSadeh.

193. For an attempt to harmonize both of Rashi's interpretations, see Maskil LeDavid, yet another commentary on Rashi.

194. Milgrom, *Numbers*, 142.

195. As rendered by Rabbi Rosenberg.

196. As rendered by Arthur Cohen, *Soncino Chumash* (London: Soncino, 1956), 885.

197. For the Rabbinic logic behind this, see the Steinsaltz Talmud (in Hebrew) to b. Yoma 44a (186), sub *'iyyunim;* cf. also the comments in Torah Temimah to Numbers 17:11.

198. For those who still feel that *kipper* in this context must be connected with atonement—despite the interpretation of leading Jewish biblical scholars, both ancient and modern—I would point out that Moses instructed Aaron to "take fire from the altar" (the very altar called by Maimonides "the altar of atonement"), hinting that even in this context, the usage of *kipper* was tied to the sacrificial altar. Baruch Levine, *Numbers 1–20*, Anchor Bible (New York: Doubleday, 1993), 420–21, translates *kipper* here with "perform a rite of expiation," explaining that "the sense is functional: the verb *kipper* does not mean 'to cleanse,' but rather to perform a rite whose *result* is a kind of purification. . . . What Aaron did on this occasion represents an adaptation of procedures involved in expiation rites, and conveyed by the verb *kipper*. There rites normally required the utilization of sacrificial blood, placed on the horns of the altar of burnt offerings and occasionally on other interior appurtenances of the Tabernacle [with reference to his earlier study, *In the Presence of the Lord*, 63–77]." His comments in the latter work, 73, n. 51, are noteworthy: "In Nu 17:11–12, the verb *kipper* conveys the apotropaic use of incense in stemming a plague. This usage is borrowed, since the incense was sprinkled or spread over the people in the manner of blood, hence the verb *natan* (v. 12), elsewhere used in connection with placing sacrificial blood on the altar (Lev 4:25, 30, 34, etc.). In Nu 25:13 the verb *kipper* characterizes the result of Aaron's action in stabbing the sinful *nasi'* [leader], thus again resembling the use of blood. We observe, therefore, that even in several cases where *kipper* does not refer directly to the use of blood from the *ḥaṭṭa't* [sin offering] and *'ašam* [guilt offering], it relates to apotropaic activity similar to it."

199. Cf. Hertz, *Pentateuch and Haftorahs*, 643, to Numbers 17:11 (English trans., 16:46); Hertz there observes that when Moses instructed Aaron to bring his censer (or fire-pan), the Hebrew literally says *the* censer, "i.e., the censer which belongs to the High Priest and which he used on the Day of Atonement (Lev. xvi, 12) when ministering in the Sanctuary." See also immediately above, n. 198.

200. For discussion of Numbers 25 (Phineas), see below, 3.15. Interestingly, although Solomon Schechter made reference to many different forms of atonement according to the Talmudic rabbis, it is clear from his discussion that none competed with or took the place of the blood sacrifices or the Yom Kippur rituals. For references see Solomon Schechter, *Some Aspects of Rabbinic Theology* (Peabody, Mass.: Hendrickson, 1998), 300–306, where he also notes that some of the statements of the relevant comments of the Talmudic rabbis are to be taken *"cum grano salis"* (Latin for "with a grain of salt") (300).

201. See already in the Torah Exodus 34:6–7, where the Lord described himself as "the compassionate and gracious God, slow to anger, abounding in love and faithfulness, maintaining love to thousands, and forgiving wickedness, rebellion and sin. Yet he does not leave the guilty unpunished."

202. There are two explanations for rendering *kipper* as "forgive": (1) It could be meaning derived from "atone, expiate," since the result of atonement is forgiveness; (2) it could reflect a more literal, older aspect of the verb, meaning, "wipe away, purge." Hence, God would forgive sin by wiping it away or removing it from his sight. See further above, n. 173 (on Jer. 18:23 and the meanings of *kipper*).

203. In 2 Chronicles 30:18–19, during a major, nationwide celebration of Passover at the Temple in Jerusalem, it is written that "although most of the many people who came from Ephraim, Manasseh, Issachar and Zebulun had not purified themselves, yet they ate the Passover, contrary to what was written. But Hezekiah prayed for them, saying, 'May the LORD, who is good, pardon [*kipper*, rendered this time in the NJPSV as "make atonement for"] everyone who sets his heart on seeking God—the LORD, the God of his fathers—even if he is not clean according to the rules of the sanctuary.'" Averbeck, *"kpr,"* 697, with attention to the Hebrew grammar (*kipper* followed by *be'ad*) explains Hezekiah's prayer as follows: "The basic idea here is that the Lord should act as the priest 'on behalf of' (*be'ad*) certain people in the congregation by wiping them clean even though they were eating the Passover in violation of the Passover purity laws (on *be'ad*, see also Lev. 9:7[2x]; 16:6, 11, 17, 24; Ezek. 45:17; also Exod. 32:30, where Moses intended to act as a priest on behalf of the congregation)."

204. For an extensive study, see my article, *"Kippēr* and Atonement in the Book of Isaiah," in *Ki Barukh Hu: Ancient Near Eastern, Biblical, and Judaic Studies for Baruch A. Levine*, ed. Robert Chazan, William W. Hallo, and Lawrence H. Schiffman (Winona Lake, Ind.: Eisenbrauns), 189–202; for a discussion of Isaiah 28:18 and 47:11, which also contain forms of *kipper*, along with Isaiah 43:3, with *kopher*, see the same article.

205. For a typical, midrashic application of this verse by the Talmudic rabbis, see b. Berakhot 57a.

206. For a discussion of Isaiah 22:14b, often cited in Rabbinic literature as a proof text for the view that there is atoning power in one's own death, see my article on *"Kippēr* and Atonement in the Book of Isaiah," 200–202, where I conclude that the text in Isaiah is saying, "This sin will not be purged away *(kipper)* till your dying day," rather than, "With death this sin will be atoned for." If, however, one feels that a case can be made for the Rabbinic position, then it would actually tie in well with our extensive treatment of the atoning power of the death of the righteous (below, 3.15).

207. For the question of why blood sacrifices will be necessary in a future Temple if Jesus already paid for all our sins, see below, 3.17.

208. For Talmudic use of Proverbs 16:6 in the context of receiving forgiveness of sins through charity and good deeds, see b. Berakhot 5b.

209. See b. Yoma 85b–86a; t. Yom HaKippurim 5(4):6–9; m. Yoma 8:8; Mishneh Torah, Hilkhot Teshuvah 1:4; cf. also below, 3.15.

210. In the new translation of Rabbi E. Touger, *Maimonides, Mishneh Torah: Hilchot Teshuvah, Laws of Repentance* (Brooklyn, N.Y.: Maznaim, 1987), 16 (with brief commentary), the Hebrew phrase *teshuvah tolah* is rendered, "Teshuvah has a tentative effect." Cf. also 18.

211. For recent discussion, see B. A. Levine, *Leviticus*, JPS Torah Commentary (Philadelphia: Jewish Publication Society, 1989), Excursus 1, "That Person Shall be Cut Off," 241–42; J. Milgrom, *Numbers*, JPS Torah Commentary (Philadelphia: Jewish Publication Society, 1990), Excursus 36, "The Penalty of 'Karet'," 405–8, with reference to D. J. Wold, *The Biblical Penalty of Karet* (Ann Arbor, Mich.: Univ. Microfilms, 1978).

212. For a discussion of Isaiah 22:14, cited as a proof text for the concept that one's own death makes final atonement, see above, n. 206. For further treatment of the Rabbinic background, see R. Avraham di Boton, Lehem Mishneh to Hilkhot Teshuvah 1:4, and see concisely in English, Touger, *Laws of Repentance*, 14–19.

213. According to Levine, "The primary sense of the verb *kipper* is 'to wipe off, cleanse,' essentially a physical process" (*Leviticus*, 110). Milgrom goes as far as saying, "'Atone' or 'expiate' is the customary translation for *kipper*, but in most cases this is incorrect" (*Leviticus 1–16*, 1079).

214. Note also Rashi's comments to Ezekiel 43:20, cited above, n. 164.

215. Hartley, *Leviticus*, renders *kpr* here with "undone" (thus, by loyal love and truth, iniquity is undone).

216. Fritz Maass, "*kpr* pi. to atone," in *Theological Lexicon of the Old Testament*, ed. Claus Westermann and Ernst Jenni, trans. Mark E. Biddle (Peabody, Mass.: Hendrickson, 1997), 2:632 (the article runs from 624–35).

217. For a discussion of Genesis 32:21, see Brown, "*Kippēr* and Atonement," 193–94.

218. As I have noted, it is extremely important to remember that the sanctuary itself could only be cleansed from the pollution of Israel's sins by blood.

219. For those looking for a technical theological exegesis of Proverbs 16:6, see Delitzsch, in Keil and Deliztsch, *Proverbs*, 338–39.

220. Jacob Milgrom has argued for the expiatory function of the burnt offering as well, with reference to similar ancient Near Eastern practices and with support from some Talmudic sources; see Milgrom, *Leviticus 1–16*, 172–76. He notes that "some medieval commentators suggest the entire range of unwitting sins (Bekhor Shor; cf. Shadal) and even brazen sins, if their punishment is not specified (Ramban)" (175). Note, however, that any list of offerings that does not include guilt offerings and sin offerings—see, e.g., Jeremiah 17:24–26—would obviously not have the issue of atonement at the forefront, even if there were expiatory functions for burnt offerings under certain circumstances. See further below, 3.17.

221. See George Buchanan Gray, *Sacrifice in the Old Testament: Its Theory and Practice* (New York: Ktav, 1971), 56.

222. Harris, "Leviticus," *EBC*, 2:547. Hartley, *Leviticus*, 78, offers several other distinctives between these sacrifices, summarizing the important studies of Levine and Milgrom. According to Levine, the guilt (or reparation) offering was primarily for personal needs, and the sin (or purification) offering was primarily for public needs. According to Milgrom, "A reparation offering is presented for desecration of sancta and a purification offering is offered to remove the contamination of sacred cultic objects from the pollution arising from inadvertent sins."

223. Hartley, *Leviticus*, 18.

224. Ibid., 32–33. Milgrom, *EJ*, "Kipper," observes that "the prescriptions of the *asham* offering ordained for cases of calculable loss to the deity stipulate that restitution must be made to the wronged party (man or sanctuary) before atonement by sacrifice is permitted. Indeed, the prophetic insistence that repentance is not an end in itself, but must lead to rectification of the wrongdoing (e.g., Isa. 1:13–17; 58:6–12; Micah 6:6–8), is only the articulation of a basic postulate of the sacrificial system." Thus, repentance and sacrifices together effected atonement.

225. Hartley, *Leviticus*, 80, commenting on the fact that Isaiah describes the self-sacrifice of the servant of the Lord with the term *'asham*, notes: "The choice of '-sh-m to describe his sacrificial death may be twofold. First, it communicates that the servant's death compensates God fully for the damages he has incurred by mankind's sin-

ning. Second, the servant's sacrifice provides expiation for every kind of sin, inadvertent and intentional. That is, the servant's sacrifice provides expiation for any person who appropriates its merits to himself, no matter how grave his sin."

226. Schechter, *Aspects of Rabbinic Theology*, 300.

227. This is the translation of Jacob Neusner, *The Mishnah* (New Haven: Yale, 1988), 622.

228. This is the rendering of Philip Blackman, *Mishnayoth* (Gateshead, England: Judaica Press, 1983), 4:340. He explains "wantonness" to mean "conscious premeditated sin by an unclean person who ate of *qadošim*, holy sacrifices, or entered the Temple," the punishment for which would be "forty stripes after warning" (340, n. 1).

229. While most English readers are familiar with the term *scapegoat*, so-called because it escaped into the wilderness, the Hebrew text at Leviticus 16:21 speaks of the goat *la'az'azel*, which some translate "to [or for] Azazel." Here, Maimonides speaks of "the goat sent," which the translator Rabbi Eliyahu Touger explains with the bracketed words "to Azazel." For a summary of the issues concerning the "scapegoat," see Milgrom, *Leviticus 1–16*, 1021–22, 1071–79, with reference to other literature. Note also Lester L. Grabbe, "The Scapegoat Tradition: A Study in Early Jewish Interpretation," *Journal for the Study of Judaism* 18 (1987): 152–67.

230. Touger, *Laws of Repentance*, 1:2.

231. Milgrom, "Kipper," *EJ* (CD ROM), 10:1039–44. He adds that "deliberate sins and impurities, however, cannot be purged by the offender's own *ḥaṭṭat* (Num. 15:30–31) but must await the annual rite of purgation for the sanctuary and the nation (Day of Atonement)."

232. See also the commentary of Bertinoro—the "Rashi" of Mishnah commentaries—to m. Shevu'ot 1:6.

233. See further Richard E. Averbeck, "*ḥaṭṭa't*," *NIDOTTE*, 2:93–103; note also the comments of Jacob Milgrom on burnt offerings (with background from Hittite sources) cited by Robinson on the Jews for Jesus web site (above, n. 177).

234. Abraham Chill, *The Minhagim* (New York: Sepher-Hermon, 1979), 200–201. The first definite reference to this custom dates to the ninth century of this era. Interestingly, Maimonides doesn't mention the custom at all in his law code, and four hundred years later, Joseph Karo spoke against the practice in his law code (Shulhan Arukh, Orah Hayyim 605). However, the expanded commentary of Moses Isserles on the Shulhan Arukh—printed as part of the law code itself—actually praised the custom of *kapparot*, to the point that Karo's negative comments were later removed from some editions of his own law code. The practice of *kapparot* was so widespread that it has continued to this day, being codified again in the early twentieth century in Yehi'el Mikhael Epstein's Arukh Hashulhan (Orah Hayyim 605, expanded to six subdivisions). It is also fascinating to see how this blood sacrifice was replaced in some communities with an offering to charity, the price of the fowl substituting for the bird itself. Once again, tradition came up with a replacement for blood sacrifices. See Chill, *Minhagim*, 200–202.

235. See above, 3.10, for references to the *mizbah kapparah*, altar of atonement, in Rabbinic literature, along with the Talmudic expression *'en kapparah 'ella' baddam*, "There is no atonement without the blood."

236. Commenting on the NIV's rendering here, R. Laird Harris offers the following useful comments: "The expression 'to sin unintentionally' (*ḥaṭṭa' bishegagah)* in v. 2 [of ch. 4] calls for some comment. The NIV reading may give the impression that there was no sacrifice for intentional sins. This would be a problem, for many of our

sins are more or less intentional though not necessarily deliberate. The word *shagag* and its by-form *shagah* and their cognates basically seem to mean 'to err,' 'go astray,' 'wander,' 'stagger.' The nouns mean 'error,' 'mistake.' Outside the Pentateuchal legislation, the NIV always translates these words with such expressions (about twenty-five times). The idea of intent is not basic to the word and ought not to be imported."

237. Milgrom, "Kipper," *EJ* (CD ROM), 10:1039–44.

238. Harris, "Leviticus," 547. He notes: "The sense of the verb *shagag* will be adequately caught if in all the verses concerned here in Leviticus 4–5, the phrase 'sins unintentionally' is rendered by 'goes astray in sin' or 'does wrong' or the like. In Numbers 15:22–29 the translation 'wrong' or 'wrongly' or 'in error' will better replace 'unintentional' or 'unintentionally.' Indeed, the NIV translates *shegagah* by 'wrong' in Numbers 15:25 (second instance) and in Leviticus 5:18. 'Unintentional' seems better to fit *shagag* and its cognates only in the manslaughter passages (Num. 35:11–22; Josh. 20:3–5), and even there 'inadvertently' or 'by mistake' would actually fit better."

239. Milgrom, *Numbers*, 125.

240. Jacob Milgrom, "The Priestly Doctrine of Repentance," *Revue Biblique* 82 (1975): 186–205.

241. Milgrom, *Leviticus*, 373.

242. For the danger of unintentional sins according to the Talmudic rabbis, see the quotes compiled by Robinson on the Jews for Jesus web site (above, n. 177).

243. As to the argument that Daniel 6:10 proves Daniel was following the oral tradition that prayer should be offered to God three times daily, see vol. 3, 6.6.

244. I could also point out that the text itself doesn't state explicitly that Daniel faced Jerusalem in prayer. It only states that the windows of his upstairs room where he prayed opened toward Jerusalem. What if he, like Hezekiah of old (see 2 Kings 20:2), faced the wall when he prayed? Then he would have been looking *away* from Jerusalem, not toward it. Of course, I have no problem with the concept of Daniel facing Jerusalem when he prayed, and I believe the text intimates that idea. However, there is no indisputable proof of this from the text.

245. Gleason L. Archer Jr., "Daniel," *EBC*, 7:80.

246. Although I cited these verses above, 3.9, they are so important to our discussion here they could not be omitted. I would appeal to every traditional Jew reading this book to carefully consider the implications of this biblical text.

247. This, by the way, answers the question of how the Jewish people secured atonement during the Babylonian exile. The answer is painful but clear: They had no assurance of atonement on a national level. They felt the weight of their sins, they recognized that they were under divine judgment as a people, and they could only hope for mercy on an individual level (or put their trust in God's promises of coming redemption, as Abraham did, being pronounced righteous by faith; cf. below, end of 3.13). While the Torah does speak of the people of Israel paying for their sins in exile (see Lev. 26:40–43; cf. also Isa. 40:1–2), it simply means receiving the due punishment for their deeds (like doing time in prison for a crime) rather than earning forgiveness. Rather, as Leviticus 26 makes plain, once they have paid for their sins and have repented and turned back to God, he would show mercy by bringing his people back to their homeland. Interestingly, biblical concepts such as these led to the Rabbinic belief that "exile atones for sins." For discussion of this, see 3.15 (on the biblical basis for the Rabbinic teaching that the death of the righteous atones). In anticipation of our discussion there, let me simply quote part of a midrash that states that in the absence of Temple or Tabernacle, God said to Moses, "I will then take one of their righteous men and

keep him as a pledge on their behalf so I may pardon all their sins." And what text is given in support of this? It is Lamentations 2:4b, "he has slain all who were pleasing to the eye," referring to God's judgment on Jerusalem when the First Temple was destroyed. So the midrash is stating that during the time of the Babylonian exile, God would take a righteous man as a pledge (meaning, he would slay the righteous), and through that righteous man's death, atonement would be procured for the nation. How closely this approximates the New Testament view of the atoning power of the death of the Messiah! See again below, 3.15.

248. It is obvious that Solomon was not countenancing *the entire population* going into exile in his prayer but rather a portion of the people. In his mind, the Temple would still be standing, hence his request that prayers offered *toward the Temple*—not towards the ruins of the Temple—would be received by God. See 1 Kings 8:46–50.

249. "Sacrifices," *EJ* (CD ROM), 14:599–615. For further discussion of this period, see Mendels, *Jewish Nationalism.*

250. Cited in Scherman, *ArtScroll Siddur,* 110, their emphasis.

251. The note in Scherman, *ArtScroll Siddur,* 110, to the phrase, "The fire-offerings of Israel" is also of interest: "Since the Temple is not standing this phrase is taken in an allegorical sense. It refers to: the souls and the deeds of the righteous, which are as pleasing as sacrifices; Jewish prayers that are like offerings; or the altar fires and sacrifices of Messianic times. Some repunctuate the blessing to read: . . . *and restore the service . . . and the fire-offerings of Israel. Their prayer accept with love . . .*"

252. According to some biblical interpreters, Lamentations 5:7 seems to teach the opposite of this: "Our fathers sinned and are no more, and we bear their punishment." I addressed this issue as follows in my article, "Lamentations: Theology of," in *NIDOTTE,* 4:884–893: "Did not the prophets declare that the saying, 'The fathers have eaten sour grapes and the children's teeth are set on edge,' would no longer be spoken in Israel (Jer 31:29–32; Ezek 18:2–4)? And did not Deut 24:16 state that sons would *not* be put to death for the sins of their fathers? Actually, the latter verse, as explicated elsewhere in the OT (cf. 2 Kgs 14:6; 2 Chron 25:4) simply refers to judicial punishment alone. Moreover, the principle of Exod 20:5ff. was never revoked, viz., that the Lord visits the sins of one sinning generation upon the next sinning generation (cf. Lam 5:7 with 5:16b). However, the 'sour grapes' oracles, coming as they do in the books of Jeremiah and Ezekiel, spell the beginning of the end of a cycle (cf. Lam 4:22a, and see also Isa 40:2). Previous generations (in particular, that of Manasseh; cf. 2 Kgs 24:1–4) sinned grievously, leaving a legacy of judgment-to-come hanging over the heads of their descendants. The sour grapes pronouncement, delivered in Jeremiah in the context of restoration promises (throughout chapter 31, and immediately before the new covenant section in 31:31–34), states that in these days of prophesied national renewal and blessing, no legacy of judgment would be left for the future. Rather, there would be immediate retribution for sin. This was to be considered a blessing! Cf. also Ezek 18:2ff., where a slightly different perspective is clarified, viz., that righteous children would not be punished for the sins of their unrighteous fathers; cf. further C. F. Keil" (890–91).

253. With regard to the verses cited in Romans, they are in the midst of a lengthy argument by Paul in which he demonstrates that we are justified by faith (see Rom. 1:16–17; 3:19–31). How wrong it would be, then, to prove from the verses cited that Paul believed we were justified by our works alone.

254. For scholarly arguments pointing to the necessity of repentance in conjunction with sacrifices—something I affirm—see the references cited above, n. 224, along with Leviticus 5:1–5; 16:21; Numbers 5:6–7.

255. For an unusual interpretation of Ezekiel that attempts to place the prophet's entire ministry in Judah, see William H. Brownlee, *Ezekiel 1–19*, Word Biblical Commentary (Waco: Word, 1986), especially xxiii–xxv.

256. "Kapparot," *EJ* (CD ROM), 10:756–57.

257. As to the controversial history of the custom, the *EJ* article notes: "This custom is nowhere mentioned in the Talmud. It appears first in the writings of the *geonim* of the 9th century, who explain that a cock is used in the rite because the word *gever* means both 'man' and 'cock'; the latter can, therefore, substitute for the former. In Babylonia, other animals were used, especially the ram since Abraham offered a ram in lieu of his son Isaac (see: *Akedah* and Gen. 22:13), or plants, e.g., beans, peas, (cf. Rashi, Shab. 81b). After the destruction of the Temple, no animals used in sacrificial rites could serve similar purposes outside the Temple (Magen Abraham to Sh. Ar., OH 605) and therefore cocks or hens were employed in the *kapparot* rite because they were not used in the Temple sacrificial cult. R. Solomon b. Abraham Adret strongly opposed *kapparot* because it was similar to the biblical atonement rites (see Azazel; cf. Lev. 16:5–22); he also considered the *kapparah* ritual to be a heathen superstition (*'Darkhei Emori,'* responsa ed. Lemberg [1811] pt. 1 no. 395). This opinion is shared by Nahmanides and Joseph Caro who called the *kapparot* 'a stupid custom' (OH 605). The kabbalists (Isaac Luria, Isaiah Horowitz), however, invested the custom with mystical interpretations. These appealed strongly to the masses, and it became very popular when the rabbis acquiesced to it. Isserles made it a compulsory rite and enjoined for it many ceremonials similar to those of the sacrificial cult; e.g., the laying of the hands upon the animal, its immediate slaughter after the ceremony, prayers of confession, etc."

258. Hertz, *Pentateuch and Haftorahs*, 562. Interestingly, it was the gospel teaching concerning God's people being a spiritual Temple that helped Messianic Jews not to lose a beat when the Second Temple was destroyed. On the spiritual imagery, see Mendels, *Jewish Nationalism*, especially 312.

259. According to ancient Jewish tradition, and based on the so-called Table of Nations in Genesis 10, there were a total of seventy (Gentile) nations in the world. See, e.g., Nahum Sarna, *Genesis*, The JPS Torah Commentary (Philadelphia: The Jewish Publication Society, 1989), 67–70. Note that the sacrifices were offered up for seven days, beginning with thirteen on the first day, then twelve, then eleven, etc., until the last seven were offered on the seventh day. Then, on the eighth and final day of Sukkot, one sacrifice was offered. According to George Foote Moore in his classic work *Judaism: In the First Centuries of the Christian Era: The Age of the Tannaim* (Peabody, Mass.: Hendrickson, 1997), 2:43, n. 2, "These burnt offerings were made, according to an often repeated explanation, in behalf of the seventy heathen nations; the *one* on the eighth day for the unique people of Israel. When the heathen destroyed the temple, they destroyed the atonement that was made for them."

260. Through this sacrifice, at one and the same time, God could be just (by exacting the punishment of the Messiah's death for those sins) and the justifier of those who believe in Yeshua (by pronouncing righteous all who put their trust in the Messiah); see Romans 3:19–31 (I have excerpted here the end of Rom. 3:26). God in his justice demanded payment for sins, but in his mercy he sent the Messiah to make that payment—with his own life!—on our behalf. So through Yeshua, God is both just and merciful.

261. See Don Richardson, *Peace Child* (Ventura, Calif.: Regal, 1974); idem, *Eternity in Their Hearts* (Ventura, Calif.: Regal, 1984).

262. Berel Wein, *The Triumph of Survival: The Story of the Jews in the Modern Era 1650–1990* (Brooklyn, N.Y.: Shaar, 1990), 14.

263. This is the rendering of Patai, *Messiah Texts*, 116.

264. According to Siftey Hakhamim, commenting on Rashi's words, just as the red heifer, which is not a real sacrifice, atones, so also the death of the righteous atones.

265. Ginzberg, *Legends of the Jews*, 3:191, cites Sifre Deuteronomy 31: "The death of the pious man is a greater misfortune to Israel than the Temple's burning to ashes." For further references to the atoning power of the death of the righteous, see Ginzberg, *Legends of the Jews*, 6:75, n. 386; 6:107, n. 602.

266. Cf. *Shnei Luhot HaBerit*, Massekeht Ta'anit, Derash LeHesped Mitat Tsadiqim uLeHorban Beit HaMiqdash, 23; 27.

267. Cited in S. R. Driver and Adolph Neubauer, eds. and trans., *The Fifty-Third Chapter of Isaiah according to the Jewish Interpreters*, 2 vols. (New York: Ktav, 1969), 2:9. The Zohar states that this explains Ecclesiasties 7:15: "In this meaningless life of mine I have seen both of these: a righteous man perishing in his righteousness, and a wicked man living long in his wickedness." Cf. also b. Shabbat 33b, "The righteous are taken by the iniquity of the generation."

268. Ibid., 1:394–95 (the numeric value for guilt offering is 341, which equals the numeric value of Menahem ben Ammiel); the emphasis in the original indicates Scripture citations. The midrash concludes with another citation from Isaiah 53: "And what is written after it? *He shall his seed, shall have long days, and the pleasure of the Lord shall prosper in his hand.*"

269. Schechter, *Aspects of Rabbinic Theology*, 310–11, my emphasis.

270. See Genesis Rabbah 56:3, cited in this context by Jon D. Levenson, *The Death and Resurrection of the Beloved Son: The Transformation of Child Sacrifice in Judaism and Christianity* (New Haven: Yale, 1993), 105.

271. See also the note of Buber in his edition of Tanhuma.

272. Vermes, "Redemption and Genesis xxii," 211. For some critical interaction with the work of Vermes—primarily relative to the dating of some of the relevant material, not the content—cf. Bruce Chilton, "Recent Discussion of the Akedah," in idem, *Targumic Approaches to the Gospels: Essays in the Mutual Definition of Judaism and Christianity* (Lanham, Md.: University Press of America, 1986), 39–49.

273. See Vermes, "Redemption and Genesis xxii," 206, cited in the Fragmentary Targum.

274. Leviticus Rabbah, 29:9, cited in ibid., 213.

275. Avraham Yaakov Finkel, *Contemporary Sages* (Northvale, N.J.: Aronson, 1994), 84.

276. Cf. the following from the *EJ* article "Death": "At death the soul leaves the body with a cry that reverberates from one end of the world to the other (Yoma 20b), to pass into a state of existence, the exact nature of which was a matter of considerable dispute amongst the rabbis (cf. Shab. 152b–153a; Ber. 18b–19a; Maim. Yad, Teshuvah 8:2, and the critical remark by Abraham b. David of Posquiires (Rabad); see also Afterlife, Body and Soul, World to Come). Whatever the nature of the world beyond, it was generally accepted that there the dead reap the desserts of the acts they performed while alive, that they were free from Torah and the commandments (Shab. 30b), and that death served as an atoning process (Sifre Num 112). One confession formula before death, particularly prescribed for the criminal about to be executed, is 'May my death be an atonement for all my sins' (Sanhedrin 6:2). The atoning value of death received greater emphasis after the destruction of the Temple, with the abolition of

sacrificial atonement, so that complete forgiveness for more serious sins was dependent, despite repentance, the Day of Atonement, and suffering, on the final atoning value of death (cf. the discussion in Urbach, *Hazal*, 380–3)."

277. This text also gives us further insight into the usage of Hebrew *kipper* in terms of turning away wrath; see above, 3.10.

278. Cf., e.g., Rashi to Exod. 32:7–13; and see Urbach (*Sages*, 508ff.) on the red heifer and atonement for the dead; the merits of the fathers (or the righteous); and atonement for the living. As pointed out by Urbach, in Rabbinic thought it is not just the *death* of the righteous that atones but also the *merits* of the righteous and the *life* of the righteous that atone.

279. Milgrom, *Numbers*, 371, my emphasis.

280. Ibid., 294. In a fascinating discussion found in Hiddushei Aggadot 4:2, further explanation of the atoning power of the death of the high priest is given. Stating that "this matter is deep," it notes that the manslayer goes into exile because he killed and cut off a soul from the body, and so he is cut off from his home. However, the death of the high priest atones because it is at a high (spiritual) level, a level at which the power of the manslayer is not found. For the death of the righteous (in general) is at a very high level, as the Talmud states in b. Mo'ed Qatan 28a (cited above, stating that the death of the righteous atones), and the spiritual level of the death of the high priest is such that cutting off and murdering are not found there, but only life and peace, which are the measure (or virtues) of the high priest.

281. See also m. Nega'im 2:1 (dealing with various skin diseases): "A bright spot appears in a German as dim, and the dim in an Ethiopian as bright [white]. R. Ishmael says, 'The children of Israel—I am their atonement!—lo, they are like boxwood'" (Neusner's translation); cf. also m. Sanhedrin 2:1, where the people say to the high priest, "Let us be your atonement."

282. This is the rendering of Neusner in his American translation; the words in the brackets reflect the universal understanding of the passage. Rashi explains Shimon bar Yohai's statement as follows: "Through my merit, I bear all your iniquities and cancel them from the judgment." Note also the comments of R. Hananel, another of the major Talmudic commentators. See also b. Erubin 64b–65a.

283. See Patai, *Messiah Texts*, 116.

284. For the Rabbinic rationale behind this, see Eliezer Berkovits, *Not in Heaven: The Nature and Function of Halakha* (New York: Ktav, 1983), 47–70.

285. According to some, the Messiah, according to others, the people of Israel; see below, 3.23 (suffering Messiah) and vol. 3, 4.5–6.

286. Interestingly, the Talmudic rabbis claimed that some of the specific regulations regarding exactly how the animal's blood was to be applied to the altar were actually in memory of the binding of Isaac. As stated in Leviticus Rabbah 2:11 (to Lev. 1:5, 11): "Concerning the ram, it is said: And he shall slaughter it on the side of the altar northward before the Lord. It is taught: When Abraham our father bound Isaac his son, the Holy One, blessed be He, instituted (the sacrifice of) two lambs, one in the morning, and the other in the evening. What is the purpose of this? It is in order that when Israel offers the perpetual sacrifice upon the altar, and read this scriptural text, Northward before the Lord, the Holy One, blessed be He, may remember the binding of Isaac." Cited by Vermes, "Redemption and Genesis xxii," 209.

287. Rosenberg, *Ezekiel*, Soncino Books of the Bible (London: Soncino, 1950), 265.

288. Rav Dr. Joseph Breuer, *The Book of Yechezkel: Translation and Commentary* (New York: Feldheim, 1993), 354. I supplied the literal translation of Maimonides, which was cited in the original Hebrew by the author.

289. Note that according to b. Hagigah 13a, it was the Talmudic rabbis themselves who sought to suppress the Book of Ezekiel because it was thought his words contradicted the words of the Torah. In contrast with this, I do not know of any Christian leaders who sought to exclude Ezekiel from the canon, indicating that they felt less threatened by Ezekiel's vision than did the Talmudic rabbis.

290. His name is sometimes given as Chananyah or Hananiah. Commenting on Ezekiel 45:22, Rashi wrote, "Our Rabbis (Hag. 13a) said that they sought to suppress the Book of Ezekiel for his words contradicted the words of the Torah. Indeed, Hananiah the son of Hezekiah the son of Gurion is remembered for good, for he sat in his attic and expounded on it. But because of our iniquities, what he expounded on these sacrifices—why a bull is brought on the fourteenth day of Nissan—has been lost to us." See Rosenberg, *Ezekiel*, 406.

291. This leads to an important principle of prophecy and fulfillment that we will return to when discussing Messianic prophecy; see vol. 3, 4.5.

292. As translated by Rosenberg, *Ezekiel*, 381.

293. Ibid., 386–87.

294. Ibid., 382–83. Rashi was following a Talmudic interpretation of Exodus 15:16 which was taken to mean that Israel would enter the Promised Land twice, once with Joshua and once with Ezra.

295. This is reminiscent of the famous Talmudic tradition we reviewed in vol. 1, 2.1, namely, that the Messiah should have come two thousand years after the inauguration of the Torah (according to many interpreters, meaning two thousand years after the time of Abraham), but because of our sins, the Messiah did not come and these years have been lost.

296. Some interpreters believe that Ezekiel's Rosh Hashanah referred to the ancient biblical calendar in which Nissan (around April) was the New Year. However, the Rabbinic view is also quite possible. For details, see Leslie C. Allen, *Ezekiel 20–48*, Word Biblical Commentary (Dallas: Word, 1990), 229. If the vision was received on the tenth day of Nissan, that would be four days before the Passover began.

297. Rosenberg, *Ezekiel*, 342.

298. For the Qumran community being a spiritual Temple, see Geza Vermes, *The Dead Sea Scrolls*, rev. ed. (Philadelphia: Fortress, 1981), 180–82; note especially The Manual of Discipline [1QS] 8:5–10; 9:4–5; and see further the references in Peter H. Davids, *The First Epistle of Peter*, New International Commentary on the New Testament (Grand Rapids: Eerdmans, 1990), 85–86. There is extensive literature on the Temple Scroll, one of the most important Dead Sea Scroll documents.

299. It is a foundational observation of the medieval rabbis, following the Mishnaic sage Rabbi Ishmael, who differed with his contemporary Rabbi Akvia, that "the Torah speaks in the language of men." However, that dictum primarily applies to grammatical forms and expressions; cf. the discussion in Moses Mielziner, *Introduction to the Talmud* (New York: Bloch, 1968), 124–28.

300. This same line of interpretation would also tie in with Ezekiel's vision of allotment of the land of Israel; according to Allen, *Ezekiel*, 215, "Land and temple become symbols of solid hope for the renewal of social identity, for full fellowship with God and for 'a kingdom that cannot be shaken' (Heb 12:22–24). The concern with the correction of pre-exilic abuses becomes God's call for the translation of theology into the

stuff of worship and of daily life, so that, 'as he who calls you is holy,' you may 'yourselves be holy in all your conduct' (1 Pet 1:15; cf. Ezek 43:10–11)."

301. For example, Messianic Jewish scholar Arnold G. Fruchtenbaum, in his book *Messianic Christology* (Tustin, Calif.: Ariel, 1998), 96, commenting on Daniel 9:24–27, can make reference to "the Jewish Temple which is to be rebuilt when Messiah comes," stating that it is "the same Temple that Daniel's contemporary, described in great detail (Ezekiel 40–48)." For a well-reasoned argument for the literal fulfillment of this passage, see Ralph H. Alexander, "Ezekiel," *EBC*, 6:942–52, although it becomes apparent from reading Alexander's position that problems remain for all interpreters. As expressed by Allen, *Ezekiel*, 214–15, "Readers will find themselves embarrassed by these chapters. . . . To some extent at least they were presumably presented as normative for the future. Yet the post-exilic community, even when adoption of its rulings was within its power, found other models for its worship, while the different orientation of the Christian faith has left these chapters outdated. [Note well what Allen is saying: When the exiles returned to Jerusalem, they could have implemented much of Ezekiel's plan, but they did not.] Must one relegate them to a drawer of lost hopes and disappointed dreams, like faded photographs? To resort to dispensationalism [which is the position held by the two previous authors cited in this note] and postpone them to a literal fulfillment in a yet future time strikes the author as a desperate expedient that sincerely attempts to preserve belief in an inerrant prophecy. The canon of scriptures, Jewish and Christian, took unfulfillment in its stride, ever commending the reading of them as the very word of God to each believing generation. Essentially they spoke first to their own generation, and one must overhear them before hearing them for oneself." For a scholarly analysis of the entire section, see Jon Douglas Levenson, *Theology of the Program of Restoration of Ezekiel 40–48* (Missoula, Mont.: Scholars Press, 1976).

302. On Rabbinic statements concerning changes in the Torah in the world to come, see W. D. Davies, *Torah in the Messianic Age and/or the Age to Come* (Philadelphia: Society of Biblical Literature, 1952), and vol. 3, 5.30.; note also Montefiore and Loewe, *Rabbinic Anthology*, 669–70.

303. Alexander, "Ezekiel," 951.

304. Hertz, *Pentateuch and Haftorahs*, 562.

305. As explained by Kenneth L. Barker, "Zechariah," *EBC*, 7:697.

306. There is no compelling reason to apply Isaiah 56:7 to a still-future time. However, even if it is yet future, it is in keeping with the other passages we have reviewed so far from Isaiah, Zechariah, and Malachi.

307. Cited in Montefiore and Loewe, *Rabbinic Anthology*, 350. The rabbis also cite Psalm 56:13 as a proof text.

308. VanGemeren, "Psalms," 608. For scriptural references to what have sometimes been called "chaos monsters" in the Hebrew Bible—representing the powers of darkness, earthly enemies, or the hostile forces of nature—see e.g., Isaiah 27:1; Psalm 89:5–12, along with Psalm 74, just cited.

309. See the article on "Salvation," in the *ODJR*, 602; see also S. Daniel Breslauer and Celia Deutsch, "Salvation," in *Dictionary of the Jewish-Christian Dialogue*, 179–85.

310. As we saw in vol. 1, 2.1–2, the purpose of the Messiah's first coming was not to establish worldwide peace or set up an earthly kingdom. Rather, that will mark the end of this transition era in which we now live.

311. *Sozo* is the verbal form; the noun *soter* means savior; *soteria* is salvation. Although it may not seem obvious to those unfamiliar with Greek, all these words are derived from the same basic root.

312. See my discussion in *Israel's Divine Healer*, 212–14. W. Radl, "*sozo*, rescue, save, preserve, help" in *Exegetical Dictionary of the New Testament*, ed. Horst Balz and Gerhard Schneider (Grand Rapids: Eerdmans, 1990), 3:319–20, notes: "That from which one is saved . . . include [*sic*] mortal danger, death, disease, possession, sin and alienation from God, and eternal ruin."

313. I have written on these themes extensively; see Brown, *Israel's Divine Healer;* idem, *"rapa',"* in *Theologische Wörterbuch zum alten Testament*, ed. H.-J. Fabry and H. Ringgren (Stuttgart: Kohlhammer, 1991), 7:618–26 (forthcoming in *Theological Dictionary of the Old Testament*); idem, with A. Kam-Yau Chan and Thomas B. Song, *"rp',"* in *NIDOTTE*, 3:1162–72; idem, "Was There a West Semitic Asklepios?" *Ugarit Forschungen* 30 (Münster: Ugarit-Verlag, 1999), 133–54.

314. Cf. the insightful comment of Warfield, cited below, n. 416.

315. See Abraham Cohen, *Everyman's Talmud: The Major Teachings of the Rabbinic Sages* (New York: Schocken, 1995), 346–89.

316. Note the Talmudic discussion about defiant sinners being punished in this world and in the world to come; e.g., see b. Sanhedrin 64b, 90b.

317. As we will see below (3.25), traditional Judaism sees this world as the portal to the world to come but stresses the importance of life in this world. As for Christianity, while stressing the importance of the world to come, it has been responsible for the building of more hospitals, the feeding of more hungry people, and the establishment of more educational institutions than all other religions of the world combined. The difference between the two is not one of substance but of emphasis.

318. See the insightful study of Yochanan Muffs, "Who Will Stand in the Breach?: A Study of Prophetic Intercession," in idem, *Love and Joy: Law, Language and Religion in Ancient Israel* (New York: Jewish Theological Seminary, 1992), 9–48; note also the implications of verses such as Psalm 99:6; Jeremiah 15:1.

319. Cf., e.g., b. Bava Bathra 12a; see, vol. 3, 6.1–6.5, for an in-depth discussion of these issues.

320. Aryeh Kaplan's claim that "Christianity . . . starts with one idea about man, while Judaism starts with the exact opposite idea of man" (*The Real Messiah?* 9) is certainly overstated, based on an exaggerated view of the fall ("What sin was so great that it required his [Jesus'] sacrifice? The early Christians answered that this was required to atone for the sin of Adam," [32]), as if all human culpability were Adam's and none was our own. More importantly, however, the question is not what Judaism or Christianity teach but rather what do the Hebrew Scriptures say? As will be seen plainly, the Tanakh does *not* support Kaplan's position.

321. See Robert Conquest, *Reflections on a Ravaged Century* (New York: W. W. Norton, 2000).

322. Notice the use of the Hebrew root *sh-h-t* (be corrupt; destroy) in Genesis 6:12–13 (I have emphasized all English words derived from the root): "Now the earth was *corrupt* in God's sight and was full of violence. God saw how *corrupt* the earth had become, for all the people on earth had *corrupted* their ways. So God said to Noah, 'I am going to put an end to all people, for the earth is filled with violence because of them. I am surely going to *destroy* both them and the earth.'" The meaning is that God will destroy the earth and start afresh before we totally destroy everything ourselves!

323. By the way, even if you take the story of the flood allegorically and not literally—although I see no compelling reason not to take it literally—the same *lesson* of
human sinfulness is still taught.

324. In fact, to underscore this point even further, we must realize that when God
gave this assessment of the inherent sinfulness of man, the only ones alive at the time
were righteous Noah and his family!

325. Just consider the recaps of our history in biblical sources such as Psalms 78
(up to David), 106, or 107. It is not a pretty picture.

326. Tragically, in Israel there are "kosher" prostitutes, women who "work" exclusively among the ultra-Orthodox. For a discussion of this unfortunate phenomenon, which is certainly frowned on and rejected by official teaching, see Samuel
Heilman, *Defenders of the Faith: Inside Ultra-Orthodox Jewry* (New York: Schocken,
1992), 106, 327–28, who notes that "a significant number of haredim [referring to
ultra-Orthodox Jews in Israel] were known to do it [i.e., go to prostitutes] late at
night" (327).

327. In b. Sanhedrin 101a, this verse is cited to refute the view that some people
mentioned in the Bible were actually sinless. See also b. Sanhedrin 46b, cited in Urbach,
The Sages, 435: "To the query, 'Do the righteous need atonement?' the Sages reply, 'Yea!
for it is written, "There is not a righteous man upon the earth, that doeth good, and
sinneth not" (Ecclesiastes vii 20).'" See also Midrash Tehillim, xvi:2, cited in ibid., 879,
n. 56. The midrash there gives an interesting twist to the verse, "As for the holy ones
that are in the earth" (Ps. 16:3), explaining, "for the Holy One, blessed be He, does not
call a righteous man 'holy' until he is placed in the earth [i.e., in death!]. Why? Because
the Evil Inclination vexes him, and (the Lord) puts no trust in him until the day of his
death. So, too, Solomon declared, 'For there is not a righteous man upon earth. . . .'"
Although some commentators read this verse differently (namely, that even righteous
people are not perfect and still sin), the interpretation most commonly found in the
Rabbinic literature is identical to the one cited here.

328. Here is another point to consider. Judaism teaches that in each generation
there are at least thirty-six totally righteous people (Jews or Gentiles), through whose
righteousness the world is preserved. (They are called the "lamed-vavnicks," based on
the Hebrew letters for 36, *lamed* and *vav*.) However, not only is this questionable based
on scriptural precedent (Jeremiah 5; Genesis 6), but it is striking too, since even traditional Judaism must recognize the deep sinfulness of our race if it thinks in terms
of only thirty-six righteous!

329. "Fall of Man," in *Encyclopedia of Jewish Religion*, ed. R. J. Werblowsky and
G. Wigoder (New York: Adama, 1986), 141. For the Talmudic tradition of Eve's cop-
ulation with the serpent, see b. Shabbat 146a; b. Yevamot 103b; b. Avodah Zarah
22b ("When the serpent went into Eve, he injected contaminating lust into her");
note also Louis Jacobs, *Theology in the Responsa* (Boston: Routledge & Kegan Paul,
1975), 49–50, discussing a responsum of Abraham Ibn David ("the mere approach
to Sinai was highly significant in that it freed Israel from the taint of 'original sin'").
It is interesting to observe that this tradition claims that it was Mount Sinai that
removed the contamination of Eve's sin from the Jewish people (but not from the
Gentiles), although only temporarily (cf. Urbach, *The Sages*, 428; 169). The New Testament teaches that it was the death of the Messiah on the cross that provided the
ultimate (and permanent) source of cleansing of this inherited filth for *both* Jew and
Gentile.

330. See Ginzberg, *Legends of the Jews*, 1:59–83.

331. See his Likutey Torah, Taamey HaMitzvot, on Leviticus 19:18, cited in Aryeh Kaplan, *Reaching Out*, 25. Based on this concept, Luria taught that "all the Jews (collectively) form a single body. Therefore, even if an individual has never committed a particular sin, he should confess it anyway. For if another Jew has committed this sin, it is the same as if he himself had done so." Thus a Jew praying alone at home should still confess in the plural, "We have sinned."

332. See Goldstein, "Shekhinah," 454.

333. "Fall of Man," *Encyclopedia of the Jewish Religion*, 141.

334. Cohen, *Everyman's Talmud*, 95.

335. Ibid., 95–96.

336. Ibid., 96.

337. See ibid., 88–93, with the primary Rabbinic references.

338. Reflecting the traditional view, Cohen notes, "part of human nature is the evil impulse which can be mastered, but all too often takes control and demoralizes" (ibid., 95). For the objection that the law of God is actually *easy* to keep, see vol. 3, 6.9; for Genesis 4:7, God's word to Cain about mastering sin, see above, 3.20.

339. For discussion of Deuteronomy 10:16 and Ezekiel 18:31, which call on God's people to circumcise their hearts or to get new hearts, see the commentaries of C. F. Keil.

340. These sayings were selected from Reuven Alcalay, ed. and trans., with Mordekhai Nurock, *Words of the Wise* (Israel: Massada, 1970), 410–12 (for the most part, using the translation as given there).

341. *Sefer Madda'*, *Hilchot Teshuvah*, The Book of Knowledge, Laws of Repentance.

342. 1:3, as rendered by Touger, *Laws of Repentance*, 12.

343. This daily prayer is called the Shemoneh Esreh, literally, "Eighteen," or the Amidah, literally, "standing," because the prayer is recited in a standing position due to its importance.

344. See Pinhas H. Peli, *Soloveitchik on Repentance* (New York: Paulist Press, 1984); Abraham Isaac Kook, *The Lights of Penitence, Lights of Holiness: The Moral Principles, Essays, and Poems*, ed. and trans. Ben Zion Bokser (Mahwah, N.J.: Paulist, 1978); Schechter, *Aspects of Rabbinic Theology*, chapter 18, "Repentance: Means of Reconciliation" (313–43). Schechter concludes his discussion by saying, "For repentance is as wide as the sea, and as the sea has never closed and man can always be cleansed by it, so is repentance, so that whenever man desires to repent, the Holy One, blessed be he, receives him" (343, with reference to Pesikta deRav Kahana 157a and Midrash Psalms 65:4). Cf. also the works cited in vol. 1, 1.11, n. 36, and note Urbach, *The Sages*, 462–71, "The Power of Repentance"; Byron L. Sherwin, *In Partnership with God* (Syracuse: Syracuse University, 1990), 119–29.

345. Rabbi Shmelke of Nikolsburg, cited in Simcha Raz, ed., *Hasidic Wisdom: Sayings from the Jewish Sages*, trans. Dov Peretz Elkins and Jonathan Elkins (Northvale, N.J.: Aronson, 1997), 301.

346. Numbers Rabbah 14:1, cited in Schechter, *Aspects of Rabbinic Theology*, 319 (see 318–19 for another important tradition regarding Manasseh's repentance). Schechter also makes reference to the notorious Israelite king Jeroboam, of whom it was said that "the Holy One, blessed be he, laid hold of him and said, 'Return (in repentance), and I and the son of Jesse [David] and thou shall walk together in Paradise.'" However, because of his arrogance—he didn't want to be second to David!—he refused to repent. See ibid., 319–20, with reference to b. Sanhedrin 102a.

347. Adin Steinsaltz, *Teshuvah: A Guide for the Newly Observant Jew*, trans. Michael Swirsky (Northvale, N.J.: Aronson, 1996). Note that *teshuva* means repentance because it speaks of a return to God; hence repentant Jews are said to "do *teshuva*." Cf. also Chaim Nussbaum, *The Essence of Teshuvah: A Path to Repentance* (Northvale, N.J.: Aronson, 1994).

348. Jacob Neusner, "Repentance in Judaism," 60–76 (here, 61–62), in *Repentance: A Comparative Perspective*, ed. Amitai Etzioni and David E. Carney (Lanham, Md.: Rowman & Littlefield, 1997). For the Hindu perspective, see Guy Beck, "Fire in the Atman: Repentance in Hinduism," 76–95; for the Jewish perspective, see Neusner's article; cf. also vol. 1, 1.11.

349. Cf. S. Y. Agnon, ed., *Days of Awe: A Treasury of Jewish Wisdom for Reflection, Repentance, and Renewal on the High Holy Days* (New York: Schocken, 1995).

350. A good summary is found in 2 Kings 17:13: "The LORD warned Israel and Judah through all his prophets and seers: 'Turn from your evil ways. Observe my commands and decrees, in accordance with the entire Law that I commanded your fathers to obey and that I delivered to you through my servants the prophets.'" See also Zechariah 1:1–6. For an older but still important discussion of the root *shuv* in the Hebrew Bible, see William L. Holladay, *The Root Šubh in the Old Testament* (Leiden: E. J. Brill, 1958).

351. Hertz, *Pentateuch and Haftorahs*, 562.

352. Collins, *Scepter and the Star*, 189.

353. Thus, scholars today commonly refer to first-century Judaisms in the plural; cf. Jacob Neusner, William S. Green, and Ernest Frerichs, *Judaisms and Their Messiahs at the Turn of the Christian Era* (Cambridge: Cambridge, 1987); see also vol. 1, 2.3.

354. To this day there are many religious Jews who hold to this doctrine of the two Messiahs, which is quite understandable in light of the fact that this belief can be traced back to the Talmud; see below, 3.23–3.24.

355. J. Immanuel Schochet, *Mashiach: The Principles of Mashiach and the Messianic Era in Jewish Law and Tradition*, expanded edition (New York/Toronto: S.I.E., 1992), 98.

356. Interestingly, Harris Lenowitz, *Jewish Messiahs*, 66, 217, points out that with regard to the rulings of Maimonides regarding the Messiah as found in his Mishneh Torah, his "conclusions have no legal bearing and do not influence messiahs or those who seek them," adding, "His 'law' here is not law. It does not have support from traditional Jewish sources or beliefs, and Maimonides himself does not require adherence to what he freely concedes is merely his opinion."

357. For Schochet's attempt to reconcile the various traditions, cf. Lenowitz, *Jewish Messiahs*, 217.

358. This is actually the term used on the front flap on the Lenowitz volume: "The word 'messiah' meaning 'anointed one,' comes from the Hebrew Bible where it refers to holy prophets and priests as well as kings. In later Judaism it is associated with a semi-divine figure whose future reign will usher in everlasting justice, security, and peace." For the more detailed statements of Lenowitz, see ibid., 11: "The biblical accounts of anointment make it clear that messiahs have a peculiar relationship with the divine. . . . Supernaturalism comes to enrich the portrait of the king-messiah, as the political necessities of the Davidic dynasty demand theological validation." For his use of the term "quasi-divine" (ibid.), see above, n. 55.

359. As translated in Driver and Neubauer, *Fifty-Third Chapter of Isaiah*, 2:9, their emphasis.

360. God promises to judge every one who is high and lofty (see Isa. 2:12–14), whereas he deserves to be called the high and lofty one (see Isa. 6:1; 57:15; cf. also Isa. 33:10; 5:16).

361. Sometimes spelled Abrabanel, Abarbanel, or Abarvanel. Note that it was the weight of tradition behind this midrash that caused Nachmanides to accept the Messianic interpretation of Isaiah 52:13–53:12. He wrote: "The right view respecting this Parashah is to suppose that by the phrase 'my servant' the whole of Israel is meant, as in xliv. 2, xlix. 3, and often. As a different opinion, however, is adopted by the Midrash, which refers it to the Messiah, it is necessary for us to explain it in conformity with the view maintained there" (Driver and Neubauer, *Fifty-Third Chapter of Isaiah*, 2:78).

362. Ibid., 2:154.

363. Ibid., 2:165.

364. I should point out here that I fully recognize the traditional Jewish position on the Messiah's humanity, articulated clearly by Joseph Klausner, *The Messianic Idea in Israel*, trans. W. F. Stinespring (London: George Allen and Unwin, 1956), 520, 523: "The Jewish Messiah is truly human in origin, of flesh and blood like all mortals. . . . Both with respect to holiness, righteousness, truth, and goodness, and with respect to might and authority, the Messiah is the 'supreme man.' . . . But with all his superior qualities, the Messiah remains a human being." Or as stated (perhaps overstated?) by Cohen, *Everyman's Talmud*, 347, "The Talmud nowhere indicates a belief in a super-human Deliverer as the Messiah." It should be kept in mind that followers of Yeshua fully affirm both his humanity *and* his divinity; see above, 3.1–3.2. For further discussion of traditional Jewish views of the Messiah, in addition to the works cited elsewhere in these notes, cf. Leo Landman, ed., *Messianism in the Talmudic Era* (New York: Ktav, 1979); Shmuel Boteach, *The Wolf Shall Lie with the Lamb* (Northvale, N.J.: Aronson, 1993); Rabbi Yehudah Chayoun, *When Moshiach Comes: Halachic and Aggadic Perspectives*, trans. Rabbi Yaakov M. Rapoport and Rabbi Moshe Grossman (Southfield, Mich.: Targum; Spring Valley, N.Y.: Feldheim, 1994); Jacob Neusner, *The Messiah in Context* (Philadelphia: Fortress, 1984); Joseph Sarachek, *The Doctrine of the Messiah in Medieval Jewish Literature* (New York: Hermon, n.d.); Julius H. Greenstone, *The Messiah Idea in Jewish History* (Westport, Conn.: Greenwood, 1972); Gershom Scholem, *The Messianic Idea in Judaism and Other Essays on Jewish Spirituality* (New York: Schocken, 1971), 1–77; Moshe Idel, *Messianic Mystics* (New Haven: Yale, 1998); cf. also James H. Charlesworth, ed., *The Messiah* (Minneapolis: Fortress, 1992).

365. Driver and Neubauer, *Fifty-Third Chapter of Isaiah*, 2:102–3, their emphasis; additional portions of Ibn Crispin's commentary, which next describes the Messiah's sufferings, are excerpted below, 3.23.

366. I am aware, of course, that these Talmudic references are generally explained to mean that the *concept* of the Messiah was created before the world began, but not the Messiah himself, or that the Messiah's soul was preexistent, remaining at the throne of God until the time came for his birth. See, e.g., Klausner, *Messianic Idea*, 520. Note also Pesikta Rabbati 152b, "From the beginning of the creation of the world king Messiah was born, for he entered the mind (of God) before even the world was created." Cf. also Robert Leo Odom, *Israel's Preexistent Messiah* (Washington, D.C.: Israelite Heritage Institute, 1985).

367. Collins, *The Scepter and the Star*, 189.

368. With reference to these verses, I noted above that neither of them make reference to the term *son*, yet here the Midrash cites them with reference to God's "son."

And these texts are among the most famous Messianic prophecies in the entire Bible, frequently cited by Messianic Jews as pointing to Yeshua.

369. See above, 3.3, for references; cf. also immediately below, n. 370.

370. In fact, this figure is so highly exalted that some interpreters have wondered if he is an angel! The most common non-Messianic view of the passage is that the term "Son of Man" refers corporately to Israel (or the righteous within Israel). For refutation of this view, see Archer, "Daniel," 90–91; see also the detailed discussions in John E. Goldingay, *Daniel*, Word Biblical Commentary (Dallas: Word, 1989), 167–72; and John J. Collins, *Daniel*, Hermeneia (Minneapolis: Fortress, 1993), 304–10. Regardless of which interpretation is followed by modern scholars, they recognize that the earliest Jewish interpreters understood it to refer to the Messiah (see Collins, *Daniel*, 306–7, n. 63, with reference to Geza Vermes, *Jesus the Jew* [Philadelphia: Fortress, 1973], 170–72; and Herman L. Strack and Paul Billerbeck, *Kommentar zum Neuen Testament aus Talmud und Midrasch* [München: C. H. Beck, 1924], 1:486). See also Chilton, "The Son of Man: Human and Heavenly," in *Judaic Approaches to the Gospels*, 75–109. He states concisely that the phrase "like a son of man" in Daniel "is no technical reference or title, but a descriptive designation of an unusual, human angel."

371. I reproduce here the relevant portion of Horbury's endnote: "Gray, *Isaiah I–XXVII* [referring to his volume in the International Critical Commentary], 173. He rightly stresses that Hebrew *el*, used here, regularly refers to the almighty God, but the importance in the Old Testament of its use in the sense of a divinity or angel from the divine assembly, probably reflected here, has since been underlined by Qumran writings (see Clines, *Dictionary*, I, 253–54, s.v. *'el*)." See William Horbury, *Jewish Messianism and the Cult of Christ* (London: SCM, 1998), 188–89, n. 94.

372. Ibid., 90. See further 112.

373. I speak here of George Buchanan Gray, cited by Horbury. The Jewish publisher Ktav reprinted some of Gray's books, most notably his famous works on Hebrew poetry and on sacrifices in the Old Testament.

374. For further discussion of Psalm 110, with bibliography, see vol. 3, 4.29.

375. See especially vol. 3, section 4 ("Messianic Prophecy").

376. Cohn-Sherbok, *The Jewish Messiah*, xvi.

377. Heilman, *Defenders of the Faith*, 303.

378. See above, n. 84, for publication information. The section dealing with the suffering Messiah runs from 104–21.

379. Gustaf H. Dalman, *Der leidende und der sterbende Messias der Synagoge im ersten nachchristlichen Jarhtausend* (Berlin: Reuther, 1888). Cf. also idem, *Jesaja 53: das Prophetenwort vom Sühnleiden des Gottesknechtes mit besonderer Berücksichtung der jüdischen Literatur*, 2d ed. (Leipzig: J. C. Hinrichs', 1914). For a thorough bibliography on the subject through the early 1980s, see Emil Schürer, *The History of the Jewish People in the Age of Jesus Christ (175 B.C.—A.D. 135)*, rev. Eng. vers. by Geza Vermes, Fergus Millar, and Matthew Black (Edinburgh: T & T Clark, 1973–1987), 2:547–49.

380. Patai, *Messiah Texts*, 104.

381. Ibid.

382. This provides an interesting parallel to the Christian belief in Messiah Jesus, who suffered, died, and rose from the dead. I should note, however, that in the Talmudic text I just cited, there is no concept of Messiah ben Joseph dying for the sins of Israel, so the parallel is hardly exact. (For the Rabbinic teaching that the death of the righteous atones, see above, 3.15.)

383. Midrash Konen, from Bet HaMidrash, 2:29–30, as translated by Patai, *Messiah Texts*, 114, his emphasis.

384. Zohar 2:212a, as translated by Patai, ibid., 116, his emphasis. For Isaiah 53 cited by the Zohar in the context of the atoning power of the death of the righteous, see above, 3.15, where another portion of this text from the Zohar is quoted as well.

385. As cited in David Baron, *The Visions and Prophecies of Zechariah* (Grand Rapids: Kregel, 1972), 442. Baron, in translating from the Hebrew, capitalized the pronouns relating to God (e.g., "me" in the phrase "They shall look unto me") as well as to Messiah ben Joseph (e.g., "himself" in the phrase "he will take upon himself all the guilt of Israel"), giving the erroneous impression that Alshekh may have viewed the Messiah son of Joseph as divine. To avoid confusion, I removed all capitalization, since, in any event, there are no capital letters in Hebrew.

386. Ibid., 110.

387. Ibid., his emphasis.

388. *Tractate Sanhedrin, Talmud Bavli,* The Schottenstein Edition (Brooklyn, N.Y.: Mesorah, 1995), vol. 3, 98a5, emphasis in original. The actual text in the Schottenstein Talmud includes the Hebrew of Isaiah 53:4, represented here by my ellipses. Nothing has been deleted from the text. Need I emphasize that once more Isaiah 53 is being cited with reference to the Messiah's sufferings, and this time in a compendium of Orthodox commentaries?

389. Patai, *Messiah Texts*, 104–5.

390. Note that Targum Jonathan, *the* Targum to the prophetic books, applied this section directly to the Messiah ("my servant the Messiah") but changed the text in a number of key points, thereby effectively removing all references to the Messiah's suffering. How odd it is that the Targum recognized that the servant of the Lord spoken of in Isaiah 52:13–53:12 was actually the Messiah—a fundamental position of the New Testament—and yet found it necessary to radically alter the meaning of the text to make it into a statement of the Messiah's military prowess and his victory over the nations. It would have been more logical to attempt to argue that the text did not refer to the Messiah at all! For a discussion of all this, see Samson H. Levey, *The Messiah: An Aramaic Interpretation: The Messianic Exegesis of the Targum* (Cincinnati: Hebrew Union College-Jewish Institute of Religion, 1974), 63–67.

391. For audio copies of the debate (including a recap with Sid Roth), contact ICN Ministries, 8594 Hwy. 98 W., Pensacola, FL 32506; 850-458-6424; fax: 850-458-1828; www.icnministries.org.

392. For the more common traditional interpretation associating Isaiah 52:13–53:12 with the people of Israel, see vol. 3, 4.5–4.6, 4.10. I find it somewhat ironic that the classic Jewish commentators who read the passage in terms of Israel's sufferings believe that Isaiah prophesied of the deaths of many Jews through the ages. Yet when the passage is interpreted with reference to the Messiah, it is normally claimed that Isaiah 53 does *not* speak of the death of the servant of the Lord! Such a contradiction in interpretations actually came to the surface in 1992 at Yale University when the campus rabbi from Lubavitch raised objections to my presentation in a public forum hosted by Christian students there. (We were comparing the Messianic credentials of Yeshua with those of the Lubavitcher Rebbe.) The inconsistency in his interpretations became apparent to almost everyone in the audience.

393. Driver and Neubauer, *Fifty-Third Chapter of Isaiah*, 2:78.

394. Ibid., 2:81, their emphasis.

395. See further vol. 3, 4.10–12, 4.14, on the prophesied death of the servant of the Lord according to Isaiah 53.

396. Driver and Neubauer, *Fifty-Third Chapter of Isaiah*, 2:84.

397. For a detailed treatment of the relevant verses, see vol. 3, 4.10–12, 4.14.

398. Driver and Neubauer, *Fifty-Third Chapter of Isaiah*, 2:103.

399. Ibid., 2:107–8, emphasis in original. Amazingly, Ibn Crispin ends his comments by saying, "This prophecy was delivered by Isaiah at the divine command for the purpose of making known to us something about the nature of the future Messiah, who is to come and deliver Israel, and his life from the day when he arrives at discretion until his advent as a redeemer, in order that if any one should arise claiming to be himself the Messiah, we may reflect, and look to see whether we can observe in him any resemblance to the traits described here: if there is any such resemblance, then we may believe that he is the Messiah our righteousness; but if not, we cannot do so." Even more amazingly, the scribe who copied out Ibn Crispin's interpretation was troubled by it, although he hoped that "an answer may be found in it against the heretics who interpret it of Jesus." And so he added that "it does not seem to me to be right or permissible to apply the prophecy to the King Messiah (for reasons which any intelligent man will easily find out); it must, in fact, be referred either to Israel as a whole, or to Jeremiah." See ibid., 2:114.

400. Ibid., 2:259. According to Alshekh, the Jewish people will say of the Messiah, "We beheld a man, just and perfect, bruised and degraded by suffering, despised in our eyes, and plundered verily before God and man, while all cried, 'God hath forsaken him;' he must surely, therefore, we thought, be 'despised' likewise in the eyes of the Almighty, and this is why he hath made him 'an offscouring and refuse' (Lam. iii. 45)." See ibid., 2:264.

401. See the quote from Mordechai Staiman, below, 3.24, with reference to the Rebbe's hoped-for return. Cohn-Sherbok, *The Jewish Messiah*, xv–xvi, summarizes some of the key events as follows: "When the *Rebbe* suffered a stroke, his followers were not deterred; indeed, the *Rebbe*'s incapacity fueled the flames of messianic enthusiasm. His illness was invested with redemptive significance: the suffering servant in Isaiah 53 was perceived as being a reference to the *Rebbe*'s debilitated state. . . . Even the *Rebbe*'s death did not daunt those who were convinced of his Messiahship. He would return! In the view of one Israeli newspaper, those who had lost faith in the *Rebbe* were like the worshippers of the golden calf who had given up hope of Moses' return from Mount Sinai. Within a few months of the funeral, two volumes appeared, explaining the grounds for continuing faith in his Messiahship. Eventually, as time passed, a number of messianists became convinced that the *Rebbe* had not in fact died: in their view he remains alive but concealed. Hence what happened on 3 *Tammuz* 5754 (the Jewish date of his death) was an illusion. The *Rebbe*'s corpse, they argued, was a test for carnal eyes; but in truth there was no passing away or leave-taking at all."

402. Patai, *Messiah Texts*, 105.

403. Interestingly, some have speculated that these chapters of Pesikta Rabbati, which is a compilation of a series of Sabbath sermons preached in the synagogue, bear evidence of Christian influence. On the contrary, these chapters remind us of just how Jewish true "Christianity" really is.

404. Schochet, *Mashiach*, 92–93, n. 2, where he also points out some overlap in terminology in the descriptive titles of the two Messiahs.

405. Cf. Yeshua's words to his disciples about suffering: "All men will hate you because of me, but he who stands firm to the end will be saved. When you are perse-

cuted in one place, flee to another. I tell you the truth, you will not finish going through the cities of Israel before the Son of Man comes. A student is not above his teacher, nor a servant above his master. It is enough for the student to be like his teacher, and the servant like his master. If the head of the house has been called Beelzebub, how much more the members of his household!" (Matt. 10:22–25). Note also John 15:18–21: "If the world hates you, keep in mind that it hated me first. If you belonged to the world, it would love you as its own. As it is, you do not belong to the world, but I have chosen you out of the world. That is why the world hates you. Remember the words I spoke to you: 'No servant is greater than his master.' If they persecuted me, they will persecute you also. If they obeyed my teaching, they will obey yours also. They will treat you this way because of my name, for they do not know the One who sent me."

406. Patai, *Messiah Texts*, 113–14.

407. Several verses from Psalm 22 are quoted in Pesikta Rabbati 37:2.

408. Cf., e.g., Sigal, *The Jew and the Christian Missionary*, 88; see further vol. 3, 5.15, for an in-depth answer.

409. It's also worth remembering that other religious Jews at the time of Jesus were looking for two Messiahs as well, one a priest from the line of Aaron, the other a Davidic king (see vol. 1, 2.1).

410. See concisely Lenowitz, *Jewish Messiahs*, 215–23, who actually makes reference to "the dual, human-and-divine status of the Rebbe" in Lubavitcher thought (see 217–18, and above, end of 3.22). Lenowitz notes that "the Rebbe's death in June 1994 received several responses among adherents of the *'moshiach*-now' movement. The most common of these followed the line developed in basic Chabad [Lubavitch] documents, finding its authority in Maimonides' theory that each generation may have a potential messiah who becomes *the* messiah if the generation is worthy—and holding that this generation did not prove to be so; but two substantial groups held (and continue to do so at this writing) that the Rebbe was not dead and/or that he would return" (216). He points to a split among the Rebbe's followers after his death arising over "the [Lubavitch] missionary program's presentation of the doctrine, that the Rebbe will be resurrected and is yet the messiah," noting that "the missionaries—who hold to this belief like almost all Lubavitch hasidim do—only wish to refrain from public discussion of it since they view it as counterproductive. Of course, non-Lubavitch orthodoxy, as represented by the Rabbinic Council of America, condemns Lubavitchers and their belief" (216).

411. *Tractate Sanhedrin*, vol. 3, 98a5.

412. Other either-or scenarios discussed in the Talmud and Jewish tradition include the views that the Messiah will come when the world is totally righteous or that the Messiah will come when the world is totally wicked. For the use of this doctrine by the followers of Shabbetai Zvi, the powerful false messiah of the seventeenth century, see the classic study of Gershom Scholem, *Shabbetai Zvi* (Princeton: Princeton, 1973). Note also that some modern, more liberal forms of Judaism, believe that the Messiah is a concept (more or less a code word for the Messianic era, synonymous with human improvement) or that the Messiah is a myth, more or less a carryover from ancient pagan beliefs.

413. Note the words of Paul and Barnabas to their fellow Jews who rejected the message of the Messiah: "We had to speak the word of God to you first. Since you reject it and do not consider yourselves worthy of eternal life, we now turn to the Gentiles" (Acts 13:46).

414. See Acts 2:23: "This man was handed over to you by God's set purpose and foreknowledge; and you, with the help of wicked men, put him to death by nailing him to the cross." See also Revelation 13:8; 1 Peter 1:20.

415. We will return to this theme in vol. 3, 4.1.

416. Scholars calls this progressive revelation. It would be similar to teaching children to count before you teach them to add, or teaching them algebra before teaching them calculus. As explained by Greek scholar and theologian B. B. Warfield, "The Old Testament may be likened to a chamber richly furnished but dimly lighted; the introduction of light brings into it nothing which was not in it before, but it brings out into clearer view much of what is in it but was only dimly or even not at all perceived before." Cited in Cotrell, *God the Redeemer*, 134–35, from his article, "The Biblical Doctrine of the Trinity," reprinted in his *Biblical and Theological Studies* (Nutley, N.J.: Presbyterian and Reformed, 1952), 30–31.

417. For relevant discussion of the hope of afterlife in the Tanakh, cf. Brown, *Healer*, 141–45 (with bibliography).

418. Simcha Paull Raphael, *Jewish Views of the Afterlife* (Northvale, N.J.: Aronson, 1994), xxxiii.

419. Cohn-Sherbok, *The Jewish Messiah*, 55.

420. For some extreme examples, presented more with wit than with sympathy, see Andrew Dickison White, *A History of the Warfare of Science with Theology* (Gloucester, Mass.: Peter Smith, 1978), especially vol. 1. For positive reflections on the life of solitude, including the paradoxical observation of Thomas Merton that the more he withdrew from the world, the more he was forced to deal with the world's pain, see Henri J. M. Nouwen, *Reaching Out: The Three Movements of the Spiritual Life* (New York: Doubleday, 1986), 59–60.

421. There is a debate concerning the meaning of Paul's teaching here concerning food. Did he mean that the false teachers told their followers *not* to eat certain *kosher* food (food "which God created to be received with thanksgiving by those who believe and who know the truth"), or was he saying that the false teachers told people *not* to eat certain *unkosher* food (whereas "everything God created is good, and nothing is to be rejected if it is received with thanksgiving, because it is consecrated by the word of God and prayer")? For discussion of this, see vol. 3, 5.29, 5.33.

422. For an extensive discussion of all Rabbinic sources, see Joseph Babad, *Minhat Hinuch* (Netanyah, Israel: Miphal Torat Hakhemei Polin, 1988), 1:1–7.

423. As explained by Gordon D. Fee, a leading New Testament and Greek scholar, "In light of all the troubles we are already experiencing, who needs the additional burden of marriage as well?" See his *1 Corinthians*, New International Commentary on the New Testament (Grand Rapids: Eerdmans, 1987), 329; for a balanced discussion of the whole issue, cf. 334–49.

424. I refer especially to 1 Corinthians 7:1–2, the beginning of the passage I've been discussing: "It is good for a man not to marry. But since there is so much immorality, each man should have his own wife, and each woman her own husband." Thus, Paul has been wrongly accused of grudgingly accepting marriage rather than seeing it as a healthy and necessary gift from God.

425. D. James Kennedy and Jerry Newcombe, *What If Jesus Had Never Been Born?* (Nashville: Thomas Nelson, 1997), 3–4.

426. For the theology of William Booth and his emphasis on twofold salvation (i.e., spiritual and physical), see Roger J. Green, *War on Two Fronts: The Redemptive Theology of William Booth* (Atlanta: The Salvation Army Supplies, 1989).

427. By way of personal example, I was involved in a church on Long Island from 1977–1982 when there was a refugee crisis from Southeast Asia (in particular, from Vietnam and Cambodia). These "boat people," as they were called, fled their homelands at great personal sacrifice—as many as half of them died at sea, and many of them who survived lost everything—only to be housed in massive refugee camps in countries like Hong Kong. When our church heard the news, almost every member began to take in one or more refugees—and most without receiving government or charity compensation—and we lived with these precious people for years as if they were our own brothers or sisters or sons or daughters. It was the natural thing to do! Why? We were followers of Jesus. (The most active organization in the area working with the refugees was, not surprisingly, Catholic Charities.) This then raised our awareness of other world needs, and we began to sponsor Ethiopian refugees, even setting up wide-ranging food and housing programs for them. Again, this was our natural response to New Testament teachings such as Matthew 25:31–46. For a recent study, see Mark and Betsy Neuenscwhander, M.D.'s, *Crisis Evangelism: Preparing to Be Salt and Light When the World Needs Us Most* (Ventura, Calif.: Regal, 1999). On page 106 they state, "The greatest Search and Rescue Team of the universe is God the Father, Son and Holy Spirit, because God so loved the world that He gave His only Son. . . . The qualities of these spiritual genes are transferred to us when we are 'born again.'"

428. It is no surprise that Rabbi Yechiel Eckstein, an Orthodox rabbi, airs a nightly thirty-minute infomercial on Christian television, seeking to raise funds to bring poor and/or persecuted Jews back to Israel.

429. It is true that there were Christian slave owners in early America, and many of them based their theological position on the Old Testament laws of slavery coupled with the fact that the New Testament did not explicitly tell masters to release their slaves (for thoughts on this usage of Scripture, see John Bright, *The Authority of the Old Testament* [Nashville: Abingdon, 1967], 49–51). However, it is equally true that Christian leaders such as Charles Grandison Finney, the most prominent American evangelist in the first two-thirds of this century, were at the forefront of the anti-slavery movement in America, that slave traders like John Newton (famous for writing the hymn "Amazing Grace") after conversion to Christianity, abandoned the slave trade and even fought against it, and that the "liberation" message of Jesus laid the theological groundwork for complete emancipation (for related theological perspectives, see Brown, *Healer*, 217–18, with bibliography).

430. Even if you hold to a pro-abortion (called pro-choice) position, my point here is simply that Christians fight for the rights of the unborn because of their high view of the sanctity of life.

431. One of the most striking examples of such a transformation occurred this century in Nagaland in northernmost India. This state was known for its brutal tribal warfare, and headhunting was commonly practiced there. Today, roughly 90 percent of its people profess Christianity, and their warring ways have been abandoned. Not only do I have associates who labored there as missionaries in recent decades, but our School of Ministry welcomed its first student from Nagaland in 1999. What a joy it is to hear their stories firsthand! For a recent assessment of the impact of the gospel on the Vikings, see "The Vikings," *Christian History* 62, vol. 18, no. 3 (1999).

432. For the New Testament's emphasis on good works, see Matt. 5:13–20; Acts 9:36; Eph. 2:10; 1 Tim. 2:9–10; 5:9–10; 6:17–19; Titus 2:7, 14; 3:1, 8, 14; Heb. 13:16; James 3:13; 1 Peter 2:12, 15; 3:10–17. Remember, it was Jesus who taught us that "it is more blessed to give than to receive" (Acts 20:35)!

433. Regarding the "sins of the church," see Kennedy and Newcombe, *What If Jesus Had Never Been Born?*, 205–23. The authors offer this honest assessment: "The Church has never been perfect, but its track record in history should be remembered for the good as well as the bad. Its sins should not be taken out of their context, blown out of proportion and remembered forevermore, as if this has been the only activity of the Church. Furthermore, the Church has seemed to learn from many of its past sins and then it moves on. We no longer engage in Crusades, except the Billy Graham type! We no longer torture alleged heretics on the rack to get them to change to more orthodox doctrine. We no longer burn or hang alleged witches" (222). Of course, while I am not absolving the church of its many sins, I would be quick to point out that most of the abuses spoken of here, in particular the Inquisitions and Crusades, were perpetrated by people who were Christian in name only, holding to a completely corrupt form of the faith. For more on this, see vol. 1, 2.4–7.

434. Kenneth L. Woodward, "A Lama to the Globe," *Newsweek*, 16 August 1999, 34.

435. Kennedy and Newcombe, *What If Jesus Had Never Been Born?*, 101; see Henry Morris, *The Biblical Basis for Modern Science* (Grand Rapids: Baker, 1984), 463–65.

436. Brown, *Healer*, 66, citing Provonsha, "The Healing Christ," in Morton T. Kelsey, *Healing and Christianity* (New York: Harper & Row, 1973), 361, 363. Provonsha contends that the Hellenistic body-soul dichotomy that strongly influenced the post–New Testament church brought about a decreased emphasis on the importance of ministry to one's physical needs, noting also that "the Post-Apostolic Church often saw the healing ministry of Jesus, and that committed to the Church, as radically opposed to the methodology of 'pagan' physicians of the period. It was miracle against scientific method—Christ's healings were miraculous, not scientific! But the early Church often failed to distinguish between 'miracle' and 'magic'" (363). On the tendency to disdain proper care of the body in certain wings of the church, see White, *History*, 67–96.

437. "Medicine," *Encyclopedia Britannica*, 23:890.

438. H. E. Sigerist, *Civilization and Disease* (Chicago: Univ. of Chicago, 1943), 69.

439. See *The Proceedings of the Consultation on the Study Program of Healing Ministry, October 30–November 1, 1980* (Seoul: Asian Center for Theological Studies and Mission/Korea Christian Medico-Evangelical Association, n.d.), 3, 5, cited in Brown, *Israel's Divine Healer*, 295, n. 4.

440. This is not to say that *only* Christian countries show tolerance. Hinduism in India has been largely tolerant throughout the centuries, although at the time of this writing there is intense, violent persecution against Christians there. On the other hand, Hinduism in Nepal—the world's only "official" Hindu nation—is totally oppressive. As for Buddhism, one of the countries in which Christians are experiencing the most severe, government-sanctioned persecution is the Buddhist country of Myanmar (formerly Burma). As for America and its Christian legacy, the Princeton theologian Charles Hodge had this to say about our country's reception of refugees (he wrote this more than one hundred years ago): "All are welcomed; all are admitted to equal rights and privileges. All are allowed to acquire property, and to vote in every election, made eligible to all offices, and invested with equal influences in all public affairs. All are allowed to worship as they please, or not to worship at all, if they see fit. No man is molested for his religion or for his want of religion. No man is required to profess any form of faith, or to join any religious association." Cited in Kennedy and Newcombe, *What If Jesus Had Never Been Born?*, 89–90 (from Hodge's *Systematic Theology*, 3:345–46). Regarding the *sins* of the church through history, see n. 433, above. As for

the rise of Nazism in "Christian Europe," while it is true that historic anti-Semitism in the so-called church helped pave the way for the Holocaust (see vol. 1, 2.9), it is important to note that Nazism was utterly *anti*-Christian, and its murderous philosophy stood in total opposition to all the fundamental tenets of the gospel.

441. For more on this, see vol. 1, 2.7.

442. As noted in "Death," *EJ* (CD ROM), 5:1420–27, "Death itself, though imbued with mystery—contact with the corpse, for instance, meant defilement in the highest degree—was thought of as that moment of transformation from life in this world to that of the beyond. In terms of the mishnaic image, 'This world is like a corridor before the world to come' (Avot 4:16), death is the passing of the portal separating the two worlds, giving access to a 'world which is wholly good' (Kid. 39b)."

443. This manifesto, together with *Humanist Manifesto I* (1933) are reproduced in Harry Conn, *Four Trojan Horses of Humanism*, rev. ed. (Milford, Mich.: Mott Media, 1982); the quote here is taken from 125.

444. This was poignantly expressed in a poem that greatly inspired Betty Stam, who, together with her husband, John, were killed as missionaries in China in 1934 (their baby daughter was spared). See Ruth A. Tucker, *From Jerusalem to Irian Jaya: A Biographical History of Christian Missions* (Grand Rapids: Zondervan, 1983), 421–25. The poem was written by E. H. Hamilton after hearing of the courage of Rev. Jack Vinson, martyred in China in 1931:

> Afraid? Of What?
> To feel the spirit's glad release?
> To pass from pain to perfect peace
> The strife and strain of life to cease?
> Afraid—of that?
>
> Afraid? Of What?
> Afraid to see the Saviour's face,
> To hear His welcome, and to trace
> The glory gleam from wounds of grace
> Afraid—of that?
>
> Afraid? Of What?
> A flash, a crash, a pierced heart;
> Darkness, light, O Heaven's art!
> A wound of His a counterpart!
> Afraid—of that?
>
> Afraid? Of What?
> To do by death what life could not—
> Baptize with blood a stony plot,
> Till souls shall blossom from the spot?
> Afraid—of that?

For further details, see James and Marti Hefley, *By Their Blood: Christian Martyrs of the Twentieth Century*, 2d. ed (Grand Rapids: Baker, 1996), 55–59; note that the authors refer to the day of the martyrdom of the young missionary couple as "Victory Day for the Stams" (56). They also note that the impact of their deaths was so great that a missionary with the China Inland Mission wrote to Betty's parents and said, "A life which had the longest span of years might not have been able to do one-hundredth of the work for Christ which they have done in a day" (59). A full and productive life need not always be a long life! See Michael L. Brown, *Revolution! The Call to Holy War* (Ventura, Calif.: Regal, 2000).

445. For the quoted material of Jim Elliot and Nate Saint, see Vinita Hampton and Carol Plueddemann, eds., *World Shapers: A Treasury of Quotes from Great Missionaries* (Wheaton: Harold Shaw, 1991), 16, 10.

446. For discussion of this verse, see the Romans commentaries of C. B. Cranfield; James D. G. Dunn; Douglas J. Moo; and Thomas Schreiner.

447. For an insightful discussion of verses in the Hebrew Bible such as Psalm 137:8–9, "Daughter of Babylon, doomed to destruction, happy is he who repays you for what you have done to us—[happy is] he who seizes your infants and dashes them against the rocks," and Psalm 139:21–22, "Do I not hate those who hate you, O Lord, and abhor those who rise up against you? I have nothing but hatred for them; I count them my enemies," see VanGemeren, "Psalms," 830–32 (Appendix: Imprecations in the Psalms). He notes that "the Old and New Testaments hold in tension the requirement of love and the hatred of evil," also pointing out that "we must appreciate the cry of the martyrs in heaven, as they pray for God's vindication (Rev. 6:10) and rejoice in the judgment of the wicked ([Ps.] 18:20; 19:1–6)." However, he writes, "indiscriminate hatred is wrong. The psalmists wrote under the inspiration of God regarding the nature of evil. They were intoxicated with God's character and name (9:16–20; 83:16–17) and were concerned with the manifestation of God's righteousness and holiness on earth. Since evil contrasts in every way with God's nature and plan, the psalmists prayed for divine retribution, by which God's order would be reestablished (109:6–21) and God's people would be reassured of his love (109:21, 26)." On a practical level, VanGemeren states that "for the Christian it is most important to uproot any selfish passions, judgmentalism, and personal vindictiveness, because those who practice these come under the judgment of God (Gal 5:15; James 4:13–16). These psalms help us to pray through our anger, frustrations, and spite to a submission to God's will. Only then will the godly man or woman be able to pray for the execration of evil and the full establishment of God's kingdom."

448. For Christian reflections on this, see the chapter entitled "Jesus, the Pearl of Great Price, the Center of Revival" in my book *From Holy Laughter to Holy Fire: America on the Edge of Revival* (Shippensburg, Pa.: Destiny Image, 1996), 186–95; for Yeshua's use of parables as compared with the Rabbinic use of parables, see Brad H. Young, *Jesus and His Jewish Parables: Rediscovering the Roots of Jesus' Teaching* (New York: Paulist Press, 1989); idem, *The Parables: Jewish Tradition and Christian Interpretation* (Peabody, Mass.: Hendrickson, 1998).

449. For Talmudic discussion on whether Job (and Abraham) served God out of love or out of fear, see b. Sotah 27b; 31a; cf. further b. Yoma 86a–b; b. Yebamot 48b; b. Sotah 22b; b. Sanhedrin 61b–62a; b. Keritot 3a.

450. By the way, as mentioned previously, hell is not just a "Christian" concept! The Hebrew Bible speaks of future damnation—see especially Daniel 12:2—and the Rabbinic writings speak of hell and future punishment; see vol. 1, 219, n. 30; and above, 3.25. Cf. further Moore, *Judaism*, 2:287–322 ("Retribution after Death").

451. See b. Shabbat 88a. Putting several midrashic accounts together in popular form, the following narrative emerges: "When Hashem [the Lord] descended upon *Har Sinai* [Mount Sinai] in a burst of fire, surrounded by a host of 22,000 angels, the earth

quaked and there was thunder and lightning [Exodus Rabbah 29:2; Yalqut Shimoni 1:283]. The *Bnai Yisrael* [children of Israel] heard the sound of the *shofar* becoming continually louder, growing in intensity until it reached the greatest volume which the people could possibly bear. The fire of *Har Sinai* rose up to the very heavens, and the mountain smoked like a furnace [see the Mekhilta]. The people trembled with fear. Then Hashem took *Har Sinai* and suspended it over the people, indicating to them, 'If you accept the Torah, good, but if not, you will be buried under this mountain!' Hashem thereby forced the people to accept the Torah, although they had previously accepted it willingly [b. Shabbat 85a]." See Rabbi Moshe Weisman, *The Midrash Says, The Book of Sh'mos* (Brooklyn: Bnei Yakov Publications, 1980), 180–81. For a lively study of the very caricature of Christianity that forms the basis of this objection (in this case, Roman Catholicism), cf. Piero Camporesi, *The Fear of Hell: Images of Damnation and Salvation in Early Modern Europe*, trans. Lucinda Byatt (University Park, Pa.: Penn State, 1991). For additional studies on the history of the doctrine of hell, cf. Alan E. Bernstein, *The Formation of Hell: Death and Retribution in the Ancient and Early Christian Worlds* (Ithaca, N.Y.: Cornell, 1993); Alice K. Turner, *The History of Hell* (New York: Harcourt Brace, 1993).

452. It is not clear from the immediate context in John whether these are Jesus' words or the words of the narrator; see the standard commentaries for discussion. In any case, what is written here is *God's* Word, utterly reliable and completely true.

453. If you are a brand-new, Jewish believer in Yeshua and somehow think that you are one of the few Jews in the world who believes in him, don't be discouraged. There are tens of thousands of Jewish believers in Jesus around the world! And there are some congregations in which several hundred Messianic Jews worship together. You are not alone! Even if you are an ultra-Orthodox Jew, know that there are others like you who believe that Yeshua is the way. I know some of them myself. Whoever you are, if you have just asked the Messiah to come into your life, we would love to hear from you. Write us, call us, fax us, or e-mail us. We will send you some free materials to help you in your new life.

Glossary

Babylonian Talmud. The foundational text for Jewish religious study, it consists of 2,500,000 words of Hebrew and Aramaic commentary and expansion on the **Mishnah.** It includes much **Halakha** as well as **Haggada,** and thus it touches on virtually every area of life, religion, custom, folklore, and law. It reached its final form between 500 and 600 C.E., and it is mainly the product of the Babylonian sages. *See also* **Palestinian Talmud.**

Five Scrolls. (Hebrew, kha-MESH me-gi-LOT) The biblical books of Song of Songs (Song of Solomon), Ruth, Lamentations, Ecclesiastes, and Esther. They were read in the synagogues on special holidays. *See also* **Ketuvim.**

Haggada. (Sometimes spelled Aggada) Nonlegal (i.e., nonbinding) Rabbinic stories, sermons, and commentaries relating to the **Tanakh** and Jewish life. *See also* **Halakha** and **Midrash.**

Halakha. A specific legal ruling ("What is the Halakha in this case?") or Rabbinic legal material in general. The word **Halakha** is interpreted as meaning "the way to go." *See also* **Haggada.**

Humash. (pronounced KHU-mash) Another name for the Five Books of Moses. *See also* **Written Torah.**

Ibn Ezra. Abraham Ibn Ezra (1089–1164). He was one of the three greatest Jewish medieval biblical commentators, especially famous for his careful attention to Hebrew grammar. *See also* **Radak** and **Rashi.**

Jerusalem Talmud. *See* **Palestinian Talmud.**

Kabbalah. The general term for Jewish mystical writings and traditions. It literally means "that which has been received." *See also* **Zohar.**

Ketuvim. Writings. This refers to the third division of the Hebrew Bible (*see* **Tanakh**) and includes Psalms, Proverbs, Job, the **Five Scrolls,** Daniel, Ezra-Nehemiah, and 1 and 2 Chronicles.

Masoretic Text. The term for the closely related Hebrew text editions of the **Tanakh** transmitted by the Masoretes ("transmitters") from the sixth to the eleventh centuries. All translations of the **Tanakh** (including the King James and *all* modern versions) are primarily based on this text. (*Note:* There is not *one* Masoretic Bible; there are thousands of Masoretic manuscripts with almost identical texts.)

Midrash. Rabbinic commentaries on a verse, chapter, or entire book of the **Tanakh,** marked by creativity and interpretive skill. The best-known collection is called Midrash Rabba, covering the Five Books of Moses as well as the **Five Scrolls.**

Mishnah. The first written collection of legal material relating to the laws of the **Torah** and the ordinances of the sages. It provides the starting point for all subsequent **Halakha.** It was compiled approximately 200 c.e. by Rabbi Judah HaNasi (the Prince) and especially emphasizes the traditions of the rabbis who flourished from 70 to 200 c.e. *See also* **Babylonian Talmud, Palestinian Talmud,** and **Halakha.**

Mishneh Torah. Systematic compilation of all Jewish law by Moses Maimonides (also called Rambam; 1135–1204). It remains a standard legal text to this day. *See also* **Shulkhan Arukh.**

Mitzvah. Commandment. The foundation of Jewish observance consists of keeping the so-called 613 commandments of the **Torah.**

Nevi'im. Prophets. This refers to the second division of the Hebrew Bible (*see* **Tanakh**) and consists of Joshua, Judges, 1 and 2 Samuel, 1 and 2 Kings (together called the Former Prophets), and Isaiah, Jeremiah, Ezekiel, and the Twelve Minor Prophets (together called the Latter Prophets).

Oral Torah. All Rabbinic traditions relating to the **Written Torah** and various legal aspects of Jewish life. The traditions were first passed on orally before they were written down.

Palestinian Talmud. Similar to the **Babylonian Talmud** but based primarily on the work of the sages in Israel. It is shorter in scope, less authoritative, and therefore, studied less than the **Babylonian Talmud.** It reached its final form in the Land of Israel approximately 400 c.e.

Radak. Acronym for *R*abbi *D*avid *K*imchi (pronounced kim-KHEE; 1160–1235). He wrote important commentaries on much of the **Tanakh.** *See also* **Ibn Ezra** and **Rashi.**

Rashi. Acronym for *R*abbi *Sh*lomo *Y*itschaki (pronounced yits-KHA-ki; 1040–1105), the foremost Jewish commentator on the

Tanakh and **Babylonian Talmud.** Traditional Jews always begin their studies in Bible and **Talmud** with Rashi's commentaries as their main guide. *See also* **Ibn Ezra** and **Radak.**

Responsa Literature. (Hebrew, she-ey-LOT u-te-shu-VOT, "Questions and Answers") A major source of **Halakha** from 600 C.E. until today, it consists of the answers to specific legal questions posed to leading Rabbinic authorities in every generation. *See also* **Oral Torah.**

Shulkhan Arukh. The standard and most authoritative Jewish law code, compiled by Rabbi Joseph Karo (1488–1575). *See also* **Mishneh Torah.**

Siddur. The traditional Jewish prayer book, containing selections from the **Tanakh** as well as prayers composed by the rabbis.

Talmud. *See* **Babylonian Talmud** and **Palestinian Talmud** (Jerusalem Talmud).

Tanakh. Acronym for *Torah, Nevi'im, Ketuvim,* the Jewish name for the Old Covenant in its entirety. Although the order of the books is different from that of the Christian Old Testament, the contents are the same.

Targum. Literally, "translation." This refers to the expansive Aramaic translations of the Hebrew Bible that were read in the synagogues where biblical Hebrew was no longer understood. They were put in written form between 300 and 1200 C.E. The most important Targum's are Targum Onkelos to the Five Books of Moses, and Targum Jonathan to the **Nevi'im** (Prophets).

Torah. Literally, "teaching, instruction, law." It can refer to: (1) the **Written Torah** (the first division of the Hebrew Bible; *see* **Tanakh**); or (2) the **Oral Torah** in its entirety (this of course includes the **Written Torah** as well).

Torah She-be-al-peh. *See* **Oral Torah.**

Torah She-bikhtav. *See* **Written Torah.**

Tosephtah. An early collection of Rabbinic laws following the division and order of the **Mishnah** but containing parallel legal traditions not found in the **Mishnah.**

Written Torah. The Five Books of Moses (the Pentateuch). *See also* **Humash.**

Zohar. The foundational book of Jewish mysticism. It was composed in the thirteenth century, although mystical tradition dates it to the second century. *See also* **Kabbalah.**

Subject Index

Index of Scripture
and Other Ancient Writings